MW00571316

PANAMÁ

3rd Edition
Marc Rigole
Claude-Victor Langlois

ULYSSES
TRAVEL PUBLICATIONS
Travel better... enjoy more

Authors	Project Director	Illustrations
Marc Rigole	André Duchesne	Stéphanie Kitembo
Claude-Victor Langlois		Lorette Pierson
	Page Layout	Marie-Annik Viatour
Editors	Typesetting	
Daniel Desjardins	Anne Joyce	Photography
Stéphane G. Marceau	Visuals	Cover Page
	Jenny Jasper	Steven Gould
English Editing	Layout Assistant	Superstock
Jacqueline Grekin	Clayton Anderson	"Kuna Woman"
Tara Salman		Inside Pages
	Cartographers	John Mitchell
Translation	Patrick Thivierge	IPAT
Christina Poole	Yanik Landreville	
Danielle Gauthier		Artistic Director
Suzanne Murray		Patrick Farei (Atoll)
Josée Olivier		
		Computer Graphics
		Stephanie Routhier

Distributors

AUSTRALIA: Little Hills Press, 11/37-43 Alexander St., Crows Nest NSW 2065, ☎ (612) 437-6995, Fax: (612) 438-5762

BELGIUM AND LUXEMBOURG: Vander, Vrijwilligerlaan 321, B-1150 Brussel, ☎ (02) 762 98 04, Fax: (02) 762 06 62

CANADA: Ulysses Books & Maps, 4176 Saint-Denis, Montréal, Québec, H2W 2M5, ☎ (514) 843-9882, ext.2232, 800-748-9171, Fax: 514-843-9448, www.ulysses.ca

GERMANY and **AUSTRIA**: Brettschneider, Fernreisebedarf, Feldfirchner Strasse 2, D-85551 Heimstetten, München, ☎ 89-99 02 03 30, Fax: 89-99 02 03 31, cf@brettschneider.de

GREAT BRITAIN and **IRELAND**: World Leisure Marketing, Unit 11, Newmarket Court, Newmartket Drive, Derby DE24 8NW, ☎ 1 332 57 37 37, Fax: 1 332 57 33 99, office@wlmsales.co.uk

ITALY: Centro Cartografico del Riccio, Via di Soffiano 164/A, 50143 Firenze, ☎ (055) 71 33 33, Fax: (055) 71 63 50

NETHERLANDS: Nilsson & Lamm, Pampuslaan 212-214, 1380 AD Weesp (NL), ☎ 0294-494949, . Fax: 0294-494455, E-mail: nilam@euronet.nl

PORTUGAL: Dinapress, Lg. Dr. Antonio de Sousa de Macedo, 2, Lisboa 1200, ☎ (1) 395 52 70, Fax: (1) 395 03 90

SCANDINAVIA: Scanvik, Esplanaden 8B, 1263 Copenhagen K, DK, ☎ (45) 33.12.77.66, Fax: (45) 33.91.28.82

SPAIN: Altaïr, Balmes 69, E-08007 Barcelona, ☎ 454 29 66, Fax: 451 25 59, altair@globalcom.es

SWITZERLAND: OLF, P.O. Box 1061, CH-1701 Fribourg, ☎ (026) 467.51.11, Fax: (026) 467.54.66

U.S.A.: The Globe Pequot Press, 6 Business Park Road, P.O. Box 833, Old Saybrook, CT 06475, ☎ 1-800-243-0495, Fax: 800-820-2329, sales@globe-pequot.com

OTHER COUNTRIES, contact Ulysses Books & Maps (Montréal), Fax: (514) 843-9448

No part of this publication may be reproduced in any form or by any means, including photocopying, without the written permission of the publisher.

Canadian Cataloguing in Publication Data
© November 1999 (see p 8)
Ulysses Travel Publications.
All rights reserved
Printed in Canada
ISBN 2-89464-129-X

"It seems that if the world were to choose its capital,
the isthmus of Panamá would be appointed this illustrious destiny"

– Simón Bolívar

Table of Contents

Symbols

🐉	Ulysses' Favourite
☎	Telephone Number
⌐	Fax Number
≡	Air Conditioning
⊗	Fan
≈	Pool
#	Screen
ℜ	Restaurant
⊕	Whirlpool
ℝ	Refrigerator
K	Kitchenette
△	Sauna
⊖	Exercise Room
tv	Colour Television
hw	Hot Water
pb	Private Bathroom
sb	Shared Bathroom
fb	Full Board (Lodging + 3 Meals)
½ b	Half Board (Lodging + 2 Meals)
bkfst	Breakfast Included

ATTRACTION CLASSIFICATION

★	Interesting
★★	Worth a visit
★★★	Not to be missed

Prices mentioned in this guide are for one adult admission.

HOTEL CLASSIFICATION

$	$25 or less
$$	$25 to $50 US
$$$	$50 to $90 US
$$$$	$90 to $150 US
$$$$$	$150 and more

The prices in the guide are for one room, double occupancy in high season.

RESTAURANT CLASSIFICATION

$	$8 or less
$$	$8 to $15 US
$$$	$15 to $25 US
$$$$	$25 to $40 US
$$$$$	$40 and more

The prices in the guide are for a meal for one person,
not including drinks and tip.

All prices in this guide are in Panamánian Balboas

Write to Us

The information contained in this guide was correct at press time. However, mistakes can slip in, omissions are always possible, places can disappear, etc. The authors and publisher hereby disclaim any liability for loss or damage resulting from omissions or errors.

We value your comments, corrections and suggestions, as they allow us to keep each guide up to date. The best contributions will be rewarded with a free book from Ulysses Travel Publications. All you have to do is write us at the following address and indicate which title you would be interested in receiving (see the list at the end of guide).

Ulysses Travel Publications
4176 Rue Saint-Denis
Montréal, Québec
Canada H2W 2M5
www.ulysses.ca
E-mail: guiduly@ulysses.ca

Thanks to: **Ariadna C. Sanchez** and **Ilka** (IPAT Panamá), **Maria Quiel** (IPAT Bocas del Toro), **Araceli R. De Cordóvez** (Director of the Museo Panamá Viejo), **Dr. Aristides Royo** (Ambassador of Panamá in Paris), **Ariadna J. Rojas** and **Jorge A. Troyano** (Embassy of Panamá in Paris) and special thanks to **Azmy J. Juarez Duarte**, **Héctor Jiménez Barsallo** and **Frédéric Beaudry** for their contribution and support.

"We acknowledge the financial support of the Government of Canada through the Book Publishing Industry Development Program (BPIDP) for our publishing activities".

We would also like to thank SODEC (Québec) for their financial support.

Canadian Cataloguing in Publication Data

Rigole, Marc 1956-

Panamá

3rd ed.
(Ulysses Travel Guide)
Translation of: Panamá.
Includes index.

ISBN 2-89464-129-X

1. Panama - Guidebooks. I. Langlois, Claude-Victor. II. Title. III. Series.

F1563.5.R5413 1999   917.28704'53   C99-940940-9

List of Maps

Map Symbols

✈	Airport	★	National Capital	▲	Mountain
🚗	Car Ferry	⚓	Port	⌂	Fort
🚤	Passenger Ferry	►◄	Lock	◎	Beach
🚌	Bus Station	)(	Bridge	✝	Church
❶	Tourist Information				

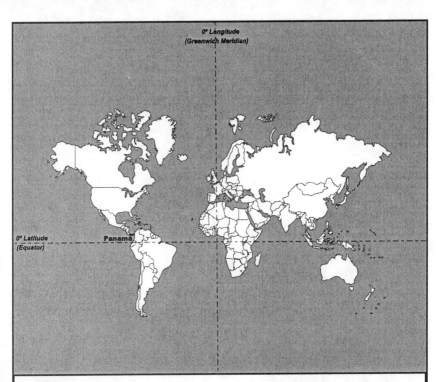

Where is Panamá?

Ciudad de Panamá

9°N

79°O

Panamá	
Capital:	Panamá City
Language:	Spanish
Population:	3,000,000 inhab.
Currency :	Balboa
Area:	75,650 km²

Atlantic Ocean

Gulf of Mexico

Mexico

Cuba

Dominican Republic

Haiti

Puerto Rico

Jamaica

Guadeloupe

Martinique

Belize

Guatemala

Honduras

El Salvador

Nicaragua

Caribbean Sea

PANAMA

Costa Rica

Venezuela

Pacific Ocean

Colombia

0° Latitude
(Equator)

Ecuador

Peru

Brazil

© ULYSSES

Portrait

Panamá, Central America's fourth largest country, with an area of 75,650 km², boasts a rich variety of landscapes.

Bordered by Costa Rica to the west and Colombia to the east, Panamá constitutes a veritable bridge in the shape of a horizontal "S", extending 750 km between the two Americas. Long and narrow (except for the Azuero peninsula), Panamá is bounded on either side by two of the world's great oceans, the Atlantic and the Pacific, and crossed by a mountain chain stretching almost its entire length. The highest peaks of this range are in the west, dominated by the 3,475-m volcano, Barú. On the east side, the highest peak is Mount Tacarcuna, at 1,875 m.

The Geography of Panamá

The Panamanian territory encompasses 2,866 km of coastline and a great number of islands, scat-

tered on either side of the isthmus. The two oceans are separated by only 51.4 km at the country's narrowest point. With 153 rivers draining into the Atlantic and 325 into the Pacific, Panamá has an ample supply of fresh water as well.

From a geological standpoint, this part of the world is relatively new, Central America having been formed only three or four million years ago. The Cocos plate began its eastward shift some

20 million years ago, colliding with the Antilles plate and sliding partway underneath it, thus causing the temporary emergence of several islands. Much later – three to four million years ago – the movement of the plates became more pronounced, and new upheavals brought forth volcanoes, mountains and new land. This formed a "bridge" between the two continents, which until that time had been separated.

Though Panamá lies on the famous Pacific fire belt, it is still the safest of all Central American countries from a volcanic standpoint. Also, thanks to its geographic location, the isthmus is spared the terrible hurricanes that regularly ravage this part of the world.

Another great upheaval, although much more modest in scale and created by humans, was the construction of the Panamá Canal. This giant undertaking altered the face of the country significantly. When the canal was dug, and the Río Chagres was diverted, a large area was flooded. The result was the 425-km^2 Lago Gatún; the mountain peaks left above water formed a number of artificial islands on which many animals took refuge (see p142).

The Flora and Fauna of Panamá

Approximately three million years ago, the two American continents (North and South America) were connected by a narrow strip of land creating a land bridge or isthmus. As a result, this bridge has been crossed not only by humans, but also by the flora and fauna from both subcontinents. Thus, Panamá, with its varied climates and location between the two land masses, is a natural "biodome" with a diverse plant and animal life. Contrary to what one might believe, the original Panamanian forest is one of the largest in Central America, because the isthmus is sheltered from devastating hurricanes. While the vegetation varies enormously depending on the altitude and the richness of the soil, the country's flora can be roughly divided into two major types: equatorial and grassland. Along with these are all kinds of variations that have developed differently according to location and altitude.

The explorer Gonzalo Fernández de Oviedo y Valdés was one of the first Europeans to describe Panamá's fauna and flora, which are detailed in his writings from his voyage in 1513 entitled *Historia general y natural de las Indias*. However, the first truly scientific expedition to the tropics was organized by the Académie Royale Française des Sciences, from 1735 to 1744, and supervised by Charles Marie de la Condamine. Condamine's aides-de-camp left a substantial amount of written information on the natural riches of the isthmus. Much later, in the 19th century, the famous German scientist Alexander von Humboldt wrote a wealth of information about the tropics, gained through his many journeys.

Fauna

Because of its microclimates and geographical location on the Central American isthmus, Panamá has the greatest number of animal species in the world. Biodiversity, or the variety of plant or animal species, is measured by the number of species found in a particular area. Panamá is particularly renowned as a birdwatching paradise, with over 900 species of birds. Many different kinds of birds can be seen without having to travel very far.

Like the tourists seeking sun and sandy beaches, many birds migrate from North America to Panamá in the winter. These include swallows, buntings, thrushes, and warblers, among others. Visitors will surely be amazed by the colours of the different toucans and parakeets. The **saffron toucan** and the majestic **scarlet macaw** are definitely among the world's most beautiful birds, and are relatively easy to spot in certain areas of the country. The bird that draws the most looks, however, is the **quetzal**. The quetzal is a rather large bird (up to 35 cm) with a long emerald tail up to 60 cm long. It lives in the humid tropical forests of the provinces of Chiriquí and Bocas del Toro. The best months for bird-watching are January to May, during nesting season. At other times of the year, it can also be seen in Parque Nacional La Amistad with the help of a good guide.

Denchobate

Curious travellers will have the opportunity more than anywhere else to see wildlife that is very much alive and very well adapted to its environment. In addition to the many different bird species, this tiny corner of the planet is also home to some 15,000 kinds of butterflies, more than 200 mammals and reptiles, about 100 species of freshwater fish and amphibians, and infinite insects. Many of these animals are indigenous to Panamá.

The animals visitors are most likely to see in Panamá are monkeys (**white-faced capucin**, **howler** and **spider**), **sloths**, **agoutis**, **coatis**, **iguanas**, **lizards**, **toads**, **crocodiles** and small brightly-coloured poisonous **frogs**. Mammals such as **anteaters**, **tapirs** and large felines (**jaguars**, **pumas**, **ocelots**) are harder to spot, but they sometimes leave their tracks behind. The country also has several kinds of snakes including **vipers** and **boas**. Four of the eight types of **marine turtles** (see box, p 264) visit Panamá's beaches, where the females lay their eggs.

Flora

According to a vegetation classification system devised by the biologist L.H. Holdridge in 1947, there are some 116 life zones on earth. These observations are based on the different types of climates, temperature changes, precipitation, as well as seasonal changes. Due to Panamá's great diver-sity in climatic conditions and the very rugged terrain, the country has 12 life zones as well as eight transition zones.

Marine Turtle

Lagoons, marshes, grasslands, mangroves, plains, dry tropical forests, tropical wet forests and subalpine plains make up the Panamanian landscape, depending on the altitude and region. The country's high mountains have some of the lowest temperatures in Central America and their rivers flow into the Atlantic and Pacific Oceans.

Although Panamá is a small country, it har-

Crocodile

bours 5% of all plant and animal species in the world. There are 10,000 species of plants (almost as much as in all of Europe), 1,000 species of trees as well as 1,200 species of orchids, including the national flower, **Espíritu Santo**, a white orchid.

While some plants produce poisons in order to protect themselves from herbivorous animals, others produce particularly rich fruit which, when eaten and excreted by animals and insects, will spread the seeds far and wide.

The two main flowering seasons are at the beginning of the rainy season, from March to June, and at the end of the rainy season, September through October. Only the first one is essential for seed production.

An Exceptional Diversity

For a long time, biologists all over the world have been wondering why there is such a wide variety of flora and fauna in these regions. How is it that there are 10 or 15 times more species of trees in Central America than elsewhere? Why are there so many different types of animals, all with such widely divergent behaviour patterns and feeding habits? What could be the cause of such an explosion of life? Also, why is it that the same type

of plant exists in several different regions, all far apart?

One possible answer might be the availability of protein in certain areas. Proteins are indispensable to every form of life. Made up of amino acids, they are found primarily in fruits, young leaves, shoots and seeds. Animals obtain amino acids by eating the shoots themselves or by eating other animals that have ingested them. In more temperate zones, where the change of seasons is pronounced, the arrival of spring heralds an awakening of nature, and a veritable explosion of young shoots yields an abundance of proteins.

The animals that depend on this type of food have adapted their way of life to the cycle. Birds migrate, and when mammals bear their young, an extraordinary abundance of food awaits the newborn. Protein production is all the greater because the seasons are short, and each plant must generate enough to ensure its own survival.

In tropical regions, however, things are different: the warm climate enables plants to develop year-round. Because of the heat and the difficulty of producing large quantities of proteins all year, species have had to find all sorts of ways to

escape predators. This has led to two phenomena: diversity and disparity. Some plants have developed means of defence, like thorns, or the production of caustic substances. Others, of the same species, have spread into various regions and flower at different times to avoid being eaten all at once by voracious birds and mammals. These different means of defence have complicated the hunt for food, thus resulting in the same disparity and diversity among wildlife. The animals have had to specialize in their search for food, either by developing a specific morphology (a beak adapted to a particular food type), or by a specific type of behaviour that could be termed mutualism – a type of association between plant and animal.

Some plants even go so far as to produce substances that are useful to certain insects, which in turn protect the plants against predators. This mutualism can also apply to the animal kingdom.

Tropical Dry Forest

The dry tropical forest is disappearing in Central America. Only about 2% of it is left, some in Panamá, more specifically in the central provinces.

Before the land was cleared, the Azuero Peninsula was made up of savannah forest. Now the land is made up of pastures, as well as cacti and other semi-arid vegetation. Deforestation has intensified the dry and rainy seasons, making the dry season, which runs from December to April, a desert-like climate where rainful is almost non-existent. Some trees have even adapted to the lack of ground water by shedding their leaves.

On the other hand, the arrival of the rainy season brings relief and makes the desert bloom again. The grass becomes green, flowers burst with brilliant colours and the trees blossom with white, yellow, red and pink flowers.

The Tropical Rainforest

The tropical rainforest is very diverse in Panamá, both on the Atlantic (Caribbean Sea) and the Pacific coasts, and even in the centre of the country. This type of forest is called "rainforest", because, like the Amazon, parts of Panamá receive at least 2,000 mm of rain each year, sometimes as much as 6,000 mm, especially in the provinces Darién, Chiriquí and Bocas del Toro. Humidity is also very high, and the annual temperature is almost steady, at an average of approximately 24 °C.

A constant supply of clean water is therefore essential to the survival of the tropical rainforest. Also, since the tropical rainforest recycles 75% of its water through evaporation, it sucks up plant and animal nutrients from the soil. Termites and mushrooms then decompose the dead vegetation so the trees can replenish it with the lost nutrients through their roots.

Altitude also plays an important role in the rainforest's vegetal composition. The tropical rainforest starts at 1,000 m in Panamá and vegetation gets sparser the higher you go. Between 1,000 and 3,000 m, the forest is extremely dense with mosses, lichens, lians, vines, bushes and trees whose canopy is shrouded in mist. Only vegetation that can adapt to the harsh climate grows here, such as stunted bushes. You can see this type of vegetation by climbing above the tree line in the high mountains of the Talamanca Cordillera, especially on the Barú volcano (3,475 m).

Deforestation

Before the Spanish conquistadors set foot on its shores in the 16th century, Panamá was almost entirely made up of rich natural forests. Only small sections had been deforested by the Amerindians to grow corn and cassava, among other crops. When the Spanish colonized the country, they began clearing forested areas to make way for towns and later for crops, such as bananas and coffee, or for pastures.

Deforestation proceeded at a relatively moderate rate until the mid-20th century, when it took off at a drastic pace. Thus, it is extremely important to protect the existing forests and implement an efficient reforestation policy. If not, the deforestation of tropical rainforest will cause an ecological disaster and it will take tens, if not hundreds, of years before anything can grow again.

Deforestation has done more than just deface some of the most beautiful natural landscapes in Panamá. Soil erosion has actually created deserts in the central provinces. During the dry season, water for domestic and industrial consumption becomes scarcer. Some rivers dry up, endangering much of their flora and fauna. During the rainy season, floods cause the most extensive damage.

Environmental Conservation

Starting in the 1960s, many grassroots environmental movements sprang up worldwide to counteract mass deforestation, realizing the importance of protecting natural resources. These groups viewed the United States national park system as the basic model for conservation. However, since the population of tiny Panamá doubled within 20 years (1950-1970) and was distributed evenly throughout the country, the forest conservation project was seen as a threat to the prosperity of farmers and breeders.

Orchids

Therefore, environmentalists had to find a good reason for the population to cooperate in protecting the forest, while maintaining their livelihood. This is the notion of "sustainable development", the combination of economic and environmental activities to promote better living. For sustainable development to be successful, the governments of each country, as well as environmental organizations, must get more involved and set up programs to better educate the public about the importance of this type of development.

A Few Examples of Panamanian Flora and Fauna

Orchids: These flowers are known around the world for their beauty and their scent. Over 35,000 different species exist. While some spring directly from the soil, others are epiphytes, attaching themselves to other plants without taking their food; still others feed on decaying plant life. Orchids are part of the group Orchidaceae, which provide us, among other things, with vanilla flavouring.

The **quetzal**: This bird has been called the most beautiful in the world, and is part of the Trogonidae family. Birds of this group are unique in that they can remain motionless for up to an hour watching their prey which, after the slightest movement, is devoured. The average quetzal is 35 cm long and its tail can reach a length of 60 cm. The bird is of great symbolic importance in

Quetzal

native culture, and its feathers were once worn by high dignitaries. Its name is also associated with the pre-Columbian god of vegetation and regeneration, *Quetzalcóatl*. The god was represented by a serpent covered with quetzal feathers. The bird has bright green feathers on most of its body and vivid red ones on its stomach. Two very long tail feathers give it a striking elegance in flight. On its head is a small crest. Males have a yellow beak, females, a black one.

Although the quetzal is very popular, especially among travel agencies, many of which tout it as one of the country's major attractions, you will have difficulty spotting one in the wild, since they make their home in isolated areas between 1,200 m and 3,000 m above sea level in the wet tropical forests from the south of Mexico all the way to Panamá, where it is mostly found in the provinces of Chiriquí and Bocas del Toro. The best months to see it are from January to May, during nesting season. The rest of the year, it can be seen in Parque Nacional La Amistad with the help of a good guide.

The quetzal digs its nest in the trunk of a tree – generally a sick tree whose wood is soft; the bird's beak is quite fragile and cannot penetrate hard wood. Then male and female build the nest and incubate the eggs together. When the male is sitting on the eggs, he tucks his long tail feathers behind his head and lets them hang out of the nest, so as not to damage them. Quetzal-watching entails an expedition into regions that are difficult to get to, and requires patience. It is therefore wise to go with an experienced guide.

The **toucan**: Next to the quetzal, the toucan is probably the most curious bird on the isthmus. There are some 40 species in the toucan family, known for their unique, colourful beaks, which grow to an impressive size (up to a third of the length of the bird's body) and appear massive and heavy, but are actually very light. The toucan's

feathers are relatively sombre compared to its beak, whose apparently striking colours serve above all to frighten predators.

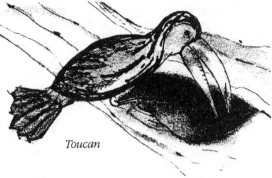

Toucan

Toucans also have the reputation of being among the noisiest birds. Observing them in the wild is not easy, since they often perch at the top of trees. They are very social, and you will often see them in little groups.

The **hummingbird**: There are some 100 species of these in Central America. Their feathers come in an infinite variety of colours. What distinguishes them most is their swiftness and agility in getting about; their wings can beat up to 79 times a second, allowing them to fly backwards. Their heart rate has been clocked at an incredible 273 beats per min!

Monkeys: Contrary to popular belief, there are not as many types

of monkey in Central America as there are in Asia or Africa. In fact, there are only six types: the howler, the capuchin, the tamarin, the spider, the squirrel and the owl. They are distinguished from monkeys on other continents by several traits. Some species have a prehensile tail with which they can grasp trees, and all have broad noses, unlike the narrow noses of monkeys elsewhere in the world.

Hummingbird

There are also behavioural differences: they generally live in groups and in some races the males take care of educating the young. These patterns are peculiar to Central American monkeys.

The **howler monkey** is also called **alouatta palliata**. Alone or in a group, it can emit sounds that would frighten the most courageous person. The noise can carry very far, and is intended to warn one group of the presence of another. It is also a means of communicating within the same group. When two groups meet, each tries to out-howl the other and frighten it away. This creates the impression of some ferocious battle between wild animals, but the confrontation is usually limited to lugubrious noise-making.

The howler monkey is one of the animal species being studied by the famous Smithsonian Tropical Research Institute on Isla Barro Colorado. Their research has revealed that the howler monkey has a very special kind of diet: about 50% of the monkeys' diet comes from at least 50 different kinds of plants, the other half being made up of fruits and flowers. This may seem like a lot of food, but howler monkey population growth is very irregular and there can be food shortages some years. Further studies have revealed another factor essential for population growth: monkeys eat only the young leaves, which are richer in vitamins and contain fewer toxins than adult leaves but only grow at certain times of year. Although the gestation period of howler monkeys usually coincides with the budding season, a variety of factors can delay the leaves from sprouting, causing an estimated 60% to 80% of young monkeys to die from malnutrition before the age of five.

Sloth

The **sloth** is a strange-looking mammal that moves extremely slowly. It has long, curved claws, and hangs from branches, where it eats leaves and fruit. Strangely, its fur is covered with algae and butterfly larva, which make for excellent camouflage. Once a week, the animal comes down from its tree to relieve itself. There are two species of sloth: one has two fingers, and the other three. Both are found mainly in the Darién forests and in isolated regions.

The History of Panamá

The Pre-Columbian Period

With the help of various objects unearthed during archaeological digs, it can be concluded that human life existed in Central America as far back as 12,000 (some say 20,000) B.C. It is reasonable to assume that this can also be said for Panamá. The oldest traces of activity to be discovered in Panamá specifically are stone arrow tips dating back to 11,000 B.C. Stone statues from before 2,000 B.C. and small stone tables on which grain was ground (*metates*) have been found in the province of Chiriquí. Certain pieces of pottery date back to the same period. While there are no large monuments like those from other native civilizations like the Mayas or the Aztecs, a number of handcrafted items tell us that the indigenous peoples of Panamá knew much about pottery and metalwork. The most ancient piece of ceramic work in Central America was discovered at the oldest known site in Panamá, the village of Monagrillo in the province of Herrera. It dates back to 2,130 B.C. The skill of the artisans is borne out in richly coloured pottery, whose handles are shaped like small animals such as frogs and lizards. Already, artisans were using a technique similar to what we call bisque. It would appear that most regions had their own style of pottery, and through various excavations it has been determined that this craft did not develop at the same rate everywhere. The provinces of Chiriquí, Veraguas and Coclé, for instance, were highly developed in comparison with Darién.

Iron and gold work were equally important, and in this, the Amerindians of the province of Coclé excelled. Their mastery of precious metalwork is evident in the magnificent specimens discovered on the archaeological site of Sitio Conte (near Natá). Among the many objects found here are numerous pieces of gold jewellery, sometimes representing animals or half-human figures. These *huacas* are on display at the Reina Torres de Araúz museum in Ciudad de Panamá (see p 92).

The use of semi-precious and precious stones, like emeralds, in ornaments tells us that countries like Colombia and Mexico were already trading in such materials. Some of these items look exactly like gold, indicating that the indigenous people were also masters at the art of preparing and applying paint.

Unfortunately, we know very little about the many tribes who lived on the isthmus in pre-Columbian times. While the settlers may have taken great care in enumerating precious things taken from the Amerindians, the writings of the time teach us very little about their native peoples' way of life. We know that in the early years of colonization most of the western territories of the country were controlled by two powerful groups, probably from the Guaymíe tribe. The Azuero peninsula was ruled by a chief named Parita, and the land even farther to the west, by one named Urracá. Little is known about the customs of this period, largely because many of the tombs have been looted. Various excavations have, however, shed some light on the subject.

During the digs near Natá, graves containing 32 human skeletons were unearthed. When an important warrior chief died, he was buried not only with his household servants but also with his wife (or wives; he was allowed several). His possesions (pottery, gems, etc.) were buried with him. Research has taught us that during the funeral, which lasted several days, the dead chief's wives went down into the

Ancient Vase

grave, sat down on a bench, and proceeded to get drunk on *chicha* (a fermented corn-based drink). After the ceremony, when the chief's body had been put into the grave along with his household servants and wives, the grave was filled with earth, and the chief's companions were buried alive. Customs varied according to the region and era.

Some graves containing large urns full of human bones have been discovered, others containing only the personal belongings of the deceased. Sometimes the dead were burned. A great deal of mystery still surrounds the many tribes and the wide variety of sites they inhabited, all of which are still being studied.

The Horn of Plenty

Not only did the Amerindians know a great deal about making pottery, they also had vivid imaginations. This can be seen in what is called the horn of plenty. It rests on three hollow feet, with a small earthen marble in one of them. When the object is shaken, the marble makes a noise, creating the impression that the horn is full.

The Colonial Period

Discovering the Isthmus

In 1500, Castilian Rodrigo Galván de Bastidas, accompanied by a young explorer named Vasco Núñez de Balboa, set sail for the New World from Cadiz, Spain in the hopes of discovering untold riches.

After sailing up the Venezuelan coast, they continued west past the Bay of Cartagena and the Gulf of Urabá (between Colombia and Venezuela) to Darién in present-day Panamá. After a brief stop there, they continued up the Panamanian coast until Nombre de Dios. From there, his ships in bad condition, Bastidas headed for nearby Hispañola (today the Dominican Republic and Haiti) for some much-needed repairs. Thus, Bastidas was the first explorer to discover the Central American isthmus.

Later that year, another expedition headed by Alonso de Ojeda and including cartographer Juan de la Costa and Amerigo Vespucci (see p23) explored Panamá's Caribbean coast before heading towards Hispañola. Despite the discovery of these new lands, no permanent settlements were established. Towards the end of 1502, accompanied by his brother Dom Bartolomé, Colombus explored the Honduran coast up to Portobelo Bay in Panamá. Colombus was warmly received by the indigenous people there and was showered with large quantities of jewellery and gold ob-jects. This led Columbus to believe there was more gold in the area and he set sail for Hispaniola, where a ship awaited him to return to Spain. However, his plans fell awry when a sudden storm ran the ship aground on a sandbank at the mouth of present-day Río Belén. Trapped for some time, he decided to establish a permanent settlement there which he named Santa María la Antigua de Belén and entrusted to his brother before departing. Shortly after Columbus's departure, a chief named Quibián attacked the colonists and destroyed the village, forcing them to flee for their lives. Thus ended the first attempt at colonization.

Vasco Núñez de Balboa, An Exceptional Destiny

Little is known about the early life of Balboa. He was born between 1475 and 1477, probably in Badajoz (Jérez de Badajoz), Galicia (Spain). Of noble but poor origin, he was presumably the son of Don Nuño Arias de Balboa and a Badajozian woman. Young Vasco was apparently educated by Don Pedro Puertocarrero, nick-named the "deaf sei-gneur" because of his hearing impairment. It was also at this time that Christopher Co-lumbus set off from the neighbouring village of Palos de la Frontrera for the New World. Balboa, fed by these rumours of gold and riches, became passionate about finding a passage to the East, particularly India.

After having finished his apprenticeship as a knight under Puertocarrero, Balboa left for Seville where he worked for explorer Rodrigo de Bastidas. Towards the end of 1501, Balboa, along with Bastidas and cartographer Juan de la Cosa, set sail from the port of Cadiz hoping to reach the mysterious *tierra incógnita* that he had dreamed off for so long.

After stopping in the Canary Islands, Bastidas followed the route of Columbus's third voyage, passing by Trinidad and Tobago, the Paria Peninsula and Isla Margarita off the Venezuelan coast. After crossing the Gulf of Maracaibo and the La Guajira Peninsula (the furthest west any explorer had ever gone before) they arrived in the Bay of Urabá, where they settled temporarily. It was during this voyage that Balboa met "Indians" for the first time. The Spanish traded the Amerindians' baubles (knives, tools, little bells, glass pearls, etc.) for what they believed to be pure gold but was actually only *guanín*, or an alloy of

gold and copper. The indigenous peoples, according to Spanish accounts from this journey, were also afraid of the conquistadors' horses, because they had never seen any before.

After leaving the Bay of Urabá, Bastidas and Balboa briefly explored the coast of Darién, then sailed to Hispaniola. Shipwrecked near Port-au-Prince, they finally reached Santo Domingo by an overland route. Because of his involvement in the conquest of Hispaniola, Balboa was rewarded by the island's governor with lands and slaves and founded a colony, Salvatierra de la Sabana. In 1510, after several disastrous years as a farmer, he secretly embarked on a ship bound for the Bay of Urabá. Finding nothing but an abandoned settlement, he headed further west, where he believed there was rich, fertile land. Soon after reaching a bay where they were greeted with hostility by the Amerindians, the crew decided to retaliate. Ignorant of local customs, the Spaniards tortured men who wore dresses. These men were supposed to supervise the work of the women, and tradition dictated that they wear long garments. The conquistadors believed them to be homosexuals instead, and punished them by burning them

at the stake. The first settlement in Panamá, La Guardia, was founded after this tragedy. The small village grew steadily because of the surrounding fertile soil and its location next to the mouth of a river creating a natural port. In November 1510, Balboa had the village renamed Santa María la Antigua del Darién. The village's rapid growth lead to a conflict of authority between Balboa and another colonist named Enciso. Taking advantage of Enciso's unpopularity in the colony, Balboa easily had him deported and took charge of the settlement. In 1511, Balboa became governor of the province of Darién.

Discovering the Mar del Sur

In May 1511, Balboa set off with 200 men to conquer a land further west called Cueva, which the Amerindians at Darién had told him was full of riches. Balboa took their chief Careta to help him find this land of riches, and in return promised to help overcome the chief's closest enemies, chiefs Ponca and Comogre. As dictated by local custom, the deal secured when the chief offered his tribe's women to Balboa's men, and his own daughter, Anayansi, to Balboa.

Next, the whole village was converted to Christianity and Careta baptised and renamed Fernado. With the help of the Amerindians, Babloa's troops succeeded in overcoming Ponca; then they continued further west to Chief Comogre's village where they were unexpectedly welcomed and given food and gold. After swearing allegiance to Balboa, the entire village was baptised and Comogre renamed Carlos. This last conquest proved to be particularly fruitful, because it was here that Balboa was told for the first time about a vast stretch of water that lay beyond the mountains, possibly another ocean. The indefatigable Balboa pushed forward with his expeditions, but at the same time native hostility was building; the region's chiefs formed an alliance to chase away the great white chiefs and thus liberate the territory of Darién.

Once again, history turned bloody as Balboa ordered the chiefs killed and their villages burned as punishment for their participation in the plot. Finally, around 1513, two caravels arrived from Spain with long-awaited supplies, horses and settlers to increase the colony's population.

Vasco Núñez de Balboa decided to return to the Cueva region in August of 1513 to find the vast stretch of water with the help of men provided by chief Careta. After a long jungle trek, they arrived in the village of Quareca on September 24 only to be greeted by a hail of arrows. Nevertheless, Balboa and his men managed to capture the village.

This time around, the victims were sacrificed to a hoard of ravenous dogs who devoured them before Balboa's steadfast gaze and the encouragement of his soldiers. The next day, the conquistadors continued on to Chief Porque's village and spotted the Pacific Ocean for the first time from the top of a nearby mountain.

What Balboa had actually seen was the Golfo de San Miguel. After resting in the seaside native vllage of Chape, the 38-year old Balboa officially claimed the Mar de Sur in the name of the Spanish king and queen, Ferdinand and Juana on September 29, 1513. Another aspiring explorer who was part of the expedition, Francisco Pizarro, had no idea of the great fate that awaited him, for it was he who would discover the Equator and Peru.

Shortly after claiming the territory, Balboa pursued his voyage along the coast as far as present-day Punta de San Lorenzo, where he once again sacked native villages and stole large quantities of their gold. Spurred on by rumours of even greater riches, he continued as far as the Las Perlas Archipelago. After landing on an island he baptised Island Rica (present-day Isla del Rey) and gathering a large quantity of pearls, he decided to return to Santa María la Antigua in November 1513 and finally arrived there on January 19, 1514.

Arrival of Pedrarías and the Era of Plots

A merchant called Pedro de Arbolancha arrived in Panamá at the end of January 1514 in search of new

Amerigo Vespucci

Portrait

Born in Florence in 1454, Amerigo Vespucci sailed with Alonso de Ojeda on his first expedition to the New World in 1499. After four expeditions along the South American coast, Vespucci was named , or chief explorer, by the Spanish crown. He used this title and his reputation in the Spanish court to pretend to be the first to discover the American continent. This is why cartographer Martin Waldseemüller of Lorraine published a map of the New World in 1507 in which he called the new continent, *Americi Terra*. However, Vespucci did discover America in a way, because unlike Columbus who believed he had found the Far East, Vespucci realized that America was indeed a new continent. Although the mistake was later rectified, the American continent still bears Vespucci's name and not Columbus's.

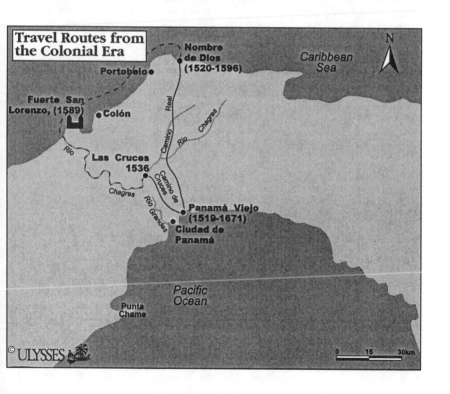

Travel Routes from the Colonial Era

markets. Arbolancha informed Balboa that the court had named him as the new governor of the Castilla d'Oro (the new name for the province of Darién). Balboa, hoping for a restitution of his authority, entrusted Arbolancha with a letter to the Spanish court claiming the discovery of the Mar del Sur in the name of the Spanish crown.

The crown answered Balboa by sending a new governor, Pedro Arias de Ávila, also known as Pedrarías, to Darién on June 26, 1514. Pedrarias arrived with about 2,000 settlers composed of bureaucrats, churchmen and workers, in addition to all kinds of supplies. Pedrarías had difficulty putting up with Balboa's governing of the colony right from the start. He blamed Balboa for the poor cramped conditions of the town: there were only 200 houses in Santa María la Antigua del Darién at the time, around which were clustered close to 1,500 indigenous people. Despite the presence of a church and hospital, Pedrarías was humiliated to be named governor of such a small colony. Although his initial reaction was to throw Balboa in jail, he changed his mind after the bishop warned him against it, citing Balboa's popularity.

Several months later, in December 1514, a new caravel arrived with a message from the court recognizing Balboa's merits (as discoverer of the Mar del Sur); the governor was instructed to consult Balboa for all important decisions. This assault on his authority made Balboa a sworn enemy in Pedrarías's eyes. Then followed a long period of intrigue and conflict during which Pedrarías plotted and schemed to get rid of his rival, even resorting to attempted murder. Jealous of Balboa's treaties with the Amerindians, Pedrarías organized a series of punitive raids against them, wiping out all previous efforts to bring peace to the region.

In addition, not content with looting their villages, he authorized their enslavement, citing disobedience to the crown. Francisco Pizarro, who participated in these attacks, would put Pedraria's principles into practice during his conquest of Peru and Ecuador.

In March of 1515, the Spanish court decided to create two new provinces, Panamá and Coiba, and put Balboa in charge of them. Humiliated once again, Pedrarías secretly began pillaging the new territories before Balboa even got there. Sensing a plot against him, Balboa sent messengers to Cuba for

help. Hearing of this on his return, Pedrarías accused Balboa of treason against the crown and proceeded to arrest him. Then followed one of the most bizarre episodes of the whole Spanish Conquest.

Fearing an uprising from Balboa's supporters, the bishop once again warned Pedrarías against executing Balboa. Instead, the bishop suggested a marriage between the two rival families. His logic was that in one fell swoop, as a relative of the governor of the southern provinces, Pedrarías would have de facto access to their riches, in addition to the court's protection. So in August 1516, the bishop married off Pedrarías's daughter, Doña María Peñalosa, to Balboa. Shortly afterwards, the newlyweds set out for the new colonies of Panamá and Coiba, where Balboa founded the town of Aclá.

The indefatigable Balboa, with the help of his men, then started *La Compañía de la Mar del Sur* to finance a new expedition to explore the Pacific Coast. It was the first example of capitalist colonization, once again highlighting Balboa's tremendous organizing abilities. As soon as the funds were gathered, the expedition set off. After crossing the isthmus for the second time, Balboa continued on towards

Isla del Rey off the Pacific coast until present-day Bahía Piña before returning to Aclá.

Assassination of Balboa

In 1518, King Ferdinand of Spain died, leaving the throne to Charles V, a native of Flanders. That same year King Charles sent a new governor, Don Lope de Sosa, to Santa María la Antigua del Darién. Afraid Sosa would blame him for bad management of the colony and violence against the local communities, Pedrarías came up with a diabolic scheme have his new son-in-law, Balboa, accused instead. With the judge's complicity and the false testimony of several witnesses, a trial was held and Balboa found guilty and thrown in jail in Aclá. Francisco Pizarro, who would go on to conquer Peru, was one of these witnesses, betraying his former friend. Aclá was chosen as the location for the trial because it was far from the major towns; the news of the sentence would not spread as quickly, thus avoiding any riots.

Balboa was condemned to death on January 21, 1519 and beheaded at dawn the next day in Aclá's public square. He was 44 years old.

After Balboa

After Balboa's death, Pedrarías de Ávila continued exploring the Panamanian coast and discovered Isla Taboga, before founding the small town of Nuestra Señora de la Asunción de Panamá on the mainland. The town prospered, while the fortunes of Santa María la Antigua del Darién declined. The town of Panamá, for its part, obtained the title of *Ciudad Real* or "Royal City" in 1521 because of its ideal location and constant development. The rest of the colonial history not only of Panamá but of the entire isthmus as well as South America is marked by infighting between governors and nobles, each wanting to control the new territories and especially their riches.

By founding the city of Panamá, the Spanish set up the first European trading post on the Pacific Coast. Beginning in 1519, the celebrated Camino Real would occupy an important place in the development of the isthmus. This road linked the city of Panamá with Nombre de Dios and Portobelo, and for years was used to carry treasures (gold, silver, precious handicrafts) from the conquered colonies in Colombia and Peru. Around 1533, another road, the Camino de Las Cruces, was built

along the Río Chagres. The Chagres was navigable at certain times of the year, and it too was used to carry merchandise. For a long time, these roads would provide the shortest access between the two oceans.

Later, as the Spanish pressed on in their search for new riches in the west, towns like Natá, Parita and Los Santos were founded. The newly acquired territory was first called *Castilla del Oro*, because of the gold mines in the province of Coclé. The gradual westward progress was not accomplished with ease, however. The names of towns like Natá and Parita, bestowed in honour of two mighty native warriors, testify to the many battles fought with the Amerindians.

Once the colony was well established, Castilla del Oro flourished on the strength of trade and the transportation of goods. With the conquest of the Inca empire and its fabulous treasures, and the discovery of the Philippines by Magellan in 1521, the isthmus acquired a new strategic importance which ensured its continued development and growth up until the 18th century. By the 16th century, goods from Asia were already passing through Panamá on their way to Europe. At the adminis-

Portrait

trative level, Spain attached Castilla del Oro to New Granada (now Colombia, Venezuela and Ecuador) in 1739.

However, the increase in riches passing through the isthmus attracted the attention of pirates and drew the envy of other powers. Acts of piracy multiplied. Even with fortifications at Portobelo and San Lorenzo, the Spanish were not able to defeat the pirates, and in 1746 Spain decided to stop shipping goods via the Camino Real and start sending them around Cape Horn. This decision had a major impact on transportation, and trade went down.

In the 18th and 19th centuries, there were many civil wars in the region, provoked largely by nationalist sentiment. The economy turned sour, and the country was poised on the brink of bankruptcy. The decision was made to break with Spain, and Panamá declared its independence on November 28, 1821, following the example of New Granada, to which it decided to annex itself. The new political entity thus formed was called Gran Colombia, and consisted of present-day Peru, Venezuela, Bolivia, Ecuador, Panamá and, of course, Colombia. Despite

these troubled times, Panamá experienced true cultural growth in the 18th and 19th centuries. The first university was created in 1749. By this time the country had become a cultural centre, teeming with activity, where grand schemes for pan-American unity were debated. The fact that this country was chosen by **Simón Bolívar** to host the first Pan American Congress testifies to the activism that reigned there.

After a long period of economic stagnation and even decline, Panamá, because of its geographical location, experienced a sort of second wind, which continued into the 20th century, thanks to the United States. The year 1848 marked the beginning of the California gold rush. The east-west roads across the U.S. were uncertain and difficult, so most of the pioneers opted for a sea voyage via Panamá. In order to speed up the westward migrations, the Ameri-

Simón Bolívar

General Simón Bolívar was born in Caracas, Venezuela, in 1783. He earned his place in history as the first person to try to bring the countries of Latin America together into one nation. After long struggles against Spanish domination, he succeeded in liberating Venezuela, Colombia, Ecuador, Peru, and Bolivia. Emboldened by his victories, he created the republic of Gran Colombia (encompassing all these states) and

became its president. Despite his military success and the first Pan American congress in Panamá, El Libertador ("The Liberator", as he became known after the liberation of Caracas) was unable to keep these countries together and died a desperate man, in Santa Marta, Colombia, in 1830. He is venerated as a real hero, and his name has been given to many places in Latin America.

cans, with the agreement of Colombia, to which Panamá was attached at the time, built a railway across the isthmus. The first train crossed the country in 1855 (see p178). The developement of the American west would prove a determining factor in the joint history of the two countries and would later lead to the digging of the canal.

Independent Panamá

While a number of revolutions took place against the centralist Colombian government, the history of independent Panamá really begins early in the 20th century, a few years before the Americans launched the second phase of building the canal (see p133). At this time, Bogotá's lack of interest in this remote province led to a feeling of frustration among the local elite, who felt far removed from the seat of power. During this time, the French, under the direction of Ferdinand de Lesseps, fresh from his triumphant realization of the Suez Canal, obtained Colombia's permission to build and manage a canal connecting the Pacific to the Atlantic.

Tropical diseases and financial troubles, however, got the better of the French project,

which failed miserably in 1889, nine years after work began. The Americans, meanwhile, were becoming increasingly anxious to see a navigable route joining the two oceans – as much to ensure the rapid development of the American west as for strategic reasons. They were unable to reach an agreement with Colombia, which was wary of the great power's appetite.

A combination of regional frustrations within Panamá and American impatience ultimately lead to the independence of the isthmus. On November 3, 1903, a rebellion broke out. Secession was proclaimed, and a provisional military government installed. The following day, the declaration of independence was drawn up, and on November 6, the United States recognized the new state. American warships, supporting the Panamanian revolution, were anchored offshore, and while the Colombians did try to recover their territory, there was really nothing they could do. Very shortly afterwards, the new republic signed a treaty with its new ally, granting it the canal zone in return for military protection and financial compensation for the territory administered (see p133).

In the wake of independence, a series of

governments succeeded each other. At the political level, only a relatively small number of influential persons (large landowners, merchants, and soldiers) played an important role. With the construction and development of the canal came a noticeable change in the evolution of political thought in the country. One aspect of this change was the nationalistic attitude of the people, characterized by a contradictory feeling: while on the one hand the people wanted total independence from the United States, on the other they enjoyed the comfort and financial advantages that resulted from the presence of the American installations.

Important Dates in Panamá's Recent Political History

In 1936, the United States stopped guaranteeing Panamá's independence, thereby granting the country complete freedom in the defence of its territory. The annual $250,000 payment for use of the canal zone was increased to $430,000.

In 1955, certain aspects of the canal treaty, including provisions on financial compensation, were amended by the Eisenhower-Remón Treaty. From that time on, the U.S. would pay about two million dollars a year to rent the canal zone.

In the 1960s, a number of student demonstrations were held demanding Panamanian sovereignty over the canal zone. As a result, the Panamanian flag began to fly over the zone.

In 1964, diplomatic relations with the U.S. were broken off in the wake of violent riots, which caused some 20 deaths. The revolt broke out when the governor of the canal decided to pull down the Panamanian flag, and resulted in a promise by President Roberto Chiari to review the dispute over the 1903 treaty unconditionally and without restriction. The U.S. thus opened the door to a possible return to the zone under Panamanian sovereignty.

On October 11, 1968, President Arnulfo Arias Madrid was overthrown in a coup d'état (he himself had assumed power in a rather undemocratic manner). The political parties and the National Assembly were dissolved, and a government made up of a military *junta* and a civilian cabinet was installed. At the end of 1969, the members of the *junta* were replaced by civilians under General Omar Torrijos, who had instigated the coup

and was also head of the National Guard. Torrijos's policies were both nationalistic and open to social reforms for the poorer classes, and he played a major part in the country's political history. His accomplishments included a review of the constitution in 1972, reestablishment of diplomatic relations with Cuba, membership in the movement of nonaligned nations, nationalization of energy and telecommunications, creation of state enterprises and many cooperatives, legislation promoting banking, and the list goes on. He was also the first to concern himself with The indigenous peoples and to grant them any benefits.

His most important accomplishment, however, came about in 1977, when the Torrijos-Carter agreement definitively marked the end of the treaty of 1903. Under the new agreement, the entire territory of the canal zone would be restored to the Panamanians, and all U.S. soldiers withdrawn from the region by 1999. Moreover, by 1979, Panamá would officially recover sovereignty over the canal zone. The official canal zone has since been dissolved and is now administered by the joint Panamá Canal Commission (see p134). In 1979, however, the U.S. Congress

passed legislation reserving for itself the right to ensure protection of the canal, even after 1999, if its security is threatened. With the Torrijos-Carter agreement and all the measures he had undertaken for the country, the general enjoyed great popularity and became a veritable hero. Although he had come to power in a rather undemocratic manner, and despite a dramatic increase in the debt, it can truthfully be said that Torrijos catalyzed Panamá's development, allowing his country to assume an important place in the world.

In July 1981, General Omar Torrijos died in an airplane accident. The military influence he left on the political scene led to a constant struggle for political control between the military and the civilian camps – a cruel test for democracy.

In 1983, Manuel Antonio Noriega was appointed chief of the Panamanian Defence Forces, formerly the National Guard.

In May 1984, the old party, which had formed a coalition (the Democratic National Union), was elected to power, with the Democratic Alliance as the opposition. Although the election was contested by the opposition on the grounds that the Democratic

National Union had been directly supported by the military, Nicolás Arditto Barletta was appointed President of the Republic.

In September 1985, the decapitated body of Hugo Spadafora was found near the Costa Rican border. Spadafora had been known for his less than flattering statements about the army, and especially about General Noriega. The military was suspected, and a little later, on the "advice" of Noriega, President N. A. Barletta was "asked to resign". He was succeeded by the first vice-president, Eric Delvalle.

In June 1986 the American press printed its first allegations that Noriega was involved in drug trafficking. Tension mounted between the General and the United States.

In June 1987, a former soldier who had been dismissed made statements to the effect that Noriega had been involved in the murder of Spadafora, had rigged the 1984 elections and was linked to drug trafficking. Riots broke out. The opposition mounted what was called a "civic crusade" to force the government and Noriega to resign. A state of emergency was called for ten days, followed by savage repression. All constitutional guarantees were suspended and the opposition press was outlawed.

In 1988 and 1989, tensions between Panamá and the U.S. continued to mount. Delvalle may still have been president, but it was mainly Noriega who controlled the situation. In the meantime, the U.S. Justice Department openly accused the General of international drug trafficking. In accordance with U.S. wishes, Delvalle asked for the General's resignation. In the wake of a failed coup d'état, however, Noriega appointed Manuel Solís Palma president. The dismissed president called upon the U.S. to boycott his country. Skillfully manipulating the nationalist trend, Noriega took an aggressive stance with the Americans, and stirred up anti-American feelings. At the same time, he founded the Battalions of Dignity in 1988. According to Noriega, this group was created to protect the country against American invasion and to preserve the integrity of the Republic. In fact, it was used to suppress all forms of opposition and to keep civilians under his thumb.

In May 1989 came a final political upset: the opposition coalition (ADOC) and its head, Guillermo Endara, were elected to power on a platform which included, among other things, the demilitarization of politics. However, the election results were cancelled, and Noriega placed his own candidate in power; Francisco Rodríguez was named president. As a result, a number of countries followed the example of the United States and broke diplomatic relations with Panamá.

In October 1989, a bloody coup d'état was mounted by the army, but it failed. In the wake of incidents implicating Panamanian soldiers and members of the U.S. Army, by mid-December the National Assembly declared a state of war with the United States. General Noriega was appointed head of State with full powers. This declaration provided the United States with an excellent excuse for an invasion: the Americans living in Panamá were now in danger.

Operation Just Cause

On December 20, 1989, 13,000 American troops invaded the country with the aim of deposing the dictator Noriega, capturing him, and placing him in the hands of American justice. The 12,500 American soldiers already stationed in Panamá joined in the operation. Noriega took refuge in the Vatican embassy, surrendering, after two weeks of siege. He was then transferred to Miami for his trial. Guillermo Endara was reinstalled as the legally elected president of Panamá.

As for the number of victims of the intervention, each side had its own set of figures. Unlikely though it may seem, these ranged from 400 dead (U.S. Defence Department) to 7,000 dead and 25,000 homeless! The number and percentage of civilians killed gave rise to much debate. For us to advance and support any particular set of figures would be impossible – in any event, it is not our role. Regardless of the number of victims, one thing remains certain: there was a breakdown in dialogue between two nations, providing more proof of the need for nations to communicate rather than fight.

While it is not our task to take a political stand on Operation Just Cause, we must still consider two points: first, the Noriega regime cared little for such concepts as democracy and human rights, and many people suffered because of this. Tension was such that in recent years it had become dangerous to make anything but positive remarks about the government, while anti-American talk was good form. Shortly before the intervention, there was a veritable climate of terror, and the Battalions of Dignity were infiltrating every level of society in an effort to better control them. People were arrested for such simple things as carrying a white handkerchief (symbol of the opposition) on their person or in a car. For members of the opposition to be physically assaulted was an everyday occurrence. It can safely be said that a majority of Panamanians longed for a return to democracy, and that Noriega's fall was greeted with relief.

The second point to be considered is that there appears to be a real problem with regard to the good-neighbour relations between some Central American countries and the United States. While an examination of all the details would take too long, one important factor would seem to be respect for democracy. As long as democratic states continue to support countries that care little for democracy and human rights (Noriega was actually trained by the U.S. Secret Service and acted as an agent for a while) solely in the interest of economic and strategic influence, aggressive relations between states will continue to be a problem. In the long term, the wisest investment is to establish relations with truly democratic countries that respect human rights.

After Noriega

Immediately following the U.S. invasion, the country suffered a rude economic awakening. A few years before Noriega's downfall, in 1987, the United States imposed a boycott on Panamá, hoping to provoke the downfall of the regime. This boycott prohibited all American enterprises from dealing with Panamanian companies. This had an extremely negative impact on tourism, among other things. The Panamanian GNP fell 16% between 1987 and 1989, and the country went heavily into debt.

In 1990, an agreement with the United States brought banking secrecy to a halt; financial institutions could now be investigated with a view to better controlling movements of money and avoiding it being laundered by the drug dealers. Then, to help the country get started again, the U.S. Congress approved humanitarian assistance; its example was then followed by the European Community and Japan. From 1990 to 1992, the GNP gradually returned to its pre-1987 levels. But even with the foreign aid, the government was forced to dismiss many civil servants and, in order to reduce the immense accumulated debt, to make major budget cuts. A number of strikes broke out. Disagreement within the coalition and allegations of presidential corruption did nothing to improve the government's position. As a result of the major disorganization which followed the American invasion, 1991 saw an increase in violence and crime. After the invasion, a number of members of former paramilitary groups set up under Noriega found themselves unstructured but still armed, and they took advantage of the reorganization of the forces of order to attack banks, businesses and other properties. The government dissolved the *Fuerzas de Defensa Nacional* and created the *Fuerza Pública*.

In 1992, the ruling coalition proposed a referendum asking for the people's agreement on various constitutional amendments, in particular abolition of the army. The reply to this particular question was "No". Also, with the departure of the Christian Democratic Party from the ruling coalition, the government was once again in a minority position in the National Assembly. Despite the failure of the referendum, and despite all the social unrest that year, the ruling power did meet with some success in its fight against crime.

Despite the many political crises within the coalition, and after reshuffling his government, Guillermo Endara remained in power, but his popularity continued to decline. He persisted in carrying out a severe policy of economic renewal at the expense of certain social programs. This renewal did produce some results, as Panamá entered a period of sustained growth. Guillermo Endara's greatest achievement, however, was to succeed in reestablishing a certain level of security in the country. Nevertheless, in May of 1994, Ernesto Pérez Balldares, candidate of the *Partido Revolucionario Democrático*, was elected president with 33.2% voter turnout. The widow of former president Arnulfo Arias, in power in the 1940s and 1950s, came second, while singer Rubén Blades had to settle for third. His movement, Papá Egoró, did however succeed in getting six deputies elected to parliament, which approves government initiatives.

The party in power, the PRD, is largely made up of politicians who supported Noriega during the 1980s. The old guard is thus making a comeback, even though it has abandoned any vague militaristic impulses. In January 1995, a coup, apparently linked to certain factions of the army, was exposed before it was too late. Superior officers promptly disassociated themselves with such non-democratic acts by making statements to that effect in the daily newspapers.

In August 1998, thinking he would reap the benefits of four years of sustained growth, President Ernesto Pérez Balladares called a referendum that would have allowed him to run for another term (according to Panamanian law presidents can only hold office for one five year term). More than 60% of voters voted not to extend his presidency. In addition to his government's involvement in several corruption scandals, the people reproached the billionaire president's running of the country like a private company, with little regard for the "little people" and the widening gap between rich and poor.

Dawn of the Year 2000

No less than 12 political parties were represented in the May 1999 elections (presidential, legislative and provincial). From these parties, three coalitions were formed: Nueva Nación (including the outgoing president's PRD party), Acción

Opositora and Unión por Panamá. Although the Nueva Nación coalition wisely allied itself with celebrities such as singer Rubén Blades and presented the son of famous general Omar Torijos (see p39) as a candidate for the presidency, this was not enough to sway the voters to once again vote for the PRD. The Unión por Panamá won the majority of votes, and **Mireya Moscoso** became president of the republic with a platform promising to pay more attention to social problems. In any case, the new president not only won a landslide victory but became the first woman president of a country with a macho culture.

No matter what social changes may be in the cards, it is clear that the management of the canal (which transfers back to Panamá at the end of 1999) as well the U.S. bases will continue to be in the forefront. In reality, Panamanians would prefer not to have an army on their soil, but are already missing the substantial capital inflows generated by the presence of American soldiers. Because of the increase in drug trafficking in the province of Darién, the Americans may establish bases in this region. A continued American presence would benefit both parties: the Americans would continue to have a certain influence in the region, and the Panamanian government would avoid losing a lot of precious U.S. capital.

The Population of Panamá

Although Panamá experienced very strong demographic growth between 1911 and 1998 (its population rose from 336,000 to 3,000,000), it is still quite scarcely populated, with 35 inhabitants per km².

As is the case in many other Latin American countries, the population is primarily young and urban. Panamá is unique, however, because of its great ethnic diversity. Aside from the native population (6%) and the descendants of the Spanish conquerors (10%), there are the descendants of the workers of various nationalities who participated in the construction of the canal.

While the great majority of Panamanians are of mixed origins (70%), there are also blacks of African descent. The black population is made up of two groups with distinct origins. The first group (mostly from Jamaica) came during the construction of the canal, and speak English primarily. The second group was brought here by force by the Spanish, to act as slaves in the early years of colonization. These individuals mostly speak Spanish. There is a high number of *Mestizos*, descendants of unions between the Amerindians and the conquerors. Finally there are many Chinese, Italians and other Europeans from Slavic or Germanic countries.

The Amerindians

Contrary to the situation in neighbouring Costa Rica, Panamá's indigenous population constitutes a sizeable minority. It is estimated at some 200,000 people, most of whom live in the western and eastern parts of the country. Today, there are seven native groups in Panamá: the **Ngobe** and **Bugle**, also called the **Guaymíes**, are the largest group; the **Tule**, also known as the **Kuna**, the **Emberás** and **Wounaan** called the **Chocoes**, and the **Tlorio** or **Teribes**. Finally, there is also a small **Bri-Bri** minority in the west of the country.

The Kunas and Chocoes have been allowed to administer their own territories, called *comarcas*, for many years now. Only defence and national security are still controlled by the Panamanian government. The Guaymíes, on the other hand, have had a hard time getting their rights recognized. Despite the

Portrait

creation of the Reserva Tabasara in 1952, their lands have been exploited by farmers and mining companies.

After going through some dark years (see p221) during which their communities' traditions and social fabric started breaking down, the Guaymíes started a long campaign for the recognition of their rights.

As a result, in 1965, following a national conference of all Ngobe-Bugle grand chiefs, the Guaymíes Free Republic was created and a president named for the new territory. However, barely three days later, the Guaymíes, under pressure from the army, were forced to give up their independence.

Despite the promise of a *Ngobe-Bugle comarca*, the Panamanian government has not stopped breaking its promises, taking advantage of the politico-religious differences within the Ngobe communities that arose shortly after their independence was quashed. Things then quieted down in the Ngobe communities until 1991 when, during the festivities for the 500th anniversary of Christopher Columbus's landing, Ngobe chief David Binns painted some graffiti on the cathedral of Panamá stating "500 years of

evangelization, enough!". The government responded by fining Binns B/. 100, thus demonstrating their ignorance of the whole native claims movement. The same year, the Panamanian government secretly signed a contract with Texaco, which would expropriate Guaymíes lands, as well as Parque Internacional La Amistad and the Bastimentos marine park, thus violating the law on national parks. In 1992, the government granted the Cerro Colorado Mine Development Corporation (an Anglo-Panamanian venture) the rights to develop a copper mine on Ngobe territory. The government subsequently granted more land to foreign mining companies (most U.S. and Canadian) despite opposition from the Ngobe-Bugle delegation.

On November 25 1996, six Ngobe and Bugle representatives, fed up with the non-recognition of their rights, went on a hunger strike in the capital's anthropological museum. They demanded the annulment of past contracts with mining companies and a legal recognition of their lands. With public opinion in their favour as well as the support of various university groups, the government finally passed a law creating the *Ngobe-Bugle comarca* in Janu-

ary 1997. Although it was a first step, the land was small in comparison to what the Guaymíes wanted. Of the 1.3 million ha claimed, the country's largest indigenous population has received only 700,000 ha. In addition, because the development of natural resources within the *comarca* remains strictly under state control, large chunks of Guaymíe territory are still held by mining companies. So long as the government grants new mining exploration rights, the situation in the Ngobe-Bugle comarca remains tense.

The Tlorios have made no official land claims up to now and the Bri-Bris are considered too small to be officially recognized as a native group; most of them live in Costa Rica. After the canal reverts back to Panamanian control, it would be good to finally see ownership of native lands revert back to its original inhabitants. The Guaymíes and the Kunas belong to the Chibchan language family. Chibchan was the spoken language of the Chibchas tribes, whose influence extended from Nicaragua to Colombia and Ecuador, before the arrival of the Spaniards. The Chibchas are estimated to have numbered 500,000, and the largest group of them lived in the high valleys surrounding what is today the city of Bogotá, in Colombia. Their society was highly centralized and especially well organized. The Chocoes, for their part, belong to the Carib language group, which originated in Guyana and Brazil.

Panamá's indigenous peoples have a highly diversified culture. This is due to cultural blending caused by migrations, forced or otherwise. Several influences are felt, including those of the Mayas, Aztecs and even the Incas. The three main groups in the country are described briefly below.

The Ngobe - Bugle (Guaymíes)

This is the largest native group in the country (estimates range from 97,000 to 150,000); it is also the most integrated and the most assimilated. Until the Spaniards arrived, the Ngobe - Bugle lived primarily in the centre and the west of the country; particularly in the provinces of Veraguas, Herrera, Los Santos and Coclé. After the land was colonized, most moved to the provinces of Bocas del Toro and Chiriquí. A warlike people, the Guaymíes apparently came from Colombia to settle in the central and western parts of the country. It is believed that before the Spaniards arrived they were

divided into several nations, each with its own supreme chief (see also the section on the pre-Columbian period) (see p18)

The Guaymíes consist of two main groups: those from the south, who live on the Pacific coast, and those from the north, who live in the mountains and shores along the Atlantic. The climates of these two regions differ greatly, and this seems to have had a considerable influence on each group's way of life and culture. Those of the north live in damp tropical forests and along the Caribbean shore; they are more isolated and their culture is said to be more "primitive".

Those of the south, unlike their neighbours, live in larger villages generally situated on hilltops. They chose this location, often to the detriment of their water supply, because they needed to have an excellent view of the surroundings. They had once been warriors, and found it important to be able to watch the enemy from afar. Since they lived in drier and less wooded areas, they became adept at farming. Today, they often work on a seasonal basis on the huge plantations in the area, or in the mines that have sprung up on their land over recent years. The women make dresses

and jewels for sale in the villages and along the Interamericana.

At the social level, the Guaymíes are now monogamous, though this was not always the case. The women wear long dresses of two colours; often blue and red or green and orange, and decorated mainly at the bottom and on the collar. Sleeves are generally short. Sometimes the women wear large necklaces (see p130) made of tiny beads of different colours. Both dresses and collars have geometric patterns, mostly triangles.

Among important rituals is the coming of age ceremony for males called "La Clarida". A group gathers in the forest near a source of water and a mountain. Then, a priest-healer or *sukia* teaches the males chants and sacred prayers. Today, however, the capitalist way of life has driven many men away from the reserves, and this has led to many social changes (see p221) in the Guaymíe community. Tribal customs are disappearing along with the influence of the *sukias*. Only time will tell if land claim efforts will in their turn be followed by attempts to preserve traditions.

The Tule (The Kunas)

The Kunas are generally smaller and more thickset than the Guaymíes. They emigrated a number of centuries ago from Colombia. About 500-1,000 of them live in Darién, the biggest group (50,000-60,000) settled in the San Blas islands. Long before colonization, they also occupied the central part of the country.

The word *Kuna* means "the people" and is applied primarily to those living on the continent; those on the islands call themselves San Blas. Although contacts with pirates profoundly influenced both groups, the continental Kunas, because of their isolation in the jungle, have maintained a more "primitive" lifestyle. The principal activities of the San Blas Kunas are fishing and farming, and the women make the famous *molas* (see p280).

The Emberás and the Wounaan (The Chocoes)

The Chocoes of Panamá, unlike their Colombian neighbours who mixed strongly with the local black populations, were opposed to all assimilation and withdrew into the forest of Darién. They have separated into two distinct groups; the Emberás who number 14,000; and the Wounaan, totalling about 3,000 people. Unlike the Kunas and the Guaymíes, the Chocoes do not live in a community, but live in an isolated manner, usually along rivers. They appear to have neither leaders nor political or economic structures, and live mainly in families. Their principal activities are fishing, hunting and farming. Little is known about their origins, though they appear to have come from neighbouring Colombia. Of all the indigenous peoples in Panamá (some would say in the world), these are the most "primitive" and the most isolated. This can be explained by their environment (the Darién jungle) and by the fact that they avoid all contact with other groups.

Politics

Panamá is a presidential-type republic. Its constitution was adopted in 1983 following a referendum, and provides for legislative power represented by a unicameral (one chamber) legislative assembly. Executive power is vested in the president of the republic, who is assisted by two vice-presidents. Both presidential and legislative elections are held every five years.

In 1989, the *Fuerza de Defensa Nacional* (formerly the *Guardia Nacional*), which represented the military power, was abolished and replaced by the *Fuerza Pública*.

Kuna woman at work on a mola

Commanding officers serve a two-year term. This "public force" also acts as a police force. The courts and the districts are governed by a Supreme Court, while the president of the republic appoints a governor for each province.

At the administrative level, the country consists of nine provinces, divided into districts and consisting of municipalities. Each province has its own cultural and geographical peculiarities. The province of San Blas, for instance, is an autonomous territory, or *comarca*. Among other features, it contains a large group of islands, and the villages are inhabited and administered exclusively by the Kunas. The province of Chiriquí is inhabited both by Guaymíes and by people of Spanish, German and Slavic descent. Both in its countryside and in its climate, it is reminiscent of Switzerland! The inhabitants are very proud of their regions; each province has its own capital; when someone talks about "the capital", s/he means the capital of his province. The population is unequally distributed, and the provinces of Panamá and Colón alone account for more than half the country's population. Nombre de Dios and Natá are among the oldest cities, dating back to the colonial period.

The Economy

From an economic standpoint, revenue from the canal still plays an important role. Many people are employed in the Zona Libre in Colón and in the administration of the canal.

Another major source of revenue is in the west of the country: the pipeline carrying oil from one ocean to the other and running from Puerto Armuelles to Chiriquí Grande. Another source of revenue related to petroleum is the oil tankers. A great many ships fly the Panamanian flag, so the country has a good-sized merchant fleet, although the original Panamanian fleet is not all that large. Farming and fishing have also developed greatly and become major activities. The main crops are corn and rice, and the country exports fruits, sugar, coffee, cocoa and shrimp. Its principal clients are the United States, Costa Rica, Germany and the European Community.

Panamá is one of the most indebted countries in the world, with respect to its GDP. The debt is $6 billion and so is the GDP. Its fiscal deficit is 7.7% of the GDP. In 1995, a portion of the interest and capital it owed to international creditors was cancelled.

Nevertheless, the country is still undergoing significant economic growth (close to 2% since 1994), and does not suffer from inflation, which hovers around 1.3% per year. However, the lifting of price controls on certain commodities and the American dollar's weakness in relation to European currencies may force the inflation rate up to 2 or 2.5%.

The recent decision made to partially or totally privatize certain public companies has brought in significant amounts of foreign investment and in some cases has allowed the quality and competitiveness of services to be improved. In addition to the total privatization of the phone company, a large part of the country's electricity is presently provided by Hydro Québec International. The Québec giant, in partnership with the *Fonds de Solidarité des Travailleurs du Québec*, owns 50.1% of the shares of the Fortuna hydroelectric generating station in the west of the country, and provides 40% of Panamá's electricity.

The government has created certain incentives to develop the country's tourism industry. A law was passed, for example, which exempts investors from paying taxes on their tourist-related ventures. With the transition of the canal to Panamá by the end of 1999, a committee called the *Autoridad de la Región Interoceánica* was also set up to oversee an ambitious real-estate development project for the canal zone. Land that used to house American military bases has been put up for sale and is expected to fetch $30 billion, or five times the total national debt! Architect Frank Gehry, famous for his design of the Guggenheim Museum in Bilbao, Spain, has been put in charge of the project.

The government hopes to attract the foreign capital necessary to realize the country's enormous potential as a tourist destination.

The unemployment rate remains high, at 13.8%. The development of tourism, an industry that employs a large work-force, should help lower that rate. On the whole, Panamá is in an enviable position compared to its neighbours: it has the highest GNP per capita, the strongest growth and the lowest inflation rate of all Central American countries.

Society

Panamá has 3,000,000 inhabitants (1998), most of them Roman Catholics. There are also Protestant and Jewish minorities. There is a social security system and the state pays old age and disability pensions. While the number of physicians stands at a little more than 1 per 100 inhabitants, the child mortality rate remains at 25 per 1,000 (versus 7 per 1,000 in Canada, and 9 in the United States). Education is compulsory from age 6 to age 15, and about 93% of the children go to elementary school. Only 28% of the population continues to higher studies and 11.9% still cannot read. The country has three universities, one of them private.

Panamá ranks among the three top Central American countries for standard of living, life expectancy and general quality of life. Still, there is a great difference between the people who work for the canal or the American military and the rest of the population. A good number of those who work in the canal zone are employed by the Canal Commission and paid according to U.S. salary scales. This leads to a certain frustration among the Panamanian civil servants (since the government cannot afford to pay the same levels of salary) and among other workers in general. With high unemployment, and a sizeable public debt, the workers in the zone are considered spoiled children.

The major challenges facing the country in the future are the reduction of the country's enormous foreign debt, returning the administration of the canal to Panamanian sovereignty, and the withdrawal of U.S. forces.

Will the many people employed by the Americans (95% of the staff operating the canal is Panamanian) agree to be paid at the same rate as the local government employees? Will the Panamanian economy be able to ensure work for the 5,000 people working on the U.S. bases? What will be the impact of the withdrawal of the U.S. Forces? According to some estimates, the spinoff derived from the presence of these forces equals close to $300 million.

Panamanians and Tourism

From the point of view of tourism, the country has suffered enormously since the dark days of the Noriega regime. The number of visitors was quite high beforehand, but now it has plummeted, although since 1992 there has been a slight upward trend. While there are a number of tourist facilities in place, these are more frequently adapted to

Panamanian families. A number of initiatives are developing, and these have the support of the government. There are also various programs aimed at attracting foreign investors (see p133).

The variety and beauty of the countryside, the exceptional diversity of flora and fauna and the endless beaches make Panamá an ideal destination. Some people maintain that Panamá is just a big American base whose culture has become largely Americanized, and that there is no room left for anything but a Coca-Cola lifestyle and anglicization. This is simply not true. The country has a real culture of its own, steeped in colonial history. The Spanish language, furthermore, is very much alive here. While some remain bitter toward the Americans (especially after the 1989 invasion), the general attitude is a mixture of malaise combined with gratitude toward the invaders: malaise by reason of legitimate pride and a feeling for their country's independence, gratitude for being liberated from a terrible dictatorship. In any case, Panamanians are generally pleasant, courteous and good-humoured. Regardless of the problem you may be facing, ask someone for help and invariably, with a smile,

Common Symbols and their Meanings:

- the turtle symbolizes fertility
- the lizard symbolizes prudence and speed
- the bird of prey symbolizes authority
- the puma and the jaguar symbolize pride, cunning, skill and strength

will come the answer *"Si, como no?"* ("Yes, of course!"). Panamanians also enjoy celebrating and having fun; there is music almost everywhere.

The Arts in Panamá

The first forms of artistic development in Panamá date back to the pre-Columbian period with the large-scale production of ceramics and jewellery in the central provinces and in Chiriquí.

This was the period of Coclé culture (see p19). From the colonial conquest until the birth of the republic, artistic activities were limited to religious demonstrations and feasts (like Corpus Christi), and the erection of religious buildings. The same applied to painting and sculpture. Many folkloric ceremonies developed as well, some of them a mixture of pagan and Catholic rituals. Native cultures

exerted their influence on these customs, mixing with those brought from Spain.

Literature

With the exception of the works of writer Victor de la Guardia and poet Darío Herrera, there was no intense literary movement until the birth of the republic as an independent country. A number of poets and writers appeared in the 20th century: Ricardo Míro, José María Núñez and Rogelio Sinán are just a few examples. A number of works of realism were produced, mostly influenced by the many sociopolitical upheavals that had a profound impact on Panamanian literature. Two fine Panamanian writers are Joaquím Beleño, whose book *Luna Verde* describes workers in the canal zone, and the poet Amelia Denis de Icaza.

Music and Dance

Panamanian folk dancing has a long and rich past. Originally brought by the settlers, it assimilated various elements from inside and outside the country as it spread among the regions. Slaves from Africa and, much later, workers from the Caribbean, also contributed much to local folklore. The dance called *Congo*, performed mainly on the coast of Colón, reflects a strong African influence. Panamá's most celebrated dances are still, however, the *tamborito* (the national dance), the *mejorana*, and the *punto*, during which the female dancers wear the *pollera* (see p206).

Music, with a long and rich tradition, developed very rapidly in Panamá, and a national symphony orchestra was created in 1941. The most celebrated Panamanian composer of the 20th century was Alberto Galimany (1889-1973). Popular, contemporary Panamanian music is in many respects highly distinctive and quite different from that of the neighbouring countries. In addition to the omnipresent accordion,

Empollerada in a pollera

characteristic shouts called *saloma* very often punctuate the songs, imparting a pleasant pastoral style. Among popular singers are Victorio Vergara, Alfredo Escudero, Dorindo Cardenas and Sony and Sandra Sandoval. Besides all of these, one performer, known around the world and praised in Panamá, stands out: Rubén Blades.

Rubén Blades

Rubén Blades was born in Ciudad de Panamá, the second of five children. He grew up surrounded by artists and musicians, with a father who played bongo, and a mother, the daughter of a Cuban and an American, who sang with one of the greatest Cuban lyricists, Ernesto Lecuona. Blades was brought up mostly by his feminist grandmother, a painter and author; one can imagine how much she influenced a young Blades.

During his childhood, Blades, like any other young Panamanian in the 1960s, was greatly impressed by American music. His view of America was shattered, however, during the events of 1964 when several students were killed.

As a result, he reconsidered his identity as a Panamanian. Until then he had been singing rock songs in small groups, but from that moment on he refused to sing in English and concentrated on Latin American music. The Argentinean singer Piero became his model, and the social themes evoked in a number of Piero's songs provided inspiration to Blades' own lyrics.

The Torrijos coup d'état occurred while Blades was enrolled in law at the University of Panamá, and brought him to another turning point in his life. The military authorities closed the university, and Blades decided to accept an offer he had received some years back from a group of New York musicians; in 1969 he emigrated to the United States. At this time the *salsa* was very much in fashion, and Blades joined the very popular artist Rodríguez. He made a record with Rodríguez, but it failed to bring him the recognition he sought. His future in the United States was now uncertain, and since the University of Panamá had reopened, he went back to finish his law studies. After two years with the Central Bank, however, Blades realized that he could never abandon music, so he returned to the States.

In New York he became very popular, but at the same time he began looking for something more. Tired of music that carried no message, he wanted songs that were more personal, a salsa that was more committed. He found this depth with Willie Colón, and their album *Siembra*, for which Blades had written most of the songs, became an immediate success.

Around 1982, after many other successes, Blades and Colón decided to go their separate ways. Blades formed a group called "Seis del Solar", and in 1984 the group's album, *Buscando América*, was released in two languages: Spanish and, for the first time, English. It was an immediate hit. On this album, Blades sings of the difficulty of living under corrupt and tyrannical regimes. One of the songs is dedicated to Cardinal Romero of El Salvador;

another, *Decisiones*, was banned in Panamá. Despite the ban, the song was still heard everywhere, even on city buses, and when Blades appeared for a concert, he was an immediate success.

After helping produce the film *Crossover Dreams* and taking a break for a law degree from Harvard, Blades returned to music. In 1985 he and Linda Ronstadt released a new album, *Escenas*. A voracious reader, Rubén Blades was an admirer of Gabriel García Márquez and became one of his friends. The writer's influence was felt in the album *Agua de luna*, which is directly based on Márquez's writings. By 1989 he had formed a new group, "Son del Solar", and put out a new album, *Antecedente*. This was followed in 1991 by *Caminando*.

While Rubén Blades is an accomplished singer and musician, he is

also appreciated, though less known, as an actor, and has appeared in such films as *Milagro Beanfield War* and *Critical*.

He travels regularly to Los Angeles, and in 1990 he was given his greatest role, in *Dead Man Out*, filmed in Québec, for which he won a prize as best actor. To date, Rubén Blades has taken part in 13 films.

As someone constantly in search of new ways and a more just and more democratic society, Blades was shaken by the tragic events in Panamá. Pleased at Noriega's departure but crushed by the American invasion, Blades is now ready to take a more active part in his country's political life. As a candidate in the May 1994 elections, Blades came in third, while six members of his party were elected to parliament.

Practical Information

M ost regions in Panamá can be explored without much difficulty, though visiting certain places, such as Darién, will require making prior arrangements.

Whatever your destination, planning ahead is always a good idea. This section is intended to help you organize your visit to Panamá by providing general information and practical advice on local customs.

Entrance Formalities

Before leaving home, be sure you have the official documents that will allow you to enter and leave Panamá. Take good care of these documents; keep them with you wherever you travel in the country.

To enter Panamá, travellers, no matter what their nationality, must have a passport, valid for at least six months after entering the country, and either a "tourist card" or visa, valid for the length of stay.

British, German, Austrian, Spanish, Swiss, Costa Rican, Chilean and Uraguayan citizens do not need a visa or a tourist card, only a valid passport. Canadian and American citizens, as well as citizens of most western European countries, must have a tourist card in addition to their passport. These cards can be obtained at customs upon entering the country, usually cost B/. 6 and are valid for 30 days. You must keep the card throughout your travels as it must be returned to customs upon departure.

When entering the country **overland** from Costa Rica or Colombia, you must present the same card or a visa and a return plane ticket. In some cases proof of sufficient funds for the duration of your stay may be required. Though the tourist card is available from the main border crossings it is strongly advised to purchase a visa ahead of time to avoid any problems. Sometimes they are out of these cards at borders. Visitors entering the country by car will also need official authorization to drive in the country. This authorization is given at border-crossings after the registration for the car and car insurance have been verified. Travellers wishing to visit Colombia or Costa Rica during their stay must follow certain formalities and are advised to check with those countries' consulates.

It is a good idea to photocopy the important pages of your passport and to write down your passport number. This will make it easier to replace this document should it be lost or stolen (do the same with all official documents, driver's license, tourist card, etc.). In the event that you lose an important piece of identification, contact your country's embassy or consulate (see p42) to have a new one issued.

As events and policies evolve rapidly, it is a good idea to make sure the formalities described above still apply **before leaving** on your trip.

Travellers wishing to stay longer than 30 days can renew their tourist card for another 30 days at the *Departamento de Inmigración y Naturalización* in Ciudad de Panamá (see address below). In addition to two passport-sized identification photos, you will need to present a ticket out of the country and a short letter explaining why you want to extend your stay. You may also be asked to prove that you have sufficient funds to support yourself on a longer visit. In addition, it is important to get an exit permit (**permiso de salida**) when you do decide to leave. They can be obtained at the *Ministerio de Hacienda y Tesoro* by asking for a *paz y salvo.*

Departamento de Inmigración y Naturalización
at the corner of Calle 28 este and Avenida 2a Sur (Cuba)
☎ *225-8925*
☎ *227-1448*
☎ *227-1175*
☎ *227-1209*

Ministerio de Hacienda y Tesoro
Calle 36 y 35 between Avenida Perú and Cuba
☎ *227-4879*
☎ *227-3033*
≈ *227-2357*

In order to avoid delay, it is preferable that you ask for an extended visa **before** your departure in the Panamanian consulate in your home country.

Departure Tax

Everyone leaving Panamá must pay a departure tax of B/. 20. The payment (to be made in cash – credit cards are not accepted) is made when reserving seats for your return flight.

Embassies and Consulates

Embassies and consulates representing your home country can provide valuable assistance in the event of health emergencies, legal problems or the death of a travel companion. However, visitors are responsible for any costs incurred as a result of services provided by these official bodies. If there is no representation in Panamá, then the closest consulate or embassy is given below.

Belgium
Embajada de Bélgica
Los Yoses
4 A Entrada 25 M Sur
Apto 3725
San José, Costa Rica
1010
☎ *(506) 225-6633*
☎ *225-0351*

Canada
Embajada de Canada
Edificio Banco Central
Hispano No.4
Ave. Samuel Lewis and Calle Gerardo Ortega
Ciudad de Panamá
☎ *(507) 264-9731*
☎ *264-7115*
≈ *(507) 263-8083*

Colombia
Consulado General de Colombia
Calle Manuel Maria Icaza 12
Edificio Grobman Piso 6
Apartado postal 4407 Zona 5
Ciudad de Panamá
☎ *(507) 264-9266*
☎ *264-9644*
≈ *(507) 223-1134*

Some Interesting Web Sites

www.ipat.gob.pa:
Official site of the Panamanian Tourist Office

www.pa:
The country's most complete site but also the slowest!

www.iaehv.nl/users/grimaldo/Panama.html:
General information on the country

www.alphaluz.com/Panama:
General information on the country

www.Panamacanal.com/index.htm:
General information on the country

www.sinfo.net/alcaldia:
Panamá City's official site

www.elecciones99.com:
Information on the elections

www.pancanal.com:
Official Canal Commission site

www.pancanal.com/photo/camera-java.html:
Live footage of the Miraflores locks

www.zonian.com:
Site that pays tribute to the builders of the canal

www.czbrats.com/cz_brats.htm:
Site dedicated to the American era of the canal

www.trainweb.org//Panamá:
Site of Panamá's only railway

www.ariPanamá.com:
Official site of the Interoceanic Region Administration

www.boyds.org/recipes.htm:
Religious site with many Panamanian recipes

Costa Rica
Embajada de Costa Rica
Calle Gerardo Ortega y Vía
España
Ciudad de Panamá
☎ *(507) 264-9237*
⊷ *(507) 264-6348*

Great Britain
Embajada de Gran Bretaña
Calle 53 y Urb. Marbella
Ciudad de Panamá
☎ *269-0866*

Italy
Embajada de Italia
Calle Primera 42, 1st floor
Parque Lefevre
Apdo 2369
Ciudad de Panamá
☎ *(507) 226-3616*
⊷ *(507) 226-3121*

Netherlands
Consulado de los Países Bajos
Calle Manuel Maria Icaza 4
Ciudad de Panamá
☎ *264-7257*

Spain
Embajada de España
Plaza de Belisario Porras
Ave. 6 No. 44
Zona 1
Ciudad de Panamá
☎ *(507) 227-5122*
☎ *227-5472*
☎ *227-5478*
⊷ *(507) 227-6284*

Switzerland
Edificio Centro Colón
10 Pisa Paseo Colón
San José, Costa Rica 1007
☎ *(506) 221-4829*
⊷ *(506) 255-2831*

United States
Embajada Americana
Avenida Balboa
Apartado postal 6959 Zona 5
Ciudad de Panamá
☎ *227-1777*
⊷ *227-1964*

Panamanian Consulates and Embassies Abroad

While consulates can sometimes provide general travel information, their main function is to issue official documents (visas, immigration papers etc.). When possible, contact a Panamanian tourist office for additional information.

Belgium
Embassy of Panamá
Avenue Louise 390
1000 Brussels
☎ *(02) 649.07.29*
☎ *649.28.79*
⊷ *(02) 648.92.16*

Canada
Consulate General of Panamá
1425 Boul. René-Levesque Ouest
Suite 504
Montréal, Québec
H3G 1T7
☎ *(514) 874-1929*
⊷ *(514) 874-1947*

Embassy of Panamá
130 Albert St.
Suite 300
Ottawa, Ontario
K1P 5G4
☎ *(613) 236-7177*
⊷ *(613) 236-5775*

Colombia
Embajada de Panamá
Calle 92, 7-70
Apdo 90094
Santa Fe de Bogota
☎ *(507) 257-5068*
⊷ *(507) 257-5067*

Costa Rica
Embajada de Panamá
Del Centro Colón 275m al norte
San José, Costa Rica 1000
☎ *257-3241*
☎ *256-5169*
⊷ *257-4864*

Germany
Embassy of Panamá
Lutzowstrasse, 1
53173 Bonn
☎ *(228) 361-036*
⊷ *(228) 363-558*

Great Britain
Embassy of Panamá
48 Park Street
London W1Y 3PD
☎ *171-493-4646*
⊷ *171-493-4499*

Italy
Embassy of Panamá
Viale Regina Margerita No. 239
Cuarto Piso, interno 11
Rome 00198
☎ *4-425-2173*
☎ *4-426-5436*
⊷ *4-426-5443*

Netherlands
Consulate of Panamá
Herman Grosterstraat 14
Amsterdam 1077 WG
☎ *20-673-6199*

Nicaragua
Embajado de Panamá
Del Hotel Colón, 1 quadre al lago y 25 varas arriba
Casa 73
Managua
☎ *(2) 78-1619*
⊷ *(2) 74-223*

Spain
Embajada de Panamá
Claudio Coello 86, 1er
Madrid 28006
☎ *(1) 576-5001*
⊷ *(1) 576-7161*

Switzerland
Consulate General of Panamá
72 Rue de Lausanne
1202 Geneva
☎ 22-738-03-88

United States
Embassy of Panamá
2862 McGill Terrace N.W.
Washington D.C. 20008
☎ (202) 483-1407
📠 (202) 483-8416

Consulate of Panamá
24 Guenway Plaza, Ste. 1307
Houston, TX 77046
☎ (713) 622-4451
📠 (713) 622-4468

Consulate of Panamá
870 Market Street, Ste. 551
San Francisco, CA 94102
☎ (415) 391-4268
📠 (415) 391-4269

Consulate of Panamá
1212 Avenue of the Americas
10th floor
New York, NY 10036
☎ (212) 840-2450
📠 (212) 840-2469

Consulate of Panamá
Rivergate Plaza
444 Brickell Ave., Suite 729
Miami, Fla 33131
☎ (305) 371-7031
📠 (305) 371-2907

Tourist Information

IPAT (Panamanian Tourist Institute)

Offices of the Panamanian Tourist Institute (IPAT) are found only in Panamá. However, Panamanian consulates and embassies in many countries can usually provide information and a small selection of brochures. The IPAT offices found throughout Panamá are there to answer questions and help visitors explore the country. Unfortunately, the documentation they have on hand is limited and dated.

The addresses and telephone numbers of IPAT regional offices can be found in the "Practical Information" section of each chapter. There is also an office at the international airport to assist visitors on arrival.

Aeropuerto Internacional Tocumen
open from 8am to midnight
near the customs offices
☎ 238-4356
☎ 238-4102

Publications

A publication called **Focus Panamá** is available free of charge in many hotels and restaurants in the capital. The magazine describes Ciudad de Panamá's nightlife and cultural activities, and provides short descriptions of interesting activities that take place elsewhere in the country. It is available in English and Spanish.

Two small English publications provide information on the latest in theatre, tourism, and dining out. These are the bilingual (English-Spanish) weekly **The Visitor**, also known as **El Visitante**, and the English-language **Panamá News**. Both are available for free in most hotels and restaurants.

The best place to get detailed maps of the country is from the **Instituto Geográfico Nacional Tommy Guardia**, located across from the University of Panamá (take the pedestrian walkway over Vía Simón Bolívar). Unfortunately, the maps are not up to date and the staff is not very cooperative. Maps of the country, including excellent ones published by the ITMB at a scale of 1:800,000, are also available in many travel bookstores in Europe and North America.

Instituto Geográfico Nacional Tommy Guardia
Calle 57 Oeste (Melchor Lasso de la Vega) y Avenida 6A Norte
Apartado 5267 Panamá 5

Entering the Country

By Plane

From Canada

At present there are no direct flights between Canada and Panamá. However, indirect flights are offered by Delta Airlines, Continental Airlines and Air Canada. The best deal seems to be with Delta, which has an arrangement with Copa (the national airline of

The Visit Central America Pass

If you plan on visiting several countries in Central America, you might consider the Visit Central America Pass. This pass allows you to start your trip in the United States and then head to one of the Central-American capital cities. You can then travel on any of the five major Central-American airlines: Copa, Lacsa, Nica, Aviateca, or Taca to the destination of your choice. A minimum purchase of three tickets is required. For information in North America dial: ☎ 800-255-8222.

Panamá). This deal is sold as a single ticket which means that in the event of a delay, the passenger is guaranteed a hotel and a restaurant meal. Chartered flights are also offered during the winter from Montreal and Toronto.

Other air travel possibilities include travelling though Mexico and most countries in Central America and the Caribbean.

Delta Airlines offers flights from Toronto and Montreal to Ciudad de Panamá, with a transfer in Miami to **Copa**.

Air Canada offers flights from Toronto and Montreal to Ciudad de Panamá with a transfer in Houston to **Continental Airlines**.

From Europe

Most airline companies flying to Panamá out of Europe make stops in the United States or in one of several Latin American countries. Depending on the point of departure, several combinations are possible.

Here are two airlines that *do* have direct flights to Panamá:

Iberia: three flights a week out of Madrid.

KLM: two flights a week out of Amsterdam.

As the fares can vary substantially depending on the season and the "fare wars" waged between competing airlines, it is a good idea to shop around.

From the USA

Panamá's national airline, **Copa**, has daily flights from Miami.

Certain American airline companies such as **Continental**, **Northwest** and **America West Airlines**, have made arrangements with Copa to provide several connections between the United States and Panamá. A number of possibilities exist for flying out of Mexico and most countries in Central America and the Caribbean.

By Car

From Costa Rica

Two regions of Panamá are accessible from Costa Rica: the province of Bocas del Toro by bus, train or boat, and the province of Chiriquí, along the Interamericana highway to Paso Canoa, the border town in the province of Chiriquí. The latter option is the most convenient for those travelling by car or bus. Remember that the Costa Rican border crossings are only open from *8am to 11pm*.

Also remember that no matter how you enter the country, certain formalities apply (see p 41). There is a time difference between Costa Rica and Panamá, so remember to put your watch ahead an hour when you cross the border into Panamá.

By Bus

From Costa Rica

Two companies provide service from the capital of Costa Rica to Ciudad de Panamá:

Tica Bus
B/. 40
in San José, Calle 9 et Av. 4
☎ 221-9229
☎ 221-8954

In Ciudad de Panamá, departures are from the Ideal Hotel
Calle 17 Oeste or Calle I
☎ 262-2084
☎ 262-6275

Panaline
B/. 42
in San José, Calle 16, Av. 3/5
☎ 255-1205
Panaline has daily departures from San José. In
Ciudad de Panamá, from the International Hotel close to the Plaza 5 de Mayo
☎ 262-1618
≈ 262-1589
There are daily departures.

Tracopa
Avenida 18, Calle 4
☎ 221-4214
☎ 223-7685
Another possibility is to take a Tracopa bus from San José to David; from David you can change buses and travel on to Ciudad de Panamá (this is the more time-consuming of the two bus routes).

The buses cross the border at Paso Canoa, a town with a number of banks and other services. Note that the border is sometimes closed for a while in the middle of the day and at night.

From Colombia

It is virtually impossible to travel across land from Colombia to Panamá. While there are a few rudimentary paths in northern Colombia that wind toward the border, and plans have been made to extend the Interamericana highway, the thick jungle in the province of Darién in southern Panamá acts as a barrier between the countries. The trip is technically possible but very risky, so it is best left to well-equipped and experienced travellers who know the region. Insects, including disease-carrying mosquitos, and poisonous snakes are just a few of the dangers likely to be encountered along the way.

In addition, passing through some Amerindian villages in the area requires authorization from village chiefs, and lodging facilities in the region are non-existent or very basic. In short, road travel between Colombia and Panamá is not recommended (unless big risks and adventure are a priority).

Airports

Besides Tocumen International Airport, there are a number of smaller airports scattered around the country. International flights into Panamá touch down at the **Tocumen** airport. The **Albrook** military airport has recently been converted to handle domestic flights.

Tocumen International Airport

The Tocumen International Airport is a relatively modern facility with most of the services expected of a major airport.

Along with a number of duty-free shops and international car rental agencies, the airport also has a cafeteria and a bar. The national tourist information bureau, IPAT, has an office in the airport open from 8am to midnight.

For arrival and departure information:
☎ 238-4322

Car Rental Agencies

Avis
☎ 238-4037
☎ 238-4056

Hertz
☎ 238-4081
☎ 238-4106

Budget
☎ 238-4069

From Tocumen International to Ciudad de Panamá, (see next chapter).

In the area around the airport there are all kinds of people offering their services or selling different merchandise. If you decide to buy something, don't open your window too wide when paying. It is safer to drive from the airport during the day.

Domestic Flights

Domestic flights have recently been transferred to Albrook, the former military airport, which is larger and better-equipped than the airport at Punta Paitilla. Only three companies currently offer regular flights within Panamá. Their offices are found at the new airport, which is also called Aeropuerto Marcos Gelabert.

For all general information: ☎ 315-1622

Mapiex-Aero
☎ 315-0344
Mapiex-Aero has regular flights to David, Bocas del Toro, Changuinola and Colón from the capital.

Aeroperlas
P.O. Box 6-3596, El Dorado
☎ 315-0303
☎ 325-0302
≈ 315-0337
iflyap@aeroperlas.com
www.aeroperlas.com
Aeroperlas is the largest company and flies to 13 destinations from Ciudad de Panamá including Isla Contadora, Colón, Santiago, Chitre, David, Bocas del Toro, Changuinola, Garachiné, Sambú, La Palma, Bahía Piña, Le Real and Jacqué.

Aero Taxi
Aeropuerto Albrook
☎ 315-0275
Aero Taxi specializes in flights to the San Blas comarca.

Insurance

Cancellation Insurance

This type of insurance is usually offered by travel agents and is purchased along with airline tickets or holiday package-deals. Cancellation insurance ensures that the cost of an airline ticket or package deal will be refunded in the event

that a trip must be cancelled as a result of illness or death. This can be useful, but one should weigh the likelihood of such an event against the cost of the insurance.

Theft Insurance

Most residential insurance policies cover a percentage of personal belongings against theft if they are stolen outside the country. To file an insurance claim for a theft incurred while on holiday, you will need a police report from the country you are visiting. If you have a residential insurance policy, you may already be sufficiently protected. If you plan to travel with valuable objects, check you policy or with an insurance agent.

Life Insurance

A number of airline companies offer life insurance with the price of a ticket. As many travellers already have life insurance policies, additional coverage may not be necessary.

Health Insurance

This is the most useful kind of insurance for travellers, and should be purchased before you leave. Recommended is a comprehensive health insur ance policy that provides a level of coverage sufficient to pay for hospitalization, nursing care and doctor's fees – keep in mind that health care costs are rising quickly everywhere. The policy should also have a repatriation clause in case the required care is not available where you become ill. As patients are sometimes asked to pay for medical services immediately, find out what provisions your policy makes in this event. If you have to pay for health care in cash, make sure to keep all documents related to the transaction so that you can present them to your insurance company later for a refund. To avoid any problems during your vacation, always keep proof of your insurance policy on you.

Climate

Panamá has a tropical climate characterized by two seasons: the dry and the rainy, or green, season. Depending on the region and the altitude, there are many possible variations, resulting in many different microclimates within the country. The Caribbean coast gets plentiful rain all year long, while the dry season on the Pacific side is more pronounced. On the Azuero Peninsula, the climate is extremely arid during the dry season, and several weeks can go by with no rain at all. At the other extreme, it can rain for two days out of three during the wet season in the mountains!

The rainy season is from May to November. Panamánians call this season *invierno* (winter), not to be confused with the cold and snow of North American or European winters. Indeed, the rainy season is generally referred to as the "green season" because of the explosive growth of greenery at this time of year. In fact, many repeat visitors prefer to come during this season, because of the incredible greenery, lack of tourists and lower prices. The dry season (*verano*, meaning summer) is from December to April; March and April are generally the hottest months.

Temperatures are relatively constant in Panamá, and variations are linked to altitude. Temperatures on the coasts regularly climb to more than 35°C. The higher the altitude, the colder the temperature, which falls about 1°C for every 150 m of elevation. For the past few years, the climate has been irregular and unpredictable. But as Panamá is a small country with many climates, there is always somewhere that is comfortable! Those who do not like the heat and humidity would be more comfortable staying in the El Valle, Boquete, Volcán or Cerro Azul regions, where the temperature is almost always cool and pleasant.

Health

Illnesses

Panamá is a wonderful country to explore, however, travellers should protect themselves against a number of health risks associated with the region. In addition to diseases found throughout the world, including AIDS and various venereal diseases, a number of illnesses specifically related to Panamá's hot humid climate pose a less familiar threat. Malaria, yellow fever, hepatitis A, typhoid and occasionally cholera are all present in most Central and South American countries, though the risk of contamination varies according to location. Other health problems travellers risk encountering include diphtheria, tetanus and polio.

Please note that this section is intended to provide general information. Since recommendations can change, see your doctor (or visit a traveller's clinic) before leaving for more complete

Practical Information

advice on the need to protect yourself) against the health risks mentioned here. It is much easier and convenient to take precautions – such as getting vaccinations and bringing along medication – than to deal with what may be a serious illness with long-term effects.

Malaria

Also called paludism, malaria is caused by a parasite in the blood transmitted by anopheles mosquitoes; it cannot be passed from one person to another.

The symptoms of malaria include high fever, chills, extreme fatigue and headaches as well as stomach and muscle aches. There are several forms of malaria, including one serious type caused by *P. falciparum*. The disease usually takes hold while travellers are still on holiday or up to 12 weeks following your return; in some cases, the symptoms will recur months later.

While most people recover from malaria, it is important to take all possible precautions against the disease. A doctor can prescribe anti-malarial medication to be taken before and after your trip (various types exist, depending on the destination, length of trip, age, etc.). Since the parasite that causes malaria is constantly evolving, anti-malarial

medication is not foolproof. As much as possible, travellers should avoid getting bitten by mosquitoes (see p51).

Diphtheria and Tetanus

These two illnesses, against which most people are vaccinated during their childhood, can have serious consequences. Thus, before leaving, check that your vaccinations are valid; you may need a booster shot. Diphtheria is a bacterial infection that is transmitted by nose and throat secretions or by skin lesions on an infected person. Symptoms include sore throat, high fever, general aches and pains and occasionally skin infections. Tetanus is caused by a bacteria that enters your body through an open wound that comes in contact with contaminated dust or rusty metal.

Yellow Fever

Like malaria, yellow fever is transmitted by infected mosquitos. The symptoms usually appear three to six days after infection, do not last long and their intensity can vary; they include headaches, a very high fever, vomiting, sore back, and a slight yellowing of the skin. An effective vaccination against yellow fever, best taken before departure, is available; consult your physician. Once again, as the vaccine is not 100% effec-

tive, so it is important to avoid getting bitten by mosquitoes (see p51).

Hepatitis A

This infection is generally transmitted by ingesting food or water that has been contaminated by fecal matter. The symptoms include fever, yellowing of skin, loss of appetite and fatigue, and these can appear between 15 and 50 days after infection. An effective vaccination, given by injection, is available. Besides the recommended vaccine, good hygiene is important. Always wash your hands before every meal and ensure that the food and preparation area are clean.

Hepatits B

Hepatitis B, like hepatitis A, affects the liver, but is transmitted through direct contact of bodily fluids. The symptoms are flu-like, and similar to those of hepatitis A. A vaccination exists but must be administered over an extended period of time, so be sure to check with your doctor several weeks in advance.

Typhoid Fever

This illness is caused by ingesting food that has come in contact (direct or not) with an infected person's stool. Common symptoms include high fever, loss of appetite, headaches, constipation and occasionally diarrhoea, or red spots on the skin. These symptoms will appear one to three weeks after infection. Besides good hygiene, there is a typhoid vaccination, which must be administered in two or three doses to be most effective. Once again, check with your doctor.

Additional Health Care Advice

Bodies of fresh water are frequently contaminated by the bacteria that causes schistosomiasis. This illness, caused by a worm-like parasite that enters the body and attacks the liver and nervous system, is difficult to treat. Swimming in fresh water should thus be avoided.

Strict controls on blood quality have been put into place by the health care systems in most countries. However, in the unlikely event that you require an emergency blood transfusion, make sure (when possible) that such measures have in fact been taken. Remember as well to use condoms during all sexual encounters.

The health problems that most often plague travellers are usually related to poorly treated water containing bacteria. In most of

the bigger hotels, this danger has been almost completely eliminated. Still, in certain high risk areas (especially along the Atlantic coast and in Darién), it is a good idea to drink only bottled water. When buying bottled water, make sure the bottle is properly sealed. Ice cubes should be avoided, as the cold does not destroy the bacteria. In addition, fresh fruits and vegetables that have been washed (especially those that are not peeled before being eaten) can also pose a health risk. Make sure that the vegetables you eat are well-cooked and peel all your fruit.

If you do get diarrhoea, several steps should be followed to treat it. First, try to soothe your stomach by avoiding solids; instead, drink carbonated beverages, bottled water, or weak tea or coffee (avoid milk) until you recover. As the resulting dehydration can be dangerous, drinking sufficient quantities of liquid is crucial. To remedy severe dehydration, a solution containing a litre of water, two or three teaspoons of salt and one teaspoon of sugar will help re-establish the body's fluid balance. Pharmacies also sell ready-made preparations to help cure dehydration. Finally, gradually reintroduce solids to your system by eating easily digestible foods. Medi-

cation, such as Imodium or Pepto-Bismol, can help control intestinal discomfort. If more serious symptoms develop (high fever, bloody stool), see a doctor.

Remember that consuming too much alcohol, particularly when accompanied by prolonged exposure to the sun, can cause severe dehydration and lead to health problems. Sunstroke is a common affliction among travellers – protect yourself with a hat and sunglasses.

Medication

Some types of medication require a prescription and can be very expensive in Panamá; in some areas they may not be available at all. Bring along whatever prescription drugs and other potentially expensive medication you may need. It is also useful to have a small first-aid kit containing adhesive bandages, disinfectant, aspirin and antihistamines.

Mosquitoes and Other Insects

A nuisance common to many countries, mosquitoes are no strangers to Panamá. They are particularly numerous during the rainy season. Protect yourself with a good insect repellent. Repellents with DEET are the most effective. The concentration of DEET varies from one product to the next; the higher the concentration, the longer the protection. In rare cases, the use of repellents with high concentrations (35% or more) of DEET has been associated with convulsions in young children; it is therefore important to apply these products sparingly, on exposed surfaces, and to wash it off once back inside. A concentration of 35% DEET will protect for four to six hours, while 95% will last from 10 to 12 hours. New formulas with DEET in lesser concentrations, but which last just as long, are available.

To further reduce the possibility of getting bitten, do not wear perfume or bright colours. Sundown is an especially active time for insects. When walking in wooded areas, cover your legs and ankles well. Insect coils can help provide a better night's sleep. Before bed, apply insect repellent to your skin and to the headboard and baseboard of your bed. If possible, get an air-conditioned room, or bring a mosquito net.

Lastly, since it is impossible to completely avoid contact with mosquitoes, bring along a cream to soothe the bites you will invariably get.

Dangerous Wildlife

A graphic description of the snakes, scorpions, spiders and other creatures native to Panamá could be enough to put off potential travellers. However, keep in mind that the presence of such things varies according to region – they are almost non-existent in cities – and that a number of simple precautions can be taken to avoid problems:

Shake out your clothes in the morning.

Shake out your shoes before putting them on.

Move your bed away from the wall by an inch or two.

Do not leave food out that could attract insects or animals.

Take the necessary precautions against mosquitoes.

Snakes

Among a country's rich and diverse fauna, there are bound to be some species that are less congenial than others. Accordingly, Panamá is home to several kinds of snakes, some of which are poisonous. There is no need to get too alarmed, as you are unlikely to cross paths with one during your visit. Nevertheless, it is important to keep your

eyes open and watch where you step. In the forest, look around before you lean against something or sit down somewhere. When hiking, be careful as you part the foliage that sometimes hangs across the path, and check the shores as well as the surface of the water if you go swimming in a river. Some people think they are faster than a snake and tease it, or poke it to see if they can make it move; needless to say, this is not a good idea! The presence of snakes should not prevent you from exploring everything that Panamá has to offer. Like most wild animals, snakes avoid contact with humans as much as possible.

Other Animals

People are sometimes tempted to pick up the coloured frogs seen throughout Central America. Avoid this. Though not all frogs in Panamá are poisonous, many do secrete a toxic substance that protects them from predators. Avoid touching any frogs and you will avoid potential problems.

The Sun

Exposure to the sun, as pleasant as it can be, can also cause a few problems – some of them serious. In recent years there has been a higher incidence of skin cancer around the world. A good sun screen is invaluable, but be aware that most dermatologists recommend buying a brand name sun screen with a minimum SPF of 15 for adults and 25 for children. To be fully effective, the cream must be applied at least 30 min before exposure to the sun and should be re-applied regularly while outside. Avoid staying in the sun for too long, especially the first few days, as it may take a little while to get used to the sun's strength. A hat and proper sunglasses will also help protect you from the sun. The longer you stay out in the sun, the higher the risk of getting sunstroke, so be careful.

The Sea

The long sandy beaches along both coasts of Panamá are among the country's most beautiful attractions; many are completely undeveloped and have no facilities.

For the sake of safety and enjoyment, beach-goers should keep the following suggestions in mind:

Choose a beach where other people are swimming – busy beaches are generally safer ones. This is a particularly good idea if you are on your own, as it means there will be someone around if you need help. A number of areas have strong undercurrents that can pull swimmers under the surface or out to sea.

If you are intent on swimming alone off empty beaches, make sure these places are safe for swimming. Certain stretches of coastline on the Pacific side are heavily frequented by sharks.

Find out about the jellyfish situation where you are. They have cycles of abundance and are present close to shore at certain times of the day.

Wear sandals or shoes rather than walk barefoot over rocks or coral. Be careful of insects at the beach as well, as some can cause painful stings.

In general, avoid venturing too far out from deserted beaches, which are deserted for a reason, probably because they are more dangerous.

Follow the example of the local inhabitants and, so as not to offend, do not sunbathe or swim in the nude (or topless).

Packing

As the temperature in Panamá varies according to altitude and season, the type of clothes to bring depends on when and where you plan to go. In general, loose-fitting cotton clothing is best in low-lying areas. Wear shoes rather than sandals when exploring cities, as they will protect you from cuts that could get infected.

Practical Information

A Packing Checklist

insect repellent
(indispensable if travelling outside Panama City)
insect coils
sun block (cream)
sink stopper
sun glasses
hat
umbrella
hiking boots
binoculars
light wind-breaker
compass (for hikers)
plastic sandals for shower and beach

During the rainy season, and in tropical forests, it is useful to have a light windbreaker. In areas of higher elevation, where the nights can be quite cool, a sweater will come in handy. Bring walking shoes or boots that cover the ankle if you plan to explore the countryside (see p52). Do not forget to bring along a cheap pair of plastic sandals to wear in the shower and at the beach. Certain restaurants and clubs (particularly those in cities) have a dress code – pack a few appropriate items.

Safety and Security

While Panamá has a reputation as a place where theft is common, it is important to put the facts in context. To the majority of Panamanians, your possessions (particularly things like cameras, video cameras, leather suitcases and jewellery) represent a great deal of money. Theft is much more common in cities because of poverty. Rural areas are generally safer. A degree of caution can help avoid problems. For example, do not wear too much jewellery, keep your electronic equipment in a nondescript shoulder bag, and avoid revealing the contents of your wallet when making a purchase. A money belt can be useful for hiding money, traveller's cheques and passports. And if your bags should happen to be stolen, you will at least have the money and documents necessary to get by. Remember that the less attention you draw to yourself, the less chance you have of being robbed.

Avoid bringing anything of value with you to the **beach**. However, if you do, keep a close eye on it. Most hotels have a **safe** where you can leave your valuables.

When driving in Panamanian cities, particularly Colón and Ciudad de Panamá, **keep your doors locked**. It is recommended that you park your car in a guarded lot or in an open area. Wherever you end up parking, **don't leave anything valuable in the car** and leave the glove compartment open.

One last piece of advice: **never** leave your bag in the checkroom of a major store, particularly in the capital. Even in the presence of a guard, you risk never seeing it again!

Transportation

By Car

The Interamericana

The Interamericana highway crosses nearly the full length of the country, from the border of Costa Rica to the village of Yaviza. However, not all sections of the road are paved. The stretch of highway leading out of the capital toward the west is in excellent condition and parts of it are wider. Heading east from the capital, the highway is paved only as far as the village of Chepo. From here to just beyond the village of Metetí, the road is paved in places but is more often covered with gravel. Beyond the village of Yaviza, the road becomes little more than a jungle track. The long-discussed plans to extend the Interamericana highway have not yet been carried out. The big price tag involved and the potential social and environmental problems involved have put the project on hold.

While the speed limit on the Interamericana is 90 km/h, a more realistic average speed is about 60 km/h.

Travel slows down considerably in the many villages and larger towns along the route and at major intersections. The speed limit is lowered to 40 km/h along these sections. There are police officers keeping an eye out for driving violations at many of the bigger intersections. The only place where the speed limit is as

Many city streets in Panamá, particularly those in Panamá City, have several names. For example, the same street can be known as both "Calle 49 Este" and "Calle Aquilino de la Guardia". In the capital, the avenues (avenidas) usually run parallel to the coast, whereas streets (calles) run perpendicular. Sometimes even local inhabitants do not know the exact names of all the streets. It is therefore easier to ask directions to a specific building (a church, monument) or well-known store near the street you are looking for.

A few streets with multiple names:

Avenida Simón Bolivar	Transístmica
Avenida 1a Sur	Perú
Avenida 2a Sur	Cuba
Avenida 3a Sur	Justo Arosemena
Avenida 4a Sur	Nicanor de Obarrio or Calle 50
Avenida Ecuador	Calle Brasilia
Calle 48 Este	Uruguay
Calle 49 Este	Aquilino de la Guardia
Calle 49 A Oeste	Veneto
Calle 50 Este	Ricardo Arias
Avenida 2a A Norte	Eusebio A. Morales
Avenida 1a A Norte	Calle D
Avenida Ricardo J. Alfaro	Tumba Muerto

These are just a few of the many examples. Perhaps the most complicated example of all is Avenida Nicanor de Obarrio, also known as Avenida 4a Sur and, more commonly still, Calle 50! To complicate matters even further, some people designate a lower or higher number, depending on their direction, to streets running parallel to well-known numbered streets. As such, Avenida 4a A Sur is suddenly nicknamed Calle 49... as it is located south of famed Calle 50. As the latter intersects Calle 49 Este, it is simply a matter of distinguishing the real 49 from the imposter! A challenging riddle to look forward to!

high as 100 km is on the section of highway between La Chorrera and Ciudad de Panamá, as well as on the newer toll highways surrounding the capital (Corredor Norte) or en route to Colón.

Secondary Roads

As a result of uneven road conditions in certain parts of Panamá, reaching some destinations requires the use of a 4WD vehicle. A description of conditions will be given for most of the roads mentioned in this guide.

In the Capital

Refer to box above.

Driving in Villages

Remember to reduce driving speed to 40 km/h when passing through villages. It is not unusual for village children to play in or along the road; it often seems that villagers see the road as their own. Drivers should also keep a look out for a host of animals including chickens, cats, dogs, horses and donkeys that often wander onto the road.

Additional Information for Drivers

As most roads in Panamá do not have street lights, make sure to plan road trips so as not to end up driving at dusk. Panamá is near the equator; darkness falls in this part of the world at about 6:30pm in January and at about 7pm in July. It can be very difficult to see signs for hotels (they are often not lit) once it is dark.

At highway intersections and on busy city streets, drivers stuck in traffic are often approached by individuals offering to wash their car windows. Even if turned down, they may clean the windshield regardless, hoping the driver will give in and pay them something. Keep in mind, that for many of them this is their only way of making ends meet and so they may get angry if their ser-

vices are refused. By agreeing to have your windows washed, and parting with a few coins in return, you will be doing a good turn and making the best of the situation. Be careful, however (particularly in Colón and Ciudad de Panamá) not to open your window more than a few inches. An appropriate payment is between B/. 0.10 and B/. 0.25. Drivers may also be asked if they want their cars watched. Pay about B/. 0.25 for this service. While this may seem a strange service, it will reduce the likelihood of theft. As a general rule, however, never leave anything valuable in your car.

Taxis

Taxis can be found just about anywhere and are probably the safest way to get around. The cars do not have meters; fares are based on which urban area you are travelling to and from. You will have to negotiate the cost of the ride, and it is a good idea to agree on a price before getting in. Normally, taxi drivers are not tipped.

In addition to many personal taxis, there are also collective taxis which offer the advantage of shared costs (even if destinations vary somewhat). Collective taxis travel in and between cities.

Buses

A number of bus companies have routes between the country's larger cities. The long distance buses are better equipped and more comfortable than the city buses, but they do stop frequently. Buses on express runs are faster and hardly stop at all. As some destinations are very popular, it is a good idea to reserve bus tickets in advance. In the countryside, travellers can flag down buses along the road and pay the driver. There are three bus stations in Ciudad de Panamá, each serving passengers heading to different parts of the country.

The locations of the various bus stations can be found in the "Practical Information#" section of each chapter.

The following are several typical one way fares on regular long distance buses (they are subject to change without notice). Ciudad de Panamá to Colón: B/. 2.20
Ciudad de Panamá to Santiago: B/. 6
Ciudad de Panamá to David: B/. 11 (Express 15)
Ciudad de Panamá to Chitré B/. 6
Ciudad de Panamá to Punta Chame: B/. 2.25
Ciudad de Panamá to El Valle: B/. 1.50
Colón to Portobelo: B/. 2

David to Boquete:
B/. 1.50
David to Chiriquí
Grande: B/. 7
David to Cerro Punta:
B/. 3

Hitchhiking

Hitchhiking is not
common in Panamá,
and for safety reasons
we avoid trying to get
around this way.

Trains

With the exception of
two small private rail-
way lines in Bocas del
Toro province, which
are mostly used for
freight, the only exist-
ing line is the one
following the canal
from Balboa to Colón.
Unfortunately, at press
time the train was
reserved for the trans-
port of freight and
occasional groups (see
p57). There are plans
underway to use it for
regular passenger
transport again in the
year 2000. For more
information:

**Ferrocarril Nacional de
Panamá**
☎ *232-6000*

Renting a Car

Renting a car in
Panamá is relatively
easy to do. Most of the
major car rental agen-
cies have offices in the
bigger towns. If you
have reserved a car,
make sure to bring the
rental reservation docu-
ment, which should
indicate the rate to be
paid. Sometimes, rental
agents in Panamá will
make up excuses in an
attempt to increase the
price previously agreed
to. If you have your
contract and are being
asked to pay more than
was earlier stipulated,
threaten (politely) to go
elsewhere or to contact
the company's head
office.

Be patient, smile, and
tell yourself that bar-
gaining is part of a
complete travel experi-
ence. Expect to pay an
average of B/. 330 a
week (with unlimited
mileage) for a small air-
conditioned car. You
will also be charged a
5% tax, a B/. 8 daily
insurance charge and a
B/. 500 deposit in case
of accident. A credit
card can be used to
cover the latter. Choose
a car that is in good
condition and prefera-
bly new. Some agen-
cies offer lower prices,
but generally their cars
are older and in worse
condition. Before sign-
ing a rental contract,
make sure that the con-
ditions of payment are
clearly laid out. You
must be at least 23
years old to rent a car.
A valid driver's license
from any country is
accepted in Panamá.
Cars drive on the right
side of the road.

The following are the
telephone numbers of
some car rental agen-
cies in the capital:

Budget:
☎ *263-8777*
⇄ *263-7721*
budgetmg@sinfo.net

Avis:
☎ *264-0722*
⇄ *264-0622*

Hertz:
☎ *264-1111*
⇄ *263-6903*

Thrifty:
☎ *214-7677*
⇄ *264-7419*

Central Rent a Car:
☎ *223-5745*
⇄ *223-6941*
gcentral@sinfo.net

National Car Rental:
☎ *265-2222*
⇄ *265-3232*

Dollar Rent a Car:
☎ *270-0355*
⇄ *226-8191*
dollar@Panamac-com.net

Road Accidents

When driving through
small towns, beware of
the livestock that some-
times wanders onto the
road. Chickens in
particular seem fatally
attracted to the front
bumpers of moving
cars. If you should
accidently kill an ani-
mal, head to the near-
est police station rather
than deal directly with
villagers who may
become aggressive. In
the case of a more
serious road accident,
contact the police and
phone your car rental
agency as soon as
possible.

Practical
Information

Highway Police

Police officers are posted at various spots along the Interamericana. They have the right to pull over anyone who commits an infraction or just to inspect their papers. If you are charged with committing a traffic violation, make sure you are given a document stipulating the nature of the infraction. All fines are to be paid to the Dirección Nacional de Tránsito y Transporte Terrestre (see below). It is a good idea to take the name and number of the police officer. The highway police in Panamá are approachable and can be helpful if you run into trouble on the road. In any dealings with the police, it is best to be patient and friendly. Knowing a little Spanish is also a definite advantage.

Dirección Nacional de Tránsito y Transporte Terrestre
Departamento de Infracciones Menores
☎ 262-5687

Gasoline

There are gas stations all along the Interamericana highway. It is still a good idea to fill up before heading too far away as gas stations can be hard to find off the highway. The price of gas in Panamá is fairly low by European standards, but a bit higher than in the United States. Expect to pay about B/. 0.60 a litre. Some gas stations do not accept credit cards; this is more often the case outside big cities, so make sure to travel with sufficient cash.

Panamanian Money: The US Dollar

Panamá's Balboa has been worth exactly $1US since 1934, and Panamá no longer prints bank notes. The bills in circulation are US dollars. Coins are the only money still minted in Panamá, making the medio-balboa (worth $0.50) a neat souvenir; American coins are accepted everywhere.

When a small country decides to adopt the currency of another, larger country, it is essentially abandoning money as a tool to influence its economy. It can no longer diminish the value of its currency to stimulate exports, or increase it to control inflation. It has been proven, however, that countries with small money supplies cannot use this tool to their advantage and that a small floating supply is easy prey to speculators. A few fortunes in Hong Kong, New York or London could lower a small money supply by 10% just like that. Panamá has thus probably made a wise choice, since its small money supply, relative to its 2 million inhabitants, would have been an easy prey for speculation.

Money and Banking

Currency

The official currency of Panamá is the **Balboa**. The Balboa is kept on par with the US dollar: 1 balboa = 1 US dollar. The national bank does not, however, print bank notes. As a result, the paper money currently in use in Panamá is American (it is best to travel with American currency – including traveller's cheques). American and Panamanian coins are both used. The balboa is divided into 100 centésimos. There are coins worth 50 (medio-balboa), 25 (cuarto de balboa), 10 (décimo de balboa) and 5 (cinco centésimos de balboa) centésimos. This last coin is sometimes called a real, and you may be asked for cinco real for something that costs B/. 0.25.

Some establishments will not accept $100 and $50 bills without personal identification because of the circulation of counterfeit money. Make $20 bills the largest denomination you carry.

Banks

Banks are open from 8am to 1pm. Try to avoid banks on Fridays, as this is the day many businesses do their banking. There are banks in all of the moderate- and larger-sized towns. Most will exchange a number of currencies, though fewer will exchange traveller's cheques.

Traveller's Cheques

It is always best to keep most of your money in traveller's cheques in American dollars. A small commission (usually 10¢ US per cheque) is some times charged in banks.

Traveller's cheques in US currency are accepted in some hotels, restaurants and stores.

Credit Cards

Credit cards, particularly Visa and MasterCard, are accepted in many businesses. Do not rely on credit cards alone, however, as many places, especially in the countryside will refuse them. Always carry some cash.

Tele-communications

Mail

There are post offices, or *Correos y telégrafos*, in every sizeable town, distinguished by a blue and yellow sign. In the capital, some hotels also sell stamps and provide mail service for guests. Post cards to North America cost B/. 0.25 and to Europe B/. 0.45.

Telephone and Faxes

Panamá's country code is 507; there are no area codes. To call Panamá, first dial the number for interna-

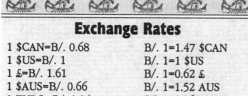

Exchange Rates

1 $CAN=B/. 0.68	B/. 1=1.47 $CAN
1 $US=B/. 1	B/. 1=1 $US
1 £=B/. 1.61	B/. 1=0.62 £
1 $AUS=B/. 0.66	B/. 1=1.52 AUS
1 EURO=B/. 1.04	B/. 1=0.96 EURO
1 DM=B/. 0.53	B/. 1=1.88 DM
1 Guilder=B/. 0.47	B/. 1= 2.12 Guilders
10 BF=B/. 0.26	B/. 1=38.74 BF
1 SF=B/. 0.65	B/. 1=1.54 SF
100 Pesetas=B/. 0.63	B/. 1=159.80 Pesetas
1000 Lire=B/. 0.54	B/. 1=1,859.65 Lire

Practical Information

tional calls (e.g. 00 from Europe and 011 from Canada and the United States), followed by 507 then the seven-digit Panamánian number.

To call abroad from Panamá, dial 00, followed by the country code of the country you are dialling, then the area code (if applicable) and finally your party's number.

For example, to call **Great Britain**, dial 00-44, followed by the area code (London 171/181) and your party's number.

For **Canada** and the **United States**, dial 00-1, the area code, then your party's number. Canada Direct (☎ *0 800 015 1161* diff. Number than in french version) will connect you directly to an operator in Canada for free. However, if you are calling from a public telephone, you must still use a calling card or insert change in order to get a line.

International telephone calls can be made from post offices and from most big hotels.

If you want to send a fax to Panamá and the fax and telephone numbers are the same, you will usually have to call first to check that the fax machine is turned on.

Newspapers

The most widely distributed newspapers are *La Prensa*, *El Siglo*, *El Universal*, *El Panamá América* and *Crítica*.

Accommodations

Many visitors to Panamá find that staying in air-conditioned rooms is necessary for maintaining a minimum level of comfort (nights in Panamá can be extremely hot and sticky). At the very least, be sure that the rooms you rent have good mosquito netting. In some hotels, the price of a

room includes breakfast. Ask about this before registering.

As in many countries, a wide range of accommodation possibilities is available in Panamá. Not surprisingly, the cheapest places – those costing less than B/. 25 a night – are also the least comfortable (they usually do not have air-conditioning, mosquito netting or private bathrooms). A 10% tax is added to the price of hotel rooms. It is often possible to negotiate a 10% to 20% reduction in the price of a hotel room. However, this may be more difficult to do on weekends, Panamanian national holidays and during vacation periods. With the competition between hotels in Ciudad de Panamá, it is often possible to negotiate a reduction of as much as 25% off the price of a room. In the beach resorts, hotels can give reductions up to 40% during low season. The bigger hotels usually accept credit cards, while smaller establishments often do not.

The school year in Panamá runs from March to December. At present, the country's tourist infrastructure is primarily geared toward meeting the demands of Panamanian holiday-makers who flock to the country's most popular sites between December and March; visitors from outside the country are

Press

www.elsiglo.com
www.sinfo.net/prensa/home.htm
www.eluniversal-pma.com
www.epasa.com/El_Panama_America/today/
index.html
www.epasa.com/critica/hoy/critica.html

advised to reserve rooms ahead of time.

Accommodation Rates and Taxes

Five price categories are used in the descriptions of the hotels and other types of lodgings mentioned in this guide (see below). The prices listed are for double rooms and do not include taxes. In most cases, a 10% tax will be added to the price of a room.

$
$25 US or less
$$
$25 US to $50 US
$$$
$50 US to $90 US
$$$$
$90 US to $150 US
$$$$$
$150 US or more

Hotels

While the range of comfort and services offered by hotels in Panamá can vary greatly, most of the places mentioned in this guide have at least a small bathroom and air-conditioning. The low budget hotels (*with nightly rates between B/. 25 and B/. 50*) provide a basic level of comfort but can be quite pleasant. Moderately priced hotels (*with rooms for between B/. 50 and B/. 150*) offer a level of comfort visitors may be used to from hotels back home. They often have a bar, restaurant and pool.

Hotels in both categories are often family run and are good places to meet Panamanians. More expensive hotels (*those with rooms costing over B/. 150 per night*) offer an range of services and a level of comfort typical of major international hotel chains and are often located in the best tourist spots.

Apart-Hotels

Apart-hotels offer a full range of services plus rooms equipped with fully functional kitchenettes (pots, pans and dishes included). This type of accommodation is most often found in larger towns (there are many in Ciudad de Panamá). Visitors planning on longer stays can save on meal costs by staying at these places. Room rates tend to be lower for longer stays (though you may have to bargain).

Cabañas

Cabañas are small huts or cabins that are usually located on or near the beach. Some are extremely basic and do not even come with mosquito netting, while others have air-conditioning and kitchenettes. Less expensive *cabañas* often have several beds in one room. On national holidays and during vacation periods, people from all over Panamá descend on the beaches. During these periods accommodation can be hard to come by (if you have not made reservations) but there is much more activity day and night. For a more peaceful stay, try to get a *cabaña* set well away from the others on the beach, as they are often poorly soundproofed.

Motels

Motels tend to be a bit less expensive than medium-priced hotels, but are correspondingly less comfortable. Despite a few drawbacks (less attractive locations, poor soundproofing), this type of accommodation can be useful to travellers in a hurry, as they are often conveniently located next to major roads and highways (though they sometimes turn out to be brothels). The more expensive motels will have a pool and restaurant.

Cottages

In the western part of the country, most often in mountainous areas in the province of Chiriquí, it is possible to rent small cottages. These fully equipped little houses are often rented to families. This is a recommended form of accommodation for visitors interested in exploring nature and enjoying the cooler mountain air. Usually, cottages can only be rented for stays of at least several days, if not weeks.

Camping

The country's very hot nights and many insects do not make this a very attractive activity. Camping in Panamá can also be unsafe because of the abundance of insects and animals.

Restaurants

Restaurants in the country's bigger cities reflect Panamá's cultural diversity by offering a wide range of cuisines. Whether you prefer Italian, French, Chinese or, of course, Panamanian cooking, you will find what you are looking for. In the countryside, the choice is much smaller and is often restricted to Panamanian food. With the heat and the big portions, it is often difficult to eat three meals a day.

Prices, Taxes and Tips

The prices mentioned in the restaurant sections of this guide are for a meal for one person, including appetizer, main course, dessert and coffee. Drinks (wine, beer,

etc.) and tip are not included, but taxes are. A 10% tip is standard in bars and restaurants. Check your bill carefully, as the tip is sometimes included automatically.

$
$8 US or less
$$
$8 US to $15 US
$$$
$15 US to $25 US
$$$$
$25 US to $40 US
$$$$$
$40 US or more

Panamanian Cuisine

Panamanian food is delicious and not too spicy. Corn, in all its forms, has a very prominent place. However, the cuisine in general is not particularly varied. Cooking is done mainly in oil. Certain dishes, especially *pollo*, *ceviche*, *patacones*, *corvina*, *camarones*, as well as corn prepared in a variety of ways, are sometimes the only things available.

While a large variety of fruits are grown in the country, restaurants serve very little fresh fruit. For example, it is very rare to be offered fresh fruit for breakfast. The best place to buy fruit is at outdoor markets and at stands along major roads.

Drinks

Horas Felizes (Happy Hour)

At certain times of the day in Ciudad de Panamá, usually between 4pm and 7pm, bars offer reduced prices on drinks. Like happy hour in many other countries, during these periods you can either buy two drinks for the price of one or pay a reduced price for a single drink.

Beer

Beer is the most popular alcoholic drink in Panamá. Most beer in Panamá is light, fairly low on alcohol content (between 3% and 3.8%), and of good quality. The most popular brands include *Panamá*, *Cristal*, *Atlas* and *Balboa*.

Wine

Wine is not very popular in Panamá and there is little in the way of local production. The French wines sometimes sold in restaurants are often very expensive. We recommend the more affordable (and usually very good) Chilean wines instead. Expect to pay between B/. 15 and B/. 20 a bottle.

Hard Alcohol

The most popular type of hard alcohol in

Panamanian Dishes Not to be Missed

Bollo: a corn-based dish which can be made with different ingredients (chicken, vegetables, beef, etc.) and is served in corn husks

Camaroncitos: small shrimp (fish, seafood and shellfish dishes are very good in Panamá)

Carimañola: pastry stuffed with manioc and meat or fish mixed with egg

Carne de Res: beef from bollo chiricano cows (beef is a speciality of the southwestern regions)

Ceviche: raw fish, usually corvina, in lemon juice and coriander

Chicharrones: pork rinds (an acquired taste)

Corvina: a white fish common to the Pacific

Empanadas: pastry (often made of corn flour) filled with meat or vegetables.

Patacones: fried plantain slices

Platanos en tentación: dessert consisting of very ripe plantains slowly cooked in cane sugar

Ropa Vieja: ground hamburger seasoned with onions, green peppers and sometimes cassava

Sancocho: soup with chicken, cassava, onions, oregano, coriander and sometimes corn

Sopa Borracha: moist rum cake with prunes and raisins

Sopa de Gloria: moist milk cake with sugar and nuts

Tamales: cornmeal mixed with chicken or pork with spices wrapped in a banana leaf – a delicacy

Practical
Information

Panamá is **Seco**, a sugarcane-based rum.

Chicha

This refreshing drink is made of milk and fruit juice. While it is generally a good idea to avoid milk products in Panamá, Chicha is usually safe to drink in the northern regions of the province of Chiriquí. The drink comes in a variety of flavours.

Ecotourism

Agencies Specializing in Ecotourism

Ancón Expeditions
Calle Elvira Méndez
Edificio El Dorado
☎ 269-9414
☎ 269-9415
≈ 264-3713
www.ecopanama.com
travel@ecopanama.com

Starlite Travel
Ave. Roosevelt et Heights L-639, Balboa
in front of the canal administration building and next to McDonalds
Apdo 6-6200
El Dorado
☎ 232-640
☎ 272-2474
≈ 232-6448
starlite@panama.c-com.net

Jungle Adventures
Calle Ricardo Arias 38
(offices of Polvani)
Apartado 871254
Panamá 7
☎ 269-6017
☎ 269-6047
≈ 263-8261
iskardup@sinfo.net
www.iskardup.com

Iguana Tours
Vía. Porras, facing Parque Omar
☎ 226-8738
☎ 226-4516
≈ 226-4736
iguana@sinfo.net
www.nvmundo.com/iguanatours/

Aventuras Panamá
Apdo 9869, Panamá 4
☎ 260-0044
☎ 236-5814
≈ 260-7535
aventuras@atba.com
www.geocities.com/ResearchTriangle/3311/

Pesantez Tours
Plaza Balboa, Oficina 2
Apdo 55-0716
Punta Paitilla
☎ 263-7577
☎ 263-8771
≈ 263-7860
pezantes@sinfo.net
www.pesantez-tours.com

Eco-Tours
Calle Ricardo Arias, 7
Apdo 465
Panamá 9a
☎ 263-3077
☎ 263-3076
≈ 263-3089
ecotour@pty.com
www.avatar.pty.com/ecotours/fra-home.htm

Miscellaneous

Women Travellers

Women travelling alone should not encounter any problems. Panamá is one of the rare Latin American countries to have had a woman as mayor of its capital (Mayín Correa) and to have recently elected a woman as president of the republic (Mireya Moscoso). Of course, a certain level of caution should be exercised, but for the most part, people are friendly and not aggressive. Generally, men are respectful toward women. Some men will show a tendency toward macho behaviour, and this includes making unwanted verbal advances or comments. However, this is not usually done in a threatening manner. You may be more likely to be left alone if you dress conservatively in this Catholic country.

Gay Life

Despite the relatively important role women play in Panamanian society, the situation for gays and lesbians is about the same as in other Latin American countries. Although there are a few gay bars in the capital (see p128), gays and lesbians are still repressed

to a certain extent. Machismo, the ideology of male superiority, remains alive and well, and its insistence upon maintaining rigid sex-based stereotypical roles is responsible more than anything else for the repression of gays and lesbians and the attempt to keep women in their traditional roles.

Electricity

Electrical appliances run on an alternating current of 110 volts (60 cycles), just as in North America. European travellers will need both a converter and an adapter with two parallel flat pins for any appliances they plan to bring along.

Smokers

There are no restrictions on smoking in Panamá, and cigarettes are very cheap.

Holidays

All banks and businesses close their doors on holidays and the country seems to function in slow-motion. Make sure you do not get caught needing to change money or buy last minute souvenirs on one of these days.

January 1
New Year's Day

January 9
Martyrs Day

May 1
Labour Day

October 12
Hispanic Day (Dia de la Raza; arrival of Columbus)

November 3
Independence Day (separation from Colombia)

November 10
Declaration of Independence Day

November 28
Independence Day (separation from Spain)

December 8
Mother's Day

Shifting
Good Friday

Panamá's famous carnival celebrations are particularly spectacular in the Azuero peninsula. They always take place from the Saturday to the Tuesday preceding Ash Wednesday.

Easter is also a time for celebration in various cities throughout the country.

Time Zones

Panamá is in the Eastern Standard Time Zone. This means that when North America is not on daylight savings, there is no time difference with the East Coast, and it is three hours ahead of the West Coast. Panamá is six or seven hours behind continental Europe, depending on the time of year.

Weights and Measures

Officially, Panamá uses the metric system. The following conversion table may be useful.

Weights
1 pound (lb) = 454 grams (g)

Linear Measure
1 inch = 2.54 centimetres (cm)

Volume Measure
1 U.S. gallon (gal) = 3.79 litres
1 U.S. gallon (gal) = 0.83 imperial gallon

Temperature
To convert °F into °C: subtract 32, divide by 9, multiply by 5
To convert °C into °F: multiply by 9, divide by 5, add 32.

Practical Information

Culture Shock

Before going on vacation, we pack our luggage and get the necessary vaccinations and travel documents, but rarely do we prepare for culture shock. The following text explains what culture shock is and how to deal with it.

In a nutshell, culture shock can be defined as a certain anxiety that may be experienced upon arriving in another country where everything is different, including the culture and language, making communication as you know it very difficult. Combined with jetlag and fatigue, the strain of orienting yourself in a new cultural context can lead to psychological stress that may throw you off track.

Culture shock is a frustrating phenomenon that can easily turn travellers setting out with the best of intentions into intolerant, racist and ethnocentric ones — they may come to believe that their society is better than the new, and seemingly incomprehensible, one. This type of reaction detracts from the whole travel experience.

People in other countries have different customs and lifestyles that are sometimes hard for us to understand or accept. We might even find ourselves wondering how people can live the way they do when their customs run contrary to what we deem to be "normal". In the end, however, it is easier to adapt to them than to criticize or disregard them. Even though this is the era of globalization and cultural homogenization, we still live in a world of many "worlds", such as the business world, the worlds of different continents, suburbia, and the world of the rich and the poor. Of course, these worlds intersect, but each has its own characteristic set of ideas and cultural values. Furthermore, even if they are not in direct contact, each has at least an image of the other (which is often simply distorted). And if a picture is worth a thousand words, then our world contains million upon millions of them. Sometimes it is hard to tell what is real and what isn't, but one thing is certain: the place you see on television is not the same when you get there.

When people interact with one another, they inevitably make sense of each other through their differences. The strength of a group, human or animal, lies in its diversity, whether it be in genetics or ideas. Can you imagine how boring the world would be if everyone were the same?

Travelling can be seen as a way of developing a more holistic, or global, vision of the world; this means accepting that our cultural fabric is complex and woven with many different ethnicities, and that all have something to teach us, be it a philosophy of life, medical knowledge, or a culinary dish, which adds to the richness of our personal experience.

Remember that culture is relative, and that people's social, technological and financial situations shape their way of being and looking at the world. It takes more than curiosity and tolerance to be open-minded: it is a matter of learning to see the world anew, through a different cultural perspective.

When travelling abroad, don't spend too much energy looking for the familiar, and don't try to see the place as you would like it to be – go with the flow instead. And although a foreign country might seem difficult to understand or even unwelcoming at times, remember that there are people who find happiness and satisfaction in life everywhere. When you get involved in their daily lives, you will begin to see things differently – things which at first seemed exotic and mystifying are easily understood in time. It always helps to know the rules before playing a game, and it goes without saying that learning the language will help you better understand what's going on. But be careful about communicating with your hands, since certain gestures might mean the opposite of what you are trying to say!

Prepare yourself for culture shock as early as possible. Libraries and bookstores are good places for information about the cultures you are interested in. Reading about them is like a journey in itself, and will leave you with even more cherished memories of your trip.

Jean-Étienne Poirier

Table of distances (km)
Via the shortest route

© ULYSSES

	Boquete	Cerro Punta	Chitré	Colón	David	Divisa	El Valle	Las Tablas	Ciudad de Panamá	Paso Canoa	Penonomé	Portobelo	Santiago	Volcán
Cerro Punta	114													
Chitré	306	350												
Colón	549	593	326											
David	35	79	271	514										
Divisa	263	307	43	289	228									
El Valle	408	452	182	200	373	145								
Las Tablas	338	382	32	358	303	75	214							
Ciudad de Panamá	473	517	250	76	438	213	124	282						
Paso Canoa	88	73	324	567	53	281	426	356	491					
Penonomé	327	371	101	225	289	64	81	133	149	345				
Portobelo	572	616	349	43	537	312	223	381	99	590	248			
Santiago	277	271	79	325	192	36	181	111	249	245	100	348		
Volcán	92	22	328	571	57	285	430	360	495	62	346	594	249	
Yavisa	757	801	534	360	722	497	408	566	284	775	433	383	533	779

Example: The distance between Ciudad de Panamá and Santiago is 249 km.

Outdoors

A wealth of highly varied natural attractions awaits the visitor to Panamá; these can be discovered through the various outings recommended in the "Outdoor Activities" section of each chapter.

During your stay you will certainly have the opportunity to try various sports, which will allow you to get better acquainted with the country's rich environment. The following is a list of the principal activities available to visitors.

National Parks

Panamá may have fewer national parks than Costa Rica, but the great variety of plant and animal life therein is extraordinary. Panamá's tropical forest has remained intact and virtually untouched, thanks to the absence of violent hurricanes. The variety of flora harboured within will delight travellers interested in botany. Despite this extraordinary stroke of luck, major ecological problems seem to be looming in the future. Like many other countries in the region, Panamá must come to grips with the problem of deforestation, the result of an aggressive expansion of agriculture. These fertile regions have attracted many peasants, who have harshly cleared the land, leading to serious erosion problems. Among the hardest hit is the province of Chiriquí, especially the region around the Volcán Barú. This problem has made Panamanians strongly aware of ecological concerns, and a number of nature preservation societies have been founded.

In addition to creating national parks and various protected zones, the Panamanian government has also established two environmental research organizations: INRENARE (Instituto Nacional de Recursos Naturales Renovables), now called ANAM (Autoridad Nacional del Ambiente) and IDIAP (Instituto de Investigación Agropecuaria de Panamá). ANAM is responsible for managing the national parks and protecting the environment, while IDIAP takes care of agricultural matters. Unfortunately, the government

National Parks

1. Parque Nacional Cerro Hoya
2. Parque Nacional y Reserva Biológica Altos de Campana (see p 157)
3. Parque Nacional Soberanía (see p 141)
4. Parque Nacional Chagres (see p 100)
5. Parque Nacional Coiba
6. Parque Nacional del Darién (see p 288)
7. Parque Nacional Volcan Barú (see p 236)
8. Parque Nacional Camino de Cruces (see p 141)
9. Parque Nacional Portobelo
10. Parque Nacional Marino Isla Bastimentos (see p 261)
11. Parque Nacional Sarigua (see p 210)
12. Parque Nacional General de División Omar Torijos Herrera
13. Parque Nacional Marino Golfo de Chiriquí
14. Parque Internacional La Amistad (see p 234, p 264)

greatly reduced its spending on environmental protection after the economic crisis that followed the Noriega affair. The crisis even forced the government to lease protected lands (see p30) for profit. Therefore, tourist facilities in the parks are not as developed as in Canada, the U.S. or even Costa Rica. Information centres, places to stay, picnic areas and hiking trails vary enormously from one park to another, and are even non-existent in many cases.

Roads to the parks are often unpaved and require a 4WD vehicle. Realizing the success of ecotourism in neighbouring Costa Rica, the Panamanian government is trying to improve the parks to draw more visitors. Despite this, here as everywhere else, government bureaucracy isn't budging much and it will probably take several years for significant improvements to be seen. However, because of the ongoing withdrawal of American military forces and the large loss of US capital, the Panamanian government will have to act more quickly. The government has made some efforts, though, such as setting up the Autoridad de la Región Interoceánica, in place to carry out a general development plan for the canal zone. This plan involves the sale of numerous lots bordering the canal as well as the issuing of tax breaks to attract investors to the former zone.
Overdevelopment of the canal is also a concern, especially for environmental organizations. In the future, the Panamanian governments will hopefully do even more to protect the country's rich heritage.

Today, there are 13 national parks, one of which is managed jointly with Costa Rica. One metropolitan park and 27 other zones have also been given special status and are classified under such names as reserve, refuge, recreational zone, recreational park, and so on. The majority of these zones are fully or partially protected and make up 22% of the isthmus. A list of the principal parks is provided (See box for a more detailed description), refer to the "Parks" section in the

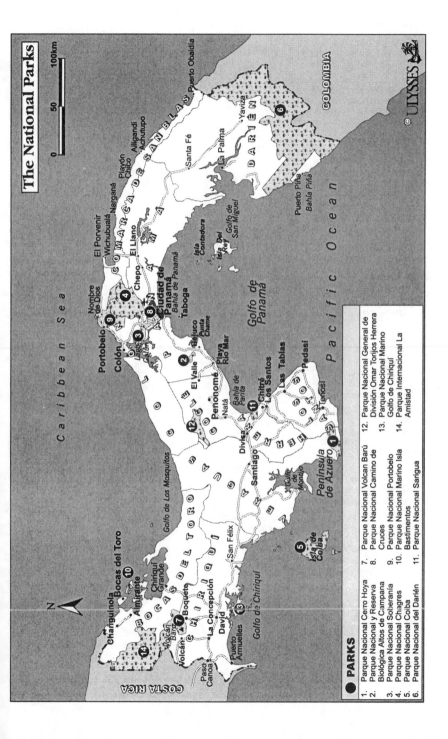

The National Parks

PARKS

1. Parque Nacional Cerro Hoya
2. Parque Nacional y Reserva Biológica Altos de Campana
3. Parque Nacional Soberanía
4. Parque Nacional Chagres
5. Parque Nacional Coiba
6. Parque Nacional del Darién
7. Parque Nacional Volcán Barú
8. Parque Nacional Camino de Cruces
9. Parque Nacional Portobelo
10. Parque Nacional Marino Isla Bastimentos
11. Parque Nacional Sarigua
12. Parque Nacional General de División Omar Torrijos Herrera
13. Parque Nacional Marino Golfo de Chiriquí
14. Parque Internacional La Amistad

© ULYSSES

0   50   100km

chapter on each province.

Today, an ANAM permit is required to visit or camp in a national park. Although permits can be obtained at certain park entrances, it is more practical to get one beforehand in the capital (see address below). ANAM regional offices are not always open when you get there and are sometimes far from the park you wish to visit. Park entrance fees vary between B/. 3 et B/. 10 per park.

For information:

ANAM (INRENARE)
Dirección Nacional de Areas Protegidas
Calle Curundú also called Vía La Amistad and Avenida Ascañio Villalaz (in front of the bus station)
Apdo 2016
Paraíso
Corregimiento de Ancón
☎ 232-7228
☎ 232-7221
⇿ 232-7220
inrenare@ns.inrenare.stri.si
.edu2.usma.ac.pa/~eco1

Among the environmental organizations working in Panamá, the following two are particularly reputed.

ANCÓN
Calle 53 Oeste or Alberto Navarro
Apdo 1387
Panamá 1
☎ 314-0060
⇿ 314-0061
ancon@ancon.org
www.ancon.org

Smithsonian Tropical Research Institute
(*only for information on Barro Colorado*)
Avenida Roosevelt n° 401
Edificio Tivoli
Ancón
☎ 227-6022
⇿ 232-5978

Swimming

Naturally, swimming is a popular activity in Panamá – after all, people come here to enjoy the sea and the sun.

Furthermore, many resort centres have been built along the country's most beautiful beaches, such as those on **Isla Taboga, Isla Contadora, the Islas San Blas** and in the region west of **Ciudad de Panamá**. The beaches on either side of the country have their own characteristics. The water on the Atlantic, or Caribbean, side is clearer, making it easier to spot interesting fish. However, this part of the country also gets more rain and is more humid. The Pacific coast has a greater number of beaches with fine sand and has drier weather, but the water is less clear. Since the country is much longer than it is wide, it has countless islands and beaches, most of which remain

completely undeveloped. Visitors seeking solitude will have no trouble finding kilometres of deserted beach in the provinces of **Los Santos** and **Chiriquí**. On the other hand, those looking for lively activity will be delighted with the beaches in the districts of **San Carlos or Isla Taboga**, which are crowded with Panamanian families during the weekends. Finally, if you would like to swim in waters ideal for observing fish and have a taste for adventure, you can head out to **Isla de Colón**.

Snorkelling

This sport requires little equipment – flippers, a mask and a snorkel, all of which are easy to rent in Panamá for just a few dollars. Anyone can snorkel, since no courses are required. It's a very pleasant way to explore the sea bottom in this wonderful part of the world. Snorkellers should note that the water on the Atlantic coast is clearer than that on the Pacific coast, although with the many islands on either side of the isthmus, the sport is just as accessible on either coast. Some beaches are skirted by superb coral reefs which add to the beauty of the underwater scenery. It is preferable to snorkel in bays and quiet waters, and a degree of caution should be taken.

Among the more beautiful places are the **San Blas islands**, **Isla de Colón** (at Bocas del Toro), **Isla Grande** (in the province of **Colón**) and **Isla Contadora** in the **Las Perlas** archipelago.

Scuba Diving

Scuba diving is a more complicated sport and requires some experience. Before diving, you must attend courses and obtain a certificate. A few tourist centres provide these courses (see below). For coastline diving, the Atlantic is your better option. The water there is clearer and the marine wildlife especially abundant. In addition, the tides are not as high, making the water safer for divers. Places like **Bocas del Toro**, the **San Blas islands** and **Isla Grande** are famous for the sport. Diving along the Pacific coast (with a few exceptions, like **Playa Venado**) is not recommended because of tidal variations, which can be as much as six or seven m in a day. The sport can, however, be practised near the great many islands along the coast.

In artificial **Lago Gatún**, divers have an extraordinary chance to explore a silent world, where some of the most unusual wildlife can be seen. Long ago, tropical forests grew here, and the sight of submerged villages only enhances the impression of having discovered some lost world. Some cities along the lake (like **Escobal** and **La Arenosa**) provide various services for this activity.

Whether you are planning to rent or buy equipment, or for information on diving guides or diving instruction, various stores in downtown Ciudad de Panamá can help you out (see p 82).

Surfing and Windsurfing

Equipment for surfing and windsurfing, like that for diving, can be rented in the capital (see p 82) or from various seaside hotels. Beginner windsurfers will particularly enjoy the beaches at **El Palmar** and **Río Mar**, scarcely half an hour's drive from the capital. Those who want a little more excitement should look for windier bays. In the province of **Los Santos, Playa Venado**, with its high waves, is one of the country's best spots for windsurfing. Unfor-

tunately, there are few services there (a restaurant and some rudimentary cabins), and the beach is isolated, two hours' drive from Los Santos.

Deep-Sea Fishing

The more luxurious hotels in the **Las Perlas archipelago** and the **Gulf of San Miquel** often organize deep-sea fishing expeditions, although you need not be a guest at one of these hotels to take part. This is a fine opportunity to sail about and enjoy the open sea, while learning about the various species of fish native to the Pacific. Equipment and advice are available on board, and an outing usually lasts half a day.

Hiking

Hiking is the best way to discover Panamá's parks, reserves and untamed wilderness. Because the country is relatively small and covered by rugged terrain, mountain hikes are particularly spectacular. In the province of Chiriquí, you can climb 3,474 m to the top of **Volcán Barú** – quite an invigorating hike! Some parks have steep jungle trails following the

Outdoor Activities

historic **camino de cruzes**, a trail formerly used by the Spaniards. This trail is difficult to hike on, not because it is steep but because of the heat and humidity, which can sometimes be suffocating. Unfortunately, marked trails on the isthmus are hard to find, so it is best to contact one of the environmental protection organizations (see p72) or one of the many ecotourism agencies for information. The addresses and telephone numbers of some of these companies can be found in the "Practical Information" chapter (see p64). Various outings are also described in the "Outdoor Activities" section of each chapter. Finally, before setting out on a hike in one of the country's numerous parks, keep in mind that a permit is required to visit them (see p72).

Bicycling

Panamá's road system includes everything from two-lane main highways with no shoulders, to small secondary roads riddled with potholes – certainly not a cyclist's dream. Cycling may be a very pleasant way of getting about, but it is fairly dangerous on these roads, especially on the Interamericana, where large trucks, not always in mint condi-

tion, travel at dangerous speeds. There are also the perpetually warm daytime temperatures and lack of shade to contend with, and few roads are lit at night. Nevertheless, outside the major urban centres, cycling can be extremely pleasant – but watch out for speeding cars.

Horseback Riding

For some Panamanians, especially those in the remote countryside, riding is more than just a sport; in the province of **Los Santos** and in the whole **Azuero peninsula**, it is still an important means of transportation. In fact, there are more horses than there are cars! Riding is a pleasant form of relaxation, and a good way to discover certain parts of Panamá. However, follow the same advice provided for nature hikes: consult an agency (see p 64, 72).

Rafting

Although Panamá is not well-known for rafting, there are nevertheless some ideal rivers for it. Among the best-known are **Río Chagres** (see p100), which runs into the gigantic artificial

Lake Alajuela (less than one hour from the capital), as well as the **Río Chiriquí** (see p221, 240) in the more mountainous and temperate province of Chiriquí. The latter is one of the few rivers where rafting can be enjoyed year-round as a result of its partially-controlled flow. However, the level of difficulty on these two rivers changes according to the time of year. The best months for rafting are from September to December.

Golf

A popular pastime in Europe and North America, golf is becoming increasingly popular in Panamá. Despite the construction of a new course on **Isla Contadora** and a few private courses in the former canal zone, the only professional course is **Playa Coronado**, barely an hour from the capital (see p155).

Birdwatching

With 900 bird species, Panamá is without a doubt one of the best places in the world for birdwatching. People come from all over the world to see the famous quetzal, which can be seen in the **Parque Internacional La Amistad** (part of which is in Costa Rica). Other good places for birdwatching are **Parque Nacional Soberanía** (known for its excellent observation platform) (see p141), and the large **Parque Nacional del Darién**, which still harbours the harpy eagle, one of the world's most powerful raptors. Hiring a naturalist guide will maximize your chances of seeing the greatest number of bird species. The forest is so dense that it can be extremely difficult for the untrained eye to spot certain birds. The Audubon Society, internationally renowned for its research on birds, regularly organizes hikes led by biologists at quite affordable prices. For more information:

Sociedad Audubon de Panamá
Calle 74 Este (close to the Parque Recreativo)
Apdo 2026
Balboa
☎/≈ **224-4740**
audupan@pananet.com
www.pananet.com/audubon

Harpy Eagle

An Abundance of Fish

There are several legends about the origin of the word Panamá. According to one, the site upon which the city was founded was full of trees bearing an edible fruit (resembling a chestnut), whose Amerindian name was panamá. Another, put forth by the Kunas, explains that the word comes from the Kuna phrase pa na ma, or pana-mai, meaning "way over there", often used in response to the Spaniard's insistent questions about where the Amerindians had found the gold with which they adorned themselves. While some people claim that the word actually means "abundance of butterflies", others say "abundance of fish". To this day, no historian has been able to determine the exact origin of the word. However, the "abundance of fish" theory has earned official status, and seems to have been unanimously adopted by the Panamanian public.

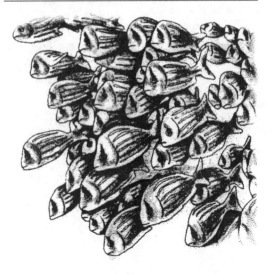

Ciudad de Panamá

The province of Panamá is the most populated on the isthmus with 1,200,000 inhabitants, some 800,000 of whom live in and around Ciudad de Panamá, the country's capital, and has a large part of the canal zone through which great quantities of merchandise are transported every year.

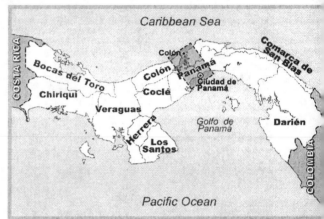

The province has much to recommend it to visitors, including the canal itself and the beautiful countryside it crosses; Ciudad de Panamá, with its colonial buildings, and the attractive islands and beaches nearby. The present chapter is devoted solely to Ciudad de Panamá. The Canal Zone and the islands and beaches in the Bahía de Panamá (Gulf of Panamá) are covered in the two following chapters.

Whatever the point of your visit to Panamá, put aside at least a few days to explore the many splendours of this province. You will not be disappointed.

The History of Ciudad de Panamá

Ciudad de Panamá was founded on two separate occasions and in two different places. Its history begins in 1519, when Pedrarias Dávila founded the small vil-

lage of Nuestra Señora de la Asunción de Panamá in a bay where today lie the ruins of Panamá Viejo. This modest settlement developed slowly at first, its main activities including fishing and the mining of small quantities of gold to the west of the territory. Later on, the discovery of the fabulous riches of the Inca Empire and the quarrying of a major silver mine in Potosí, Peru ensured the expansion of the Ciudad. The opening of trails linking Ciudad de Panamá to both

Nombre de Dios and the Fuerte San Lorenzo on the Atlantic coast made the isthmus a crucial transshipment point for goods in transit between the two oceans. Because of its strategic location, Ciudad de Panamá gained the status of the first European commercial trading post on the Pacific coast; the city was designated a Ciudad Real as early as 1521. The busy overland trade route through which precious merchandise was conveyed soon made the city prosperous and, as early as the mid-17th century, it attracted the attention of both the colonial powers and pirates, who regarded it as a choice prey. Thus in 1671, the city was stormed by Welsh pirate Henry Morgan, who bled the capital dry and left it in ruins (see "Panamá Viejo") (see p96).

In 1673, under the orders of Governor Fernando de Córdoba, a second city was established a few kilometres west. It did not, however, grow at the same pace as Panamá Viejo. Construction was slow, and the city was damaged by numerous fires. The largest of these took place in 1737 and 1756, sending many buildings up in smoke, including the former Convento de Santo Domingo. The city's development was further hindered by

Spain's decision to stop transporting goods across the isthmus once again, and by New Granada's declaration of independence. It was not until a rail link was established between Colón and Panamá (1855) and work was begun on the canal (1880) that the city finally began to thrive.

Modern-day Ciudad de Panamá boasts a wide variety of architecture. These different styles reflect two distinct periods: the colonial era, from which several lovely buildings still exist in Casco Viejo; and the period coinciding with the opening of the

Old Panamá

railway between Colón and Panamá, and the opening of the canal. Accordingly, buildings similar to those found in Europe, and more

specifically, in France, began to appear, soon followed by the newer styles popular in the United States in the 1900s. Thus, Neoclassical, Art Nouveau and Art Deco style buildings now stand side by side in Casco Viejo, the old city, and bear witness to its rich past. In the 1940s, development in the capital was concentrated mainly in the suburbs, and the large residences in the heart of the old city were gradually abandoned. Many were then divided into small apartments for low-income families, resulting in a deterioration of their façade and interior. At the end of the 1970s, however, the public began to show a certain interest in preserving the city's historic buildings. Since then, many restoration projects have been carried out, a number of which are still in progress. The great challenge facing authorities in the future will be to continue this urban renewal while protecting the fragile social fabric of the neighbourhoods.

Finding Your Way Around

By Car

From the Airport

For the time being, the quickest way into the city is to take Avenida Domingo Díaz and at the first big intersection turn left onto Vía Cincuentenario. Follow this street to Vía España and turn right. Downtown Ciudad de Panamá is straight ahead. As the route from the airport passes San Miguelito, a potentially unsafe area, keep your car doors locked. While driving through this area, all kinds of people may offer you their services or try to sell you something. If you decide to buy something, do not open your windows too wide while paying. It is safer to drive through this area during the day.

Several major public-works projects have been planned in recent years, including the **Corredor Sur** and **Corredor Norte**, two major toll highways which were meant to alleviate traffic congestion in the capital. The latter, now completed, is situated north of town, allowing motorists to reach the city of Colón without having to go through

the city centre. The *Corredor Sur,* currently under construction, will take motorists straight to Avenida Balboa from the international airport. Unfortunately, the thoroughfare will run right past the historic site of Panamá Viejo across a viaduct that is to overhang the bay (see p 96) all the way to Punta Paitilla! Say goodbye to lovely photos of the ruins against the backdrop of the bay. Environmental organizations are, needless to say, strongly against the project and are mounting a major opposition movement. In the meantime however, construction seems to be progressing at a rapid pace because several columns were already built when we were there. Should the Corredor Sur be completed, it will be the most convenient and fastest route to the city centre, albeit a highly destructive one.

Driving in Ciudad de Panamá

The traffic in Ciudad de Panamá is often heavy, but finding your way around town is not particularly difficult. Here are a few hints for getting around the city.

On certain days, several major downtown arteries become one-way streets. For example, the Las Americas bridge, becomes one

way at certain points during the weekend to facilitate getting in or out of town. On weekdays, some of the main roads leading into town from the east also become one-way.

The direction of certain roads is not always clearly indicated with signs.

To Islas Naos, Perico and Flamenco

From Avenida de los Mártires, take Avenida Amador, which will take you to the peninsula of the same name and onto the islands via the Calzada de Amador, a guarded spit of land which costs B./ 0.25 to cross.

To Panamá Viejo

Take Punta Paitilla-bound Avenida Balboa, which becomes Avenida 6a Sur or Vía Israël after the small viaduct that overhangs the Monumento a Las Madres roundabout. This road, becomes Avenida Cincuentenario after the Atlapa Convention Centre, goes all the way to the ruins.

To Cerro Azul

To get to Cerro Azul you have to take the road to the airport first. Just before the airport, turn left at the Riande Aeropuerto hotel and take the main road for 6.5 km until you get to an intersection with Supermercado Xtra on

the right. Turn left at
this intersection and
drive 1.8 km until you
see a sign on your left
indicating the road to
Cerro Azul. Take this
road for 15 km until
you reach a gate and a
sign indicating Portón
Las Nubes. Turn left
again and follow the
main road until the
summit.

By Bus

Note: the following
schedules and rates are
provided for reference
only and are subject to
change.

From the Airport to Downtown

There is a bus going
between the airport
and downtown every
15 min. Though this is
the least expensive way
of getting downtown,
the trip is long (about
an hour). The down-
town bus stop is lo-
cated on Plaza Cinco
de Mayou. Fare: B/.
0.35.

In the City

Ciudad de Panamá
does not have a
government-run public
bus company; several
small companies ser-
vice different parts of
the city. The buses
tend to be old and
drivers sometimes
show a disregard for
the safety of pedestri-
ans. Buses are always
crowded, especially on
weekends. Stops are
frequent, so this is not

the best mode of trans-
portation if you are in a
hurry. It is best to
travel on buses with as
little baggage as poss-
ible; theft, pick-pocket-
ing, usually, is not un-
common, so be careful.
Despite these inconve-
niences, bus travel is
cheap and can be a
good way to meet peo-
ple.

Generally, buses keep
to the main streets of
the city, such as
Avenida Central,
Avenida 3a Sur (Justo
Arosemena), or other
less busy streets in
shopping and hotel
areas. To get off, you'll
have to yell (buses are
noisy) "*la parada*".

The terminus for in-
ner-city travel, **Panamá
Viejo**, **Amador** and **Isla
Naos**, **Perico** and **Flamenco** is located on
Plaza 5 de Mayo, on
Avenida Central. Desti-
nations are indicated
on the windshields and
most trips within the
city centre cost B/.
0.15. To catch a bus
from anywhere other
than the terminus, ask
someone to point out
the closest bus stop,
because they are sel-
dom indicated.

For safety reasons, trav-
ellers heading to **Mi
Pueblito** (see p95) or
Parque Metropolitano are
advised to take a taxi.

By Taxi

From the airport to downtown

Taxis from the airport
to downtown cost
B/ .20 per person and
B/ .8 if you share the
taxi with other passen-
gers. In the latter case,
make sure to tell the
driver that you are
sharing the taxi.

In the City

Taxis can be found just
about anywhere and
are probably the safest
way to get around
town. The cars do not
have meters. In Ciudad
de Panamá, taxis work
by zone instead of with
meters. Sharing a cab
ride with another per-
son costs B/. 1.25 to
B/. 2.50 each for trips
within the city centre.
You will have to nego-
tiate the cost of the
ride, and it is a good
idea to agree on a price
before getting in. Taxi
drivers are normally
not tipped.

There are also collec-
tive taxis which offer
the advantage of
shared costs (even if
destinations vary some-
what). Collective taxis
travel in and between
cities.

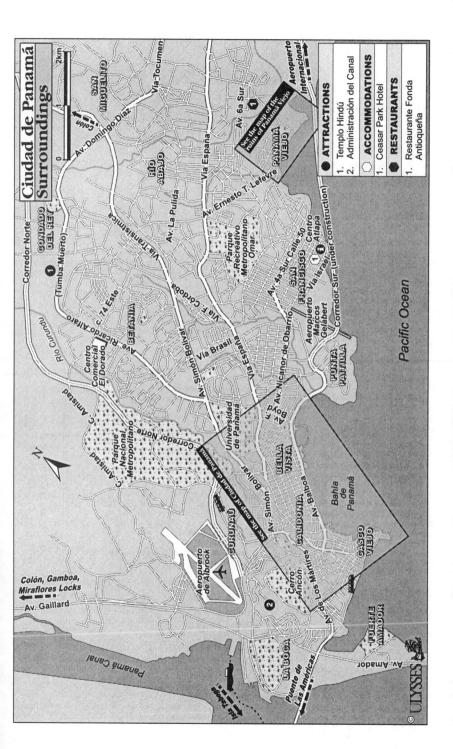

Ciudad de Panamá
Surroundings

0   2km

Corredor Norte

CONDADO DEL REY

Colón (Tumba-Muerto)

Río Curundú

C. Amistad

C. Amistad

Corredor Norte

Parque Nacional Metropolitano

Aeropuerto de Albrook

CURUNDÚ

Colón, Gamboa, Miraflores Locks

Av. Gaillard

Panamá Canal

LA BOCA

Puente de Las Américas

FUERTE AMADOR

Av. Amador

Av. Ricardo Alfaro

c. 74 Este

Av. BETANIA

Vía F. Córdoba

Centro Comercial El Dorado

Vía Brasil

Av. Simón Bolívar

Universidad de Panamá

See the map of Ciudad de Panamá

Bolívar

Av. Simón

Av. de Los Mártires

Cerro Ancón

CALIDONIA

BELLA VISTA

Av. Balboa

Av. Boyd

Bahía de Panamá

GASCO VIEJO

SAN MIGUELITO

Vía-Tocumen

Av. Domingo-Díaz

RÍO ABAJO

Av. La Pulida

Vía España

Vía-Transístmica

Parque Recreativo Metropolitano Omar

Av. Ernesto T. Lefevre

Vía España

Av. Nicanor de Obarrio

Aeropuerto Marcos Gelabert

Corredor Sur (under construction)

Av. 4a Sur Calle 50

SAN FRANCISCO

Centro Atlapa

Vía Israel

PUNTA PAITILLA

Av. 6a Sur

PANAMÁ VIEJO

See the map of the ruins of Panamá Viejo

Aeropuerto Internacional

Pacific Ocean

N

© ULYSSES

ATTRACTIONS
1. Templo Hindú
2. Administración del Canal

ACCOMMODATIONS
1. Ceasar Park Hotel

RESTAURANTS
1. Restaurante Fonda Antioqueña

Practical Information

Post Office (Correos y Telégrafos)

La Exposicíon:
Avenida Balboa and
Calle 30 Este

El Cangrejo:
Vía España and Vía
Argentina

City Tour

La **Chiva Parrandera** is a
very colourful,
open-sided bus that
offers passengers the
opportunity to listen to
tropical rhythms and
sip a cool drink en
route to a number of
possible destinations.
Itineraries include a
three-hour tour (*B/.20*)
during which three
stops are made: in Mi
Pueblito, at the Pedro
Miguel locks and on
Calzada Amador. For
more information,
contact **Chiva Parrandera**
(*Calle 46 Este, near
Parque Urrucá,*
☎ *263-3144*).

Pharmacy (Farmacia)

The *Farmacia Arrocba*
(Aquilino Guardia,
south of Vía España) or
the pharmacy in the
Supermercado Rey (Vía
España) can help you

deal with those little
scrapes, scratches and
pains.

Theatre

For information on
various Span-
ish-language produc-
tions:

Teatro Nacional
☎ *262-3525*
☎ *225-4951*

Teatro en Círculo
☎ *261-5375*

Teatro La Cúpula
☎ *223-7516*
☎ *264-1989*

For information on
English-language per-
formances:

Theatre Guild of Ancón
☎ *264-4271*
☎ *272-6786*

Bookshops

Librería Argosy
Vía Argentina
on the left-hand side of the
street when heading toward Vía
España.
Spanish, English and
French dictionaries,
books and magazines.
☎ *223-5344*

Cybercafés

**Cybercafé de Panamá
Torres de Alba**
Vía España (behind the El
Panamá hotel)
Calle Eusebio A. Morales
☎ *265-1257*
**Cibercentro In-
ternet@cafe**
B/. 4 an hour

Edificio Sun Tower Mall
Second floor, Suite 32
Avenida Ricardo J. Alfaro or
Avenida Tumba Muerto
☎ *236-5033*
⇌ *236-3290*
www.ccp.pty.com

Stratos
B/.4 an hour
Vía Argentina
Edificio Don Julio
Bella Vista, El Cangrejo district
☎ *612-9174*
www.stratos-cafe.com

Language Courses

**ILERI-Language & Interna-
tional Relations Institute**
Altos del Chase, El Dorado
Casa G-42
Vía La Amistad
Apdo 6-6331
☎/⇌ *228-1687*
☎/⇌ *260-4424*

Scuba-diving courses and equipment rental

Vía España
Edificio Rómulo Remo,
Burbujas
☎ *229-4200*
☎ *229-4201*
⇌ *229-4202*

Neptuno
Calle 73, n°12 (between Vía
Porras and Calle 50)
San Francisco
☎/⇌ *226-2020*
rperalta@ancon.up.ac.pa

Scubapanamá
Urb. Herbruger
Calle 6a. 4a. Norte, n°29
☎ *261-3841*
☎ *261-4064*
⇌ *261-9586*

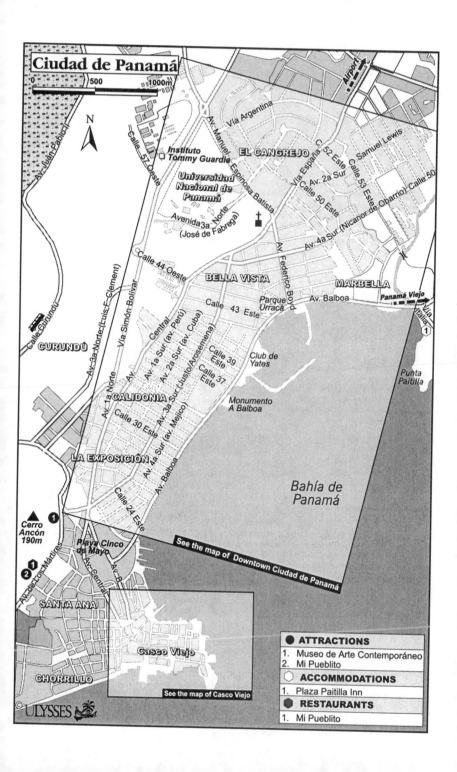

Ciudad de Panamá

0   500   1000m

N

Instituto Tommy Guardia

Universidad Nacional de Panamá

Avenida 3a Norte (José de Fabrega)

EL CANGREJO

Vía Argentina

Av. Manuel Espinosa Batista

Vía España

Av. España

C. 52 Este

Calle 53 Este

Samuel Lewis

Av. 2a Sur

Calle 50 Este

Av. 4a Sur (Nicanor de Obarrio) Calle 50

Calle 51 Oeste

Av. Juan Pablo I

Calle 44 Oeste

BELLA VISTA

Av. Federico Boyd

Av. 4a Sur

MARBELLA

Calle 43 Este

Parque Urracá

Av. Balboa

Panamá Viejo

Vía Italia

1

Calle Curundú

Vía Simón Bolívar

Av. 3a Norte (Luis F. Clement)

CURUNDÚ

Central

Av. 1a Sur (av. Perú)

Av. 2a Sur (av. Cuba)

Av. 3a Sur (Justo Arosemena)

Calle 39 Este

Calle 37 Este

Club de Yates

Punta Paitilla

Av. 1a Norte

Av. 1a Sur

Av. 2a Sur (av. Mejico)

CALIDONIA

Calle 30 Este

Monumento A Balboa

Av. Balboa

LA EXPOSICIÓN

Av. 1a

Calle 24 Este

Bahía de Panamá

Cerro Ancón 190m

1

Playa Cinco de Mayo

Av. de Los Mártires

Av. Central

Av. B

See the map of Downtown Ciudad de Panamá

1

2

SANTA ANA

Casco Viejo

CHORRILLO

See the map of Casco Viejo

© ULYSSES

● ATTRACTIONS
1. Museo de Arte Contemporáneo
2. Mi Pueblito
◇ ACCOMMODATIONS
1. Plaza Paitilla Inn
⬡ RESTAURANTS
1. Mi Pueblito

Burbujas
Vía España
Edificio Rómulo Remo
☎ *229-4200*
☎ *229-4201*
🖷 *229-4202*

Hospitals

Clínica de Paitilla
at Avenida Balboa and Calle 53
Marbella
☎ *265-8800*
☎ *265-8888 (emergencies)*

Tourist Office

IPAT
Ciudad de Panamá
Centro de Convenciones ATLAPA
Avenida 6a Sur (Vía Israel)
☎ *226-7000*
☎ *226-7614*

The entrance to the ATLAPA building is in front of the road. Once inside, ask the guard at the reception desk to show you where the IPAT office is, because it is hard to find.

Exploring

Ciudad de Panamá's most important historical area is San Felipe, commonly known as Casco Viejo (the old city). This is where most of the city's buildings dating from the colonial period are found.

The lively Avenida Central, parts of which are reserved for pedestrians only, is a good base for touring; from here the area can be explored fully in a day. There are other interesting buildings in parts of Bella Vista and Calidonia. To help you make the most of your time in the city, we have included descriptions of several interesting sites and suggested a walking tour of Casco Viejo. Nevertheless, before heading off to explore this fascinating city, take note that with regard to your personal safety, be careful in the Casco Viejo area, and in the Santa Ana and Calidonia neighbourhoods. To avoid drawing attention to yourself, wear little or no jewellery and keep your camera and any other valuables (video camera, walkman) hidden. Be on your guard in crowds, as pickpockets may be on the prowl. Stay away from Chorrillo, in the southwest part of the city. This area, heavily damaged by the American invasion, is still scarred and it is **highly inadvisable** to go there, especially at night.

Furthermore, do not walk around after dark in Casco Viejo, Santa Ana and Calidonia unless you absolutely have to. The safest neighbourhoods at night are Bella Vista, El Cangrejo, Campo Alegre and Marbella, which have many pleasant bars and restaurants. Keep to the major well-lit streets when walking after

sundown. Taxis are very cheap here, so do like most Panamanians, and take one.

Casco Viejo (San Felipe)

To fully appreciate the old part of Ciudad de Panamá and its beautiful monuments we recommend starting off by taking in a bit of bustling Avenida Central, starting from Playa 5 de Mayo, in the Santa Ana neighbourhood.

Transformed into an attractive pedestrian street, **Avenida Central** is a long commercial artery crowded with Panamanians, thus offering a wonderful, kaleidoscopic view of the capital's residents. Trees have been planted all along the avenue, and you can relax on one of a number of benches. As you walk down the street, the music streaming out of the stores will plunge you right into the lively Latin American ambiance. Although the appearance of most storefronts has been marred by placards and neon lights, some are still worth a second look. For example, the building on the first corner on the right side of the street is graced with a lovely Moorish-style façade with elegant wrought-iron balconies. Also, make sure not to

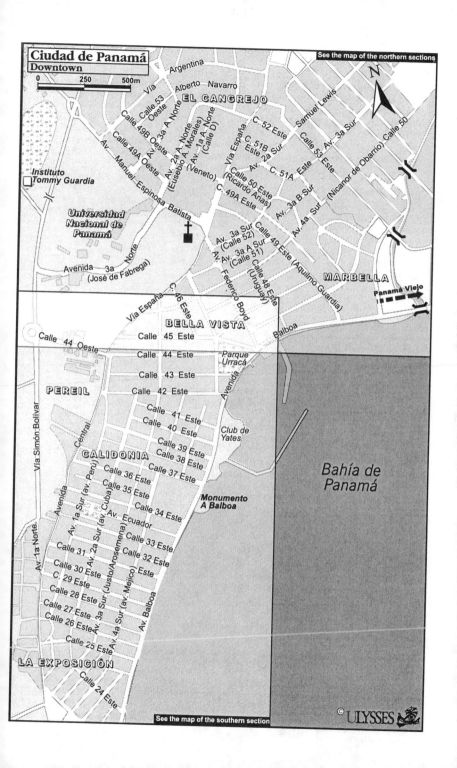

miss the beautiful ceramic **frescoes** ★ adorning the façade of the unusual building beside the Banco Nacional, farther along on the right. They cover three typically Panamanian themes: the Spanish discovery of Panamá, the construction of the canal and the operation of the locks. Finally, the most recent addition to Avenida Central, which is so much more interesting than all its shops would indicate, is the house at the corner of Calle 13a Este. Its blue façade, featuring Moorish elements and adorned with small, wrought-iron balconies, seems tailor-made for this tiny pedestrian street, nick-named "*Sal si puede*" (Leave if you can). It is so narrow and so full of shops that

passers-by do indeed seem to have a hard time moving about.

You can start your tour of the historic centre by stopping at Plaza Ana, the square at the end of the pedestrian street.

Plaza Ana. Many Panamanians gather in this pretty, verdant little square to discuss all sorts of topics, generally related to politics. The place is always full of life. Here, you will find the charming façade of **Iglesia Santa Ana**. Although the interior of the church has been completely renovated, certain parts of its walls date back to the 17th century.

Continue along Avenida Central to Calle 10 Este.

Iglesia de la Merced ★ (*at the corner of Avenida Central and Calle 10 Este*). This church is of interest mainly for its very pretty baroque façade, which dates back to 1680. The interior was entirely renovated after a fire and is not very interesting.

Just opposite, the **Casa de la Municipalidad** (*at the corner of Avenida Central and Calle 10 Este*), once the home of an affluent family, has a lovely classical façade, which has been beautifully restored. An underground passage once connected the building to the cathedral and the city's former fortifications.

The Art Deco **City Bank** Building, located on the other side of the street, is yet another example of the great variety of architectural styles found on Avenida Central.

Continue along Avenida Central to Plaza Central, also known as Plaza de la Independencia, where you will find a number of interesting buildings.

Erected between 1688 and 1796, the **Iglesia Catedral** ★★★ (*Plaza de la Independencia/Plaza Central*) is one of the city's architectural showpieces. Its most notable feature is its façade, whose central portion was built with stones from the former church of the Convento de la Merced in Panamá Viejo. The monks decided to use the stones of the destroyed church to symbolically wipe away the affront they had suffered at the hands of pirate Henry Morgan and his men. Not satisfied with

Iglesia Catedral

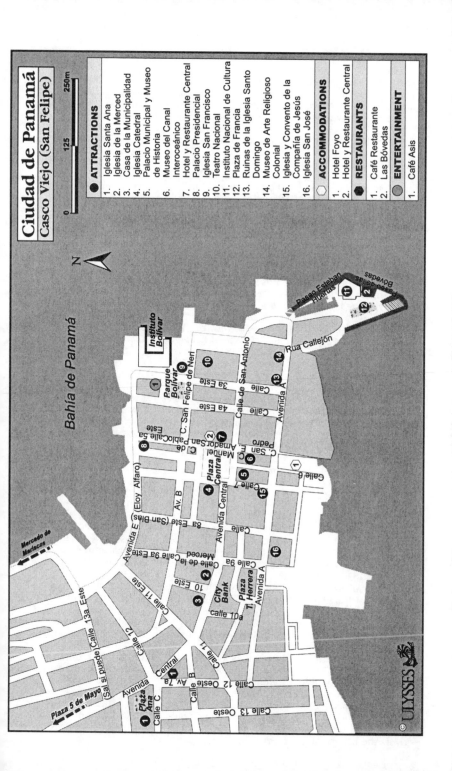

Ciudad de Panamá
Casco Viejo (San Felipe)

0   125   250m

N

Bahía de Panamá

● ATTRACTIONS

1. Iglesia Santa Ana
2. Iglesia de la Merced
3. Casa de la Municipalidad
4. Iglesia Catedral
5. Palacio Municipal y Museo de Historia
6. Museo del Canal Interoceánico
7. Hotel y Restaurante Central
8. Palacio Presidencial
9. Iglesia San Francisco
10. Teatro Nacional
11. Instituto Nacional de Cultura
12. Plaza de Francia
13. Ruinas de la Iglesia Santo Domingo
14. Museo de Arte Religioso Colonial
15. Iglesia y Convento de la Compañía de Jesús
16. Iglesia San José

○ ACCOMMODATIONS

1. Hotel Foyo
2. Hotel y Restaurante Central

⬢ RESTAURANTS

1. Café Restaurante
2. Las Bóvedas

● ENTERTAINMENT

1. Café Asis

Instituto Bolívar

Parque Bolívar

C. San Felipe de Neri

C. de San Pablo

Calle 5a Este

Av. B

8a Este (San Blas)

Avenida E (Eloy Alfaro)

Calle de la Merced

Calle 9a Este

10 Este

City Bank

Plaza T. Herrera

Avenida A

Avenida Central

Calle

Calle

Calle

3a Este

4a Este

Calle de San Antonio

Avenida A

Rua Callejón

Paseo Esteban Huertas

Paseo de las Bóvedas

Mercado de Mariscas

Plaza 5 de Mayo

Calle C

Plaza Ana

Avenida Central

Av. 7a

Calle 11

Calle 12 Oeste

Calle 13 Oeste

Calle 12

Calle 13a Este

(Sal si puede)

Calle 11 Este

calle 10a

Calle 9a

C. San Pedro

C. de Manuel Amador

Plaza Central

© ULYSSES

sacking the city, these men had no qualms about using the church as their headquarters.

The building is flanked on either side by pyramidal towers, which are painted white. The belfries have been inlaid with pearly shells to enhance their beauty. There is a curious legend surrounding the bells themselves, which are also from the old church. It is said that when they were being made in Toledo (Spain), Isabella of Portugal, who was passing through the city, threw her ring into the molten metal. Because of this, supposedly, the bells have a distinctive sound. The airy interior of the cathedral features a few lovely stained-glass windows, which could use some fixing up. You will also find a few paintings from the Seville school.

Erected on the same site as the former municipal building in which the Panamanian isthmus's declaration of independence was signed in 1821, and again in 1903, the **Palacio Municipal y el Museo de Historia de Panamá** (*B/. 1; Mon to Fri 8:30am to 3:30pm; Plaza de la Independencia/Plaza Central and Calle 7a Oeste, ☎ 228-6231*) now houses a museum of Panamanian history. Located on the third floor, this museum covers the history of

the Panamanian isthmus from the colonial era, through independence and the birth of the republic, and up until the Torrijos-Carter agreements of 1977. Unfortunately, little background information is provided in most of the rooms. The building itself is neoclassical in style, reflecting a distinct Italian influence.

Right next door, the **Museo del Canal Interoceánico de Panamá** ★★★ (*B/.2; Tue to Sun 9:30am to 5:30pm; Palacio Municipal, Plaza de la Independencia or Plaza Central, between Calles 5a Oeste and 6a Oeste, ☎ 211-1649 or 211-1650, www.sinfo.net/pcmuseum/index_eng.html, pcmuseum@sinfo.net*) is one of the most interesting museums in the capital. Before heading inside, however, take the time to admire the building's beautiful proportions. Erected in 1875 in an architectural style that reveals its French influence, the building is steeped in history.

After housing the aptly named Grand Hotel for 16 years, it was sold to the Compagnie Universelle du Canal Interocéanique, which used it as its headquarters throughout the French period of the construction of the Panamá Canal. After the dismal French failure under the aegis of Ferdinand de Lesseps,

the U.S. took over the construction of the Canal in 1904 and purchased the building for its administrative offices. The Panamanian government acquired it in 1910 and housed various administrative services under its roof until very recently, when it was converted into a museum, thus reviving its historic link to the canal.

The museum offers a chronological view of the country's history. The museum's exhibits include the outstanding *La Ruta-El Agua-La Gente*, which chronicles Panamá's development and its historic role as an interoceanic route from the pre-Columbian era to the 20th century.

A particularly informative section is devoted to the building of the Panamá Railroad, which preceded the construction of the Canal. One learns that in 1889, no less than 1,200,000 people crossed the isthmus by train, a number all the more surprising as, at the time, a first-class ticket cost as much as B/. 25 (*B/. 10 in second class*)! The section devoted to the Canal itself, also very instructive, highlights the French and American construction periods. The quality and originality of its presentation make this exhibit an absolute must. Explanations are provided in both Spanish and English.

Hotel y Restaurante Central (*Plaza de la Independencia/Plaza Central and Calle Manuel E. Amador*). This run-down hotel is worth visiting for its architecture, typical of houses built in the Caribbean in the colonial era. It has a large indoor patio, where you can admire an elegant wooden staircase leading to the upper floors. The lovely three-storey galleries give the place an airy look despite its imposing structure. Once known as the most luxurious hotel in town, it was frequented by key players in the construction of the canal.

If you are fond of Art Deco architecture, before leaving Plaza Central, make sure to take a look at the white building known as **Casa Al Ansa** located on the northeast corner of the square. Although its modern-looking windows detract somewhat from its overall appearance, this building is an example of Art Deco architecture in its purest form. Admire the sizeable entrance and the vertical lines on either side leading up to a balcony.

Continue your tour by walking away from the post office along Calle 5 Este/de San Pablo, then take Avenida E/Eloy Alfaro, to the waterfront.

If the national guard lets you, head to the front of the **Palacio Presidencial ★** (*Avenida E/Eloy Alfaro, corner Caller 5 Este*). As the name suggests, this is the official residence of the president of the republic. The building, which has characteristics typical of Andalusian architecture, dates from 1673 and was restored in 1922. It originally served as the home of the governor. The central courtyard, Moorish in design, contains a small fountain around which herons preen. The birds have long been a fixture in the building; indeed, the palace is also known as Palacio de las Garzas (Heron Palace). The interior is unfortunately not accessible to the public, unless of course you are invited by the president himself!

Nearby, on the same street, several upper class houses which date from the early 20th century have been restored particularly successfully. One of them is home to the famous singer Ruben Blades.

Double back toward Plaza Central, and take Calle San Felipe de Neri/Avenida B, located to your left. This street will lead you straight to Parque Bolívar.

Iglesia San Francisco ★★ (*opposite Parque Bolívar*). The belfry of this charming white church offers a 360° view of the city (to visit the bell tower, inquire at the office behind the church, to the right). The interior is fairly austere overall, but features a pretty choir decorated with a large, gilded mosaic. Originally erected in 1673, the Iglesia San Francisco was twice destroyed by fire, in 1737 and in 1761, and then rebuilt in 1766. In those years, it was one of the largest churches in Panamá. From the belfry, you can gaze off into the distance at the ships awaiting their turn to enter the canal.

The sheer number of vessels of such impressive sizes is a good indication of the importance of the canal on an international level. Other interesting views include the Paseo de Las Bóvedas and Plaza de Francia, the ruins of Santo Domingo church and its arch (*Arco Chato*), the Cathedral square, Iglesia Catedral, Puente de las Américas, Cerro Ancón and Punta Paitilla. This is a great place to get a feel for the layout of the city and to take photographs. On your way out of the church, make sure to take a look at the former monastery next door, which has been converted into a secondary school called the **Instituto Bolívar**. Its remarkable architecture is of Salamancan inspiration. The beautiful portal made of carved wood is particularly

Ciudad de Panamá

noteworthy, as is the main courtyard (ask the gate-keeper for permission to tour the premises), which features various coats of arms. Each represents one of the republics that participated in the congress of 1826, held in this very place and presided over by Simón Bolívar.

Some of the grand houses bordering Parque Bolívar, such as the former Colombia hotel, have recently been or are currently being restored. The current focus on the city's colonial history promises to make Casco Viejo the next "*Cartagena*" of Panamá. Let's hope that the city will also breathe new life into the Instituto Bolívar by restoring it to its original splendour and avoiding additional eyesores like the atrocious garage door with which it is currently afflicted.

The **Teatro Nacional** ★★★ (*ask the security guard for access into the theatre; Calle 3a Este, beside the Iglesia San Francisco; since half of the building is used by the Ministry of Justice, the entrance to the theatre is located opposite the bay*) was built between 1903 and 1908. Its interior bears a strange resemblance to La Scala in Milan – not surprisingly, since both buildings were designed by the same architect, Ruggieri. The celebrations marking the opening of the theatre were attended by Sarah Bernhardt. The garnet-red and gold interior, with its small, suspended balconies (make sure to take a look at the centre, or presidential, balcony, adorned with the national coat of arms) will send you off into a reverie. The crystal chandelier, imported from France, is also striking. The painting on the vault was executed by Roberto Lewis in 1907; it glorifies Panamanian patriotism and features the national colours. During the renovations carried out in the 1970s, Roberto Lewis's own son was in charge of restoring the painting. The richly furnished foyer, for its part, reveals a clear French influence. Concerts are presented in the theatre from May to October.

For information:
☎ *262-3525*
☎ *225-4951*

Continue the walking tour by going left on Calle San Antonio. Shortly after the street curves to the right, take the small staircase to the left. These stairs lead to Paseo de la Bóvedas.

The **Paseo de las Bóvedas** ★★ is a charming rampart-walk overlooking the walls built to protect the city. From here, you can enjoy a stunning view of the sea, with the ships waiting to enter the canal off in the distance. The Paseo de las Bóvedas is extremely romantic, and is frequented by large numbers of Panamanian couples; indeed, it seems to be the place of choice for lovers.

Continue walking along the ramparts until you reach the Plaza de Francia, located below.

Plaza de Francia ★★★
This lovely square has an old-fashioned charm about it. An obelisk topped by a proud French cockerel, erected in honour of the French workers and engineers involved in digging the canal, stands at the end closest to the sea.

Behind the monument is a semicircular gallery, below which the history of the construction of the canal is engraved right into the walls. Another monument, erected in memory of Carlos Finley, the celebrated Cuban who discovered the cause of yellow fever, stands in the centre of the square. Various military buildings were once located here. All that remain today, however, are the dungeons used to confine prisoners, which now house a private art gallery and an excellent restaurant called Las Bóvedas (see p112).

Right next door, the imposing Courthouse, which is crowned with a bizarre dome, now houses the **Instituto**

Nacional de Cultura (*Mon to Fri 10am to 4pm*). Temporary exhibits featuring works by Panamanian artists are housed on the main floor.

Also facing onto the square is the lovely colonial residence that serves as the **French Embassy**, and a little further, on the left, another newly renovated upper class home, which testifies to the current revitalisation of the district.

Those who are passing through the wonderful Ciudad on July 14 should make sure to drop by, as the French embassy organizes a big outdoor party here every year, complete with fireworks.

Take Rua Callejón, located to the left of the French embassy, then turn left to head back up Avenida A.

Ruinas de la Iglesia Santo Domingo ★★★ (*Avenida A and Calle 3a Oeste/San Francisco*) These are the ruins of an old monastery and adjoining chapel built by the Dominicans in 1678. What remains of the church façade makes it clear that it was once an impressive building. This delightfully peaceful site features an incredibly wide arch, known as **Arco Chato**. Built entirely of brick and mortar, with no internal reinforcements, it has stood

here for centuries, miraculously seeming to defy gravity. This feat attracted the attention of those in favour of building the canal in Panamá, who viewed it as irrefutable proof that the country was ideal for the project, being subject to minimal seismic activity. To visit the grounds, ask the caretaker of the religious art museum to let you in.

Museo de Arte Religioso Colonial ★★ (*B/. 1; Mon to Fri 9am to 4pm; Avenida A and Calle 3a Oeste/San Francisco*). This little museum, set up inside a church right alongside the ruins of the Iglesia Santo Domingo, exhibits sacred paintings and sculptures from various parts of the country, dating from the 16th, 17th, 18th and 19th centuries.

There is also a lovely collection of metalwork. The most impressive piece on display is the remarkably beautiful 18th century altar from the former chapel of the monastery, which is covered with gold leaf. Actually, throughout the exhibit, and in many churches, you will notice that colonial art is almost exclusively baroque. This is probably because the baroque style is particularly expressive, and thus well-suited to depicting scenes with an educational content. The church used this type

of art to spread its moral doctrine and establish its power. Humility, devotion and sacrifice, three signs of submission, were the watchwords in those years.

Nearby, on the same street, you will find the ruins of the **Iglesia y Convento de la Compañia de Jesús** (*Avenida A and Calle 7a Oeste/Santos Jorge*). Founded in 1749, this was once home to the largest Jesuit community in Panamá. A university was even established here in 1767. The buildings were destroyed by fire around 1781, but since then the ruins have remained more or less intact.

Erected in 1671, the **Iglesia San José ★★★** (*Avenida A and Calle 8/de San Blas*) has a rather modest exterior, and is interesting mainly for its beautiful Altar de Oro. This magnificent gold altar, which originally graced the former church of the same name in Panamá Viejo, dates from the 17th century, and is one of the few treasures to have survived the destruction of the old city. According to legend, the Recollect friars saved it from the pirates by painting it black, thus concealing its true value. In any case, even though the altar is still covered with gold, it is most striking for its style. Essentially baroque, it

Ciudad de Panamá

includes a number of unusual elements relating to Amerindian culture in the colonial era (exotic fruit, physical traits). The altar forms an extremely harmonious whole, and is perhaps Panamá's most prestigious sacred object from the colonial era.

To end your tour of the old city, take Calle 9/de la Merced to Avenida Central.

Santa Ana

The **Museo Antropológico Reina Torres de Araúz** ★★★ (*Plaza 5 de Mayo*, ☎ *262-0415*) is set up inside an imposing former railway station erected in 1913. During our visit, the museum was closed for renovation. It is supposed to reopen its doors early in the next century, 2000, that is! This is the most important anthropological museum in the country due to the quantity of objects on display, as well as the quality of these pieces. Although many treasures were destroyed by grave robbers, and others have been dispersed to museums around the world, a number of remarkable pre-Columbian pieces can be found here. A leisurely tour of the museum's five rooms reveals a great deal about Panamá's past. You are sure to spend at least

two hours discovering how the isthmus has evolved over the centuries. In addition to some lovely pottery and sculptures, an interesting collection of *Huacas* (pre-Columbian jewellery) is exhibited.

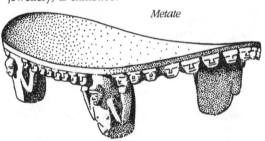

Metate

Regrettably, the management does not seem very concerned about preserving the works on display, and the overall presentation is somewhat outdated. The inadequate lighting and more or less legible commentary don't help matters. The following is a brief description of the various rooms.

The **Sala de Síntesis de la Cultura Nacional** gives visitors an overview of the pre-Columbian history of the region, of life in modern Panamá and of the country's place in the modern world. There is also an exhibit on ethnic minorities.

The **Sala Arqueología** is exclusively devoted to pre-Columbian artifacts found on archaeological digs. The objects are organized according to the cultural and ethnic groups that once

lived on the isthmus. Of particular note is the remarkable pottery and the small stone tables (*metates*) that were used to grind corn.

As the name suggests (oro means gold), the exhibit in the **Sala de Oro** focuses on gold artifacts, including valuable jewellery. Various techniques used by the region's indigenous population to make objects with precious metals are briefly explained in the exhibition. The lighting is poor, and, unlikely as it may seem, a number of objects have apparently been pilfered. During our visit, some of the display cases still showed signs of vandalism.

The **Sala de Contacto de las Culturas** deals with the pre-Columbian culture of the central region and presents objects found on certain archaeological digs, including the famous site of El Caño and the Sitio Conte in Coclé, excavated between 1930 and 1950 by Harvard University

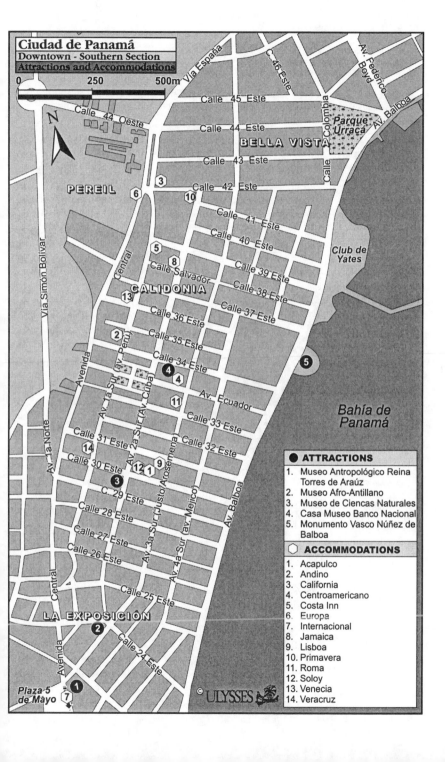

Ciudad de Panamá
Downtown - Southern Section
Attractions and Accommodations

0   250   500m

N

Via España
Calle 44 Oeste
Calle 45 Este
C. 46 Este
Av. Federico Boyd
C. Colombia
Parque Urracá
Av. Balboa
BELLA VISTA
Calle 44 Este
Calle
Calle 43 Este
PEREIL
Calle 42 Este
Calle 41 Este
Calle 40 Este
Club de Yates
Via Simón Bolívar
Central
Calle 39 Este
Calle Salvador
Calle 38 Este
CALIDONIA
Calle 37 Este
Calle 36 Este
Calle 35 Este
Av. Perú
Calle 34 Este
Avenida
Av. Cuba
Av. Ecuador
Av. 1a Sur
Calle 33 Este
Bahía de Panamá
Calle 32 Este
Av. Arosemena
Calle 31 Este
Av. 2a Sur
Av. Justo
Calle 30 Este
Av. 1a Norte
C. 29 Este
Av. Mejíco
Av. Balboa
Calle 28 Este
Av. 3a Sur
Calle 27 Este
Av. 4a Sur
Calle 26 Este
Central
Calle 25 Este
LA EXPOSICIÓN
Calle 24 Este
Avenida
Plaza 5 de Mayo

© ULYSSES

● ATTRACTIONS

1. Museo Antropológico Reina Torres de Araúz
2. Museo Afro-Antillano
3. Museo de Ciencas Naturales
4. Casa Museo Banco Nacional
5. Monumento Vasco Núñez de Balboa

◯ ACCOMMODATIONS

1. Acapulco
2. Andino
3. California
4. Centroamericano
5. Costa Inn
6. Europa
7. Internacional
8. Jamaica
9. Lisboa
10. Primavera
11. Roma
12. Soloy
13. Venecia
14. Veracruz

and the University of Pennsylvania. The rare pieces of fabric and wooden objects found on these sites are of particular interest. A few articles used by the Spanish conquerors are also on display. Lastly, in another part of the room, you will find a model of a working-class village, as well as various objects and pieces of clothing from mestizo and Afro-Caribbean communities.

The **Sala de Etnografía** is devoted to the social, cultural and economic aspects of various indigenous groups in Panamá (Chocoes, Guaymíes, Bokotas, Kunas, Teribes, etc.).La Exposicíon

The **Museo de Ciencias Naturales** (*B/. 1; Tue to Sat 9am to 4pm; Calle 30 Este and Avenida Cuba;* ☎ *225-0645*) exhibits a selection of stuffed animals (mammals, reptiles and birds) along with an interesting section on geology that contains a number of fossils. With the exception of a pamphlet sold at the entrance, the museum

provides little information on the exhibits.

The **Museo Afro-Antillano** (*B/. 1; Tues to Sat 8:30am to 3:30pm; Avenida 3a Sur/Justo Arosemena near Calle 24 Este;* ☎ *262-5348 and 262-1668*) contains various objects related to the Afro-Caribbean community at the time of the construction of the Panamá canal.

Calidonia

Erected in honour of Balboa, the freshly repainted **Monumento Vasco Nuñez de Balboa** ★ (*Avenida Balboa*) is a statue of a globe held up by four individuals of different races. Above them, Balboa points his sword toward the Pacific (which he "discovered" in 1513 A visit to the site can also include a walk along

Monumento Vasco Nuñez de Balboa

the promenade by the bay, from which there are beautiful views of

Casco Viejo and Punta Paitilla.

West of the monument, the stroll becomes all the more pleasant as the sidewalk that skirts the sea wall was recently refurbished. Amusing little mosaics with thalassic designs now adorn the low wall bordering it, and benches and new lighting have been set up. All that is needed now is an effort to reduce the non-stop traffic on this lovely avenue. Indeed, Avenida Balboa has become a veritable highway, as motorists speed along unimpeded by traffic lights (or police controls). Crossing the avenue at certain times of day is challenging!

Casa Museo Banco Nacional de Panamá (*Mon to Sat 8am to 12:30pm and 1:30pm to 4:00pm, Calle 34 and Avenida Cuba;* ☎ *225-0640*). An exhibition of coins and stamps in a lovely upper-class residence.

La Cresta

Iglesia del Carmen (*at the corner of Vía España and Avenida Manuel Espinosa Batista*). It is worth taking a few moments to admire the neo-Gothic architecture of this church. The interior is airy and harmoniously proportioned, but otherwise of little interest.

Campo Alegre

Built in 1949, the **Santuario Nacional ★** (*at the corner of Calle 53 Este and Avenida 2a Sur/Samuel Lewis*) merits a visit. The church has an interesting façade fashioned out of travertine marble, which makes it look much older than it really is. There is not much to see inside.

Ancón

Museo de Arte Contemporáneo ★ (*B/.1; Mon to Fri 9am to 4pm, Sat 9am to 12pm, Sun 11am to 3pm; Avenida de los Mártires and Calle San Blas in the Ancón area; ☎ 262-8012 or 262-3380*) This is a very interesting museum with a collection of more than 450 works by artists from Panamá and other Latin American countries. The pieces include paintings, sculptures and drawings, most of which were donated to the museum. A few paintings should not be missed, three in particular are *Los Satiros* by Humberto Ivaldi (1909-1947), as well as *The Unseen Eye is Watching You* and *Salutación al Pajaro Sagrado* by Guillermo Trujillo. Travelling exhibits by well-known artists from around the world are also presented on the ground floor.

The museum also has a boutique that sells interesting and inexpensive (*B/. 10*) T-shirts and works by local artists.

Located in the Cerro Ancón area, **Mi Pueblito ★★★** (*Tue to Sun 10am to 10pm; Avenida de los Mártires between Calle Julio A. Sosa and Calle J. De la Ossa; ☎ 228-7178; sinfo.net/alcadia/main.htm*) is a life-sized re-creation of small rural villages that can still be found in Panamá today.

Panamá's three main ethnic groups are represented here, each in a space set up to reflect their culture in the most realistic manner possible. For example, the **Mi Pueblito** section, which represents the colonial culture, features a typical central square, surrounded by a small church, a barber shop, a grocery store and a set of traditional houses like those still seen today on the Azuero peninsula. Also on site is a small museum devoted to the traditional Amerindian dress (*pollera*) and a pleasant restaurant (see p123). Finally, folk evenings featuring music and dancing are organized here every Thursday and Friday from 7pm (*reservations recommended;* ☎ 228-2124, 228-7178 or 228-7714). Created in 1994, this section should not be missed.

Nearby, the **Pueblito Afro-Antillano** follows the same concept, encompassing a church as well as shops and dwellings typical of people of West Indian ancestry, most of whom came to Panamá during the construction of the Canal. This display is particularly colourful and remarkably similar to a small Caribbean village.

A little farther still is the **Pueblito Indígena**, which features various traditional dwellings of indigenous peoples, namely those of the Kuna, Guaymíe (or Ngobe-Bugle) and Choco peoples. While the latter are set up in a jungle-like environment, those of the Kunas make up a veritable little village, similar to those that still exist on the San Blas Islands. The "village" is staffed by actual Kunas. The Pueblito Afro-Antillano and Pueblito Indígena were added in 1999.

Every shop on site carries the handicrafts of each culture represented, though the prices are distinctly higher than elsewhere. This place is a must for those with little time to spare while in Panamá, as it offers a quick introduction to the country's ethnic wealth. What's more, the very colourful Chiva Parrandera party bus (see p82) makes getting here half the fun!

Condado del Rey

Visiting an East Indian temple in Panamá? Not only is it possible, it is recommended, particularly for those who appreciate millennial Asia and its fascinating religions. Those who wish to pay their respects to Shiva, Ganesh or Vishnu should visit the **Templo Hindú** ★ (*free admission; Ave. Ricardo Arias, or Tumba Muerto, at Calle 12C Norte, on the left-hand side when heading toward the USMA*), where, besides a smiling welcome, an interesting view of the Ciudad awaits.

Panamá Viejo

This area, which covers several kilometres is so called because it is the site of the first city in Panamá (Panamá Viejo). Historically speaking, it is interesting to note that around the 1600s, when the total population of the city was about 4,000, only 850 people of Spanish origin were considered residents. The rest of the population consisted of slaves, mostly from Africa. These individuals were later sent to the Caribbean islands and the colonies to the south. Furthermore, although the city was strategically located, making it a required point of passage between the mother country and the new colonies to the south (Peru and Ecuador), its population grew very slowly. According to some, this was due to the many vast swamps nearby, which fostered the development of numerous illnesses, and also to the lure of gold, which had been discovered in other regions.

The park-like setting of the site, complete with descriptions before each of its ruins, is like an open-air museum. The site was listed as a national monument by the Panamanian government back in 1976 and, since 1995, has been administered by the Patronato Viejo foundation, which ensures its protection and carries out excavations. Before setting off to explore this wonderful historical park, be sure to visit the **Museo de Panamá Viejo** ★★ (*B/.1.50; Mon to Sat 9am to 4pm, Sun 9am to 1pm; Ave. Cincuentenario, opposite Plaza Mayor and the ruins of the Catedral*, ☎ 224-2155, *www.panamaviejo.org, patropan@pty.com*), where, in addition to various artifacts unearthed during excavations, there is a magnificent model of the city as it was in 1671, which helps visitors decipher the ruins on display. Small temporary exhibits are also presented here on a regular basis. Be sure

to check out their excellent Spanish-language web site, which features a very detailed description of the ruins. Below are some of the most interesting ruins (from west to east):

Fuerte la Navidad (The Fort of Nativity) was erected in 1658 to protect the entrance of the city. Fifty men were permanently stationed here, with six canons at their disposal.

Located just before the above fort, the **Puente del Matadero**, built in the 17th century, still spans the Río Algorroboa. It was constructed to make it easier to transport goods from the port to the city centre.

In 1552, the Mercedarian friars (a Catalan order originally instituted to ransom Christians imprisoned by the Moors) settled here and built a monastery and later a church facing the Gulf. These structures called **Iglesía y Convento La Merced** were amongst the very few to be spared from Morgan's wholesale destruction of the city. Soon after the city's devastation however, the monks chose to settle in the new city of Panamá, dismantling the church façade in order to build that of the cathedral, which can still be seen on Plaza de la Independencia. Unfortunately, the remains

The bell tower of Panamá Viejo's cathedral, ruins of a rocky colonial past.
- *John Mitchell*

The traffic never stops on Via España.
- *John Mitchell*

A pensive white-faced capuchin monkey.
- *courtesy of IPAT*

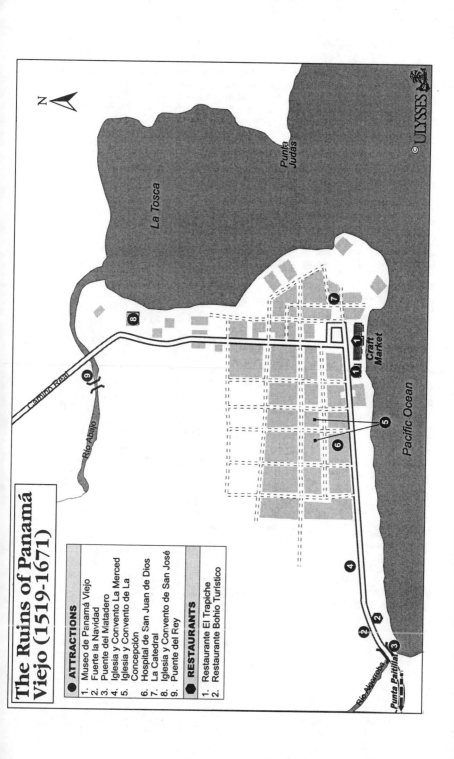

The Ruins of Panamá Viejo (1519-1671)

● ATTRACTIONS

1. Museo de Panamá Viejo
2. Fuerte la Navidad
3. Puente del Matadero
4. Iglesia y Convento La Merced
5. Iglesia y Convento de La Concepción
6. Hospital de San Juan de Dios
7. La Catedral
8. Iglesia y Convento de San José
9. Puente del Rey

⬢ RESTAURANTS

1. Restaurante El Trapiche
2. Restaurante Bohío Turístico

La Tosca

Punta Judas

Pacific Ocean

Craft Market

Camino Real

Río Abajo

Río Algarrobo

Punta Paitilla

N

© ULYSSES

do not give a very good idea of the scale of the original buildings, particularly since Avenida Cincuentenario awkwardly bisects the existing ruins.

The impressive ruins of **Iglesía y Convento de La Concepción**, along with those of the bell tower from the old cathedral, are among the best-preserved on site. The other ruins here are those of the temple built by the very prosperous Conception order of nuns.

Hospital de San Juan Dios is the site of handsome ruins of the city hospital which date from 1620.

Begun in late 1619, **La Catedral** took 6 years to complete. Rather than facing the main city square, as was the custom at the time, the church was built alongside the square and faced the sea. The ruins of the enormous clock tower suggest how impressive the original building must have been.

The well-preserved ruins of **Iglesia y Convento de San José** are located slightly to the north of the main site. The famous altar that now stands in the San José church in Casco Viejo originally came from this building. Along with the Iglesia la Merced, this is one of the few in the city not destroyed by Morgan's fire.

Near the ruins of the San José convent, the **Puente del Rey**, built in 1617, was vital to the city since it connected the city to the famous road known as Camino Real, which led to Portobelo, on the Caribbean Coast.

Cerro Azul

The climb to Cerro Azul is a lovely excursion and a great way to escape from the sometimes stifling heat of the capital without straying too far from the city. Those with a car can benefit not only from cooler temperatures (20 to 24°C), but also see flora similar to that found in most of the country's major national parks, all just a short ride away. It is a wonderful opportunity to observe a great diversity of flora and photograph beautiful panoramas.

The Destruction of Panamá Viejo

In February of 1671, pirate Henry Morgan sailed up the Río Chagres from the Fuerte San Lorenzo (see p78) with a fleet of several ships and an army of over a thousand, with the aim of plundering Panama City. After several days' rough sailing, the pirates reached the gates of the city, where they settled to regain their strength. Determined to defend the capital, thengovernor D. Guzman, leading nearly two thousand soldiers, resolved to head off the predator. Although they markedly outnumbered the pirates, the Spanish retreated after several hours of hardfought battle, leaving the city to the invaders. According to certain historians, this defeat can be explained by the fact that Guzman's garrison was then largely made up of slaves, who obviously had little motivation to defend a power that had subjugated them. Morgan seized the undefended capital and committed abominable acts of pillaging, murder, rape and desecration. Devastated, Panamá Viejo was then ultimately destroyed by a rash of fires, leaving behind only ruins to impress the visitor.

Keep in mind, however, that the higher the altitude, the more the climate changes, and rather quickly too. Grey and rainy skies are commonly encountered at a high altitude, even when blue skies and a blazing sun illuminate the plains below. Several tourism agencies in the capital offer guide services (see p 82) taking those who wish to explore the flora and fauna in greater depth off the beaten track. Those who choose not to will still find this little jaunt very peasant, particularly for the good restaurant along the way (see p124).

Parks

Parque Natural Metropolitano

This large park is one of only a few nature preserves in a very urbanized area. Lush tropical rain forest covers 192 of the park's 265 ha. The park is only 15 min from downtown, and is inhabited by monkeys, iguanas, exotic birds, sloths, tortoises, etc.

Sloth

For a map or additional information on the park's plant and animal life, head to the welcome centre near the parking lot. A guide service is also available to the public. The park is open every day from 6am to 5:30pm, and the entrance is located on Avenida Juan Pablo II (near Calle de la Amistad). If you are interested in observing the wildlife, it is best to get here early in the morning, when the animals come out to look for food.

Parque Natural Metropolitano
☎ 232-5552
⊠ 232-5615
www.sinfo.net/pnmetrop
pumetrop@sinfo.net

Punta Culebra

Centro de Exhibiciones Marinas ★★★
B/. 0.50; Tue to Fri 1pm to 5pm, Sat and Sun 10am to 5pm
Calzada Amador
☎ 227-4918
☎ 227-6022
www.stri.org/web5.html
On Isla Naos, more specifically on Punta Culebra, the Smithsonian Institute has opened an educational and well laid-out interpretation centre: the Centro de Exhibiciones Marinas, which is devoted to the understanding and preservation of the thalassic environment. Explanatory signs on a trail skirting the island's headland introduce visitors to various aspects of the marine life, from the formation of different kinds of sand and coastal vegetation, such as mangrove swamps, to the animals encountered here (birds, crustaceans, mollusks, etc.). The site also has quite a history! Visitors may be surprised to learn that several cannons were set up on Naos as well as on its sister islands (Perico and Flamenco) during World War II in order to protect the canal. Among them was a huge cannon that could be moved to the mouth of the canal along the 6-km-long causeway! Two small museums devoted to marine life are also an integral part of the site.

Farther on, the trail leads to the heart of a small dry forest where, here too, visitors are provided with ample information about the flora and fauna. With a little luck, sloths or iguanas can be spotted. The entire Centro de Exhibiciones Marinas can easily be explored in a morning or an afternoon, and a visit can be topped off with a pleasant meal at one of the restaurants on the island (see p123) or a swim at one of its beaches.

Ciudad de Panamá

Parque Nacional Chagres

Panamá boasts some 140 endemic species, no less than 80 of which have been seen in the Chagres National Park alone. Created in 1984, the park covers close to 1,290 km² and encompasses countless waterways, which now supply almost 50 per cent of the fresh water necessary to the functioning of the canal. Salt water is unsuitable as it leaves deposits which would eventually block the mechanisms of the locks. Moreover, these waterways provide drinking water for the capital, only 52 km away. The famous Río Chagres has its source in the park. A dam was built on this river in 1935, creating an enormous reservoir known as Lago Alajuela, which serves as a reserve for the operations of the canal.

Thanks to its rather limited accessibility, the park has managed to protect very rare species to which it remains home, such as the jaguar, a species of tapir and the harpy eagle. The animal and plant life here is so diverse that scientists find additional species every year.

The closest entrance to the park from the Ciudad de Panamá is Cerro Azul, where there are various trails. However, due to the presence of dangerous animals and few marked trails, it is best to go with a guide. Also, remember that authorization is required to enter the park (see p 72).

Beaches

Isla Naos, Isla Perico and Isla Flamenco

These islands are located off the Amador peninsula and are connected to the mainland by a long spit of land, though visitors are not allowed on Isla Flamenco. While the beaches on the other two islands are not very clean, the area is worth a visit for the lovely views and the more interesting attraction, Le Centro de Exhibiciones Marinas (see above), located within a small park. The narrow stretch of land connecting the

islands and the mainland is bordered by palm trees and a number of benches, and until recently was an ideal place to go for a bicycle ride or a morning jog. On our last visit work was being done around the park to prepare for the development of future buildings. We can only hope that it will once again return to the outdoor-lovers oasis it once was. If you like lively places, head to La Playita on Isla Naos, where a great atmosphere is guaranteed on weekends.

Outdoor Activities

Hiking

Parque Natural Metropolitano

This vast 265-ha park is one of the few nature reserves within city limits. No less than four trails are accessible here, including the 1,000-m-long *Sendero La Cienaguita* and *Sendero del Mono Tití* (named after the Tití monkeys who live in the park), which are linked together and thus allow visitors to enjoy a strenuous hike. These trails can be tackled alone with the

Jaguar

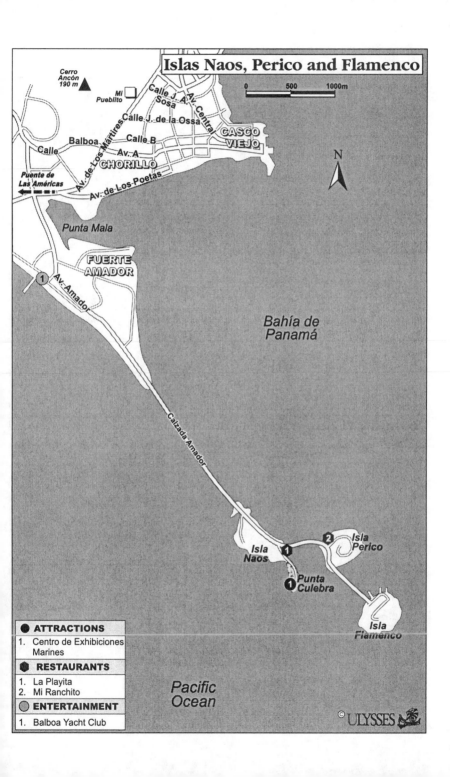

Islas Naos, Perico and Flamenco

Cerro Ancón 190 m

Mi Pueblito

Calle J. A. Sosa

Av. Central

Calle J. de la Ossa

CASCO VIEJO

Balboa

Calle B

Calle

Av. de Los Mártires

Av. A

CHORILLO

Av. de Los Poetas

Puente de Las Américas

Punta Mala

FUERTE AMADOR

Av. Amador

Bahía de Panamá

N

0   500   1000m

Calzada Amador

Isla Naos

Isla Perico

Punta Culebra

Isla Flamenco

Pacific Ocean

● ATTRACTIONS
1. Centro de Exhibiciones Marines

🍴 RESTAURANTS
1. La Playita
2. Mi Ranchito

◉ ENTERTAINMENT
1. Balboa Yacht Club

© ULYSSES

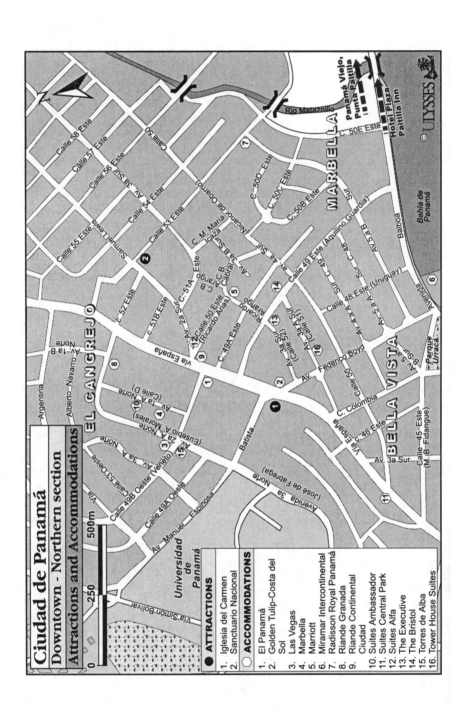

Ciudad de Panamá
Downtown - Northern section
Attractions and Accommodations

● **ATTRACTIONS**

1. Iglesia del Carmen
2. Sanctuario Nacional

○ **ACCOMMODATIONS**

1. El Panamá
2. Golden Tulip-Costa del Sol
3. Las Vegas
4. Marbella
5. Marriott
6. Miramar Intercontinental
7. Radisson Royal Panamá
8. Riande Granada
9. Riande Continental Ciudad
10. Suites Ambassador
11. Suites Central Park
12. Suites Alfa
13. The Executive
14. The Bristol
15. Torres de Alba
16. Tower House Suites

0   250   500m

Universidad de Panamá

Vía Simón Bolívar

Argentina

Alberto Navarro

Av. 1a B Norte

EL CANGREJO

Av. 3a Norte
Av. 2a Norte (Eusebio A. Morales)
Av. 1a Norte (Calle D)

Calle 49B Oeste (Venelo)
Calle 53 Oeste

Vía (José de Fabrega)

Ay. Manuel Espinosa

Avenida 3a Norte

Via España

Batista

C. 52 Este
C. 51B Este
C. 51A Este
C. 50 Este
C.49A Este

Calle 58 Este
Calle 57 Este
Calle 56 Este
Calle 55 Este
Calle 54 Este
Calle 53 Este

Samuel Lewis
AV. 3a Sur
(Nicanor de Obarrio)

C. M. María
Icaza
Av. 2a B Sur
C.B. Arango
C.B. Cabrano
Ricardo Arias
Ricardo Arango

Calle 50

C. 50D Este
C. 50C Este
C. 50B Este

MARBELLA

Calle 49 Este (Aquilino Guardia)
Av. 5a B

Calle 48 Este (Uruguay)
Av. 5a A Sur
Av. 5a B

Balboa

Bahía de Panamá

Río Matasnillo

Panamá Viejo,
Punta Paitilla

Hotel Plaza
Paitilla Inn

C. 50E Este

Av. 3a Sur
Av. 3a A Sur
Av. (Calle 51)

Av. Federico Boyd

C. Colombia
C. Calle 50

BELLA VISTA

Av. 5a Sur

Parque Urracá

Calle 46 Este
Calle 45 Este (M.B. Fidangue)

Av. 3a Sur

Vía Veneto
Vía Espa

© ULYSSES

help of a leaflet published in both English and Spanish. For the more adventurous, the Mono Tití trail leads to the park's summit, Cerro Cedro, at about 140 m in altitude. At the lookout on top there is a beautiful view of the Gulf of Panamá, the Panamá Canal and the gulf islands in the distance. Less adventurous types can take the *Los Momótides* and *Los Caobos* trails, both of which are easier.

Rafting

Parque Nacional Chagres

For some time now, the Aventuras company has been organizing rafting expeditions down the Río Chagres, in the park of the same name. Needless to say, this activity is for very fit people with rafting experience (level 2 or 3). It is a one-of-a-kind experience, as it goes through the very heart of the park where a variety of animals and particularily lush vegetation can be observed. There are four stages to this activity: first, a drive in an all-terrain vehicle to reach a camp located north of Cerro Azul, then a two-hour walk through uneven terrain to reach the river, followed by a six-hour descent down

the river to the artificial lake called Lago Alajuela. Finally, the last leg of the trip consists of a 30-minute lake crossing by motorboat to reach the road, where a car awaits to drive weary adventurers back to their hotel. Expect to pay about B/. 110 per person for a party of four. Though rafting is possible all year round, the best time to go is from September to December.

For more information:

Aventuras Panamá
Apdo 9869, Panamá 4
☎ *260-0044*
⇋ *260-7535*
www.geocities.com/Research Triangle/3311/
aventuras@atba.com

Accommodations

Casco Viejo

Although Casco Viejo is extremely charming, and the efforts made by authorities to revitalize the area are admirable, the historic centre of town still has no middle-range or luxury hotels to speak of. All you will find here are a few boarding-houses and outdated places offering only the most basic level of comfort. Furthermore, the neighbourhood is not safe after nightfall, and it is highly inadvisable to wander about here.

Those staying in Casco Viejo should either get there before dark or take a taxi. Despite these inconveniences, we have listed below a few of the most inexpensive places to stay in the capital.

Hotel y Restaurante Central
$
bw, ℜ
Avenida Central and Calle 5 Este, on Plaza de la Independencia/Plaza Central
This hotel, where the engineers working on the canal used to stay, still has a certain charm about it. Its wide patio, three-story galleries and large wooden staircase all bear witness to its glorious past. The rooms, separated from one another by simple wooden panels, are very basic, however. Those at the front of the building are the most pleasant, as they are connected to a small balcony with a view of Plaza Central.

Foyo
$
sb/pb, ⊗
Calle 6a Oeste, near Ave. A
☎ *262-8023*
Among the budget hotels in town, Hotel Foyo is a good choice, with 39 high-ceilinged rooms equipped with fans, which do not always work, however. Though clean, the place offers only rudimentary comfort. Hotel Foyo is nonetheless a decent alternative for those who do not wish to spend more than B/.10 per night.

Santa Ana

Hotel Internacional
$$
pb, hw, ≡, *tv*, ℜ
Plaza 5 de Mayo, Apartado 2751,
Balboa
☎ *262-9760*
☎ *262-4948*
↹ *262-4933*

A few steps away from
the Museo
Antropológico Reina
Torres de Aráuz, the
Hotel Internacional
offers comfortable
rooms, which are
hardly luxurious but
nevertheless decently
decorated. On the roof
of the building, there is
a bar with a terrace,
where you can enjoy
the warm Panamanian
nights. Another plus is
the free shuttle service
to the beach at Isla
Naos (see p 80, 100),
where a variety of
services are available,
including a bar, a
restaurant and chaise
longues, pedalboat and
parasol rentals. The
hotel's only drawback
is its proximity to the
heavily trafficked Plaza
5 de Mayo and equally
busy Avenida Central,
which make for a
rather noisy atmo-
sphere. Also, it is safer
to get about by taxi
after dark. In spite of
these inconveniences,
this hotel is a good
choice for travellers on
a limited budget.

La Exposición

This bustling area is not
very safe after dark, so
it is best to get about
by taxi.

Hotel Acapulco
$
pb, hw, ≡, ⊗, ℜ, *tv*
Calle 30 Este, between Avenida
Cuba and Avenida Perú
☎ *225-3832*

Located near busy
Avenida 3a Sur, the
Hotel Acapulco rents
out simply decorated,
reasonably comfortable
rooms at attractive
rates.

Hotel Andino
$
pb, hw, ≡, K, *tv*
Calle 35 Este, west of Ave. 1a Sur
or Ave. Perú
☎ *225-1162*
↹ *227-7249*

Located at the far end
of a somewhat
run-down alley, the
Hotel Andino is a good
alternative for budget
travellers, who can stay
here for less than
B/. 20 a night. Al-
though the long corri-
dors resemble those of
a hospital and the de-
cor of the rooms is
old-fashioned, overall
the place is clean and
decent. Each of the
rooms is equipped with
a small kitchen area
with sink, refrigerator
and a cooking burner,
so guests can prepare
their own meals.
Though the area sur-
rounding the hotel is
not very attractive, this
is compensated for by
the staff's smiling and
warm welcome.

Gran Hotel Soloy
$$
pb, hw, ≡, ℝ, ≈, ℜ
Avenida Perú and Calle 30 Este,
Apdo 3385, Panamá 4
☎ *227-1133*
↹ *227-0884*
hgsoloy@pan.gbm.net

Gran Hotel Soloy has
200 comfortable, spa-
cious rooms decorated
in an unoriginal style
that borders on kitsch.
In addition to its ca-
sino, the hotel has two
bars, a nightclub, a
roof-top terrace with a
panoramic view and a
24-hour restaurant. The
prices are reasonable
as well. The only draw-
back is that it is not
safe to walk around in
this area after dark.

Hotel Veracruz
$$
pb, hw, ≡, ℜ, *tv*
Avenida Perú and Calle 30 Este,
Apartado 4944, Zona 5
☎ *227-3022*
↹ *227-3789*

A modern building
with Spanish touches,
this hotel has comfort-
able rooms decorated
in a conventional mod-
ern style. It is conve-
niently located near the
old city. However, al-
though the neighbour-
hood is quite pleasant
during the day, it is
best to be cautious
here at night.

Hotel Roma
$$$
pb, hw, ≡, ℜ, ≈, *tv*
at the corner of Avenida 3A
Sur/Justo Arosemena and Calle
33 Este
☎ *227-3844*
↹ *227-3711*

The Roma is a large
hotel (160 rooms) that
offers the kind of com-

fort expected of a luxury establishment, including a bar and a nightclub. The rooms are comfortable and the service is friendly (though the decor is not great). Be careful in this area at night.

Lisboa
$
pb, hw, ≡, tv
Ave. 2a Sur or Cuba, between Calles 30 Este and 31 Este
☎ 227-5916
☎ 227-5917
↩ 227-5919
Situated in a new building, the Lisboa hotel has modern and comfortable rooms whose cleanliness seems to be one of the staff's main concerns. Fortunately, lovely dark-hued rustic wooden furniture provides a little warmth to the somewhat cold surroundings made sterile by the stark white walls. Despite the rather uninviting welcome, the Lisboa is one of the district's better establishments.

Calidonia

Residencial Primavera
$
pb, hw, ⊗
Avenida Cuba, near Calle 42 Este
☎ 225-1195
Although the rooms here are very basic, this place has the advantage of being located in a relatively safe area, not far from the residential neighbourhood of Bella Vista.

Hotel Centroamericano
$$
pb, hw, ≡, ℜ, tv
Avenida Ecuador and Av 3a, near Justo Arosemena
☎ 227-4555
↩ 225-2505
This reasonably comfortable hotel has 61 well-kept rooms, which are decorated in a conventional manner. It is located near a small park and numerous restaurants. Although this area is quite pleasant during the day, it is not the safest of place after dark, so visitors are advised to be cautious. Nevertheless, this hotel offers good value for your money.

Hotel Residencial Jamaica
$$
pb, hw, ≡, tv
Avenida Cuba, between Calle 38 Este and 39 Este
☎ 225-9870
The Hotel Residencial Jamaica is a modern colonial-style villa with comfortable, well-decorated rooms. The hotel's attractive woodwork and wrought iron styling bring to mind classical Spanish design. Though rooms can also be rented by the hour, this hotel is worth considering.

Costa Inn
$$$
pb, hw, ℜ, ≡, tv, ≈, ⊘, ⌂
at the corner of Avenida Perú and Calle 39 Este
☎ 227-1522
☎ 225-6700
↩ 225-1281
costainn@panama.phoenix.net
The Costa Inn hotel is a modern 130-room hotel with a number of ser-

vices, including a restaurant, swimming pool, bar, gymnasium and sauna. The rooms are comfortable, and the decor is modern but unexceptional. The pool is in good condition but is rather small for a hotel of this size. Good value for the money.

Hotel Venecia
$
pb, hw, ≡, tv, ℜ
Ave. Perú, between Calles 36 and 37
☎ 227-7881
↩ 227-5642
hvenecia@usa.net
On the upper floors of a new building with neocolonial-inspired balconies, the Hotel Venecia offers one of the best quality-to-price ratios in the capital. The long, tiled and somewhat cold-looking corridor leads to charming little rooms that are tastefully decorated.

Ask to see several rooms before renting one, as some have particularly elegant colonial-style furnishings. Unfortunately, none offer a truly interesting view. Also, a swimming pool would be a welcome addition. On the other hand, for as little as B/. 20 a room per night, there is hardly cause to complain. The staff is welcoming and the place is kept spotlessly clean.

Bella Vista

The Hotel California
$$
pb, hw, ℜ, ≡, tv
at the corner of Avenida Central
and Calle 43 Este, Apdo 61-93,
Zona 5
☎ 263-7736
⚏ 264-6144
Located in a fairly safe
neighbourhood, not far
from Bella Vista, this
hotel has 60 modestly
decorated but quite
comfortable rooms.
The staff is friendly and
the owner is from
Madrid. The rooms are
old-fashioned but a
good value. The only
drawback is that the
building faces onto
noisy Vía España. It is
therefore wise to ask
for a room at the back,
preferably on one of
the upper floors, which
offer a more pleasant
view. The hotel also
has a cafete-
ria/restaurant.

Hotel Europa
$$$
pb, hw, ≡, ≈, ℜ, tv
Avenida Central, opposite Calle
42 Este, Apdo 7511, Panama 5
☎ 263-6369
☎ 263-6911
⚏ 263-6749
Located on noisy Vía
España, the Hotel
Europa has about a
hundred comfortable,
but rather unattractively
decorated rooms.
There is also a con-
ference room, a res-
taurant, bar and
kitchy reception
area. Friendly
service.

Miramar Intercontinental
$$$$$
pb, hw, tv, ≡, ≈, ℜ, ☉, ✪
Ave. Balboa, Apdo 7336,
Panamá 5
☎ 214-1000
⚏ 223-4891
*www.interconti.com/pages/p/
panica.html, pan-
ama@interconti.com*
One of the newest ad-
ditions to the capital's
major-hotel scene, Ho-
tel Miramar Interconti-
nental is housed in one
of the two huge twin
towers recently erected
between busy Avenida
Balboa and the bay.

The lack of urban plan-
ning is obvious here,
and the ill-considered
development of sky-
scrapers that once
seemed to be confined
to Punta Paitilla and the
Marbella district now
seems to be spreading
to the downtown area.
The Miramar Interconti-
nental is thus the only
hotel in the capital to
offer a direct view of
the Gulf of Panamá.
Despite its choice loca-
tion, most of the rooms
lack balconies, and
guests must be content
with observing the
islands of Naos, Perico
and Flamenco, as well
as the many ships wait-
ing to enter the Canal,
through enormous but
inoperable windows.

The building offers 206
rooms and 13 suites, all
of which are tastefully
decorated, and come
with a clock radio, a
mini bar, an
in-room safe, and
a very
quiet
air

conditioner. The sinks
are separate from the
toilet in the fully mar-
bled bathrooms, which
are stocked with all the
amenities of a first-class
hotel. Of course, nu-
merous services and
facilities are available
to clients, including
several restaurants, a
bar with panoramic
view, a spa, various
shops, a tennis court as
well as a fitness centre.

Also, among the estab-
lishment's most impor-
tant assets is its very
large swimming pool
(the largest of any hotel
in the capital), com-
plete with a spacious
terrace which looks out
on the gulf and the
yachts in the marina.
Unfortunately, despite
the hotel's ideal loca-
tion and irrefutable
level of comfort, the
rooms are not well
soundproofed for this
grade of hotel, and the
restaurant offers low
value for the money
and amateurish service.

Campo Alegre

Aparthotel Suites Alfa
$$$
pb, hw, ≡, tv, K, ℝ
Calle 50 Este/Ricardo Arias,
near Vía España
☎ 263-4022
⚏ 223-0724
Alfa@sinfo.net
The four-story
Aparthotel Suites Alfa
has 65 comfortable
rooms with modern
furnishings and kitch-
enettes. The place is
somewhat depressing,
however, for several
reasons: there is no

view, the rooms are somewhat stark with tinted windows, and the decor is unoriginal. In contrast with the austerity of the premises, the staff is not only efficient, but also very friendly.

Tower House Suites
$$$
bkfst incl.; pb, hw, ≡, tv, K, ≈
Avenida 3a A Sur also called Avenida Frederico Boyd. Apdo 55-0309, Pta. Patilla
☎ *269-2244*
⇌ *269-2869*
The Tower House Suites rents out 40 nondescript modern suites, each equipped with a kitchenette. The rooms are comfortable and quiet.

Golden Tulip Hotel
$$$$
pb, hw, ≡, ≈, ℜ, ℝ, K, ⊙, △, tv
at the corner of Avenida Federico Boyd and Avenida 3a Sur/Ricardo Arango, also known as Calle 52, near Vía España. Apdo 8572, Panamá 5
☎ *223-7111*
⇌ *223-6636*
Costasol@sinfo.net
The Golden Tulip offers beautiful, comfortable little apartments with all the modern conveniences and a tasteful modern decor. On the roof, which offers a particularly interesting view of the church and Iglesia Del Carmen, you'll find a small swimming pool surrounded by a garden, and a bar-restaurant. In the evening, you can drink in a magical nightime view of the Ciudad de

Panamá from this terrace. There is also a tennis-court on the roof.

The Executive
$$$$
bkfst incl.; pb, hw, ≡, ℜ, tv, ≈, ℝ
at the corner of Avenida 3a Sur and Calle 49 Este/Aquilino de la Guardia, near Avenido Ricardo Arango, Apdo 5370, Panamá 5
☎ *265-8011*
☎ *264-3989*
⇌ *269-1944*
www.cjhotels.com /executive.htm
This big building contains 96 comfortable, well-kept rooms with classic, tasteful decor in warm colours. Also, most of the rooms have a small balcony and all have a fridge and coffee maker. The cafeteria is open around the clock.

Riande Continental Ciudad
$$$$
pb, hw, ≡, ≈, ℜ, tv
Calle 50 Este/Ricardo Arias, corner of Vía España. Apdo 8475, Panamá 7
☎ *263-9999*
☎ *265-5114*
⇌ *269-4559*
Larger than its little brother (see p109), the Riande Continental Ciudad is also more luxurious and more expensive. A 200-room complex, it offers all the services you could dream of – a conference room, a casino, a bar, a nightclub, a 24-hour cafeteria, restaurants, as well as a small swimming pool. The decor is quite attractive, and most of the

rooms have a balcony. Ask for a room on the pool side as they are nicer and offer a better view. This hotel is popular with business people.

The Bristol
$$$$$
pb, hw, ≡, ⊙, ℜ, tv
Ave. Aquilino de la Guardia or Calle 49 Este, Apdo 810-542, Zona 10
☎ *265-7844*
US ☎888-767-3963
⇌ *265-7829*
www.thebristol.com, talu@pty.com
Among the many skyscrapers sprouting up in the Campo Alegre district, The Bristol is absolutely charming. Although modern, the exterior of the building is adorned with French-style windows with decorative fittings and pastel hues, giving it a touch of refinement. The interior is classically decorated with elegant furnishings and intricate woodwork that give it a distinguished look. The rooms themselves, each unique and opulent, boast a comfortable sofa, a small desk with a telephone, a fax ma-

chine, Internet access and a CD player. To top it all off, luxurious fabrics, attractive curios and fresh orchids add to the almost aristocratic surroundings. Moreover, each of the fully marbled bathrooms comes with either a shower with glass doors or a bath with many complimentary bath oils. Newspapers, fruit, mineral water, coffee and tea are also offered daily, and there is a small fitness centre where guests can keep in shape. The only drawback is that there is no swimming pool, always pleasant in the tropics.

Panamá Marriott
$$$$$
pb, hw, ≡, ≈, ℜ, ☺, ◻
at Calle 52 and Calle 50 Este or Ricardo Arias
☎ *210-9100*
US and Canada ☎
800-228-9290
↪ *210-9210*
www.marriotthotels.com/PTY PA
Open since January 1999, the Panamá Marriott Hotel, part of the giant hotel chain is the new kid on the block in the business district. Though it constitutes yet another mammoth building in a city already teeming with skyscrapers, its architects have succeeded in giving the building a certain cachet evoking the Roaring Twenties. The interior is an entirely different story, however, with its very classical and opulent decor

characteristic of Marriott-chain hotels.

As might be expected, guests here will find everything they could possibly wish for, from the sauna and fitness centre to the swimming pool, bar, restaurant and many other services. The same holds true for the spacious guestroom which, with a coffee maker, alarm clock, mini bar, iron and in-room safe, will make guests feel right at home. Several rooms are for non-smokers, and the major English-language dailies are delivered to your door every morning. In short, nothing but the best, for those with a high credit limit on their credit card, of course.

El Cangrejo

Aparthotel Las Vegas
$$
pb, hw, ≡, ⊗, ℜ, K
Avenida 2a Norte/Eusebio A. Morales, Apartado D, Balboa,corner of Calle 49B West.
☎ *269-0722*
↪ *223-0047*
www.hotelvegas.com, lasvegas@pan.gbm.net
Located in the pleasant neighbourhood of El Cangrejo, the Aparthotel Las Vegas has a brand new lobby; about a hundred studios, each equipped with a little kitchenette; and several suites, which include a living room and laundry machines. Although decent enough, the furnishings are plain

and somewhat outmoded. Furthermore, the air conditioners, in wall units, are noisy.

Despite these drawbacks, this place offers an acceptable level of comfort, and ensures the safety of its guests. Moreover, renovations are presently under way, and a number of units have already been completely overhauled; ask for one of these. The hotel is also conveniently located in the heart of a pleasant neighbourhood, near many excellent restaurants and stores. TV addicts will be delighted to learn that they can pick up as many as 33 channels. International news is broadcasted in English on ICN. A good deal.

Aparthotel Torres de Alba
$$$-$$$$
pb, hw, ≡, tv, ℝ, K, ≈
Avenida 2a Norte/Eusebio A. Morales and Calle 49b Oeste/Veneto;
Apdo 10213 Zona 4
☎ *267-7770*
↪ *269-3924*
Built in 1994, the Aparthotel Torres de Alba rents out modern, spacious studios with kitchenettes equipped with range hoods, microwaves, washers and dryers. The studios are tastefully decorated mostly in marble, which also adorns the bathrooms. Guests also have use of a swimming pool and a workout room.

Aparthotel Suites Ambassador
$$$$
bkfst incl.; pb, hw, ≡, ≈, tv, ℝ, K
Avenida 1a A Norte/Calle D,
Apdo 5364, Zona 5
☎ 263-7274
⇆ 264-7872
This 40-unit modern hotel is in a pleasant, quiet area near numerous shops and restaurants. The studios and apartments are modern and nondescript. A small rooftop swimming pool adds to the pleasure of staying at this pleasant, but slightly expensive place.

Hotel El Panamá
$$$$
pb, hw, ≡, tv, ℜ, ≈, ⊘, ◠
Vía España and Calle 49b
Oeste,Apdo 1753, Panamá 1
☎ 269-5000
☎ 269-5421
⇆ 269-5990
⇆ 223-6080
*www.elpanama.com,
reservas@elpanama.com*
Hotel El Panamá is set back slightly from the road, and is therfore not easily reached by foot. This huge complex, equipped with 340 units, offers all of the extras one would expect from a hotel in this category: bars, restaurants (including one open 24 hours a day), a casino, luxury boutiques, a nightclub, a gym, etc. Guests also have access to a large swimming pool surrounded by a garden. The main building has tastefully decorated, spacious rooms, and a split-level side wing spans a pretty garden

with a bar and a swimming pool. Although this part of the complex is a veritable tropical oasis, the rooms here are much smaller and decorated in a rather dull manner. This area is also much noisier, and does not offer much privacy, since the rooms face each other. Three rooms are reserved for handicapped travellers.

Riande Granada
$$$$
pb, hw, ≡, ℝ, ≈, ℜ, tv
Avenida 2A Norte/Eusebio A. Morales, near Avenida 1a A Norte/Calle D
☎ 264-4900
☎ 263-7477
⇆ 263-7197
Part of a chain of hotels, the Riande Granada has 177 rooms, which are simpler and less luxurious than those of its counterpart in Bella Vista, the Riande Continental Ciudad (see p106), but nevertheless offer all the necessary comforts. In addition to a casino, a bar and a 24-hour restaurant, there is a large swimming pool surrounded by an attractive garden. Furthermore, the place is not only less expensive than the Riande Continental Ciudad, but is also located on a quieter street.

Hotel Marbella
$$
pb, hw, ≡, tv
Ave. 1a A Norte or Calle D
☎ 263-2220
⇆ 263-3622
Located on a quiet street, a stone's throw

from the Aparthotel Suites Ambassador and Vía España, the small Hotel Marbella will mainly suit those looking for a quiet place right downtown. The rooms are clean and comfortable but the decor, as well as the space, are minimalist. Though the rooms are small, they are reasonably priced. Good value for the money.

Marbella

Radisson Royal Panamá Hotel
$$$$$
pb, hw, tv, ≡, ≈, ℜ, ⊘
Calle 53 Este, at Ave. 5a B Sur, Apdo 8-320239
☎ 265-3636
US ☎ 800-333-3333
⇆ 265-3550
*www.radisson.com,
radisson@sinfo.net*
In the heart of the chic Marbella district, right next to the World Trade Centre, the tower of the Radisson Royal Panamá Hotel is not particularly attractive at first sight.

Once inside, however, guests will be delighted to find a pleasant, beautifully appointed lobby graced with a harmonious blend of glass, marble and woodwork. Conversely, the rooms' decor is somewhat disappointing, as the functional furniture shows a distinct lack of originality. The rooms are nevertheless comfortable and come with all the amenities required by businesspeople

Ciudad de Panamá

(Internet access, modem hookup and in-room safe). A swimming pool and exercise room, unfortunately both very modest, are also at guests' disposal.

La Cresta

Hotel Suites Central Park
$$$$
*buffet bkfst incl.; pb, hw,
≡, ≈, ℜ, tv*
67 Vía España, La Cresta, Apdo 873707, Panamá 7
☎ 223-3100
US ☎ 800-528-1234
↪ 223-2586
*www.suitescentralpark.com,
besuescp@pty.com*
Located on noisy Vía España, the Hotel Suites Central Park is part of the Best Western chain. Housed in a rather unattractive building, the 68 suites, all of which are luxuriously and classically if unoriginally decorated, include a guestroom and a separate living room. Indeed, comfort has priority here.

Though the place has a swimming pool, its small size and lack of verdant surroundings are regrettable. Despite these drawbacks, businesspeople will appreciate the hotel's central location and the various amenities offered, such as a computer with printer (on request; service available for free in executive deluxe suites) as well as Internet access.

Punta Paitilla

🛥️**Hotel Plaza Paitilla Inn**
$$$$
*buffet bkfst incl.; pb, hw,
≡, tv, ℝ ≈, ℜ*
Vía Italia, Punta Paitilla, Apdo 1807, Panamá 1
☎ 269-1122
☎ 269-1069
↪ 223-1470
↪ 263-6998
ppinn@ns.sinfo.net
Cylindrical in shape and resembling a large, modern guard tower, this hotel has several things going for it. The rooms are large, particularly well soundproofed and have large French doors leading out onto small balconies, some of which have unobstructed views of the gulf and the city centre. Each room also comes with an alarm clock, a table and chairs as well as a refrigerator that is far more practical than the standard mini bar. Unfortunately, the rooms do not have safes and the antiquated air-conditioners are noisy.

Noteworthy among the hotel's other assets is the spacious swimming pool with terrace. Although the large on-site restaurant is worth mentioning and has an engaging staff, prices are too high and furthermore, the large glass doors surrounding it do not provide an interesting view and the old-fashioned decor needs to be

refurbished. Despite these drawbacks, the hotel remains a good choice for its quality service and location.

San Francisco

Caesar Park Hotel
$$$$
*pb, hw, ≡, ≈, ℜ, tv, ☉,
△, ℝ*
Vía Israel and Calle 77, San Francisco, Westin Hotels & Resorts, Apartado 6-4248, El Dorado, Panamá 6A
☎ 226-4077
↪ 226-0116
Canada and U.S.
☎ 800-228-3000
www.caesarpark.com
This big, modern hotel, located near the Atlapa convention centre, has 400 fully equipped and tastefully furnished rooms. Non-smoking rooms are also available In addition to a wide range of facilities, including tennis courts, a work-out room, a casino and a nightclub, there are no less than four restaurants on the premises, one of which is open 24 hours a day (Las Hamacas). A number of luxury shops and galleries can also be found here.

The hotel does have a few drawbacks, however. First, it is located far from the downtown area, which makes it somewhat tedious to get about. Also, its unique swimming pool seems very small for a complex with so many rooms. Lastly, the international atmosphere could almost be termed sterile, making a stay here rather uninteresting, except for those attending conventions at the Atlapa centre.

Cerro Azul

Cabañas 4X4
$$$-$$$$
Vía Principal de Cerro Azul
☎ 226-6206
≈ 226-7616
www.cabanas4X4.com,
pmacab@sinfo.net
Those in search of a total retreat in the heart of the wilderness will enjoy the Cabañas 4X4. This establishment is comprised of four wooden cabins as well as five *bohios* (Amerindian-style huts) surrounded by lush tropical vegetation and only accessible by all-terrain vehicle. The rustic cabins' interior layout consists of a simple kitchen with all the necessary cooking utilities, a shower room, one or several guestrooms and a living room.

Rates vary from B/. 80 to B/. 145, depending on the size of the cabin (*for 2 to 8 people*). As for the *bohios* (*$$*), they are simple, basic one-room cabins on stilts with beds for four people. The "main floor" of the *bohios*, with an outdoor table and benches, serves as a dining area. The kitchen and showers are communal. Remember to bring insect repellent, as the mosquitos are particularly attentive here!

Hostal Casa de Campo
$$$$
bkfst incl.; pb, hw, tv, ≈, ℜ, ⌂
Ave. Los Cúmulos, 3-G Las Nubes
☎ 226-0274
☎ 270-0018
☎ 270-0019
≈ 226-0336
www.sinfo.net/casadecampo,
casacamp@sinfo.net
In a completely different style, Hostal Casa de Campo has several comfortable rooms in two buildings on a 4-ha estate, where several interpretive trails have been marked out. The rooms set up in the main building, a grand villa, are very tastefully decorated with magnificent antiques. Each room has a unique style, and the lovely antiques make them even more charming. The same holds true for the common areas, where paintings, carpets and chandeliers bring to mind Old Europe.

Unfortunately, the rooms in the new section, though comfortable, lack charm and are not tastefully decorated. So is the area around the pool, where the bizarre Greek-style columns look somewhat out of place. Different health packages are offered here, ranging from the "eco-stay" (including lodging, meals and fauna- and flora-observation hikes) and the "anti-stress workshop" (including lodging, meals, massages, sauna and many other treatments) to the "anti-aging workshop" (including meals and lodging as well as massages and revitalizing treatments). In addition to the pool, there is also an outdoor sauna and whirlpool, though these are not so large. For those seeking adventure, the establishment organizes several expeditions, including a hike to the top of Cerro Azul, a visit to a Kuna reserve and a kayak trip down the river.

Near the International Airport

Continental Riande Aeropuerto
$$$
pb, hw, tv, ≡, ≈, ℜ
Vía Aeropuerto Carretera Interamericana, Apdo 6-999, El Dorado
☎ 220-3333
from the U.S. and Canada
☎ 800-241-8955
☎ 800-RIANDE1
Situated near the Tocumen International Airport, the Continental Riande Aeropuerto hotel is primarily suited for a stopover in Panamá. The rooms are located in a two-storey U-shaped building that surrounds a garden and a pleasant swimming pool. Though the hotel looks more like a motel, the rooms are comfortable, if somewhat lacking in intimacy. Guests can have a game of tennis or volleyball while awaiting their flight.

Ciudad de Panamá

Restaurants

Casco Viejo

Restaurante Las Bóvedas
$$$
Mon to Sun 7pm to 11pm
Plaza de Francia
☎ *228-8058*
☎ *228-8068*
Adjoining pretty Plaza de Francia, inside some of the city's 18th century fortifications (see p84), the Restaurante Las Bóvedas serves quality French cuisine in an extremely attractive setting. Be careful as there is no sign on the restaurant, which is located on the west side of the Plaza. In a lovely vaulted room, away from the heat, you can savour a fish or meat dish served with a thick sauce and baby vegetables. For those who prefer to be out in the sun, there is a small terrace where you can quench your thirst. Live jazz music from Thursday to Saturday, starting at 9pm. Friendly service.

Santa Ana

Café Restaurante
$
every day 7:30am to midnight
at Calle 12 and Ave. Central
Among the least expensive restaurants in Ciudad de Panamá, Café Restaurante is probably the best.

Located on a street corner, a stone's throw from busy Avenida Central, this crowded establishment is very popular with locals who come here to eat for a reasonable price. The daily menu costs as little as B/. .3, including soup, a main course and coffee (alcoholic beverages not available), which you can eat while seated in lovely leather chairs. More than a good deal, a true wonder!

La Exposición

Mi Salud
$
Mon to Sat 7am to 6pm
Calle 31, near Avenida 4a Sur/Mejico
Located in a simple little house, this restaurant offers a small selection of vegetarian dishes in a rather nondescript dining room. The decor is accentuated by arches, and livened up by bright, colourful tablecloths. One the few vegetarian restaurants in the capital.

Rincón Griego
$
at Calle 32 Este and Ave. Cuba
The small Rincón Griego restaurant-cafeteria has just six or seven tables and a very modest decor, but dishes out very affordable Panamanian fare.

Indeed, a meal can be had here for less than B/. 3. Although it is not located in a very appealing neighbourhood, the boss's charming welcome soon puts everyone at ease.

A Casa de Fernando
$$
Calle 30 Este, between Ave. 3a Sur or Justo Arosemena and Ave. 2a Sur or Cuba
In a rustic Portuguese-style setting, Restaurante A Casa de Fernando offers patrons *sancocho de Gallina* for B/. 1.75, *sopa de mariscos* for B/. 2.75, *cazuela de mariscos* for B/. 11.25 or *pargo rojo* for B/. 9. A real bargain! Also featured on the menu are *calamares, camarones, langostinas* and *pulpos* in all its forms and with a variety of sauces at very reasonable prices. The best place in the district, with Panamanian music to boot!

Comedor Las Palmas
$$
every day noon to midnight
at Ave. Perú and Calle 30 Este, on the main floor of the Veracruz hotel
In a simple and somewhat impersonal setting, Comedor Las Palmas offers very simple *corvina*, chicken and spaghetti dishes. Its long opening hours are especially convenient.

La Cascada
$$$

Mon to Thu 4:30pm to 11pm, Fri and Sat 3pm to 11:30pm, Sun 11am to 11pm

Avenida Balboa and Calle 2

☎ 262-1297

The truly unusual restaurant La Cascada merits a short visit, if only to see its amusing decor. Guests dine near a series of pools and little fountains adorned with a number of fake swordfish. All the water comes from a reconstructed waterfall that looks like the real thing!

As if the decor was not kitschy enough already, coloured Chinese lanterns have been put up all over the place, creating a carnival-like atmosphere. The menu is equally peculiar, made up of 16 pages of jokes and games referring to the food, which consists mainly of seafood and grilled meats. There is another branch of this restaurant in El Cangrejo (see p120). Finally, La Cascada is also unusual in that its staff is made up exclusively of young Panamanian women.

Calidonia

El Viejo Pipo
$$$

Tue to Sun noon to 3pm and 6pm to 11pm Calle 42 Este, near Avenida Balboa; on the right as you head toward the avenue

☎ 225-7924

Set up inside a little villa surrounded by greenery, the Italian restaurant El Viejo Pipo has a pretty decor, whose wooden shutters, earth-coloured floor tiles and quaint little tablecloths evoke all the charm of Italy.

The menu features a refreshing *insalata de Mozarella*; curiously enough, the chef here prepares it without the traditional tomatoes. As for the main course, a choice of pasta dishes is naturally offered, as well as a delicious *corvina a la gorgonzola*, served with broccoli. What a treat! The clientele consists mainly of business people, and proper dress is expected. The only drawback is the slow service. After all, though, who cares about a little lost time when the food is so delectable? Friendly, cheerful staff.

Restaurante Hotel Costa Inn
$$$

at the corner of Avenida Perú and Calle 39 Este

☎ 227-1522

☎ 225-6700

This cafeteria-restaurant is most notable for its quality breakfasts, including an excellent fruit salad -- a rarity in the capital. During the rest of the day, predictable international cuisine is served. The restaurant has a bright dining room with a view of the neighbourhood's greenery and is open 24 hours. Prices are on the high side.

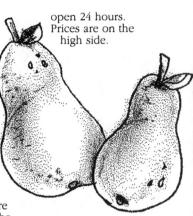

Restaurante Hotel Europa
$$$

Avenida Central, near Calle 42 Este, facing the Bella Vista theatre

☎ 263-6369

This restaurant is located in the hotel of the same name, serves generous portions of several types of cuisine: Panamanian, Italian and French. The food is good but the modern decor is a little cold. The service makes up for any small shortcomings.

Marbella
$$$$

every day 11am to 11pm Avenida Balboa, between Calle 38 and 39 Este

☎ 225-9065

Located inside a chalet, The Restaurante Marbella will delight fish and seafood lovers. The chef prepares corvina and gambas in all sorts of sauces, as well as excellent paellas. The decor is decent but somewhat dull.

Ciudad de Panamá

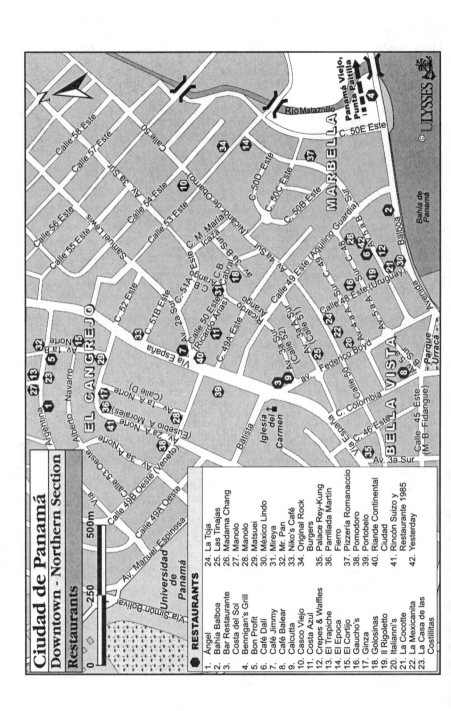

Ciudad de Panamá
Downtown - Northern Section

Restaurants

0   250   500m

RESTAURANTS

1. Angel
2. Bahía Balboa
3. Bar Restaurante
   Costa del Sol
4. Bennigan's Grill
5. Bon Profit
6. Café Dalí
7. Café Jimmy
8. Café Balear
9. Calcutta
10. Casco Viejo
11. Costa Azul
12. Crepes & Waffles
13. El Trapiche
14. El Epoca
15. El Cortijo
16. Gaucho's
17. Ginza
18. Golosinas
19. Il Rigoletto
20. Italianni's
21. La Cocotte
22. La Mexicanita
23. La Casa de las
    Costillitas

24. La Toja
25. Las Tinajas
26. Madama Chang
27. Manolo
28. Manolo
29. Matsuei
30. México Lindo
31. Mireya
32. Mr. Pan
33. Niko's Café
34. Original Rock
    Burgers
35. Palace Rey-Kung
36. Parrillada Martín
    Fierro
37. Pizzería Romanaccio
38. Pomodoro
39. Portobelo
40. Riande Continental
    Ciudad
41. Rincón Suizo y
    Restaurante 1985
42. Yesterday

© ULYSSES

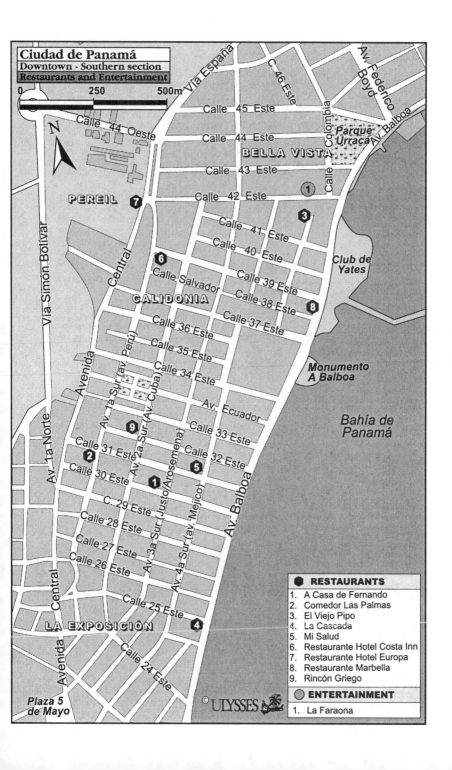

Bella Vista

Palace Rey-Kung
$$
Vía España, near Calle 46
☎ *269-0956*
The Palace Rey-Kung is an attractive, if over-priced, Chinese restaurant. The fare is made up of slightly expensive, but classic, Chinese dishes. Wine from B/. 14 to B/. 18.

Café Balear
$$$$
Mon to Sat noon to 3pm and 7pm to 11pm
17 Calle Colombia, between Ave. 4a A Sur and Ave. 5a B Sur
☎ *269-2415*
Mainly frequented by businesspeople, the lovely family-run restaurant Café Balear serves typical Spanish cuisine complimented by a few more exotic dishes, such as the *dorado* with mushrooms and port or sweet-and-sour *corvina* with coconut and tomatoes.

A *tapas* menu is also offered for B/. 24, as is an extensive wine list (*from B/. 17*). Though the food is of good quality and well presented, desserts are rather inconsistent. For example, while the *biscocho con almendra* is excellent, the chocolate cake is particularly disappointing. The decor is quite formal, despite a few plants and scores of paintings by Panamanian artists, including one by contemporary artist Antonio Alvarado.

Campo Alegre

Niko's Café
$
Calle 51b Este/Eg. Ortega, just south of Vía España
This self-service cafeteria is a good place for a light, inexpensive meal. Besides serving a large selection of dishes like shrimp, cutlets, crayfish and corvina, the place makes pitas, gyros and sandwiches to go. For breakfast, you can enjoy an omelette, corn tortillas, croissants stuffed with meat, etc. for as little as B/. 2.50. Simple, tasty food in modest but comfortable surroundings, reminiscent of Manolo's (see p119). Cappuccinos and expressos are available. The place also has a large terrace. Very popular with the locals.

Café Jimmy
$
Avenida 2a Sur/Samuel Lewis, south of Vía España, near the Riande Continental hotel; attention motorists: there are no signs to warn you, but this is a one-way street!
In the same price category, but with a less elaborate menu, the self-service Café Jimmy also offers light, simple meals in an equally simple decor. Local clientele. Terrace.

Mireya
$
Mon to Sat 6am to 8pm
at the corner of Calle 50 Este/Ricardo Arias and Avenida 3a/Ricardo Arango
☎ *269-1876*
Located in a pleasant and relatively calm neighbourhood, Mireya is a vegetarian restaurant that serves good, light dishes, perfect for breakfast or lunch. It has a pretty terrace adorned with wrought-iron furniture and all sorts of plants, where you can sample things like *torrejas de maíz nuevo*, *changa de maíz con queso* and *empanadas de maíz con queso*. Various fruits are also available. Soy coffee and herbal tea are offered instead of regular coffee. Although the menu is fairly limited, this is a pleasant place to enjoy a healthy meal. Give it a try!

Costa Azul
$$
7am to 11pm
Calle 50 Este/Ricardo Arias, left side of the street on the way to Vía España
☎ *269-0409*
Panamanian cuisine and sandwiches in a simple but comfortable setting. Small but pretty terrace. Draft beer at B/. 0.75.

Costa Del Sol
$$
Avenida Federico Boyd and Avenida 3a Sur/Ricardo Arango/Calle 52, near Vía España
☎ *223-7111*
The restaurant Costa del Sol, located on the roof of the hotel of the

time to try delicious cocktails including *banana coladas*, and *sunsets* (made with a lot of rum). The restaurant serves traditional fish (grilled *corvina*) and chicken dishes. The hanging garden is a beautiful addition to the decor.

Calcutta
$$$
Open Tue to Sun
below the Costa del Sol hotel; at the corner of Avenida Federico Boyd and Avenida 3a Sur/Ricardo Arango, also known as Calle 52, near Vía España
☎ *263-8536*
As its name suggests, the Restaurante Calcutta serves traditional Indian food. The decor, made up essentially of fabric attached to the ceiling, screens made of carved wood and prints hanging on the walls, is both tasteful and original. The service, however, is exceptionally slow; it seems to take an eternity for the food to arrive at the table. Set aside an entire evening to dine here. Furthermore, a few extra little dishes quickly lead to a fairly hefty bill. Despite these drawbacks, this place is worth keeping in mind for its quality Tandoori cuisine.

Riande Continental Ciudad
$$$
Calle 50 Este or Ricardo Arias, near Ave. España
The restaurant of the Riande Continental Ciudad hotel has nothing special to offer, but is worth the trip none

theless for its good, typically Panamanian breakfast. Called *desayuno Montuño*, this hearty breakfast is composed of *yuka*, *platano* and a *bollo de maíz*, cheese and an omelet. Its terrace with swimming pool and an assortment of green plants provides a pleasant little oasis in the heart of the city.

Restaurante Golosinas
$$$$
Mon to Sat
Calle Beatriz M. de Cabal/Ricardo Arias, near Avenida 3a B Sur
☎ *269-6237*
☎ *269-2028*
The Restaurante Golosinas which has a new location on a more pleasant street, serves fine, innovative international and Panamanian cuisine. The dishes are served with excellent vegetables, and the presentation is simply beautiful. Although the building is new, the decorators skilfully succeeded in concealing its concrete structure. The decor is post-modern, and pastel colours soften the harsh, cold look of the walls, which are adorned with a few contemporary paintings. Business people and consulate employees make up the lunchtime clientele. Unfortunately, since our last visit, the restaurant seems to be suffering from its own success as the quality and speed of service has declined.

Las Tinajas
$$$$
Mon to Sat
22 Avenida 3a Sur/Calle 51, near Avenida Frederico Boyd
☎ *263-7890*
Las Tinajas is a restaurant in a Spanish-style villa that offers an excellent variation on traditional Panamanian cuisine. *Lengua fría con alcaparras* (beef tongue with capers), *guacho de marisco* (a shellfish dish) and *pastel de yucca* (a soufflé with yucca, corn, chicken and peppers) are a few of the delicious specialities. The desserts are equally good and include coconut flan and *sopa borracha* (a rum, plum, and raisin cake). For the level of quality offered, the careful preparation and the pleasant service, the prices are good.

The decor of the restaurant is attractive and features objects from various regions throughout the country and from various time periods, including the pre-Columbian and colonial periods. Every Tuesday, Thursday, Friday and Saturday, starting at 9pm, the restaurant showcases traditional Panamanian dancing (the dancers wear the beautiful pollera). The restaurant also has an overpriced souvenir shop.

Ciudad de Panamá

Casco Viejo
$$$$
Mon to Fri noon to 3pm and 6pm to 11pm, Sat 7pm to 11pm
Avenida 4a Sur/Nicanor de Obarrio, also known as Calle 50, near Calle 53 Este
☎ *223-3306*
☎ *223-3316*

Once located in Casco Viejo, the Restaurante Caseo Viejo now occupies a large villa that has a garden terrace. As far as the interior design is concerned, the dining room is tastefully decorated in classic French style, and the tables are set in the traditional French manner.

The main attraction here, however, is the excellent, innovative cuisine prepared by the friendly chef, Pascal Finet. His Breton origins should already give you an idea of the quality of the food. The menu includes smoked duck salad, tomato tartare on a bed of spinach, crayfish on a bed of leeks and *corvina* with crayfish mousse and champagne. Talk about a treat! To perfectly accompany your meal, you can choose a bottle of Chilean wine from the restaurant's excellent and affordable selection. The Sauvignon blanc is particularly good. Finally, top off your meal–undoubtedly the best you will have in Panamá–with a marquise de chocolat with strawberry coulis. There is only one little

snag: although the trilingual menu lists a wide choice of dishes, few of these actually seem to be available. Good value for your money.

Matsuei
$$$
Mon to Sat noon to 11:30pm, Sun 6pm to 11:30pm
12-A Avenida 2a Norte/Eusebio A. Morales, opposite the Riande Granada hotel
☎ *264-9562*

This Japanese restaurant, the Matsuei serves the famous *Bento* boxes, as well as a few other typical dishes. Besides the *Obento Matsuei*, essentially a mixture of raw fish and seafood, the *Obento Sushi* is worth trying for the chicken sushi with nuts. The food is excellent and served in generous portions; one Bento box is easily enough for two people. Though the decor may be less sophisticated than Ginza's (in El Cangrejo), the room at the back is nonetheless decorated in typical Japanese fashion. Although the quality and freshness of the fish are exemplary, it is generally better to avoid raw fish in the tropics.

El Cortijo
$$$$
Mon to Sat noon to 3pm and 6:30pm to 11pm
Avenida 1a B Norte, near Calle 53 Oeste/Alberto Navarro ☎ *269-6386*

If you appreciate a sophisticated decor, make sure to try the El Cortijo, where you can

savour classic international cuisine in the most elegant of settings. A pleasant surprise and ideal for a business lunch. Proper dress required.

Restaurante Portobelo
$$$$
Vía España and Calle 49b Oeste
☎ *269-5000*
☎ *269-5421*

Situated inside the El Panamá hotel, the Restaurante Portobelo serves French and Panamanian cuisine, including excellent *langostinos bahia piñas*, in a slightly flashy setting. There is a seafood buffet on Fridays and Monday to Friday afternoons you can listen to some light piano music while enjoying a coffee. The prices are a bit high, but impeccable service is guaranteed. Proper dress required.

Rincón Suizo y Restaurante 1985
$$$$$
Mon to Fri 11am to 3pm and 6pm to 10pm, Sat and Sun 11am to 3pm and 5:30pm to 11pm
Avenida 2a Norte/Calle Eusebio A. Morales
☎ *263-8571*
☎ *263-8310*

Rincón Suizo y Restaurante 1985 is actually two very good restaurants in one. The first offers French cuisine in luxurious surroundings and has an elaborate menu; expect to pay B/. 15 to B/. 30 per dish. The second restaurant is simpler in design and is reminiscent of a Swiss chalet. The menu is equally imaginative, with cucumber salad, *quenelle* of *corvina* mousse with basil sauce, and for dessert, the famous *sachertorte* (chocolate cake flavoured with passion fruit) and chocolate crêpes. By choosing carefully, you can eat for B/. 25 per person. There is a good selection of wines; the service is impeccable and the decor attractive.

Restaurante Angel
$$$$$

every day noon to 11 p.m
68 Vía Argentina facing Parque Andres Bello
☎ *263-6411*
☎ *263-6868*

For a quiet evening or business dinner in a comfortable, refined setting, head to the Restaurante Angel, where you will be served delicious Spanish cuisine and seafood specialties by a courteous staff. The high-ceilinged dining room is exceptionally elegant. The ambiance calls for formal dress

El Cangrejo

Mr. Pan
$

Mon to Sat 7am to 8pm
Vía Argentina, near Vía España, on the right-hand side when heading toward the university

The little Mr. Pan Bakery is just the place for early risers who like simple breakfasts. Brioches and coffee can be enjoyed at one of the few tables here, as can various very

affordable sandwiches and ice creams at lunch time.

Manolo
$

every day
at Calle 49B Oeste-Veneto and Ave. 1a A Norte or Calle D

Those who like lively places should have breakfast at Manolo where they can take in the endless comings and goings of passers-by in the bustling neighbourhood from the street-corner terrace. Be sure to try the excellent fruit plate along with an egg dish. Breakfast is a good deal here as the generous portions are easily enough for two! You can also enjoy typical Panamanian fare, or the pizza for B/. 5 or some tasty spaghetti for as little as B/. 4.50. The coffee, moreover, is excellent, and both espresso and cappuccino are available. The only weak point is the slow service.

Manolo
$

at Vía Argentina and Ave. 2a B Norte

Not to be confused with the restaurant of the same name above, this Manolo is also a pleasant and reasonably place for breakfast. Also situated on a street corner, its terrace is smaller but just as pleasant, particularly since Vía Argentina is greener and quieter. Typical Panamanian food, pizzas, pastas and many other dishes are offered.

Restaurante Pomodoro
$$

every day noon to 11pm
Calle 49B Oeste or Veneto, near Ave. 2A Norte or Eusebio A. Morales, next to the Aparthotel Las Vegas
☎ *269-5836*

Despite its somewhat kitschy exterior, Restaurante Pomodoro is a delightful place. In a small room decorated by a few frescos and plants, patrons can sample good and very affordable Italian cuisine. The extensive menu features a wide selection of pastas (*spaghetti dishes from B/. 5.95*), fish (*corvina* or salmon) and meat dishes. For more intimate dining away from the noise of the street, sit out in the verdant terrace in back of the restaurant.

El Trapiche
$$

every day 7am to 10:30pm
10 Vía Argentina, corner of Avenida 2a B Norte
☎ *269-4353*

This restaurant is notable mainly for its charming terrace, which is covered with a tile roof and adorned with rustic wooden furniture. You can enjoy a variety of typical Panamanian dishes here; try the *guacho de mariscos* (seafood platter). This is also a pleasant spot to have a drink and nibble on some yucca chips, patacones or an appetizer of *surtido de Picadas* (assorted

Ciudad de Panamá

finger-foods) for only B/. 1.50. Very popular with Panamanians.

Parrillada Martin Fierro
$$
Avenida 2a Norte/Calle Eusebio A. Morales
☎ *264-1927*
☎ *223-1333*
This restaurant is an Argentinean restaurant in a Spanish-style house. It specializes not only in grilled meats, but also in seafood and fish. Most meat dishes come with the salad bar. The decor is simple, service friendly and the food reasonably priced.

Bon Profit
$$
Tue to Sat noon to 3pm and 6pm to 11pm
5 Vía Argentina, just before Avenida 1a B Norte
☎ *263-9667*
For classic Spanish cuisine, the Bon Profit restaurant is a pleasant place with an elegantly decorated little dining room. The room is a little somber but you can admire the old photographs of the city adorning the walls. Their tiny terrace (2 tables) allows you to watch the bustle of the city while enjoying a cold drink. Make sure to take advantage of the lunch special (*Mon to Fri 11am to 3pm*), which includes the dish of the day and dessert for only B/. 6.50. With a bargain like that, this restaurant truly deserves its name!

La Casa de las Costillitas
$$$
Tue to Thu 4:30pm to 11pm, Fri and Sat 3pm to 11:30pm, Sun 1pm to 10pm
Vía Argentina, just before Avenida 1a B Norte
☎ *269-6670*
On the other side of Bon Profit is La Casa de las Costillitas, a branch of the restaurant La Cascada (see p 113, 120) with a similar menu based on a large selection of grilled meat dishes. Fish and seafood are also served. Although the decor is just as "colourful" as the main restaurant's, La Casa de las Costillitas is located in more attractive surroundings on verdant Vía Argentina, in a pleasant part of town.

Restaurante Ginza
$$$
every day noon to 3pm and 6pm to 10pm
at the corner of Avenida 1a A Norte/Calle D and Avenida 2A Norte/Eusebio A. Morales
☎ *269-1389*
The Restaurante Ginza is an authentic Japanese restaurant complete with teppanyaki tables. The decor is elegant, but a bit austere. Excellent vegetarian dishes starting at B/. 12 are also available. Proper dress required.

Marbella

La Mexicanita
$
every day 11am to 11pm
Ave. 4a Sur or Nicanor de Obarrio, between Calles Uruguay and Aquilino de la Guardia
☎ *213-8952*
Restaurante La Mexicanita serves tacos, enchiladas and quesadillas at unbeatable prices. The decor, however, is simple to a fault and without any real charm.

Original Rock Burgers
$
every day 11am to 11:30pm
Calle 53 Este and Avenida José de la Cruz Herrera
Craving an old-fashioned hamburger? Head to the supertrendy Original Rock Burgers restaurant, where you can grab a tasty snack.

Pizzeria Romanaccio
$$
every day noon to 3pm and 5pm to 11pm
Calle 50c Este
☎ *264-9482*
The nearby Pizzeria Romanaccio serves huge pizza and pasta dishes. If you are still hungry, try the tiramisu. The portions are gigantic! The decor is attractive but a bit cold. Distinguished clientele. The lovely covered terrasse allows you to enjoy the beautiful weather out of the sun's reach.

Crepes & Waffles
$$
everyday noon to 11pm
22 Ave. 5a B Sur or
Calle 47, between
Calles Uruguay and 49
Este or Aquilino de la
Guardia
☎ *269-1574*
The Crepes & Waffles,
needless to say, serves
a variety of crepes and
waffles. Worth men-
tioning, however, is
that both are tasty and
inexpensive. Moreover,
it is surprising to learn
that this is not your
standard Bel-
gian-Breton concept,
but a Colombian chain
already well estab-
lished in its mother
country.

The setting is impres-
sive. Upon entering the
futuristic-looking build-
ing, a streamlined room
with a harmonious
blend of stainless steel,
brick and glass meets
the eye. Daylight
streams in through
large French windows
graced with large lat-
eral wooden slats to
subdue the bright rays
of sunshine. Elegant
wooden furnishings as
well as a few giant
posters reminiscent of
the works of Botero
round out the very
successful interior de-
cor. Those who prefer
to eat outdoors can sit
on the pleasant terrace
in comfortable rattan
chairs sheltered from
the sun beneath large
parasols. The place is
mainly frequented by
families on the week-
end. A not-to-be
missed restaurant,

even if only to admire
its decor.

Restaurante Bahia Balboa
$$$
*Mon to Fri 11:30am to
10pm, Sat 5pm to 11pm,
Sun 11:30am to 10pm*
Avenida Balboa, between Calle
48 Este/Uruguay and Calle 49
Este/Aquilino de la Guardia
☎ *223-7751*
Seafood and meat
dishes in a sophisti-
cated but slightly
kitschy setting.

Italianni's
$$$
*every day noon to mid-
night*
Ave. Frederico Boyd, near Ave.
4a A Sur or Calle 49
☎ *223-7760*
Housed in a luxurious
villa, Italianni's has two
large dining rooms
spread over two levels,
with a modern, nonde-
script decor. The tratto-
ria will satisfy the
heartiest of appetites,
as the portions served
here are positively gar-
gantuan! While the
presentation of the
dishes lacks flair, the
meals are of high qual-
ity, notably the excel-
lent eggplant au gratin
and the creamiest of
tiramisus. The perfect
place to satisfy your
appetite!

El Epoca
$$$$
*Mon to Sat noon to 3pm
and 6pm to 10pm*
Calle 53 Este, at Ave. 5a B Sur
☎ *265-3636*
In the heart of the styl-
ish Marbella district,
next to the World
Trade Centre, the tower
of the Radisson Royal
Panamá Hotel is, at first

sight, somewhat unat-
tractive. Once inside,
however, visitors will
be pleasantly surprised
by the elegant El Epoca
restaurant, which offers
moderately priced in-
ternational-style cuisine
in an exquisite setting.

La Toja
$$$
Mon to Sat noon to 11pm
at Calle Uruguay or 48 Este and
Ave. 4a A Sur
☎ *269-3004*
The Galician owner of
the La Toja restaurant
offers diners excellent
cuisine proudly featur-
ing the bounties of the
sea. Indeed, fish lovers
should not miss out on
the absolutely delicious
*Mero alla salsa de
pimienta verde*. For
those who prefer meat
and poultry, the *mignon
de pollo con hongos* will
please the most dis-
criminating of palates.
Dishes are lavish and,
for the most part,
served with a refresh-
ing little salad. The
excellent flan is a won-
derful way to round off
a meal.

In addition to the re-
fined furnishings and
tables set in the great-
est culinary tradition,
the decor includes
many paintings cele-
brating the beauty of
Galicia. Flawless ser-
vice. Good value for
the money.

Ciudad de
Panamá

Madame Chang
$$$$
every day noon to 11pm
Ave. 5a A Sur or Calle 48, between Calles Uruguay and 49
Este or Aquilino de la Guardia
☎ 269-1313
☎ 269-9654

Although Chinese cui-
sine is renowned for its
diversity, the same can
seldom be said for the
design of its restau-
rants. In fact, they are
often overly decorated
to the point of being
kitsch. The Madame
Chang restaurant
proves that there are
exceptions to the rule.

The dining room boasts
a modern decor accen-
tuated by elegant col-
umns and archways
and embellished by
various original Asian
curios for a final touch
of refinement. In this
delightful setting,
diners can enjoy the
Chinese vegetable
salad, delicious tofu
with eggplant, or crispy
Peking duck, while
seated at a table with
subdued lighting. To
accompany this feast,
the Chilean Cabernet
Sauvignon is a good
choice, especially since
it is reasonably priced.

Finally, another pleas-
ant surprise seldom to
be found in Chinese
restaurants is the good
selection of desserts
with which to top off
an excellent meal. Try
the creamy cheesecake,
the enormous *cassata*
or the rich chocolate
Cesibón. Of course, tea
and espresso are also
available.

Friendly and efficient
service. A fine evening
to look forward to!

Il Rigoletto
$$$
Calle 48 Este or Uruguay, be-
tween Ave. 5a A Sur and Ave. 5a
B Sur
☎ 214-9632

Housed within a large
villa, Ristorante Il
Rigoletto offers patrons
an Italian menu on
which pastas have
pride of place. Spa-
ghetti *carbonara,
fettucine Alfredo, tutti
quanti* and much more
await. The decor is
modern, even a little
cool, but the
Italian-style welcome
soon warms things up.
Unfortunately, as is too
often the case in the
restaurants of the
Ciudad, it is excessively
air conditioned. A ter-
race would also be
welcome.

Café Dalí
$$$
every day
Ave. 5a B Sur or Calle 47, between Calles Uruguay and 49
Este or Aquilino de la Guardia
☎ 265-0182

Across from Crepes &
Waffles, the Café Dalí
bar-restaurant features
a colourful, heteroge-
neous and fittingly
Dali-esque decor of
painted columns and
metal sculptures with
wrought-iron tables
and chairs. Conversely,
the menu, composed of
Tex-Mex-style dishes
and a few Italian offer-
ings, is rather hum-
drum. Gilded youth as
well as young execu-
tives congregate here.

Just the place for those
who wish to see and
be seen.

México Lindo
$$$
Mon to Sat 7pm to 11pm
Ave. Balboa, at Calle Uruguay
☎ 265-4746
☎ 265-4743

For genuine Mexican
ambiance, head to
Mexico Lindo, located
on the second floor of
a rather unattractive
building. This restau-
rant boasts beautiful
decor, and warm blue
and orange walls are
complemented by
lovely ceramics and
little paper lanterns that
create a welcome feel-
ing of intimacy.

The menu features all
the favourites of Mexi-
can cuisine, from *pollo
al mole poblano* (the
famous chicken with
chocolate sauce) to the
standard *enchiladas,
tacos, quesadillas* and
fajitas. Unfortunately,
prices are higher than
in Mexico itself; a sim-
ple serving of *guaca-
mole,* for instance, costs
as much as B/. 5.50. As
far as the ambiance is
concerned, diners will
have no reason to com-
plain as *música en vivo*
enlivens the place ev-
ery night.

Restaurante Yesterday
$$$
every day
Ave. 5a B Sur or Calle 47, between Calles Uruguay and 49
Este or Aquilino de la Guardia

Right next door,
Restaurante Yesterday
features an Amer-
ican-influenced

English-pub-style decor. In a large dining room where woodwork is omnipresent and numerous Tiffany-style lamps provide subdued lighting, diners can choose from salads, burgers, Tex-Mex dishes or pastas. To avoid the noisy televisions on the ground floor, sit upstairs on the verdant terrace, prettily laid out with parasols.

Gaucho's
$$$$
every day noon to 3pm and 6pm to 10:30pm Ave. 5a A Sur or Calle 48, at Calle Uruguay
☎ *263-4469*
Grilled meats, steaks, cutlets, brochettes and many other meat selections are served here in a pleasant and modern, if somewhat lukewarm Argentinian decor.

Bennigan's Grill
$$$$
Ave. Balboa, just before Punta Paitilla
☎ *214-7022*
On the fourth floor of the new Extreme Planet building, Bennigan's Grill is, in quintessential Irish-American-pub style, a place to devour a burger along with – as is only right and proper – a good helping of fries and a pint of beer. Tiffany-style lamps, opulent chairs and an overwhelmingly flowered wall-to-wall carpet make up most of the decor, not to mention televisions all over the place airing the major American channels. In short, it's the next "best" thing to

being in the Unites States. There is even a large parking lot outside. Be careful when entering the building not to get run over by the constant stream of (big) cars!

La Cocotte
$$$$$
Mon to Sat noon to 3pm and 7pm to 10:30pm Calle Uruguay, between Ave. Balboa and Ave. 5a B Sur
☎ *213-8250*
For French cuisine, head to La Cocotte, where the great classics are served in a very conventional setting. Unfortunately, sampling its most noble offerings necessitates loosening one's purse strings, as the prices are sky high. To circumvent this difficulty, come by for lunch, at which time a full meal can be had for B/. 18. Practically a bargain!

Amador

Isla Naos

La Playita
$$
Mon to Thu and Sun 9:30am to 6pm, Fri and Sat 9:30am to 10pm on Isla Naos
☎ *228-0540*
The modest La Playita restaurant serves regular Panamanian fare (chicken, *patacones*, *ceviche*, etc.), yet it is a rather pleasant place in which to have a refreshing drink while watching Panamanian families enjoying a day at the beach. *Horas Feliz*

(happy hour) every Friday.

Isla Perico

Mi Ranchito
$$
Mon to Fri 10am to 9pm on Isla Perico, on the Isla Flamenco-bound road
☎ *228-4909*
Though right on the roadside and a little set back from the beach, Restaurante Mi Ranchito offers a truly pleasant setting. Whether beneath its large straw roof or one of its charming *palapas*, savour a refreshing *ceviche de corvina* as a starter, followed by an excellent dish of *gambas* or meat while seated at one of the lovely little tables, with a little Panamanian music thrown in!

Ancón

Mi Pueblito
$$$
Tue to Sun 10am to 10pm El Pueblito (see p95)
☎ *228-7714*
☎ *228-2124*
While visiting Cerro Ancón, make sure to go to the Restaurante Mi Pueblito, in the small, reconstructed rural village of Mi Pueblito. Here, many different Panamanian specialities can be sampled, including *lombo machado* (ground beef) and excellent *pargo* fish. A nice stop on a sightseeing trip!

Panamá Viejo

Bohío Turístico
$
*Mon and Tue from 4pm
on, Wed to Sun from
11am on*
Vía Cincuentenario, to the left
after the ruins of Fuerte de la
Natividad
☎ 226-5166
For those who enjoy
dining outdoors, the
Bohío Turístico is a
pretty, circular restau-
rant with a roof made
of palm fronds. This
appealing spot, located
right beside the ruins,
serves tasty, traditional
Panamanian dishes in
extremely exotic
surroundings. Parrots
and monkeys make up
a miniature zoo! The
menu features *sancocho
panameño* (chicken
stew), *chimi-churri
sauce* (a delicious sauce
with an indescribable
flavour), *patacones*
(fried plantain slices)
and all sorts of other
light dishes.

El Trapiche
$$$
*Tue to Fri 11:30am to
11pm, Sat and Sun
8:30am to 11pm*
in the Merdado Artesanal, near
the ruins of the cathedral of
Panamá Viejo, Vía
Cincuentenario
☎ 221-5241
Right next to the Puerto
Viejo Museum, El
Trapiche offers typical
Panamanian and inter-
national cuisine as well
as seafood at reason-
able prices. This is also
a good place to take
some refreshment after
touring the nearby

ruins and to enjoy the
terrasse on the bay.
Very popular with Pan-
amanians.

Fonda Antioqueña
$$$
Vía Cincuentenario, on the left,
shortly after the ruins of
Panamá Viejo
☎ 221-4261
☎ 221-1268
This authentic Colom-
bian restaurant serves
specialties like *chorizos
Antioqueños con arepa
de maiz blanco* (wild
pig with white corn) or
*lechon asado al carbon
con yuca jancocada*
(char-broiled pork
served with yucca).
The daily *ejecutivo*
menu, available from
11am to 3:30pm, is a
real bargain at as little
as B/. 5.

Besides a giant televi-
sion showing Colom-
bian programs, you will
find a warm, colourful
decor. The place also
has a nightclub, which
makes for a lively
atmosphere on week-
ends (see p128). Since
the Fonda Antioqueña
is located outside the
city in an area that is
not very safe at night, it
is best to get here by
taxi (*B/. 3.5*).

Cerro Azul

🌴La Posada de Ferhisse
$$
every day 9am to 10pm
Calle Principal Domingo Diaz
☎ 297-0197
Located on a hill, La
Posada de Ferhisse is a
wonderful place to eat

surrounded by exotic
countryside and a
beautiful panorama.
The very charming
owner, Mr. Ferhisse
Jabbour, has family in
many countries and
enjoys chatting with
interested patrons at
their table. He is well
acquainted with the
region and can provide
information about the
richness of the sur-
rounding flora and
fauna.

The menu itself fea-
tures a variety of
dishes, including won-
derful little stuffed
crabs, curry chicken,
"brandade" (a puree of
salt cod, garlic, oil and
cream), and a dish of
combined rice pre-
pared Cuban style, just
like it is made in
Jabbour's native land.
What's more, a lovely
swimming pool (*B/. 2*)
has been set up below
the terrace for those
who wish to take a
refreshing dip.

Entertainment

Panamá has an active
nightlife; many places
have a good selection
of bars and nightclubs.
In general, big hotels
have their own clubs
(busiest nights are
Wednesday to Saturday
– traditionally, Sundays
are for family visits and
resting). Some of the
more expensive hotels
even have a casino.

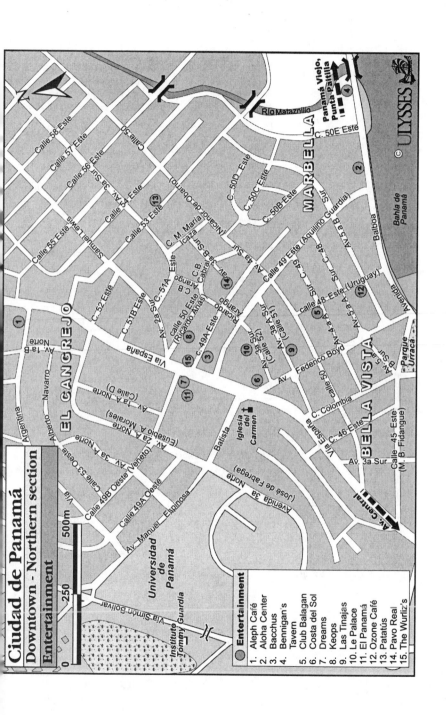

Ciudad de Panamá
Downtown - Northern section
Entertainment

Entertainment

1. Aleph Café
2. Aloha Center
3. Bacchus
4. Bennigan's Tavern
5. Club Balagan
6. Costa del Sol
7. Dreams
8. Keops
9. Las Tinajas
10. Le Palace
11. El Panamá
12. Ozone Café
13. Patatús
14. Pavo Real
15. The Wurliz's

© ULYSSES

Río Mataznillo

Bahía de Panamá

Panamá Viejo, Punta Paitilla

MARBELLA

BELLA VISTA

EL CANGREJO

Parque Urracá

Universidad de Panamá

Instituto Tommy Guardia

Iglesia del Carmen

0 250 500m

N

occasionally have a cover charge and may refuse people wearing jeans. In Ciudad de Panamá, certain restaurants double as bars or clubs. In some, shows are presented. The following are a few good places to finish off the day.

Casco Viejo

⚓Café Asis
at Calle 3a Este
In the very heart of Casco Viejo, facing the delightful Parque Bolívar, Café Asis is a successful initiative in the revitalization of the capital's historic district. In a small space decorated with contrasting colours, patrons can sip one of the many drinks available while seated at a candlelit table. In the evening, several tables are set out by the adjacent square, offering patrons a theatre-like setting.

The beautiful façade of the Instituto Simón Bolívar, on one side, and the square planted with trees and surrounded by a few grand houses, on the other, offer a romantic atmosphere. Although the neighbouring streets are rather unsafe at night (getting around by taxi is a wise idea), this magnificent café is perfectly safe. In fact, it would be a real shame to miss out on such an opportunity. Very busy on the weekend. An absolute must!

El Cangrejo

⚓Aleph Café
Vía Argentina, on the left-hand side when heading toward Ave. España, a little before said avenue
With its original little candlesticks on the tables, colourful decorative hammocks suspended from the ceiling, metal sculptures and scores of paintings, the Aleph Café is worth a visit for its imaginative and tasteful decor alone. Moreover, several musicians perform here on a regular basis, offering music for all tastes. For those feeling a little peckish, a good choice of both savoury and sweet crepes is offered on the menu. Young and hip clientele.

Hotel El Panamá
Vía España and Calle 49B Oeste
☎ *269-5000*
☎ *269-5421*
The Hotel El Panamá has a casino, a bar (the **Coco Club**, happy hour 4pm to 6pm) and a club on the roof with a view of the city. There is also a cafe that is open 24 hours a day.

Dreams
B/. 5 to B/. 10
every night 9pm to 3am
under the Hotel El Panamá, enter on Vía España, 1st floor
This multi-level nightclub, which has a very modern decor and features numerous videos, can easily compete with the trendiest hot spots. The cover charge is fairly

high, so the place is mainly frequented by an affluent clientele and members of the gilded youth. On Wednesdays, admission and drinks are free for women from 9pm to 1am. Like most nightclubs, this place is for night owls, and the atmosphere does not heat up until way after dark. Proper dress required.

Campo Alegre

Bacchus
cover charge
Calle 49a Este, near Ave. 3a Sur or Ricardo Arango
Among the most popular nightclubs in town, Bacchus welcomes a youngish clientele (25 to 35 years old) to the varied sounds of salsa, merengue, rock, disco, etc. Wednesday is karaoke night.

Keops
cover charge
Calle 50 Este or Ricardo Arias, near Ave. España
Set up on the main floor of the Riande Continental Ciudad hotel
Keops is primarily frequented by an older crowd (40 and over) and businesspeople who come to dance to salsa.

Las Tinajas
22 Avenida 3a A Sur/Calle 51
☎ *263-7890*
☎ *269-3840*
This is a restaurant that has traditional Panamanian dancing several nights a week wuith beautiful Panamanian costumes, including the

famous *pollera* (see p206). Shows are presented every Tuesday, Thursday, Friday and Saturday starting at 7pm. Reservations are strongly recommended.

Sunset Bar
at the corner of Avenida Frederico Boyd and Avenida 3a A Sur Calle 52
☎ *223-7111*
To enjoy a lovely panoramic view of the capital by night, while sipping an excellent, reasonably priced cocktail (*happy hour from 6pm to 8pm*), head to the Sunset Bar at the Apart-Hotel Costa del Sol, which has an elegant roof-top bar with a terrace. People also come here to dance on Friday nights.

Pavo Real
B/. 3
Monday to Saturday
Avenida 3a B Sur, left on Calle 51 A Este, after Ave. Nicanor de Obarrio
This small, English-style pub is frequented mainly by English-speakers between the ages of 25 and 45, along with a few Panamanians, including the capital's gilded youth. The place serves English beer, as well as meals for about B/. 20. The atmosphere is relaxed, and live music is presented every Wednesday evening and occasionally on

weekends, too. Happy hour from 3pm to 7pm.

Wurliz' Bar
open daily
Calle 50 Este/Ricardo Arias, near Vía España
Whether it be for drinks or to listen to the rare Wurlitzer organ (a pipe organ designed specifically for theatres), the Wurliz Bar in the Riande Continental hotel is quite a pleasant spot. Happy hour from 6pm to 8pm. The clientele consists mainly of business people.

Pollera

Le Palace
at the corner of Avenida 3a Sur/Ricardo Arango and Calle 49 Este/Aquilino de la Guardia
☎ *269-1844*
Le Palace is a bar popular for its dance shows where the dancers' costumes range from simple to sophisticated. Parisian strip tease performed at 10:30pm every Wednesday and Saturday. Minimum purchase required.

Coffee

Patatús
B/. 20 unlimited domestic drinks
Tue to Sat from 4pm on
Calle 53 Este, near Avenida Nicanor de Obarrio/Calle 50, on the second floor of the Plaza New York shopping centre
Patatús, located inside the Plaza New York shopping centre, is one of the most popular nightclubs in town, and is crowded with young Panamanians on weekends.

Marbella

🏛Ozone Café
Calle Uruguay or 48 Este, between Ave. 5a A Sur and Ave. 5a B Sur, on the right-hand side of the street when heading toward Avenida Balboa
☎ *214-9616*
Located behind a home-decor and antique shop, the Ozone Café serves excellent fresh-ground coffee, cocktails and various little nibbles. The decor is worth a visit in itself as, oddly enough, you can see right into the shop through its back windows. Various old artifacts thus seem to be part of the setting, treating patrons to an amusing and somewhat bizarre view. Unfortunately, as is too often the case, a television set tends to spoil the muted ambiance. Hip crowd of night owls.

Ciudad de Panamá

Aloha Centre
Ave. Balboa, near Calle 49 Este or Aquilino de la Guardia
In tropical climates such as this one, a terrace is always welcome and that of the Aloha Centre has a magnificent view of the gulf, though noisy Avenida Balboa spoils the mood a little. Various dishes and seafood starters are also available to satisfy sudden hunger pangs. Simple but pleasant.

Bennigan's Tavern
Ave. Balboa, just before Punta Paitilla
Those in search of an establishment with an "Irish-American pub" ambiance, need look no further than Bennigan's Tavern, located on the fourth floor of the Extreme Planet building. Here, you can knock back several pints of blond or amber beer while indulging in a game of pool. The music is distinctly non-local – in fact Panamá feels like a distant memory here! Watch out for the endless stream of (big) cars on their way to the parking lot near the entrance.

Amador

Balboa Yacht Club
at the entrance to the Calzada Amador, also known simply as "The Causeway"
☎ 228-5794
Although the Balboa Yacht Club is both a restaurant and a nightclub, but its bar is the main attraction for its terrace, where patrons can enjoy a beautiful view of the Canal and the Puente de Las Américas while sipping drinks. This is the place to watch sailors waiting to cross the Canal or to find a job as a crew member aboard a ship.

Panamá Viejo

Fonda Antioqueña
Fri and Sat
Vía Cincuentenario, on the left, shortly after the ruins of Panamá Viejo
☎ 221-4261
This authentic Colombian bar/restaurant contains a large nightclub, where you can kick up your heels to Latin American tunes every weekend until 6am. Guaranteed ambiance. Because this place is located outside of the city in a neighbourhood that is not very safe at night, we recommend taking a cab here (B/. 2).

Gay Bars and Nightclubs

Boy Bar
Fri B/. 5, Sat B/. 10 with open bar, Sun B/. 4
Avenida Ricardo J. Alfaro/Túmba Muerto
At the time of our visit, this was the only gay nightclub in the capital. Because it is complicated to get here, and the streets are poorly lit, you are much better off taking a taxi (B/. 3). If you do go by car, take Avenida Túmba Muerto, then, shortly after the Esso station, the street immediately to the right of the Plasticos Internacionales René Miró company. The club is located on the second street to the right as you head downhill. Set up inside an old warehouse, the Boy Bar has a large dance floor, part of which is elevated. This place has everything–loud music, a light show, a mezzanine where you can relax and watch the attractive clientele shake their thing on the dance floor, and a small outdoor terrace, which offers a temporary escape from the deafening music. All this makes the Boy Bar one of the best gay nightclubs in the world. As for the music, the Latin American and English beats heard here are enjoyed by customers of all ages.

El Hidalgo
Vía Brazil, between Vía España and Calle 50, opposite the Texaco station
Locals call this dance club Passos, though there is no sign to tell us this. Why not call El Hidalgo by its proper name? Your guess is as good as ours! In this somewhat remote dance club, patrons can groove to Latin-American music and take in a drag-queen show. The clientele is mixed and bound to include some pickpockets, therefore caution is essential.

The hidden face
of Darién – the
Chocoes.
– *courtesy of
IPAT*

Deserted
beaches and
tropical
vegetation,
some of
Panamá's many
attractions.
- *John Mitchell*

Molas – the pride of Kuna women.
- *John Mitchell*

La Faraona

Calle 42, between Colombia and Ave. 3a Sur or Justo Arosemena
Located a stone's throw from Parque Urrucá, the modest La Faraona welcomes a mixed crowd into a dark room with rather kitschy decor.

Club Balagan
cover charge with open bar
at Calles Uruguay and 4a A Sur
The latest trendy gay bar/nightclub is none other than Club Balagan. While a hip mixed crowd clusters around the oversized central bar to order drinks, dance-floor divas gather on one of two dance floors (one on the mezzanine and the other in the basement). Guaranteed ambiance from 1 o'clock (in the morning, naturally) on.

Shopping

Casco Viejo

Second-hand Goods

Festival de Antiguedades
Sat and Sun 10am to 5pm
Parque Simón Bolívar
Right next to the Café Asis, the somewhat pompously named Festival de Antiquedades (Festival of Antiques) has a few second-hand goods of no great value on display in a modest space.

The place is nevertheless fun to visit and, by doing a little digging, you may yet find a little gem. Good luck!

Santa Ana

Food

Mercado de Mariscos
Avenida Balboa, before Ave Eloy Alfaro
If you are staying in the capital for a while and have access to a kitchen, you can go to the Mercado de Mariscos, a brand new fish market set up inside a modern building and run by the City of Panamá. Open to the general public, it offers a wide selection of fish at reasonable prices.

Handicrafts

Mercado de Buhonería y Artesanía
every day 7am to 7pm
Plaza 5 de Mayo
The Mercado de Buhonería y Artesanía, located behind the Reina Torres de Araúz archeological museum, has a number of little stalls containing a variety of crafts from all over the country (*molas*, pottery, wooden sculptures, the famous Panamá hats, etc.), as well as all sorts of junk ranging from lighters and pens to watches, all at very attractive prices. Bargaining is standard here. Of course, in a crowded place such as this, you should be very wary of thieves.

Miscellaneous

Avenida Central
between Plaza 5 de Mayo and Parque de Santa Ana
Avenida Central is the main shopping street in Casco Viejo, with stores for just about anything (clothes, shoes, jewellery, electronic equipment...). The prices are negotiable. Pay at least 20% to 30% less than what is asked for.

Calidonia

Fishing Gear and Apparel

Abernathy and **El Capitán**
Ave. Balboa
entrance at Calle 40
For anything and everything connected to fishing, head to the Clube de Yates y Pesca on Avenida Balboa, where the Abernathy and El Capitán shops offer shoppers a wide array of goods, from simple swimsuits and reels to that indispensable fishing line. Don't forget your credit card!

Bella Vista

Food

Supermercado Rey
open 24 hours a day
Vía España, on the right side as you head north, near the footbridge overhanging the street
Visitors who want to do their own cooking can shop at the Superercado Rey, where they'll find everything they need at inexpensive prices.

Ciudad de Panamá

This place is like any other big North American supermarket.

Campo Alegre

Jewellery

Reprosa
at the corner of Avenida 2a Sur/Samuel Lewis and Calle 54
☎ *269-0457*
Reprosa is a store specializing in reproductions of antique (pre-Columbian) jewellery.

Souvenirs

Gran Morrison
Vía España, near Calle 50 Este, across from the Banco Nacional
☎ *269-2211*
Gran Morrison is a large store with a good choice of Panamanian arts and crafts and souvenirs of every kind. They also sell records, books, clothes etc. The traditional crafts sold here are more expensive than outside the city, but here you can find everything under one roof.

El Cangrejo

Bookstore

Librería Argosy
at the beginning of Vía Argentina, on the right side as you head away from Vía España
☎ *223-5344*
This general bookstore, run by a friendly woman named Luz Maria, sells a good choice of Spanish- and English-language books, as well as a few books in French. A very pleasant place to pore over books at your leisure.

Clothing

Adams
every day 9am to 7pm
on Vía España, north of Figali, infront of Supermercado Rey
A clothing store for men, Adams offers a vast array of reasonably priced shirts in original styles, as well as a number of other articles.

Ancón

Handicrafts

In the heart of the little village of **Mi Pueblito Cerro Ancón** (see p95) you will find a number of craft shops with products mainly from the central provinces and the Azuero peninsula. The setting is extraordinary and the selection, vast; however, the prices are considerably higher here than elsewhere.

Panamá Viejo

Handicrafts

Mercado Nacional de Artesanias
every day 9am to 6pm
near the ruins of the cathedral bell tower, beside the Museo Panamá La Viejo
Located right beside the ruins of the former capital, the Mercado National de Artesanias has two floors of handcrafted objects, including pottery, carved wood and a number of articles (*chaquiras* necklaces worn by Guaymíes, Kuna *molas*) reflecting the richness of Panamanian culture.

Chaquinas Necklace

The Panamá Canal

T he story of the canal zone is directly linked to the creation and development of the Republic of Panamá.

The idea of finding a passage across the isthmus from one ocean to the other is ancient. In 1534, Emperor Charles V asked his scientists to devise a trans-isthmus seaway, but this never got beyond the stage of a few sketches. Much later, during the second half of the 19th century, it was the Americans who began toying with the idea of a direct passage between the two oceans. This was of particular to interest to them as a means of reaching the west since there were no road or rail links at the time. In the 1870s the U.S. Navy mounted an expedition across the isthmus in order to evaluate the possibilities of dredging a canal through Darién. Of the 27 men who took part in this expedition, only

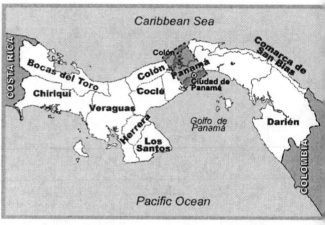

a few survived the rigours of the terrible jungle. It is clear that this territory had long been pegged as the site of one of the largest ever human undertakings. Though it is understandable that some Panamanians might be tired of hearing about the canal (after all, Panamá is much more than a canal!), travellers making their way through the country should not miss an opportunity to marvel at this feat of technology. In fact, the canal zone merits a visit in its

own right, as it is full of interesting sights.

A Brief History of the Panamá Canal

The Panamá Canal adventure began with the construction of a railroad (see p26) between Colón, on the Caribbean Coast, and Ciudad de Panamá, on the Pacific Coast. Originally intended to allow the rapid transport of goods between the two oceans, the line was destined to carry a great many adventurers heading off to settle in the American West.

Soon there was such a flood of people going west that the United States government began to consider once again the creation of a seaway. The choice of location was still undetermined; Nicaragua was being considered as well as the isthmus. Meanwhile, heady from the success of the Suez Canal, the French took advantage of the delay and procured the approval of the Colombian government for the construction of a maritime passageway.

The concession allowed not only for the construction of the canal, but also the administration and the transfer of 5 km of land on either side of it. The contract extended over 100 years. In 1875, the *Société Civile du Canal Interocéanique du Darién* was established in Paris. Its principal mandate was to collect funds in order to complete the construction of the canal.

The president of this company was Viscount **Ferdinand de Lesseps**, already well known as the author of the Suez Canal. In 1879, he had the final plans for the Panamá project approved. The canal would follow the route of the Río Grande and the Río Chagres, running from the Bahía de Limón to the Bahía de Panamá, thus linking Colón and Balboa. The work, which would take an estimated eight

years to complete, would begin in 1880, supervised by the *Compagnie Universelle du Canal Interocéanique* (which had bought the *Société Civile*).

Nine years after work began, disaster struck. The partnership was in financial difficulties and declared bankrupt by the French government. Following this failure, the press attacked the founders of the project; several of the company's directors, along with some politicians, were called before the French courts.

A number of reasons for the failure were put forth: unexpected technical difficulties, corruption, financial problems – the list went on. One thing, however, is certain: ignorance about the transmission of malaria led to a veritable plague breaking out among workers. The legs of hospital beds were placed in containers of water to keep crawling insects away. Unfortunately, the doctors and nurses did not realize that the mosquitoes that carried the disease were breeding in these very pots. In 1885, conditions were so bad in Colón that over 5,000 people died of yellow fever and malaria.

Looking back at the limited technical means of the time, we cannot help but feel great respect for the many

workers who died during the massive project. Consider what they were up against: moving some 259 million m³ of earth (the Suez Canal had only involved 75 million) through hilly countryside blanketed by a dense, insect-ridden jungle, and all of this in humid tropical heat. In addition to the victims of illness, a number of workers died in landslides. As many as 22,000 in all are thought to have perished while the French were building the canal.

Meanwhile, in France, an attempt was made to revive the project with the creation of the *Compagnie Nouvelle du Canal de Panamá*. The people of France, however, had lost all confidence. There was insufficient interest in the canal, and the company had to abandon the project once and for all.

In the wake of the French failure, the Americans re-entered the story of the canal. The *Compagnie Nouvelle* offered to sell its concessions to the United States for $40 million. In the meantime, the Americans had concluded that Nicaragua was too risky a canal site because of earthquakes, so they bought the concession and signed an agreement with Colombia (at the time Gran Colombia) in 1903. That same year, however, Colombia did an about-face and criticized the treaty as being too favourable to the Americans. This marked a new turning-point in the history of the region. The Panamanian merchant class felt removed from power and wanted to see the region develop. They reacted by provoking a revolt against the central government, resulting in the proclamation of the Republic of Panamá on November 3, 1903.

The young republic, eager to maintain its newly acquired independence, quickly proposed new negotiations with the Americans, and the Hay-Bunau-Varilla treaty (named after the principal negotiators) was signed on November 18, 1903.

The negotiations leading up to the signing of this treaty had been swift and, according to some, partisan: Panamá granted the Americans the right to build and administer the canal, as well as a zone stretching 5 miles on either side of it. These rights were granted in perpetuity! Furthermore, the United States would be able to act as owners of the land, thus opening the door to possible intervention in Panamá's internal affairs. In exchange, the Americans agreed to guarantee Panamá's independence from Colombia, which had plans to recover its former territory. The compensation package included a $10 million indemnity and an annuity of $250,000 to take effect ten years after the ratification of the treaty.

In 1904, work resumed under the leadership of Colonel George Washington Goethals, chief engineer. The project included the construction of three groups of locks and the creation of an artificial lake (Lago Gatún). The work was executed much more effectively than it had been under the French, largely because the means of transmission of yellow fever had been discovered (by Carlos Finley, a Cuban). The task of wiping out yellow fever and malaria from the region fell upon Colonel William C. Gorgas. With the help of local authorities and by spraying great quantities of chemicals all along the region of the future canal, Gorgas was able to complete the mission.

The railroad was another major factor reason for the success of the project. Huge "shovels" were used to excavate tons of earth, which were deposited directly into gigantic hopper-cars. An incredible 259 million m^3 of land were displaced in this way. Considering that only 75 million m^3 had to be removed to create the Suez Canal, this was truly a tremendous feat!

Nevertheless, the success of the undertaking required the support of a large workforce. During the French phase of the canal many workers arrived from Barbados, as well as some from Trinidad and the French Antilles. Their European co-workers came mainly from France, Spain and Italy. As of 1906, there were 24,000 people (mostly men) involved in the construction of the canal.

When the American company bought out the French company's rights it inherited dilapidated workers' housing. For this reason, the immigration of families was discouraged at first and a call was sent out for Chinese labourers, hired only for the duration of the project. In fact the expense of the long trip made it almost impossible for employees to send for their families. In response to protest demonstrations mounted by the discontented workers, the company reversed its policy and authorised the installation of entire families. Consequently, many social and administrative services were put into place, creating a veritable microcosm of American society (see p 27).

The work was terminated in 1914, and on August 15, the canal

The Panamá Canal

was inaugurated on the deck of the *Ancón* by the President of Panamá, Belisario Porras, and a contingent of American officials.

In February of 1919, legislators from the Dakotas brought forth a congressional bill that would have renamed the canal after former President Theodore Roosevelt. After several demonstrations in the isthmus and protest by the legislature of Panamá, the motion was rejected.

Oddly enough, is was not until 1931 that ferries rejoined the east and west sides of the artificially divided area. They could transport up to 30 cars at a time and made the crossing every half-hour at no charge. This service stayed in effect until 1942 when a rotating bridge was constructed over the Miraflores locks. On October 12, 1962 the impressive bridge Puente de las Américas was finally inaugurated, re-establishing a definitive link between the two parts of the isthmus.

As soon as the canal was opened, traffic began pouring into it, and the region started to thrive. The statutes governing the zone were later amended several times. The most important modification came with the Torrijos-Carter agreement, under which Panamanian

sovereignty over the canal zone was re-established (see p 27).

The Canal Today

With the Torrijos-Carter agreement of 1977, the canal zone was abolished and its territory restored to Panamá. The new treaty also provided for joint Panamanian–U.S. administration of the various military zones along the canal. The land immediately beside the canal would be administered by the Panamá Canal Commission. This commission, whose mandate would run for 20 years, was made up of nine members, five American and four Panamanian. A president and a vice-president were also named, the two positions to alternate after ten years.

Until December 31, 1989, the president was American and the vice-president Panamanian. Once the Commission's mandate has expired – on December 31, 1999 – administration of all canal installations will be completely transferred to Panamá. Revenue linked directly to the activity of the canal now represents 10% of Panamá's GNP.

In accordance with agreements signed in 1979, the number of American employees of the Panamá Canal Commission has de-

clined steadily. By 1990, they numbered fewer than 900. Today, 87% of the commission's 8,000-strong workforce is Panamanian. By the year 2000 almost all of the jobs on the canal will be reserved for Panamanian nationals.

The commission's bureaucrats, who have always been highly paid, are concerned about the effect that the return of the canal to Panamá will have on their salaries. Indeed the Panamanian government has often stated its intent to reduce salaries to avoid problems with its more modestly paid civil service. Time will tell how the Panamanian government will resolve this delicate situation. As far as the American armed forces are concerned, they are supposed to leave the country by the same date, except for a few soldiers mandated to insure military co-operation between the two governments.

Finding Your Way Around

By Car

Miraflores Locks
There are two ways to get to the Miraflores locks from Ciudad de Panamá: the first is by

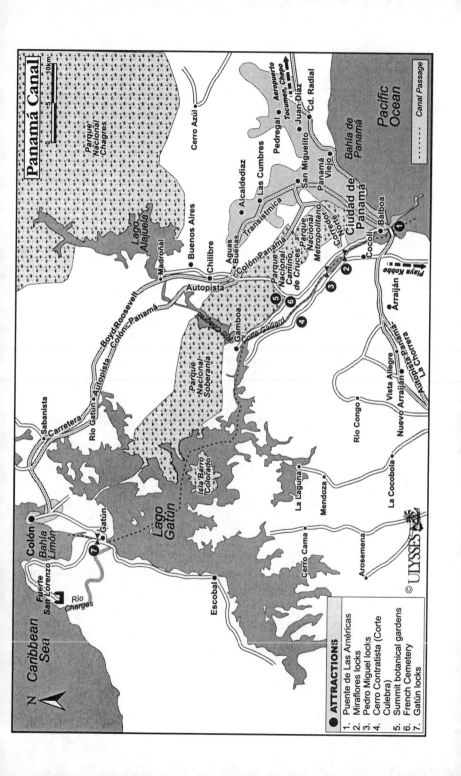

Panamá Canal

N

Caribbean Sea

Pacific Ocean

Bahía de Panamá

Lago Gatún

Lago Alajuela

Parque Nacional Chagres

Parque Nacional Soberanía

Parque Nacional Camino de Cruces

Parque Nacional Metropolitano

Isla Barro Colorado

Ciudad de Panamá

Colón
Bahía Limón
Fuerte San Lorenzo
Río Charges
Escobal
Gatún
Sabanista
Carretera
Río Gatún
Boyd-Roosevelt
Autopista Colón–Panamá
Autopista
Madroñal
Buenos Aires
Chilibre
Aguas Buenas
Colón–Panamá
Transístmica
Las Cumbres
Alcaldediaz
Cerro Azúl
San Miguelito
Pedregal
Juan Díaz
Cd. Radial
Aeropuerto Tocumen, Chepo
Panamá Viejo
Corredor Norte
Cocolí
Balboa
Arraiján
Nuevo Arraiján
Vista Allegre
Autopista Panamá–La Chorrera
Río Congo
La Laguna
Mendoza
La Cocobola
Cerro Cama
Arosemena
Cerro Cama
Gamboa
Corte Gaillard
Corte Culebra old
Playa Kobbe

Canal Passage

0   5   10km

© ULYSSES

ATTRACTIONS

1. Puente de Las Américas
2. Miraflores locks
3. Pedro Miguel locks
4. Cerro Contratista (Corte Culebra)
5. Summit botanical gardens
6. French Cemetery
7. Gatún locks

Avenida Gaillard from the Calidonia sector, and the second is by Calle Balboa, south of the Cerro Ancón (not to be confused with Avenida Balboa), which later becomes Calle Diablo and then joins Avenida Gaillard (also called Carretera Gaillard). In both cases, head north. The road to the locks lies on the left of the Carretera Gaillard. After passing a small bridge that crosses the Río Cárdenas, a small sign on the left side of the road, facing Fort Clayton, provides directions to the locks.

Pedro Miguel Locks

The Pedro Miguel locks are on the same road as the Miraflores, a little more to the north. On the way, a pleasant lookout on the left side of the road provides a view of ships coming out of the locks. A little farther north along the same main road, past the locks and on the left, is the modest **French cemetery**. Most of the men who died while working on the first phase of the canal's construction are buried here.

Parque Nacional Soberanía and the Jardín Botanico Summit

To get there, follow the directions to the Miraflores and Pedro Miguel locks (see above) and after pass-

ing them, continue on the main road. The entrance to the park is indicated on the left side of this road, and is at the first main intersection after the **French Cemetery**. Drive 1.2 km beyond the intersection to get to the entrance of the botanical gardens, located on the right. If you keep going along this road you will arrive at **Gamboa**.

Back on the main road to Colón, 4.5 km beyond the intersection leading to the gardens, there is a pleasant resting area with a picnic table and waterfall. The **Camino de Cruces** trail lies on the left side of the road, 1.4 km farther on.

To get to **Canopy Tower**, take the same Gamboa-bound road leading to the Jardín Botanico Summit and after passing it, take the second road on your right. Continue straight on along the main road which climbs toward the old radar station.

Cerro Contratista Mirador (Contractor's Hill)

To reach Contractor's Hill take the Puente de las Américas. After the bridge turn right at the signs for Camp Cocolí and Rousseau, in the direction of Coco Solo village. There is a checkpoint 4 km ahead. State your destination and you

will be issued a visitor's permit which you will have to hand in when you leave. Keep going on the main road for 11.9 km, then turn right. The Cerro Contratista Mirador (*daily 9-5*) is 0.5 km farther on.

Isla Barro Colorado

You can reach the island of Barro Colorado and the Smithsonian Scientific Institute from the harbour at the village of Gamboa. To visit the island, you need authorization from the Smithsonian (see p72), which must be requested in advance.

By Bus

To get to any point in the **Canal Zone** (including the locks) from Ciudad de Panamá, go to Plaza 5 de Mayo in front of the Reina Torres de Araúz museum, the departure point for numerous buses. The destinations are indicated (although not always legibly) on the windshields of the vehicles and the cost is between B/. 1 and B/. 3, depending on the destination. Be aware that when going to the Miraflores locks, the bus stop is on the main road and there is a walk of 1 km to reach the site. The same holds true for the **Summit Botanical Garden**.

Note: a new bus station in under construction near the Albrook Airport and, if all goes according to plan, all bus services should be transferred there by the year 2000.

Since there is no bus service to **Canopy Tower**, contact the establishment's staff who will pick you up at the Summit Botanical Garden (see above) which is just a few kilometres away from it.

By Taxi

In the downtown capital there is no problem finding a taxi to go to the locks, the Summit Botanical Garden or any other place in the Canal Zone. The cost is between B/. 20 and B/. 30, depending on the destination.

By Train

Unfortunately, the famous railroad along the canal, the Ferrocarril de Panamá, is only used for occasional shipments of merchandise or special events (see p141).

Exploring

Puente de Las Américas

This elegant cantilever bridge (a bridge with no cables and extending horizontally well beyond its vertical supports), 118 m high, was built by the Americans between 1958 and 1962, and affords a magnificent view over the Bahía de Panamá. It was built at a cost of $20 million. You can of course visit the bridge by car, though the swift traffic doesn't leave much time for admiring the sights, or you can cross it on foot. The latter option is certainly the most spectacular, due to the fine view of the bay and its constant stream of boats, although the noise of the traffic and the restricted

walking space detract somewhat from the enjoyment of the walk. Finally, for those who would rather go by car or prefer a quieter spot, there is a parking area with no facilities but a good view of the bay just past the bridge on the right as you head west out of the city (follow the signs for *mirador*).

Miraflores Locks

Of the three groups of locks in the canal zone, the Miraflores locks are the most interesting. A special area has been developed above the locks, from which visitors have an unobstructed view of the operations (*every day 9am to 5pm*). As the ships pass, commentaries can be heard from the loudspeakers in Spanish and in English. You will learn, for example, that a ship might contain 4,000

Puente de Las Américas

The Panamá Canal

The Panamá Canal: A Few Facts

The canal is 80 km long, and has three series of locks: the Miraflores locks, the Pedro Miguel locks and the Gatún locks. The Miraflores locks are the highest because the tides are higher in the Pacific.

For 11 months of the year, the water levels of the two oceans differ because of tides and climatic conditions; only in February are they about the same. While the Pacific tides are very high (up to seven metres), those in the Atlantic are quite low.

Since the canal opened on August 15, 1914, over 725,000 ships have passed through it. Traffic is continuous and since 1966 the canal has been lit up at night to ensure greater safety.

Lago Gatún's surface area (425 km²) makes it the second-largest artificial lake in the world.

In the Gatún locks, ships are lifted 26.52 m above sea level. The doors of the locks weigh 750 tons.

In the Miraflores locks, a ship can be raised nine metres in 15 minutes. Over 100,000 tons of fresh water from Lago Gatún are needed to fill the locks for this purpose. Thus, each time a boat passes, more than 100 million litres of fresh water spill into the ocean.

Little trains, or *mulas* (mules), as the Panamanians commonly refer to them, tow ships through the locks.

They each weigh 47 tons and their function is to stabilize the ships on their way into the locks. On average, ships take 24 hours to pass through the canal. About half this time, 12 hours, is spent waiting to enter the canal. The longest boat to go through the canal was the 299-m San Juan Prospector.

The highest passage fee ever levied was $141,088, paid by the Regal Princess in October 1992. The lowest passage fee was paid by Richard Halliburton, who shelled out 36 cents to swim through the canal! The fees are determined according to the vessel's weight and size. Ships flying the Panamanian flag are charged a special rate.

cars from Sweden, oil from Venezuela, or a great variety of other cargo. You can also take in a 15 min audio-visual presentation on the operation of the canal in the **little lock museum** (*every day 9am to 5pm*). The sight of a

huge ship moving a few metres away is truly impressive. Electric locomotives move alongside ships that dwarf them, guiding and stabilizing vessels by means of steel cables. What power!

Operations are carried out with the utmost precision, and once a ship has passed through, the locks empty then fill back up at an astonishing speed – a process that involves several million litres of water.

A Record Year for the Canal

A record number of ships passed through the Panamá Canal in 1994: close to 14,000 ships sailed from one ocean to the other, which is an average of 37 per day. This traffic generated $436 million US for Panamá and represents the transportation on the canal of some 216.4 million tons of cargo. The record levels in 1994 came after several years where traffic had actually been decreasing. Exceptionally good crops in the eastern United States combined with bad crops in Australia and Taiwan are a major reason for the increase in the transportation of grain.

Urgent repairs to the locks and an inordinate number of ships in January 1995 pushed the waiting time, both on the Pacific and Atlantic sides, up to a week, another record! This ludicrous waiting time was nevertheless quickly returned to the average 12 hours.

The success of canal operations is of interest to many people, first of all to Panamanians, 10% of whose GNP depends on the canal. But worldwide trade would suffer from complications in the functioning of the canal. The year 2000 signals the complete transfer of the administration of the canal to the Panamanians, and as that year approaches, many wonder whether the Panamanians are ready to take control. In any case, people seem to be getting ready; the issue is a major topic in the media and on the political scene. Panamá plans to undertake work to increase the capacity of the canal and to decrease the waiting time. This would involve, among other things, enlarging the *Corte Gaillard*, the narrowest point of the canal where it passes through the mountains.

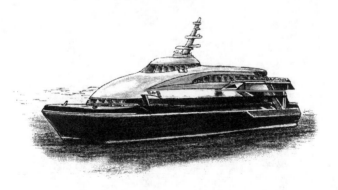

For technical reasons, this water is fresh, and comes from Lago Gatún (saltwater could jam the machinery of the locks). The extent of these operations is even more impressive when you take into account that the locks were built over 70 years ago! Those interested in actually passing through the locks and sailing on the canal can contact one of the following agencies:

Tropic Tours
☎ *264-7895*
☎ *269-3147*
☏ *269-3216*

Argo Tours
☎ *228-6069*
☎ *228-4348*
☏ *228-1234*
pcanal@panama.c-com.net,
www.big-ditch.com
Argo Tours is the tourist agency offering the widest choice of excursions. There are two interesting possibilities to mention. Those with limited time can choose a half-day cruise (*B/. 75 buffet-meal and drinks included; Sat 7:30am to12pm*) that passes through the Miraflores locks and goes down to the Panamá Bay in the region of Calzada Amador, passing under the impressive Puente de las Américas. Alternatively, you might devote a full day to a complete cruise through the three canal locks (*B/. 135, buffet-meal and drinks included; several departures monthly, 7:30am to 5:30pm*) to the city of Colón with return to the capital by bus.

Cerro Contratista (Contractor's Hill)

The passage made through the mountain to allow the canal to pass can be seen from Cerro del Contratista, a 115 m hill overlooking Gaillard Cut (Corte de Gaillard or Corte Culebra), which was

named for the engineer who supervised the work.

Porcelaine Rose

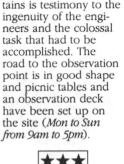

Opposite, you can see how the hill (Cerro de Oro) was levelled: it was reduced in size to minimise the risk of land slides into the canal. Literally overhanging the canal, this spot offers an impressive view of the passing ships from 199m above sea level. The sight of vessels navigating between the moun-tains is testimony to the ingenuity of the engineers and the colossal task that had to be accomplished. The road to the observation point is in good shape and picnic tables and an observation deck have been set up on the site (*Mon to Sun from 9am to 5pm*).

Summit Botanical Gardens

In this fine garden (*B/. .25; every day 8am to 4pm; Sat and Sun and summer until 6pm*) laid out in the Parque Nacionál Soberanía, there are more than 15,000 species of trees and plants. Summit Garden was built by the Americans in 1923 and handed over to Panamá in 1979. A number of trails have been cleared, and the various trees and shrubs are identified. It is tempting to stay here for hours looking at all the tropical species. A section of the garden (near the entrance to the park) is occupied by a small zoo and contains most of the wild animal and bird species that live in Parque Soberanía. A map showing the various routes for walking can usually be obtained at the entrance to the park, though copies are not always available.

An original way to get to the Botanical Garden is to use the old railway line, the Panamá Ferrocarril. For several years now there has been no regular service, but for about B/. 400 the company will organize a round trip from Balboa to the Summit Botanical Garden. For those travelling in a group, this is a unique outing on an exceptional railway line (see p 178)

For detailed information contact:

Ferrocarril Nacional de Panamá
Departamento de Comercialización
☎ *232-6018*

Gamboa

The main attraction here is the small marina on the Río Chagres – a good spot to begin an enjoyable boat ride. The marina is 8.4 km from the highway intersection at the entrance to Parque Soberanía. A little farther on the same road, you will come to a narrow bridge with an interesting view of Lago Gatún and the ships in the canal.

Balboa

At the foot of Cerro Ancón, the imposing **Administratión del Canal** building (*Mon to Fri*

9am to 4pm) is flanked by a monumental staircase that lends it an air of formality. Inside, an equally impressive 100 m² painting depicts four scenes in the important stages of the canal's construction.

On the initiative of engineer George W. Goethals, American painter William B. Van Ingen, already well known for his paintings of the Library of Congress in Washington, was commissioned for this work. The canvas was painted on several panels in New York and later reassembled here by the artist himself in 1915. The work was restored in 1993.

Parks

Parque Nacional Soberanía and the Camino de Cruces

The **Parque Nacional Soberanía** covers an area of 220km² and consists primarily of an impressive rain forest containing an extremely rich plant life.This forest is also home to a great variety of birds. Bird-watchers will be interested to know that the Panamá Audubon Society spotted over 525 different species between December 1992 and January 1993! Not only are the Summit Botanical Gardens (see p140) located here, but part of Parque Soberanía is crossed by Camino de Cruces. This well known route, in use since colonial times, (see p 23) is now a part of the **Parque Nacional Camino de Cruces**, created in 1993. Covering an area of almost 4,500 ha, it provides the link from the Parque Soberanía to the Parque Metropolitano.

Today the path is no longer entirely accessible, as part of it was submerged when the canal was built. The section of the trail that crosses Parque Soberanía, which used to be paved, is excellent for walking. Along it, outdoor enthusiasts can admire the richness and variety of the Panamanian flora.

Further information can be obtained from:

ANAM
The Parque Nacional Soberanía Office
☎ *229-7885*

The Panamá Canal

Isla Barro Colorado

This island was created in Lago Gatún when the valley was flooded. Some years later it became an exceptionally rich natural reserve. During the flooding, many animals took refuge here – so many that the island was classified a protected area. Because of this abundance and the island's small size (54 km²), the Smithsonian Institute built a research centre there to study the evolution of the island's animal and plant species.

The island has an impressive number of plants and shrubs, as well as different types of forests, some of which contain trees over 200 years old. As many as 1,300 different species of plants have been catalogued on these 1,500 ha. In fact, 300 different species of trees have been identified in a space of less than 26 ha. There are many trails (a total of some 40 km), including a 2.5 km-long path called the Nature Trail for people with little time or little hiking experience. It is recommended that you wear long, light clothing as protection against the many insects (see p51). However, Barro Colorado is accessible only with authorization from

the Smithsonian or as part of a guided tour organized by the various agencies promoting ecotourism (see p64). While there is accommodation on the island, it is reserved for the scientific staff.

The best way to see the island is to join a tour organized by
The Smithsonian Institute
☎ 227-6021
☎ 227-6022
✐ 232-5978
arosem@tivoli.si.edu,
www.stri.org

Frigate

The only inconvenience is that space is limited, and all sorts of conditions apply. Group tours are Thursdays and Sundays (*B/. 28; departure Thurs 7:15am; Sun 8am; return 4:10pm and 3:40 respectively; maximum 15 people*) and Saturdays (*B/. 28 per person, departs 8am, returns 3:30pm*). The tours include the boat trip (*Gamboa - Barro Colorado, return*), the services of a guide and a meal at the island's cafeteria. Payment must be made two weeks before your visit. It is also strongly recommended to reserve well in advance. Reservations and payment can be made by

mail. Children must be at least 12 years of age.

Another way to visit, which is more expensive but much less complicated, is with Eco-Tours, an agency that organizes day-trips from Ciudad de Panamá. The tour is led by an experienced guide who provides all sorts of interesting information on the flora and fauna. Besides a pleasant hike through the island's dense vegetation (*about 90 min*), the trip includes a boat tour along the shores of several coves to admire birds that are often hard to spot in the forests because they are usually perched at the tops of the trees.

When close to shore, the boat is powered by an electric motor so as not to scare away the animals. You may spot numerous bird species, including toucans, as well as iguanas and monkeys. This excursion is open to everyone and is very safe, though you will have to sign a waiver. Both life-jackets and binoculars are provided. The cost is B/. 175 per person, or B/. 90 each when there are at least two people. This price includes return transportation from your hotel (*departure at 6am, return at 3pm*), the guided tour and a light lunch on the island.

Eco-Tours
7 Calle 50 Este or Ricardo Arias, near Vía España
☎ 263-3077
☎ 263-3076
≈ 263-3089
www.avatar.pty.com/ecotours/fra-bome.btm
ecotours@pty.com

Outdoor Activities

Hiking

Parque Nacional Soberanía

Among the short hikes that can be undertaken without a guide is the nature interpretation trail **El Charco** (*3.8 km from the entrance to the Summit Botanical Garden, on the right side of the road going towards Gamboa*). Along the pleasant 2 km loop walk, there are explanatory signs denoting the origins of the trees and plants. Do not forget your insect repellent, as the mosquitoes are very much at home here.

Canopy Tower
by appointment only
Semaphore Hill Road
☎ 264-5720
≈ 263-2784
arba@pananet.com
www.canopytower.com
For the uninitiated,

even those with a great deal of patience, observing animals in the wild is not always easy and often requires the services of an experienced guide. The proprietor of the Canopy Tower and his team offer a number of original and instructive tours

Coqui

(in Spanish and English) of this extraordinary site. Some of these excursions are described below. Prices are provisional and excursions are subject to change due to diverse conditions. Call to confirm before heading out.

"The Awakening of the Forest" (*B/. 25/pers.; departure 6am, return 10am*), is the name of the almost four-hour hike suggested for very early risers. This morning excursion allows one to discover the animals of the park during the peak of their daily activities. Rates include entry to the park, a meal, access to the summit of the old radar tower and

use of a telescope. The "night version" of this hike (*B/. 55/pers.; departure 5am, return 1am*) allows one the unique experience of discovering the park's nocturnal animals, set to the music of screaming monkeys, chorusing frogs and all sorts of strange sounds that the guides are happy to explain. Guaranteed thrills!

Those "early to bed and *late* to rise" types can take a two-hour guided tour along the **Semaphore Hill Road** (*B/. 15/pers.*), which, although paved, is surrounded by dense vegetation. The guide will point out a surprising number of animals. The road slopes downhill all the way, but rest assured: a little electric car will bring you back to the starting point!

Fishing

Gamboa

The little marina is the perfect spot for people who like to fish in calm water. Boats and tackle may be rented there.

Pirogue

Life as a Zonian

Hired for the most part in the United States, employees in the Canal Zone had state-run stores selling goods that were imported directly from the States at subsidised prices. Curiously, it was mainly the Chinese who supplied fresh produce. Hired on for the duration of construction, they subsequently settled with their families and became the "market gardeners of the canal"

by cultivating fruits and vegetables. In terms of accommodation, the housing was erected by the administration of the Zone and residents were unable to purchase their own houses. Thus, over the course of 75 years of American management, schools, churches, social clubs, golf courses and public swimming pools have created a veritable microcosm of

the United States, completely separate from the host country and its citizens. For Americans born in the Canal Zone and those who have spent most of their lives there, returning to the United States entails a serious culture shock, not unlike that experienced by the colonists repatriated back to Europe during the 1960s.

Accommodations

Parque Nacional Soberanía

Canopy Tower
$$$$$ all incl
pb/sb, hw, ⊗
Semaphore Hill Road
☎ 264-5720
⌨ 263-2784
arba@pananet.com
www.canopytower.com
Enthralled by nature, fascinated by ornithology or simply keen on peace and quiet? Opt for a stay at the Canopy Tower for a taste of paradise! Located at the summit of a 900 m hill,

this old radar tower has been cleverly transformed into a small hotel by the proprietor, Paúl Arias de Para. Long before it was possible to buy it back from the American army, he had taken note of the tower's unique site.

Indeed, isolated at the heart of Parque Nacional Soberanía and completely surrounded by lush vegetation, this spot provides an exceptional lookout for those enthralled by virgin forest. At the moment, the industrial appearance of the entrance is somewhat disappointing. There are plans to create a museum here. After several years of intense

restoration, the old radar tower has six comfortable rooms in a rotunda on the second floor. All are charmingly decorated and are enhanced by windows looking out over the forest.

The third floor has a large circular room, entirely glassed-in, where guests can admire the dense vegetation. There is a pleasant living room corner and a library filled with books on birds and other animals of the isthmus.

Finally, on the top floor, paradise awaits! There is an oval terrace at treetop-level surrounding the old radar dome. From here the

Philippe Jean Bunau-Varilla
(1859-1940)

This Parisian engineer worked on the canal until 1888, when the project was finally abandoned by the French. Bunau-Varilla, unable to accept the defeat, tried to strike up a partnership with the Russians. The project was finally picked up by the Americans, who entrusted him to reach an agreement with Colombia on their behalf, so that they would be granted the concession. While Bunau-Varilla was a skilled negotiator, his project did not meet with success. Determined not to give up, he sought help by stirring things up among Panamá's merchant class, a revolt that ultimately lead to the country's independence. Later, as Panamá's first ambassador to the United States, he led the negotiations that would later result in the famous Hay-Bunau-Varilla Treaty. After the canal opened, he returned to France, where he took part in the First World War.

360-degree view of the park is simply extraordinary. Besides a wide view of the park one can see in the distance the immense ships navigating the canal. From this vantage point they appear to be gliding across the forest; this is truly an astonishing spectacle!

Guests can relax, sit comfortably and observe through binoculars the innumerable birds that live in the canopy. Dusk and dawn are among the noisier moments of the day; at dawn the birds are at the peak of activity and at dusk the screaming monkeys exercise their tenor and baritone voices.

Unfortunately, dreams have a price. The "all-inclusive" plan (*B/. 145/pers., three meals and drinks*), includes two hikes per day with a guide, the use of a telescope and binoculars and entrance to the national park. The less affluent need not despair, as the proprietor has different excursions at more affordable prices (see p 143).

Restaurants

Pizza Hut
on the left side of the main road leading to the locks
There are almost no restaurants near the Miraflores locks. If you feel peckish, your only choice is the Pizza Hut.

Try the Taco Pizza, with *frijoles* (beans) and cheese.

Shopping

At the Miraflores locks you will find a few vendors selling T-shirts (*B/. 10*), straw hats and many other small souvenirs of the canal. A little bargaining is in order.

The Panamá Canal

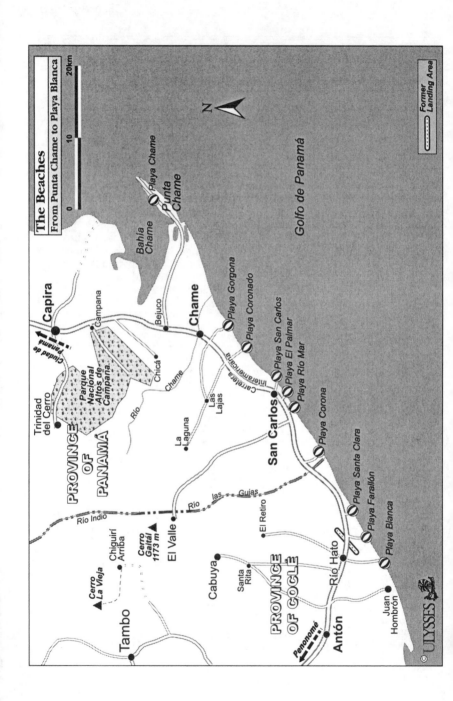

The Beaches
From Punta Chame to Playa Blanca

0   10   20km

N

Golfo de Panamá

Former
Landing Area

Punta Chame
Playa Chame
Bahía Chame

Capira

Ciudad de Panamá

Campana

Parque Nacional Altos de Campana

Trinidad del Cerro

PROVINCE OF PANAMÁ

Chicá

Río Chame

Bejuco

Chame

Las Lajas

La Laguna

Carretera Interamericana

San Carlos

Playa Gorgona
Playa Coronado
Playa San Carlos
Playa El Palmar
Playa Río Mar
Playa Corona

Río Indio

Cerro La Vieja

Chiguirí Arriba

Cerro Gaital 1173 m

El Valle

Río las Guias

El Retiro

Playa Santa Clara
Playa Farallón
Playa Blanca

Tambo

Cabuya

Santa Rita

Río Hato

PROVINCE OF COCLÉ

Antón

Penonomé

Juan Hombrón

© ULYSSES

The Islands and Beaches of the Province of Panamá

The many islands and beaches of Panamá's Pacific coast are, like its rich flora and fauna, too often overlooked by travellers.

Isolated and only accessible with difficulty, the islands of the Archipiélago de las Perlas are the largest group. Among these, the best-known is undoubtedly Isla Contadora, the only island with an international-class hotel and enough rooms to accommodate large numbers of tourists. It is also the only island in the archipelago with several daily flights to the capital. Aside from the islands of the Las Perlas group, Isla Taboga is very popular with Panamanians. Barely an hour's boat road away from the Ciudad, it is literally invaded on weekends by families who come to enjoy the sand and sun and get away from

Caribbean Sea

COSTA RICA

Bocas del Toro

Chiriquí

Veraguas

Herrera

Los Santos

Colón

Coclé

Panamá

Ciudad de Panamá

Chepo

Comarca de San Blas

Golfo de Panamá

Darién

COLOMBIA

Pacific Ocean

the city. There is a detailed description of these two islands in this chapter.

The many beaches along the Bay of Panamá from Punta Chame to Playa Santa Clara are more accessible, located less than a 100 km from downtown. Each of the ten has its own personality and is worth visiting. Despite their beauty,

the huge international hotel chains have not yet moved in, as these beaches are still a bit off the beaten path. Though throngs of people on weekends (from Friday to Sunday afternoon), and entire families on statutory holidays, travel to the beaches, there are limited services available. The few restaurants fill up quickly and accommodation is difficult to come by. As a general rule, all you can expect is average comfort, and not necessarily the best value for your money. Most accommodations are set up for large families who bring along their own food, so it can be very advantageous to rent by the week or several days, at which point the price will drop considerably. A room can cost B/. 50 the first night, but only B/. 35 the other nights. Also, it is much easier to bargain for weekday accommodation because the beaches are virtually empty then. The price rates below do not take these reductions into account and are for a single night's accommodation.

El Valle de Antón, less than an hour away from the beaches, is a bit cooler and greener and offers a wide variety of restaurants and hotels, as well as a craft market. Finally, also at less than an hour's drive from the coast, there is the Parque Nacional Altos de Campana for lovers of the great outdoors.

Finding Your Way Around

Note: the following schedules and rates are provided for reference only and are subject to change.

By Boat

To reach **Isla Taboga**, head to pier 18, located in the Balboa area. Ferries depart from here twice a day during the week, and several times a day on weekends and holidays. The crossing takes 90 min each way. Since departure times have a tendency to change often (sometimes the boat simply leaves when it is full) and service is irregular, it is a good idea to check the schedule the same day you plan to leave.

On weekends, the best way to make sure you get on the boat is to reserve a spot, since Panamanians by the boat-loads will also be heading to the island. Argo Tours offers the most regular service for the best price (*B/. 7.50 return*). Their schedule (at press time) and phone number are listed below. The best way to reach the port is by taxi since there is no guarded parking lot

and the area can be unsafe. An army of taxis will be waiting for your return, which gives you the advantage of being able to negotiate a price. From the pier to Bella Vista, for example, should cost B/. 3 for one person and B/. 4 for two.

Argo Tours
☎ *228-4348*
☎ *264-3549*
☎ *228-6069*
⇌ *228-1234*
⇌ *221-0844*
pcanal@panama.c-com.net
www.big-ditch.com

Boat Schedule:

From Ciudad de Panamá
Departure: Mon to Fri
8:30am and 2pm
Sat and Sun 8:30am,
11:30am and 4pm

From Taboga
Departure: Mon to Fri
10:00am and 3:30pm
Sat and Sun 10:00am,
2:30pm and 5:00pm

Calypso Queen
☎ *232-5736*

By Plane

Aeroperlas is currently the only airline with daily flights to the island
Travel Time: 20 min
Cost: B/. 46

Ciudad de Panamá to Contadora
Departure: Mon to Fri
8:30am and 5pm;
Sat 8am, 8:50am,
9:45am and 5pm;
Sun 8:50am, 3:50pm,
4:40pm and 5:30pm

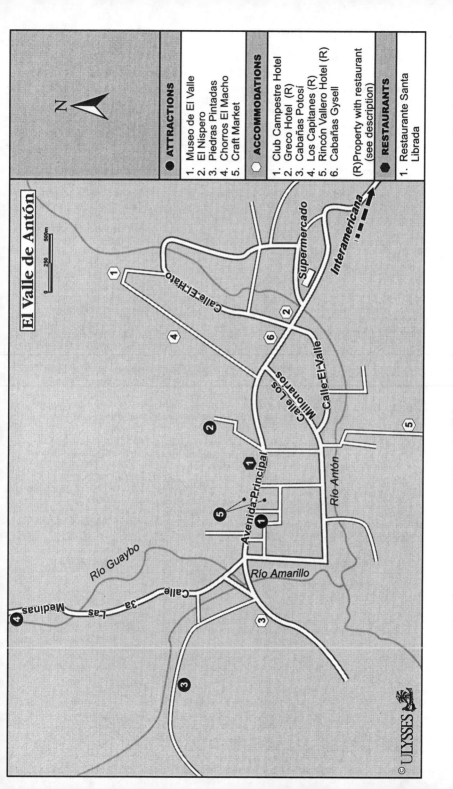

El Valle de Antón

N

0 250 500m

● ATTRACTIONS
1. Museo de El Valle
2. El Nispero
3. Piedras Pintadas
4. Chorros El Macho
5. Craft Market

⬡ ACCOMMODATIONS
1. Club Campestre Hotel
2. Greco Hotel (R)
3. Cabañas Potosí
4. Los Capitanes (R)
5. Rincón Vallero Hotel (R)
6. Cabañas Gysell

(R)Property with restaurant
(see description)

● RESTAURANTS
1. Restaurante Santa Librada

© ULYSSES

Río Guaybo
Río Amarillo
Río Antón
Calle Las Medinas
Calle 33
Avenida Principal
Calle Los Millonarios
Calle El Valle
Calle El Hato
Supermercado
Interamericana

Contadora to Ciudad de Panamá

Departure: Mon to Fri 8:55am and 5:25pm; Sat 8:25am, 9:15am and 5:25pm; Sun 9:15am, 4:15pm, 5:05pm and 5:55pm

There are also flights from **Colón**, **David**, **Chitré** and **Bocas del Toro**.

For information:

Aéroport de Contadora ☎ 250-4022

By Car

To reach the *interior* (the area to the west of the capital) of the country, take the Puente de las Américas, and continue straight on the main highway. From Arraiján, a toll highway (*toll booth is 26 km from the bridge; B/. 1*) leads to La Chorrera. Shortly after La Chorrera, the highway merges onto the Interamericana. Keep left here, since there are actually two roads, and no sign to tell you how to join the Interamericana.

To reach **Playa Chame**, take the Interamericana from the capital to the village of Bejuco and follow the signs for Punta Chame at the entrance to the village, on the left. Keep going for about 25 km.

For **Playas Gorgona**, **Coronado**, **San Carlos**, **Río Mar**, **Santa Clara** and **Corona**: these beaches are all easily accessible from the left side of the Interamericana as you drive from Panamá.

To reach **Parque Nacional Altos de Campana**, turn right off the Interamericana 5 km after Capira when coming from Ciudad de Panamá. The road is in very bad shape and is only driveable in the dry season. Though you can reach the park in a small rental car, it is advisable to have a 4WD vehicle.

To get to **El Valle** from Ciudad de Panamá, take the Interamericana westward. The exit for El Valle is on the right side of the Interamericana, 2.3 km west of the turnoff for Playa Río Mar. The road to the village has been recently redone and passes a number of attractions. At 14.8 km, you will see a small lake in an old crater. Farther on, at 22.7 km, an interesting observation point has been laid out. Farther still, at 27 km, there is another observation point with a sign showing the altitude of Cerro Gaital (1,185 m).

By Bus

To get to **El Valle de Antón** and the **beaches** to the west of the capital, go to the bus station on Calle Curundú (also known as Vía La Amistad or Calle Ascañio Villalaz) in the Curundú district. Because of its distance from downtown, it is best to take a taxi. Unfortunately, other than the one going to El Valle, most buses will let you off on the Interamericana as they continue their route west. To get to the beach, you must then take a taxi or walk. To go to **Punta Chame**, take a bus as far as Bejuco, where there are many daily departures for this destination. Keep in mind, however, that buses stop at the beginning of the peninsula, at the Punta Chame Motel.

Note: a new bus station is under construction near the Albrook Airport and, if all goes according to plan, all bus services should be transferred there by the year 2000.

Exploring

Isla Taboga

In the early days of the colony this island, located about an hour from the capital, was a major port of call and many ships anchored here, including pirate vessels.

From here Francisco Pizarro also set forth to discover new South American territories.

The village of Taboga was established around 1549 and was quickly populated by freed slaves and Chinese people. The former cultivated pineapples while the latter were mostly involved in commerce.

Early in 1885, during the Lesseps canal construction period, the French built a sanatorium and the island became a place for convalescence. In 1904, shortly after the Americans took over work on the canal, the centre was enlarged and most of the island's income came from the sanatorium's patients. When work on the canal was completed, the government transformed the sanatorium into the Aspinwall Hotel, which was privatized in 1921.

After a brief prosperous period during which sumptuous receptions were organized by Panamanian high society, the island's fortunes slumped. With the coming of World War II and the installation of a military base, the "Island of Flowers" enjoyed a brief period of vitality. After the war the island returned to its peaceful origins until it was reawakened by tourism.

The trip to Taboga is a journey of discovery in itself, even today. The boat that sails the canal passes under the Puente de las Américas, which offers good views of the bridge and the Bahía de Panamá. You will also see all the boats waiting to get into the canal. Cars are forbidden on the island, and the quiet is conducive to relaxing walks. This island is blessed with a stunning array of flowers. Colourful bougainvillea, orchids, hibiscuses, etc. are just a few of the types that grow here, making it no wonder the Panamanians call Taboga the "island of flowers". Taboga is also known for its beautiful white-sand beaches, dotted with palm trees and littered with pink and brown seashells. Unfortunately, these idyllic beaches fill up rapidly on the weekends. Come mid-week if you are searching for serenity.

The village, with its whitewashed houses and narrow streets, extends from the harbour to the slope of the mountain and is a pleasant place to stroll. Among the buildings of interest is the small church on the central plaza, the architecture of the Chu hotel and a bit farther west, the house known as the *La Concha*, decorated with shells (the owner sells shells).

Part of the island is classified as a nature reserve. The reserve is on the other side of the island from the village, and harbours many species of animals, among them iguanas and a colony of

"Island of Flowers" and Gaugin

The island's exoticism has inspired many artists over the years, particularly the Panamánian painter Roberto Lewis and the famous Paul Gauguin. The latter, who visited the island many times in 1887 while nursing his malaria, even considered building a house there.

However, his meagre salary as a canal construction worker was not enough to buy the land. Disappointed at not being able to buy "a piece of paradise", Gauguin left for the French Antilles before eventually ending up in Polynesia.

pelicans. You can visit the reserve but you must first obtain authorization from ANAM (INRENARE) (see p72), which will assign you a guide. The institute has a local office (often closed, unfortunately) on the road to the Taboga Hotel where you can obtain general information on the reserve. There are pleasant hikes off the reserve; two of the most interesting are described below (see p100, 157). If you prefer the beach, the Taboga Hotel complex offers an interesting package. Its water is excellent for snorkelling; unlike other beaches on the island, this one has almost no waves.

Archipélago de las Perlas

Isla Contadora is part of the Archipiélago de las Perlas (archipelago of pearls) which is made up of more than 220 islands and islets. The largest of the islands, Isla del Rey, has a surface area of close to 240 km^2 and a population of approximately 2,500 people. Its capital, San Miguel, was established in 1607. Although the archipelago was discovered by Vasco Núñez de Balboa in 1513, it was only in 1515 that his successors Francisco Pizarro and Gaspar de Morales invaded the island. After subduing "King

La Peregrina

This is the name of the largest pearl ever discovered. Shaped like a droplet or, according to some, a teardrop, La Peregrina was found in the Archipiélago de las Perlas and sold by the wife of the then-governor to the wife of Charles Quint,

Doña Isabel. After passing through the hands of several English royals, a French emperor, numerous nobles and business people, it is today owned by the famous American actress Elisabeth Taylor.

Toe", the Spaniards exploited the island's indigenous peoples in order to harvest pearls from the surrounding oyster beds. The Amerindian population very quickly died off and became extinct as early as 1518. Black slaves were then imported to make up for their loss. It was during this period that the slaves rebelled; many of them escaped and made their way towards Darién in 1546. These *cimarrones* formed bands of looters who, with the help of French and English pirates, would trouble colonial powers on numerous occasions.

When the oyster beds were exhausted colonial powers lost interest in the archipelago, and abandoned it to the pirates. Today, Isla del Rey's main industry is the production of

shrimp, which are exported internationally. Only two of the islands are accessible by plane, Isla del Rey and Isla Contadora, and the accommodation possibilities in the archipelago are minimal. Touring the other islands, therefore, is only possible for travellers with a boat. Those who do will enjoy a multitude of virtually deserted islands and isles, each ringed by spectacular beaches. Not to mention that rich underwater fauna makes this a prime area for scuba diving and deep-sea fishing.

★

Isla Contadora

Isla Contadora is the most easily accessible of the islands. While small, (only 1.2 km^2) it is the most developed, and a regular connection to the mainland (see p148) is guaranteed several times a day. The presence of a large hotel complex makes it the most popular island in the archipelago. This popularity is due mainly to the beauty of its white-sand beaches, low cliffs, calm sea perfect for swimming and of course its crystal-clear waters.

In the 1970s, notable personalities, like the former Shah of Iran, chose to exile themselves on this island. Its name was established once and for all in 1983 when the presidents of Mexico, Venezuela, Colombia and Panamá met to restart negotiations for peace in Central America.

Among the best beaches on the island, **Playa Cacique** is particularly beautiful and virtually deserted, even in the high season. For a swim in calm, safe waters, **Playa Larga** facing the Contadora Resort is a better choice. The latter is, however, busier. Nudists tend to congregate on **Playa Suecas**, north of the hotel complex. Wildlife abounds on the island, and it is not unheard of to see hummingbirds near the beach, or even deer bounding by farther inland.

The same is not true of the vegetation, and during the dry season, what little exuberance it has essentially dries

up. In fact, water supply problems are common at this time of the year. Contadora is an exceptional site for those in search of beaches and limpid waters and nothing else. If catching some rays isn't really your thing, you might consider limiting your stay to one day – plenty of time to explore the island. If you want to rest, or play water sports, this is the place. But if you want to save money, it is not.

El Valle de Antón

This little village, located 600 m above sea level in a resort area frequented by wealthy inhabitants of the capital, is renowned not only for its fresher climate and its greenery but also for its little local market. On Sundays, peasants come from neighbouring regions to sell all kinds of things, many from Andean countries (Ecuador, Peru, etc.).

There are bargains on carpets, sweaters, handbags, pottery, sculptures, etc., and the products are of high quality. Panamanians also flock to the El Valle market for the exotic plants and flowers, like the celebrated flower of Panamá, the white orchid known as *espíritu santo*.

Ranas doradas (golden frogs) can also be found in this region. These strange and impressive-looking creatures are orange with black spots. Their long, thin feet and slightly wrinkled skin make them appear undernourished. However, although they may seem weak and fragile, they are able to jump or climb on any surface. Unfortunately, they are not easy to find, particularly as they are threatened with extinction. They are on display, however, at the Hotel Club Campestre (see p166) or the El Nispero Zoo where you will discover another curiosity, the *arboles quadradas*, trees with square trunks that grow behind the hotel (access through the building, payment required), and do not seem all that square in reality. According to hotel advertisements, this is the only place where such trees can be seen.

The little village of El Valle is beautifully decorated with flowers and the road there leads through lush green countryside. As an added attraction, people sell handicrafts (especially baskets and pottery) along the road. Several hikes and horseback rides are possible from the town. A visit to El Valle is thus a good opportunity to take a short breather from the beaches on the Gulf of Panamá.

For those who want to know (a bit) more about village history, the **Museo de El Valle** (*B/. 0,25; Sun 10am to 2pm; Av. Principal, beside the Iglesia San José, in the center of the village*) has five rooms devoted to the history of El Valle de Antón and the surrounding area. There are very small collections of petroglyphs, pre-Colombian urns and folk costumes on display. Although the exhibits are very simply presented, a visit would be worthwhile, if only to provide much-needed encouragement to Panamá's museums.

No visit to El Valle would be complete without at stop at **El Nispero** (*B/. 2; 8am to 6pm; when coming from San Carlos, turn right at the Intel and right again at the police station*), a private hacienda that is both a zoo and a botanical garden. As well as "golden" frogs, monkeys, tapirs, pheasants and exotic birds, there is a pond full of many different species of fish. El Nispero is also famous for its orchids.

Crossing El Valle village on the main road in the direction of the church, you will end up at a little bridge over the Río Amarilla. Continue on the main road and turn left at the intersection and right at the next street. Keep

walking straight until you reach a sign for **Piedras Pintadas** (the petroglyphs). Once there, you must follow a small dirt path going through a wooded area that runs along a river for a bit. This little hike takes barely 5 min. If you are concerned about getting lost or want to have a chat with the locals, accept one of the many offers from the local children to guide you. As little as B/. 0.50 will get you many appreciative looks, bursts of laughter and explanations of all kinds – not very scientific, perhaps, but always entertaining! Opinion is divided as to both the petroglyphs' historical importance as well as their interest to visitors.

Although there are many waterfalls in the area, **Chorro El Macho** (*entrance fee, B/. 5*) are the best-known and most accessible to the

Orchids

general public. To get there, first follow the same directions as for the petroglyphs but continue straight ahead in the direction of the village of La Mesa at the first intersection. There will be a sign on the left pointing out the 35-m falls, which are surrounded by lush vegetation and fall into a basin in which some visitors swim. Unfortunately, access to the falls has become more expensive than they are worth. There are a variety of other outdoor activities offered on-site (see p158).

As you continue westward, do not be surprised to discover a landing strip along the Interamericana, between Playa Santa Clara and Penonomé. This was built by the Americans during the Second World War. Ironically, nearby on the left side of the road, there are a number of old military buildings used in the days of Noriega. Quotations from the former dictator can still be read on the walls. This area is slated for major development in the near future. Plans include the construction of large hotel complexes on the beach, while the airport may be renovated and upgraded to an international airport for charter flights. A sort of Panamanian Cancún... why not?

Beaches

★★

Punta Chame

This peninsula, jutting like a finger into the sea, has immense, white sand beaches. The road to get there is a delight, with superb views of the neighbouring mountains.

If you are lucky, you will see dolphins from the beaches on the inside coast of Bahía de Chame. Also, the beach on this side slopes gently toward the ocean, whereas on the Bahía de Panamá side, the waters get deep quickly and the resulting stronger currents make swimming risky. The latter beach is not as nice, and a favourite spot of pelicans. To get to either beach, take any road perpendicular to the main road. Only about a 100 km from Ciudad de Panamá, this place is ideal for swimming and sunbathing. Be careful, however, as swimming at low tide is highly discouraged because of the strong undertow and the presence of stingrays. Before diving in, check if there are other people swimming or ask some locals.

Playa Gorgona

Extremely busy on weekends, Playa Gorgona has a nice, though narrow, beach of white and black sand. This place is particularly ideal for travellers who thrive on throngs of people or who want to hang out with suited Panamanians and their families. Music, crying, laughing kids and lots of activity are the general rule on weekends. Two small hotel complexes with pools, showers, bars and various other services are located on site (see p162). The beach fronting the Gorgona complex is less appealing because of the barbed wire which was installed to stop intruders from entering the complex.

★★

Playa Coronado

This resort area, which lies along an interesting beach where black and white sand intermingle, is the site of many second residences belonging to wealthy Panamanians from the capital. Pretty villas surrounded by vibrant gardens overflowing with vegetation and exotic flowers line the road from the Interamericana and all the way to the beach.

A "Halt, who goes there" attitude seems to prevail, though, as just a few kilometres beyond the Interamericana you will come upon a security gate. You will have to state your name and the reason for your visit. However, since all beaches in Panamá are public, after this checkpoint you may continue on your way unheeded.

A luxury hotel with a golf course, the Coronado Club Suites Resort (see p162) opened several years ago just a few kilometres from the beach. It is a pleasant place for a drink or breakfast.

Unfortunately, the numerous villas that have been built bordering the beach have gradually made access to the beach difficult. Visitors must therefore look for an access path between two houses, which is not easy because most private lots are contiguous. One of the paths that is still accessible is near the Club Gaviota. Follow directions to the club and an Ipat sign just before it will indicate the way from there. For those who wish to quench their thirst by the sea, the friendly Club Gaviota (see p165) offers a popular pub and pool at the western end of the beach.
Although this is supposed to be a private members-only club, a B/. 3 cover charge will

get you in and even give you access to the swimming pool. Be aware, though, that the club closes at 5pm on weekdays and 7pm on weekends.

Playa San Carlos

Along with Playa Gorgona, this is probably the most popular beach along this part of the coast. After driving through the picturesque village of San Carlos, a tiny road leads to the shore where there is a restaurant run by IPAT (see p45). A handful of palm trees line the waterfront beside a ribbon of beautiful white sand. Beachgoers have a lot of room on this wide beach, despite the crowds. Plus, just off the Interamericana, numerous little shops have everything you need for a picnic on the beach.

Playa Río Mar

The waterfront of Playa Río Mar is not as wide, but the surrounding landscape of jagged cliffs and palm trees more than compensates. The sloping beach is blanketed with white sand with a few rocks and streams of black sand. A little river

empties into the sea right next to the beach, making the setting particular charming. Though you may see a few people swimming, remember that it is not a good idea to swim in untreated freshwater because of the risk of infection from schistosomiasis (bilharziasis) bacteria. A simple hotel complex on site has a few facilities, including a good restaurant with a view of the sea, *cabañas*, as well as a lovely terrace and swimming pool (see p165).

Playa Corona

Beyond Río Mar, there is endless white sand, framed by low cliffs and palm trees. However, the difficult access and the lack of services there are inconvenient. To reach the coast you have to go through the Playa Corona Hotel, since

this whole section of the coast is lined with private homes which block access to the beach. By way of compensation, the hotel is surrounded by lush vegetation and a nice little restaurant and bar (see p169) where you can enjoy fresh fruit juice or an inexpensive meal. A series of stairs leads right to the beach from the hotel's location atop a cliff.

Playa Santa Clara

Along with neighbouring Playa Farallón, Playa Santa Clara is probably the most delightful beach along this part of the coast. Lined with lovely residences, blossoming gardens and a small hotel complex with *cabañas*, the fine white sandy beach extends for several kilometres. Tourists in search of tranquillity and a change of scenery will spend hours wandering along the coast in this idyllic spot far from the weekend vacationers.

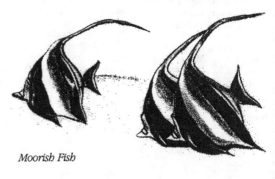

Moorish Fish

A wonderful place to rest and catch up on some reading.

Parks

★★

Altos de Campana

The Parque Altos de Campana was Panamá's first national park (1966) and has an area of more than 4,800 ha. Although human activities have greatly affected the park's flora and vast areas have undergone extensive deforestation, today there are still at least 20 native species. The average annual temperature of 24°C is conducive to the growth of epiphytic, bromeliaceous and orchidaceous plants. In addition to the numerous species of rare birds, various kinds of sloths and innumerable small mammals, you will also find the country's most amazing frog, the *rana dorada* or "golden frog", in an area close to the village of El Valle de Antón.owever, seeing it in the wild requires a great deal of luck as well as an experienced guide. Once in the park, you are guaranteed magnificent views of the coast, with the Punta Chame peninsula visible in the distance.

For access to the park, see (see p150).

Outdoor Activities

Hiking

★★★

Isla Taboga

Of the many hikes possible, we have chosen two which will allow you to see most of the island. But first a few tips:

• wear insect repellent: the mosquitoes can be bothersome in the undergrowth.

• do not forget bottled water, sunglasses and a hat.

• this island is home to many lizards, frogs and iguanas, many kinds of birds, and two types of snakes: the first is small, thin and slender, and almost looks like a dead branch, the second, the boa, can grow to an impressive size. Neither of these snakes is poisonous and both, in fact, are rather cowardly!

• avoid this island during the weekend

when it is literally overtaken by city residents and the beaches are strewn with litter.

Hike No. 1

This hike leads to the highest point on the island, Cerro Vigia (307 m), and offers splendid views of the island and of Ciudad de Panamá in the distance. While the climb is not difficult, some effort is required. Allow a maximum of two hours to reach the summit. For this hike, begin at the central plaza, in the middle of the village. Take the street to the left of the church (going toward the center of the square) and start climbing. You must first take some small village streets to get to the trail. Keep going up and away from the Hotel Taboga.

The villagers can show you the way (ask for "*el sendero por el Cerro Vigia*"). Once you reach the base of the trail, walk to the old reservoir on your left (just past an overhanging house) then turn right. Keep going upwards to the next house and just in front of it climb the "steps" on the right. Keep following the main trail to the top. (See the map on p 163). Hiking boots that cover the ankles are recommended for this hike.

Hike No. 2

Requiring less exertion than the first hike, this one takes you along the coast. Begin facing the entrance to the Hotel Taboga and take the road to the left. After 50 m, take the concrete road to the right. A few metres beyond this you will notice a bunker on the left (barely visible under leaves) and then shortly after a second bunker, also on the left. These bunkers were built by the Americans during the Second World War (don't forget the strategic importance of the canal!). Turn right, and take the dirt path facing the bunker. A water pump that serves the Hotel Taboga is located here.

The trail continues past a house and then opens onto a lovely, isolated beach. To return, retrace your steps to the second bunker and take the small trail opposite it, to the left of the trail. This trail, steep at the beginning (a rope makes the climb easier), leads through some dense vegetation. A short distance farther on, you will come to some rocks, where if you wait a bit you can spot dozens of little frogs: black with bright green spots. They are not poisonous, and you may even try to touch one. Don't forget, however, that they are among the protected

species and that it is strictly prohibited to bring one with you.

The trail then reaches the main road to the hotel. Allow an hour to complete the tour.

Parque Nacional Altos de Campana

This magnificent park, located 58 km from the capital (see p150), offers some excellent hiking opportunities.

Two lovely hikes can be organized: fans of long hikes can head off from the Interamericana and hike up to the park warden's office (at 6.1 km); those who prefer shorter hikes can drive directly to the warden's office (the road is in very bad shape, strewn with potholes and rocks) and then hike to the summit from there (about 4.4 km). Several unmarked trails depart from the summit. A 4WD vehicle is preferable for reaching the warden's office. Once there, ask for a map of the trails (unfortunately not always available). Hiking boots that cover your ankles are a good idea because there are venomous snakes in the park. Both hikes provide the opportunity to enjoy some terrific scenery, mostly made up of steep mountains. A vibrant palette of colour un-

folds on these verdant slopes, dotted here and there by darker green trees and shrubs. Adding to the scenery are occasional glimpses of the Pacific Ocean. Don't forget that you need permission from ANAM (☎ 244-0092) before visiting the park.

El Valle de Antón

El Valle is an ideal base for travellers looking to do some hiking. What better way to discover the wonders of the tropical forest, and keep fit at the same time? Be careful though, as the trails are rarely marked. Also, unless you plan on heading far from the villages, it is a good idea to enlist the services of a guide who can provide all sorts of information on the flora and fauna of the region... and also give you a chance to practise your Spanish! The locals are very friendly, and it's easy to find a guide.Among the region's particularly educational hikes is the one to **El Macho Falls**. For a fee of B/. 10, naturalist guides will bring you to the top of the falls on a path that passes many types of vegetation and where, with a bit of patience, you will be able to see many birds. The hike lasts approximately two hours and the path is quite easy for most people to follow. To get to the falls see (see p154).

Swimming

El Valle de Antón

Pozos de Aguas Termales
(*B/. .50; every day 9am to 5pm*)
Who would have believed that a hot bath in these climes could be pleasant? For a change from the climactic "rigours" of El Valle, a little dip in the Pozos de Aguas Termales will do you a world of good. The little pools of hot water (40°C) are fed by a volcanic spring a stone's throw from the Río Antón. According to locals, the murky waters possess curative powers. Say goodbye to arthritis, rheumatism and other joint disorders; the important thing is to believe!

To get to these miraculous waters, follow the main road through El Valle heading towards the church and take the first left just after the supermercado at the entrance to the village. Continuing straight ahead, there will be signs leading the way to the waters.

Scuba Diving

Isla Taboga

Hotel Taboga
about 300 m to the right of the pier
☎ 250-2122
☎ 264-6096
☎ 264-1748
Scuba gear can be rented for a reasonable price on this lovely, white-sand beach. On site you can safely explore the shores and rich marine wildlife of tiny Isla de Morro de Taboga. And for about B/. 5 you can also use the facilities (shower, beach shacks, etc.) of the hotel and get an item from the menu (drink or dish) equal to the fee. Unfortunately the island's beaches are packed on weekends and the cleanliness of the area suffers accordingly.

Isla Contadora

Captain Morgan's Playa Galeón
☎/= 250-4029
Beyond the airstrip is where you will find everything you need for a host of

Brown Pelican

aquatic activities. Besides renting the necessary equipment for scuba diving (wetsuit, tank, mask, weights, flippers, etc.), the centre offers various excursions with or without a guide, as well as a three-day trip for B/. 225 per person, including boat rental, tanks, and weights for a minimum of two sea dives per day (other equipment not included). Various courses are also offered (*expect to pay about B/. 325 per week*), as well as water skiing and jet-ski rentals (*about B/. 60 per hour*).

Golf

Playa Coronado

Coronado Club Suites Resort
Playa Coronado, on the main road leading to the beach, after the guardhouse and just before the bombeiros station, turn left at Avenida P. Prieta and continue for 1 km
☎ 240-4444
☎ 264-3164
USA and Canada
☎ 800-267-6465
= 223-8513
= 240-4380

Close to the beautiful beach at Coronado, this 18-hole course is a golf lover's dream. It is a part of the hotel and therefore normally reserved for the use of clients or club members, nevertheless the manager may allow access to outsiders for a fee.

Motorcycling

Isla Contadora

Right next to the airfield, near the pier, is a small counter where you can rent motorcycles and scooters (*expect to pay B/. 17.50 for two hours or B/. 40 for 24 hours*). This is a great way to explore the back roads of the island and check out all the beaches.

Personal Watercraft

Isla Contadora

Mar y Diversión
Playa Larga, close to the Contadora Resort Hotel
If you are a Sea-doo fan and not on a tight budget, do not pass up an opportunity to go to Mar y Diversión where there are beach buggies as well as sea-doos for B/. 50 per hour.

Fishing

Around Capira

Cafetería Parque El Lago
every day 10am to 9pm
Located 1.8 km west of the small village of Capira, near the Interamericana
The Cafetería Parque El Lago offers the bounty of a large artificial lake full of fish. You can fish (*B/. 0.50 per pound*) along with other Panamanian fishing enthusiasts. You can also rent a boat for B/. 2 per half-hour. A good restaurant with a large terrace adjoins this neat little spot.

Climbing

El Valle de Antón

Canopy Adventures
B/. 40; every day 8am to 10am and 1pm to 3pm
☎ 983-6547
☎ 264-5720
arba@pananet.com
www.canopy.mit.edu
If you are a budding Tarzan and not afraid of heights, you may be be tempted by an excursion to the El Macho Falls, the only trip of its kind in Panamá. Here, you can swing between tree tops, secured by a harness and pulley system. You must first hoist yourself up to a platform perched on a tree top, then glide along a set of cables from one tree to another, all the while watching the vegetation whizzing by beneath your feet. Clearly, this adventure is for people in good physical shape and demands suitable footwear (running or walking shoes). To get to the falls, (see p154).

Horseback Riding

Sr Victor Muñoz
☎ 993-6360
El Valle is a wonderful spot for riding. This pretty, garden-filled town is set in a valley framed by mountains and enjoys warm temperatures year-round. Here, you can rent horses for B/. 3.50 per hour. You can also hire a guide for B/. 5 per two hours. In four hours you can see the Chorro del Macho, Las Mosas and Las Piedras Pintadas (Amerindian petroglyphs) (see p 154).

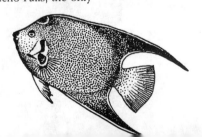

Accommodations

Isla Taboga

Hotel Chu
$
ℜ
on the main street of the village, 200 m to the left of the pier, take the road going up
☎ *250-2035*
☎ *263-6933*
Hotel Chu is a charming old colonial-style hotel, made completely of wood. Rudimentary comfort (badly sound-proofed, no private baths or screens), although each room has a small balcony with a fine view.

Hotel Taboga
$$$
pb, hw, ≡, ℜ, tv, #
about 300 m to the right of the pier, Taboga, Apdo 55-0357
☎ *269-1187*
☎ *264-6096*
☎ *264-1748*
⇄ *223-0116*
⇄ *223-5739*
A fine hotel on a superb private beach facing the small island of Morro de Taboga. The rooms are only adequately comfortable, but tastefully decorated. People not staying at the hotel may use the beach for B/. 5, which includes a shower, changing room, and a drink or snack worth the same price as the entrance fee. Snorkelling equipment for rent.

Isla Contadora

Villa Ernesto
$$
bkfst incl.
Apartado 55-0398, Pantilla
☎ *250-4112*
⇄ *250-4029*
A charming German couple runs the Villa Ernesto near Playa Caracol. Eduard and Marie Ernst rent out two pleasant and well-maintained rooms to tourists passing through. Besides a warm welcome, guests enjoy an excellent German breakfast, a real treat! There are also lounge chairs in the small flower garden. Besides German of course, the owners speak English and Spanish.

Contadora Resort
$$$$ all included
pb, hw, ≡, ≈,⊙, ℜ, tv
☎ *250-4033*
☎ *269-5269*
⇄ *250-4000*
Apdo 9728, Zona 4
contadora@pananet.com
pananet.com/contadora/
Overlooking the most beautiful beach on the island is the Contadora Resort with 354 rooms housed in several buildings surrounded by gardens. Though all the rooms are comfortable, some stand out for their lovely decor. In the newer buildings the interior layout seems to have been an afterthought and the decor has suffered because of it. Furthermore, because of the extreme dryness which dominates the island periodically, the hotel seems to have difficulty providing a steady supply of running water and its purification system is not up to par. There are four restaurants, a nightclub, a casino, a gym, two pools (one with a bar) and showers close by.

Besides an aquafitness courses, a nine-hole golf course and a tennis court are also available for guests. The management seems to prefer the all-inclusive formula offered by travel agents. Travellers without reservations can nevertheless get a one-day pass (*B/. 40, without lodging*) including a buffet meal and access to the bar, the pool and the showers.

A one-night and one-day package (*B/. 180*) is also available which includes meals, accommodation, and a variety of services. All the packages provide guests with unlimited access to snorkelling, badminton, volleyball, pedal-boats and kayaking equipment. Those in search of peace and quiet would do well to avoid the rooms around the pool, since the music that accompanies the aquafitness classes is quite loud; plus with the bar in the pool, the latter stays busy well into the night. A small beach at the end opposite the hotel is reserved for nudists. Finally, there is a doctor at the hotel to tend to your health concerns. This hotel will delight especially those in search of entertainment, the beach and engaging evenings.

Punta Chame to Playa Santa Clara

Motel Punta Chame
$$$
pb, ≡, ℜ, #
on the left, at the end of the road leading to the point
☎ 264-4036
☎ 223-1747
☎ 264-7560
www.plateadas.com/puntach ame
All kinds of lodgings are available, including small, basic but comfortable cabins (*B/. 60*), small houses with living rooms and kitchenettes (*B/. 70-75*), and a comfortable villa for four with a private pool (*B/. 80*). A hotel restaurant voucher of B/. 10 comes with all rentals. Some are along the beach and offer a pretty view of the bay.

Cabañas Playa Gorgona
$$-$$$ Mon to Fri
$$$-$$$$ Sat, Sun and holidays
≈, K
Playa Gorgona, 2.2 km from the Interamericana, to the right of the road when heading to the beach
☎ 269-2558
☎ 269-2433
↔ 223-1218
This row of small cabins is admittedly not very comfortable and poorly soundproofed. Music, laughing children crying are

guaraneed, but a friendly and charming Panamanian family atmosphere more than makes up for it, honestly! Guests have the use of a private parking lot.

Hotel Gorgona Jayes Resorts
$$ Mon to Fri
$$$ bkfst incl. Sat Sun and holidays
ℜ, ≈, ≡, *hw, tv*
Playa Gorgona, 2 km from the Interamericana via an unpaved road
☎ 223-7775
☎ 240-6095
↔ 264-3487
This small, simple hotel complex offers 44 equipped rooms set around a charming interior garden. The decor of the rooms is a bit old and could use some sprucing up. Athletes will enjoy the tennis and volleyball courts and the mast for *pelota basca*, while party types will delight in the nightclub and the *bohío* with its bar and large terrace. Part of the facilities, including the pool and showers, are located next to the beach, about a 10-min walk from the hotel. Staff are particularly attentive.

Apartamentos Río Lajas
$$$
pb, ℝ, K, #, ≡, *tv*
head towards Playa Coronada, then follow the signs to Club Gaviota
☎ 220-1863
☎ 220-2447
Fully equipped studios overlooking the beach lie in a particularly calm, verdant setting.

Ideal for those in search of rest and relaxation. The beach is accessible through a pretty flower garden. Friendly staff.

Coronado Club Suites Resorts
$$$$
pb, hw, ≡, ≈, *tv,* ℜ, ☉;
Playa Coronado, on the main road leading to the beach, after the guard post and just before the bombeiros station, turn left on Avenida P. Prieta for 1 km, Apartado 4381, Panamá 5
☎ 240-4444
☎ 264-3164
from North America
☎ 800-267-6465
↔ 223-8513
↔ 240-4380
carogolf@sinfo.net,
www.coronadoresort.com
Coronado Club Suites is a new resort with 76 suites, all furnished with a large living room with sofa and dining table. The bedroom is cleverly separated from the rest of the suite by a series of shutters, and has a safe. The combination of modern and bamboo furniture makes for a harmonious and pleasant decor. Though a large window looks out over the garden, the room could use a terrace. The bathroom is well-equipped but the harsh fluorescent lighting and noisy fan are bothersome. While the all-inclusive plan is offered at a seemingly attractive price, it is not particularly worthwhile because too many extras are added to it. Among the various facilities available are two large pools, an

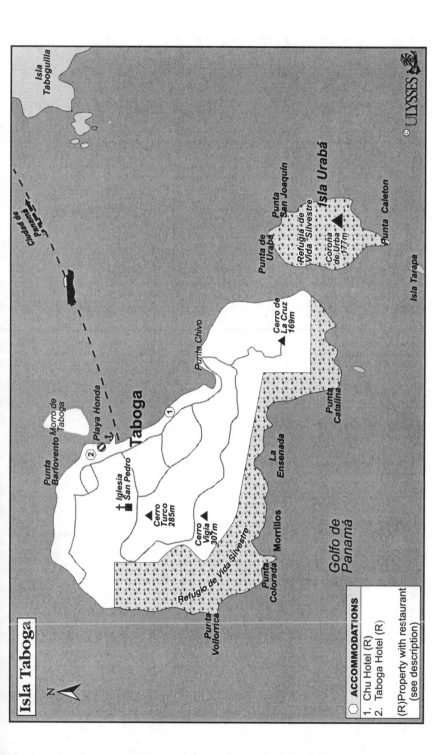

Isla Taboga

ACCOMMODATIONS
1. Chu Hotel (R)
2. Taboga Hotel (R)

(R) Property with restaurant (see description)

© ULYSSES

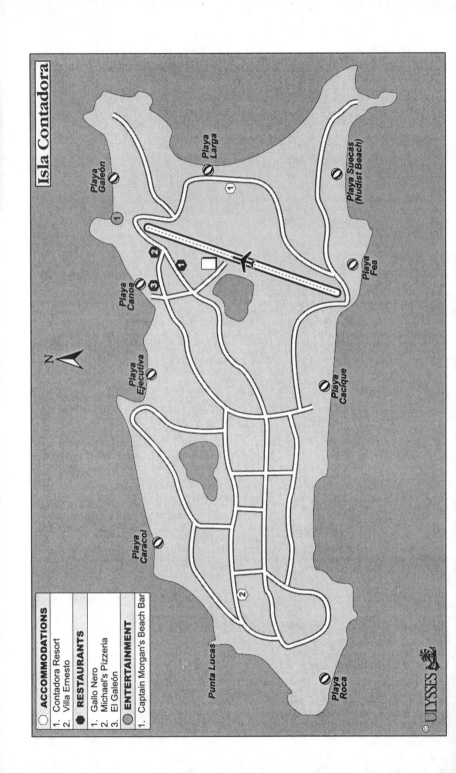

Isla Contadora

ACCOMMODATIONS
1. Contadora Resort
2. Villa Ernesto

● **RESTAURANTS**
1. Gallo Nero
2. Michael's Pizzeria
3. El Galeón

◉ **ENTERTAINMENT**
1. Captain Morgan's Beach Bar

N

Playa Galeón
Playa Larga
Playa Suecas (Nudist Beach)
Playa Fea
Playa Canoa
Playa Ejecutiva
Playa Cacique
Playa Caracol
Punta Lucas
Playa Roca

© ULYSSES

exercise room with a trainer, a tennis court and a golf course. Also, small whirlpool baths scattered throughout the blossoming gardens provide private relaxation. A casino will delight gaming enthusiasts, and shows are regularly organized for those who like to stay out late. These occasionally showcase well-known folklore performances.

Since the hotel is quite far from the beach, a shuttle transports guests along a bumpy road to the Beach Club (*Mon to Thu 9:30am to 5:30pm, Fri to Sun until 6pm*). This charming *bohío* is right by the beach and has a bar, restaurant (small selection of dishes) and a small pool. Even if you aren't staying at the Coronado Club Resort, do check out this neat spot, and enjoy a good meal (see p168) or just a refreshing drink on the pool-side terrace.

The Shangri La
$$$$$
pb, hw, ≡, ≈, tv
Playa Coronado, Apdo 8357, Panamá 7
Mon to Fri
☎ 223-8597
☎ 223-0895
Sat ☎ 264-6317
≈ 269-0633
The Shangri La is an interesting form of lodging for families or small groups. Overlooking the beach and framed by greenery, the four villas have large plate glass windows looking out onto

the gardens and the sea. Each villa is two storeys high and has three bedrooms, two bathrooms, direct beach access and a shoreside terrace. There is also a small pool available for those who prefer not to swim in the sea. In order to benefit from reduced rates, go during the week, when prices can drop by as much as 50%.

Club Gaviota
$$$$-$$$$$
Mon to Fri 8am to 5pm, Sat and Sun 8am to 7pm
Playa Coronado, from the main road leading to the beach, turn right after the little chapel, then follow the signs for the Club; Apdo 5929, Panamá 2
☎ 227-4929
≈ 227-4969
The owner of the Club Gaviota is in charge of renting out second homes in the area. There are many fully-equipped homes available in a particularly quiet and lush setting. Although this is a rather expensive option, it may appeal to those traveling in a group. All of the club's equipment and services are available to clients.

Hotel Río Mar
$$$
pb, hw, ≈, ≡, ℜ, #
Playa Río Mar, 3 km from the Interamericana
☎ 223-0192
≈ 264-2270
Hotel Río Mar rents out semi-detached *cabañas*. These are simple and adequately comfortable. Some have no

bathrooms, are poorly soundproofed and lack screens. Ask for a *cabaña* away from the restaurant and the noise. For a fee of B/. 5 per family, visitors can use the showers as well as the locker room; pool access costs B/. 2 per adult.

Hotel Playa Corona
$$-$$$
pb, hw, ≡, ℜ, K, tv
Playa Corona, 2 km from the Interamericana
☎ 250-8037
Set in a particularly pleasant location, this hotel overlooks the beach and offers several types of accommodation, from small, cute rooms with two beds to apartments with two or three rooms. There are also large suites and air-conditioned trailers for those on a tighter budget, all of which is surrounded by verdant grounds.

Cabañas La Veraneras
$$-$$$
sb, ⊗, K, ℝ, ℜ, tv
Playa Santa Clara ☎
993-3313
☎ 230-1415
≈ 993-3313
The Cabañas La Veraneras are little houses perched on a hilltop that can accommodate from two to six people. The kitchenette and living room are on the ground floor while the bedrooms are on the second floor. The cabañas offer peace and quiet, and a small terrace with a view of the sea in the distance. Hammocks are also

available. Good price/quality ratio.

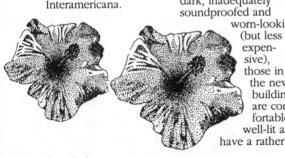Cabañas Las Sirenas
$$$ for 5 people
$$$$ for 7 people based on a 2 night minimum
pb, ≡, tv, K
Playa Santa Clara, 3 km from the Interamericana, in Ciudad de Panamá
☎ 232-5841
⇆ 232-5842
in Santa Clara
☎ 993-3235

This small hotel complex with 11 semi-detached units is located in a superb flowery setting next to the beach. The decor inside the small houses is tasteful and the landscaping is particularly well done. The kitchenettes are well-equipped but there is no hot water. For the setting and facilities, this is a good deal. There is no restaurant on site, but there are two supermarkets (*supermercados*) close by so you can stock up for a reasonable price. The first one is located at the intersection of the Interamericana and the main road leading to the beach; the second is in Río Hato, about 8 km farther west on the Interamericana.

El Valle de Antón

Cabañas Potosí
$
pb
☎ 993-6181
in Ciudad de Panamá
☎ 229-4240

These small, very simple cabins are located in a lovely setting, and are ideal for travellers on a tight budget.

Hotel Greco
$
pb, hw, ≡, ℜ, #, ≈
in El Valle on the right side of the main road at the entrance to the village
☎ 993-6149

Small *cabañas* in a pretty, natural setting. A simple but clean hotel.

Hotel Club Campestre
$$-$$$
pb, hw, ⊗, ♯, tv, ℜ
Calle El Hato, at the entrance to the village, on the right side; shortly after passing the supermercado, take the second road to your right
☎ 983-6146
☎/⇆ 983-6460

The somewhat passé charm of the Club Campestre has rooms with various comfort levels. While those in the main building are dark, inadequately soundproofed and worn-looking (but less expensive), those in the new building are comfortable, well-lit and have a rather

pleasant decor. Unfortunately, the bathrooms are too small and lack privacy because their windows look out directly onto the passageway leading to the rooms. Although the hotel claims to have a pool, during our visit it had been neglected and looked more like a swamp! Also, the old-fashioned restaurant with its outdated decorating style was reminiscent of a large school cafeteria and not conducive to convivial dining. Despite these inconveniences, the hotel is acceptable because of its lush green environment and impressive mountains nearby. Speaking of impressive, you can also have a look at the *ranas doradas* or "golden frogs", for which the area is famous, in a (too) small cage to the right of the hotel entrance.

The Cabañas Gysell
$$-$$$
sb, hw, ⊗
at the entrance to the village, on the right side after the supermercado, corner Calle El Hato and Av. Principal, El Valle
☎ 983-6507
☎ 232-6604

Located at the entrance to the village, the Cabañas Gysell has a few rooms that can accommodate from two to six people. It is clean, relatively comfortable and quiet, despite its proximity to the main road. Decoration is adequate but very basic.

Los Capitanes
$$$-$$$$
sb, hw, tv, ⊗, ℜ
Calle de la Cooperativa, Apdo
87-4381, Panamá 7
☎ *983-6080*
↔ *983-6505*
Whether in the main circular building or one of the outbuildings, the bedrooms of the hotel will charm you. There are many types of accommodations offered, from rooms for two people to apartments for four with a separate day room. The rooms in the main building, which also houses a restaurant, come with a small but pleasant balcony. Regardless of where you stay, you can rely on tastefully decorated and comfortable rooms. In addition to the tranquility, visitors can enjoy the view of the beautiful, well-maintained gardens with the mountains in the background.

Hotel Rincón Vallero
$$$-$$$$
bkfst incl.; sb, hw, ⊗, tv, ♯, ℜ, ≈
at the entrance to the village, just after the supermercado, take the first two lefts
☎ *983-6175*
☎ *226-7554*
↔ *226-6567*
Bearing a curious resemblance to a *hacienda*, the Hotel Rincón Vallero consists of several lodgings within a small flowered garden complete with a small fish pond where ducks and fish peacefully cohabit. Charmingly decorated rooms can accommodate from two

to four people. Unfortunately, they are somewhat poorly soundproofed and their proximity to each other as well as to the restaurant and pool does not help matters. In addition, the mattresses are not too comfortable. These little inconveniences detract from the comfort of this establishment, but its country charm compensates for them. The hotel is at least worth a look.

Restaurants

Around Capira

Cafeteria Parque El Lago
$$$
every day 10am to 9pm
located on the Interamericana, 1.8 km west of Capira
The Cafeteria Parque El Lago is a popular meeting place for fishermen who frequent the artificial lake. Inside a quaint, gabled building decorated with pretty tables and wood and leather chairs, the cafeteria has a distinctly country atmosphere. Good meat dishes, *ceviche* or *corvina* for B/. 10 each, await at the counter. For a quick snack, the *bollo de maiz* (a sort of corn mousse, enveloped in a banana leaf) is delicious, or you can try a plate of fried *platanos* for as little as B/. 5. Those who would like

to sample some of the lake's offerings (duck, oysters and fish), a pretty terrace with a view of the lake provides a wonderful setting. The staff are very courteous and friendly.

Isla Taboga

Restaurant Chu
$
on the main street of the village, 200 m to the left of the pier, take the road going up
☎ *250-2035*
☎ *263-6933*
This small restaurant is located in the hotel of the same name, overlooking the beach. In a lovely old-fashioned colonial setting, you can enjoy traditional fish and chicken dishes on the pleasant terrace. Good fruit juice too - try it!

Restaurant Hotel Taboga
$
about 300 m to the right of the pier
☎ *250-2122*
☎ *264-6096*
☎ *264-1748*
In addition to the hotel's restaurant which serves a selection of Panamanian and international dishes, the hotel also has a cafeteria where you can order simpler meals.

Isla Contadora

Gallo Nero
$$$
☎ *250-4061*
The small, unpretentious Gallo Nero restaurant offers a variety of meat and fish dishes,

and above all a view of the island's airfield! This means you have front row seats for the take-offs and landings of the small planes from the covered terrace. If you aren't too hungry, you can also just enjoy an excellent imported beer or share a delicious chicken and mushroom pizza in the relaxed and pleasant atmosphere. The owner speaks English and German.

Michael's Pizzería
$

close to the airport runway
A simple, unpretentious place for inexpensive pizza and ice cream.

El Galeón
$$$
every day 3pm to 10pm
on the Paseo de los Guaymíes, to the northwest of the airport runway
The small El Galeón restaurant features various fish and seafood daily specials in a non-existent decor (notwithstanding the pleasant view of the sea). Inconsistent quality and a little expensive.

Punta Chame to Playa Santa Clara

Bar Restaurante Punta Chame
$$
Punta Chame, on the left at the end of the road leading to the point
Very pleasant restaurant in an enchanting setting, with palm trees, a good view and a covered terrace. The

interior of the restaurant is charming, with orchids on every table. Their *Langostinos al Ajillo* or *a la Parilla* (B/. 8) is good, as is their steak (*B/. 4*) and *pollo al Horno (barely B/. 4.50)*. For die-hard *fast food* lovers a *queso hamburguesa* is available for B/. 3.50. Finally, a good *flan de la casa* to finish up a meal that is not quite gourmet, but certainly filling.

Gorgona Jayes
$$
2 km from the Interamericana on an unpaved road
☎ *223-7775*
☎ *240-6095*
The restaurant at the Gorgona Jayes hotel serves basic Panamanian cuisine, so it is essentially for the pretty terrace adjoining a small flower garden that people come here. The staff is courteous and friendly.

Los Ches
$
to the right on the Interamericana going west, just before the turnoff for Playa Coronado
This small, charming, well-decorated restaurant has tables set on a covered terrace. Simple cuisine (grilled chicken, spaghetti, etc.) and generous portions.

Parrillada Malibu
$$
Thu to Tue 8am to 11pm
at the intersection of the Interamericana and the turnoff for Playa Coronado
Located on the left side of the main road lead-

ing to Playa Coronado, the small restaurant has a large terrace covered with tiles and surrounded by trees and flowering plants. Among the various meals on the menu, you can try *corvina* (served with many different sauces!), octopus, chicken or just simply spaghetti. You can also enjoy delicious fresh fruit juices (a rarity) in lovely verdant surroundings for as little as B/. 1.

The Club
$$$$
Tue to Sun 6pm to 10pm
Playa Coronado, on the main road leading to the beach, after the guards station and just before the bombeiros station, turn left on Avenida P. Prieta for 1 km
☎ *240-4444*
☎ *264-3164*
Set in a residential neighbourhood in the heart of the Coronado Club Suites Resort complex, the Club restaurant serves elaborate cuisine. *Yuca sanchoco, calamares a la romana, ceviche, rollitos de pato a la naranja, corvina en salsa de coco, lenguado a la champaña, medallones de langosta en finas herbas* or *centallo gratinado* are just some of the possibilities.

A half-moon-shaped window offers a view of the gardens from the refined decor of the dining room. Service is professional and attentive.

La Terraza
$$$$
every day 6am to 10pm
in the same hotel as The Club (see above); facing the pool
For those who prefer a lighter meal, La Terraza is another restaurant in the Coronado Club Suites that serves international and Panamanian cuisine. This is also an interesting place for breakfast. Besides the fact that both restaurants are set in particularly luxurious setting, they might be considered the best restaurants of the region.

Club Gaviota
$$
Playa Coronado, on the main road leading to the beach, turn right at the little chapel and follow the signs for the club; Apartado 5929, Panamá 2
☎ ***225-1559***
☎ ***227-4969***
This private club with its pretty pool is a lovely place to enjoy a meal or just a drink. They offer simple but delicious chicken, fish and seafood dishes. The restaurant is tastefully furnished and the bar is located under a traditional *bohío*. The setting, overlooking the beach, offers unending spectacular views of the coast, much to the delight of photographers. Since access is reserved for members of the club, an admission fee of B/. 3 is charged. Courteous and friendly staff do their utmost to put you at ease.

Restaurante San Carlos
$
from the Interamericana turn left onto the main road at the flashing light for the turnoff for Playa San Carlos; once in the center of town, turn right opposite the Palacio Municipal, then left opposite the chapel and the Caja de Securidad Social, and follow the signs to the beach where the restaurant is located
This restaurant is set up in a very interesting way. After passing through the large, curious jaguar-shaped doorway, you'll find yourself in a circular room, decorated with pre-Columbian inspired frescoes, that opens onto the beach. The restaurant has been taken over by IPAT and was undergoing renovations during our visit in January, 1999. It is scheduled to re-open in early 2000.

Río Mar
$$
every day, 9am to 11pm
Playa Río Mar, 3 km from the Interamericana
☎ ***223-0192***
With a solid reputation among Panamanians for its seafood, the Río Mar offers a variety of dishes served with rice in a lovely setting. Savour the *camarones* or *langostinos* that have made this place's reputation, on the large terrace (called the Rancho Bar), facing the sea. Though the menu seems extensive, the choice is actually limited and the dishes are prepared rather simply.

Restaurante Hotel Playa Corona
$
Playa Corona, 2 km from the Interamericana
☎ ***250-8027***
This small beachfront restaurant in the hotel, with its kitschy decor, serves simple, classic Panamanian cuisine in a particularly lush and leafy setting.

Los Camisones
$$
every day 10am to 10pm
4.8 km west of the turnoff for Playa Corona, turn right off the Interamericana on an unpaved road
Located up on a hill away from the Interamericana, Los Camisones serves Panamanian cuisine under a pleasant *bohío* decorated with plants and flowers.

Restaurante Don Jacobo
$$$
every day 8am to 10pm
turn left off the Interamericana at the "Centro Turistico Salud y Felicidad" sign shortly after the turnoff for Playa Santa Clara
☎ ***993-3536***
For travellers who crave the sea's bounty, the Restaurante Don Jacobo, also a fish and seafood wholesaler, has the distinct advantage of stocking exceptionally fresh goods and a good selection of dishes. The restaurant has a lovely covered terrace with finely crafted leather chairs. This is a good address to remember for a meal and drink, and is close to the Interamericana.

Las Veraneras
$$
every day 8am to 7pm
Playa Santa Clara
☎ *993-3313*
The pleasant Las Veraneras restaurant receives its guests be neath a giant beachside *palapa* reached from the hotel (see p165) by a series of stairs and a long footbridge. Al though there is nothing fancy on the menu (mostly fish and sea food), the view of the ocean from the particu larly long, lovely beach makes dining very pleasant.

El Valle de Antón

Restaurante Santa Librada
$
on the right when coming from San Carlos, between the Intel and the post office
The Restaurante Santa Librada boasts a good reputation for its Pana manian cuisine and its friendly service.

Los Capitanes
$$
Calle de la Cooperativa
☎ *983-6080*
Set in a circular, open-air room, the Los Capitanes hotel's res taurant is worth a detour. For less than B/. 10, guests can enjoy a meal including soup, main dish and dessert. In addition to typical Panamánian foods, the restaurant also serves German specialities, as the owner is of German descent. Good home-style cooking. After

eating, you can relax in the garden and admire the majestic mountains encircling the valley in the distance.

Rincón Vallero
$$$
at the entrance to the village; just after passing the supermercado, take the first two lefts
☎ *983-6175*
Facing a garden with a fish pond, the Rincón Vallero hotel's restau rant features classical Panamánian dishes. There are no surprises and the prices are a bit expensive, but the country-style decor is quite pleasant.

Restaurante Hotel Greco
$
in El Valle, on the right side of the main street, at the entrance to the village
☎ *993-6149*
This small, unpreten tious restaurant offers a daily menu of local cuisine. The choice is limited (only three or four dishes), so it is better to arrive relative ly early.

Entertainment

Isla Contadora

Captain Morgan's Beach Bar
Mon and Tue, Thu to Sat 3pm to 3am, happy hour from 9pm to 10pm
For a beer and a great beach-side location, head to Captain Mor-gan's Beach Bar where,

besides a guaranteed good time in the eve-ning, you can see the planes taking off over your head. The bar is actually located just down from the end of the airfield. Lots of fun!

El Galeón
$$$
every day 3pm to 10pm
on the Paseo de los Guaymíes, to the northwest of the airport runway
The small El Galeón restaurant has a pool table as well as a small terrace with a view of the sea.

Shopping

Isla Contadora

Playa Canoa
every day 9am to noon and 3pm to 4pm
Playa Canoa
Shell collectors won't want to miss a stop at the Playa Canoa shop, where for about B/. 10 you can pick up some fine pieces. Very pretty sculptures created by the Guaymíes people are on sale, though they are pricey.

El Valle de Antón

If you are ever passing by El Valle on a Sunday, do not pass up an opportunity to go to the **Mercado Artesanal** (*Sun 7am to 5pm*), where people, mostly Amerindian, from the surrounding country-side come to sell soap-stone sculptures, rugs, sweaters, pottery, hats, leather items, basketwork and many other crafts. There is also a wide selection of orchids. This market will appeal to those who want to bring back a few souvenirs without spending (too) much.

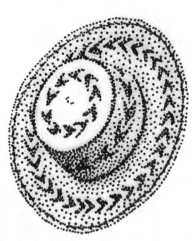

Panama Hat

Old Canons - Portobelo

Province of Colón

The Province of Colón (pop. 168,000) has a glorious past, for the Central American isthmus was "discovered" here.

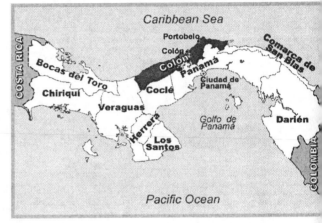

It was also the site of the first colonial settlements in Central America: Nombre de Dios and Portobelo on the Atlantic coast. Because these two towns were linked to the Pacific coast by overland trails, significant trade developed with the mother country, Spain.

Indeed, the new colony was ideally located along the trade route between South America and Europe, and riches from Peru and Ecuador passed through it. However, due to piracy and other troubles in Europe, Spain abandoned this route for good in 1746, after which the area began to decline. It was not until the mid-19th century that the province of Colón became important again, first with the creation of a railway line linking the two oceans, then with the titanic excavation work of the Panamá canal.

Today, the province's main economic activity is still linked to the canal and Colón's Zona Libre, one of the largest free zones in the world. Moreover, the province's tourist industry has been experiencing significant growth over the last few years. More and more people are visiting Portobelo, a World Heritage Site, and Isla Grande. Unfortunately, Colón, the capital of the province, is still the country's most crime-ridden city, thus curbing the attractiveness of a region worth visiting nonetheless. Much like Bocas del Toro, the region is characterized by its population, largely composed of descendants of African slaves and Afro-Caribbean immigrants hired for the construction of the canal.

Here more than elsewhere, English is widely spoken. During festivities such as the carnival, you can admire a one-of-a-kind folk dance, the *Congo*, whose rhythm and instruments recall the population's African origins.

Finding Your Way Around

By Plane

Two airlines offer direct flights between Colón and Ciudad de Panamá:

Mapiex-Aero

Ciudad de Panamá to Colón
*Departure: Mon to Fri 6:30am, 9:15am and 4pm;
Sat and Sun 7am and 4pm
Travel time: 1 hour
Cost: B/. 55 one way*

Colón to Ciudad de Panamá
*Departure: Mon to Fri 7:45am, 10:30am and 5:15pm;
Sat and Sun 8:15am and 5:15pm*

Colón Airport
☎ *721-0841*
☎ *721-0843*

Aeroperlas

Ciudad de Panamá to Colón
*Departure: Mon to Fri nine morning flights (first at 7am, last at 9:45am);
five afternoon flights (first at 4:45pm, last at 5:40pm);
no weekend flights
Travel time: 15 min
Cost: B/. 26 one way*

Colón to Ciudad de Panamá
*Departure: Mon to Fri five morning flights (first at 7:25am, last at 9:05am);
five afternoon flights (first at 4:20pm, last at 6:05pm);
no weekend flights*

Colón Airport
☎ *721-1195*
☎ *721-1230*

By Car

There are two roads to reach **Colón** from the capital. The faster way is to take the *Corredor* toll highway north from Albrook Airport or from Avenida Simón Bolívar in the La Cresta district. It will lead you straight to the Transístmica, which links the city of Colón to Ciudad de Panamá. At press time, another toll highway was under construction and slated to be open at the beginning of the year 2000.

The longer route is on a beautiful road that goes through the countryside and Parque Nacional Soberanía.

From Ciudad de Panamá, take the Carretera Gaillard and keep going north toward the Miraflores and Pedro Miguel locks. This highway runs past the Soberanía park entrance. About 10 km after the intersection for the entrance to the park, turn left before the overpass, then, at the top of the hill, turn left again on the main road. Here the road becomes busier, less beautiful and more commercial. 19 km from the turnoff for the park, you will pass over a branch of the Río Chagres, then at 39.8 km, the Río Gatún. Upon entering the city, keep going straight ahead at the sign "Zona Libre".

For **Portobelo**, the turnoff is about 66 km along the *Transístmica* on the right-hand side of the road when coming from Ciudad de Panamá, at the village of Sabanista. Keep a sharp eye out, for the road is not very well posted. Once past a footbridge overhanging the Transístmica, you will notice the Supermercado Rey; make a right turn after it.

Proceed along the main road that runs through the village for close to 2.8 km, then turn right toward Maria Chiquita, then Portobelo. The road was recently repaved and is thus in excellent condition.

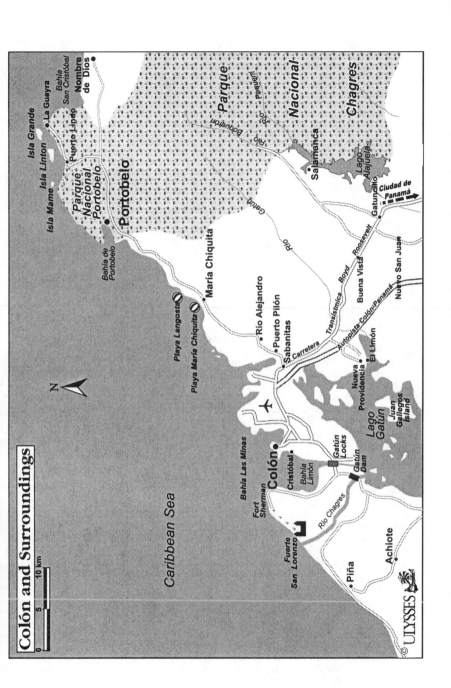

Colón and Surroundings

0 5 10 km

Caribbean Sea

Isla Grande
Isla Linton
Isla Mame
La Guayra
Puerto Lindo
Bahía San Cristóbal
Nombre de Dios

Parque Nacional Portobelo
Portobelo

Bahía de Portobelo

Parque Nacional Chagres

Río Pequení

Río Boquerón

Río Gatún

Salamanca
Lago Alajuela

Gatuncillo
Ciudad de Panamá

María Chiquita

Playa Langosta
Playa María Chiquita

Río Alejandro
Puerto Pilón
Sabanitas
Carretera

Autopista Colón-Panamá
Transístmica
Boyd
Roosevelt
Buena Vista

El Limón
Nueva Providencia

Nuevo San Juan

Bahía Las Minas

Colón
Cristóbal
Bahía Limón

Gatún Locks
Gatún Dam

Lago Gatún

Juan Gallegos Island

Fort Sherman

Fuerte San Lorenzo

Río Chagres

Piña

Achiote

N

© ULYSSES

For **Fuerte San Lorenzo**, at the exit for Colón, drive toward the Gatún locks and follow the main road, always keeping to the right. Later you will see an intersection with signs to the fort.

Just before you arrive at the locks, some 3 km from the sign, you will see a control post with a gate straight in front of you. Tell the people at the post where you are going, and you will be asked to cross a small bridge right at the foot of the gates of the lock. The drive over this bridge is most impressive, especially when you consider that those turn-of-the-century gates are holding back thousands of tons of water. Continue for 13.7 km to Fort Sherman, an important military base used as a checkpoint, then cross the town of Fort Sherman. Turn left at the end of the street (14.6 km), and then left again 200 m farther on. Soon after, the asphalt gives way to dirt and gravel. At a turnoff 21.9 km farther on, you have a choice: to the right, the road leads directly to Fuerte San Lorenzo (22.4 km); to the left it leads to the seaside, where you can enjoy a fine view of the fort from below.

To get to **Isla Grande**, take the road leading to the village of Portobelo (see above) and, once past the village, continue along the main

road for close to 9 km to the turnoff for Nombre de Dios. Once there, take the left road at the turnoff, which runs to the village of Puerto Lindo (11 km farther), then, 5 km beyond, the village of La Guayra; from here a small boat goes to the island. The crossing, which costs B/. 1, takes a little over 5 min. The road from Portobelo to Isla Grande is in dismal condition and impassable with a touring car after heavy rain. The trip takes at least 45 min.

By Bus

To get to **Colón** from Ciudad de Panamá, go to the bus stop at the corner of Avenida Perú and Calle 30 Este (*in front of the Gran Hotel Soloy*). Buses leave about every 20 min from Monday to Friday, and every hour on weekends.

Depending on the type of bus (regular or express), the trip takes 2 to 2.5 hours and costs from B/. 2 to B/. 2.50. The opening of the new toll highway should cut the trip down by 30 min to an hour.

Note: a new bus station is under construction near the Albrook Airport and, if all goes according to plan, all bus services should be transferred there by the year 2000.

There are two ways to get to **Portobelo**. The first is to take a bus from Colón (*B/. 2.50; Mon to Sun, Ave. del Frente; travel time: about 1 hour*), which stops in Sabanista. The second way is to take a bus from Ciudad de Panamá to Sabanista, and from there take the bus from Colón to Portobelo.

To get to **Isla Grande** you first have to go to the little village of La Guayra, where plenty of ferrymen can take you to the island for B/. 1 per person. Though there is bus service to La Guayra from the cities of Colón, Sabanista and Portobelo, bear in mind that it is irregular and depends on weather conditions, among other things. An alternative way is to go to Portobelo and take a taxi to La Guayra. Because the roads are not paved east of Portobelo, they can become impassable after a few days of heavy rainfall, thus it is best to get there in an all-terrain vehicle.

Exploring

Colón

The present-day town of Colón was founded as recently as 1850. It owes its origins to the Trans-isthmian Panamá

Railroad, on which work started in Limón Bay, just a few metres offshore on a small island then named Manzanillo. With the arrival of scores of workers, the place quickly turned into a genuine town and many shops opened for business. The island was soon reunited with the mainland by a major jetty and was thus transformed into a peninsula.

While the town took on the name of Colón, a port was built and named Cristóbal. The first train to cross the isthmus from coast to coast did so on January 28, 1855, and to commemorate the event, the U.S.-based Panamá Railroad Company asked permission to rename the town Aspinwall City, after the initiator of the project, American William H. Aspinwall, a wealthy businessman from New York City (see box). The request was denied, however, and the city's name henceforth remained unchanged.

Later on, though the city experienced some expansion, it really started to develop with the construction of the canal, begun by the French in 1880. Thousands of people of all backgrounds worked on the canal, contributing to the development and prosperity of Colón. With its busy port, the city prospered and developed a repu-

William H. Aspinwall

In 1850, a wealthy New York merchant, William H. Aspinwall, along with various associates, created the Panama Railroad Company to build a railway line linking the Atlantic to the Pacific coast of Panama. With a milliondollar budget, these entrepreneurs likely did not expect the bill to reach just under a whopping $9 million before the exceedingly difficult and downright deadly work was completed!

Fortunately, the operating permit was valid for a period of 99 years. A oneway train ticket was priced at $25 in first class and $10 in second class – the most expensive train fare on the planet for such a short distance (about 50 km)! The railway turned out to be a success, however: between 1850 and 1869 no less than 600,000 travellers a year took this line and a record 1,200,000 passengers was reached in 1889.

Province of Colón

tation as a city full of shops and restaurants, with an exciting nightlife. Beautiful homes were built here, many neo-colonial in style, giving Colón the appearance of a Louisiana city.

In the 1980s, various factors (economic crisis, fewer cruiseships) resulted in the city becoming progressively poorer. The city's decline was accentuated by a series of economic and social factors, such as the establishment of financial centres in the capital, by-laws that discouraged effective urban management, and an increase in un-

employment. The situation was further aggravated by a significant migration to the nearby capital.

Today, Colón is still Panamá's second most populated city (pop. 140,000), but it is also in a state of decay. Poverty, social hardship and unemployment (almost 46%) are increasing in alarming proportions. Nevertheless, the city does not lack attractions – its historical buildings with their old-world charm; its Zona Libre (free zone), where activity is beginning to pick up; its shops with unbeatable prices; its view of

The Panama Railroad Company

The French were the first to draw up plans for a railway that would cross the Central American isthmus, but in 1848, after presenting the project to the government of New Grenada (which was made up of the Republic of Colombia and Panamá), they abandoned the project because of the enormous expense it entailed. At the same time, gold was discovered in California, and many adventurers in the eastern United States began to move west to seek their fortunes. The fastest way to reach the western United States back then was through Panamá. In order to develop the West more quickly, Congress commissioned George Law and William H. Aspinwall to create two private steamship routes. The first route was to run between New York, New Orleans and the Bay of Chagres, and the second from the Ciudad de Panamá to the west coast of the United States. However, because crossing the isthmus overland was long and difficult, Aspinwall and his associates decided to build the railroad right across it, creating the first transoceanic railroad in the world. After the government of New Granada granted Aspinwall and his associates ownership of the railroad for 49 years in 1850, the Panama Railroad Company was born.

Work quickly started on the Atlantic coast on the island of Manzanillo, in the Bay of Limon, just metres away from the mainland. With the arrival of many workers, the site soon grew into a small town called Colón. Though an agreement was reached with the government of Granada that the railway be completed within six years, the workers had to overcome enormous obstacles: rugged terrain, extreme heat and humidity and jungle-like vegetation. Despite these troubles, the railroad was finished one year ahead of schedule. On January 28, 1855, the first train crossed the isthmus, and the transoceanic railroad was a success!

Despite its rapid success, the Panama Railroad Company began to see its profits decline in the 1880s and was bought by the French *Compagnie Universelle du Canal* in 1887. One of the reasons for its decline was the heavy transportation taxes levied by the government of New Grenada in 1863, after extending the Panama Railroad Company's concession from 49 to 99 years. But the main reason for the company's decline was the competition from new railway lines in the United States. Under the French, the transoceanic railway ceased to be a passenger train and was used to help build the canal instead. Then in 1889, history repeated itself when the *Compagnie Universelle du Canal* went bankrupt and lost control of the canal and the railway. The Americans took over once again by buying the canal from the French in 1904 and continued to use the railway to build the canal. Shortly before the canal's completion, the railway was relocated to a higher level of the canal, where it can still be seen today.

the Caribbean and its crystalline waters... Given all this, if a serious social and urban renewal policy were implemented, Colón could become a very appealing city. The new owners of the beautiful Washington Hotel have demonstrated this, and a number of other buildings could be used as examples, proving that the city is worth renewing. For the moment, however, a visit to Colón can bring on a sense of unease – what any sensitive tourist would feel at the sight of such poverty-stricken neighbourhoods.

Despite all this, in recent years, with help from the local authorities and merchants' associations, various people have decided to take the future of the city into their own hands seeing that the city could benefit greatly from its Zona Libre. A first step was taken with respect to legislation that prohibits the service sector, for example banks, insurance or security companies, from conducting business in the Zona Libre. These companies, by necessity, must be located near the zone and should contribute greatly to an economic renewal. The existing Zona Libre is truly isolated from the city, and with global trade on the rise it is undergoing unprecedented commercial development.

There is every reason to believe that this new measure, once adopted, along with the present opening up of world markets, can only benefit Colón and restore its past prosperity and *joie de vivre*. Many people already see a brighter future for Colón, as numerous houses and properties have supposedly been bought by Asians, Arabs and East Indians. New apartment buildings have also cropped up in certain neighbourhoods.

Some guides advise against visiting this city, for safety reasons. While safety is indeed a real concern, and not to be ignored, it is our impression that as long as certain guidelines are respected (see p 54), a visit to this city is a must. In addition to dropping in at the Hotel Washington or the cathedral, you will be able to shop at extraordinarily low prices, and thus make a small contribution to the city's prosperity.

Also worth mentioning is that the city prides itself on having spawned nine world boxing champions, a sport that has always enjoyed popularity here. It was also in Colón that Isabel Perón, a singer in one of the city's many cabarets, met the Argentinian dictator then living here in exile.

The Hotel Washington ★★

(*beside the sea, at the end of the Avenida del Frente*). This very handsome, churrigueresco building was recently renovated and painted pink and white. Its architecture alone makes it worth a visit. The lobby is of interest not only for its luxurious decor, but also for its sheer size. Outside, at the back of the building, you can enjoy a fine view of the ships off in the distance, waiting to enter the canal. Even if you do not stay here, have a drink on the terrace, and take some time to admire this magnificent building, where Peron, Argentina's former dictator, once lived in exile. On the left side of the hotel is the house where Ferdinand de Lesseps lived while he supervised the building of the canal.

El Catedral

(*on Calle 5, near Avenida Amador Guerrero*). This cathedral is worth a visit for its handsome pediment. The harmonious interior is adorned with a lovely altar.

At the corner of Avenida Bolívar and Calle 6 is another fine building, graced with handsome wrought-iron columns. Although it has not been restored, it shows that the city still has significant architectural potential.

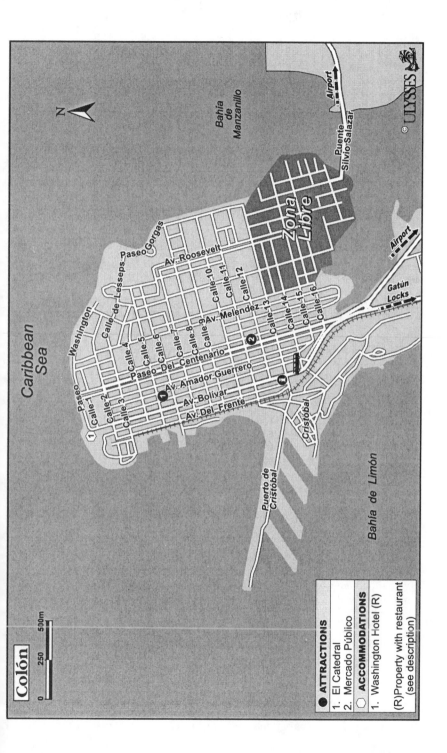

Colón

0 250 500m

Caribbean Sea

Bahía de Manzanillo

N

Airport

Puente Silvio Salazar

Paseo Gorgas

Av. Roosevelt

Calle-10
Calle-11
Calle-12

Paseo de Lesseps

Washington

Paseo

Calle-4
Calle-5
Calle-6
Calle-7
Calle-8
Calle-9
Av. Melendez
Calle-13
Calle-14
Calle-15
Calle-16

Paseo Del Centenario

Calle-1
Calle-2
Calle-3

Av. Amador Guerrero

Av. Bolívar

Av. Del Frente

Zona Libre

Airport

Gatún Locks

Puerto de Cristóbal

Cristóbal

Bahía de Limón

© ULYSSES

ATTRACTIONS
1. El Catedral
2. Mercado Público

ACCOMMODATIONS
1. Washington Hotel (R)

(R) Property with restaurant (see description)

The Zona Libre
(*Mon to Fri 8am to 5pm, closed Sat and Sun; entrance on Avenida Roosevelt*) is in fact a giant distribution centre. Vast quantities of goods arrive here from the countries where they are produced (like Japan), and are then combined with other in-coming goods and shipped out to a multitude of countries. Essentially, the Zona Libre functions as follows:

First, a freighter from Japan arrives full of fax machines; a freighter from Taiwan arrives full of colour televisions; a freighter from Korea arrives full of cars; a freighter from Australia arrives full of aluminum ingots.

Then, some of the fax machines, colour televisions, cars and aluminum ingots are loaded onto five freighters heading to Brazil, Argentina, the east coast of the United States, Chile and Morocco, respectively.

And that's how the zone works. Since the merchandise can be imported here without duty as long as it is immediately re-exported, this place is like a huge international zone where companies can redistribute goods and even package them.

For this reason, a number of companies take advantage of this trans-

shipment to put the appropriate instruction manuals with the appliances depending on where they are being shipped. In our example, instruction manuals in English, Spanish, Brazilian, and Arabic were included with the fax machines and colour televisions before the merchandise was shipped out. The Zona Libre is also a huge warehouse. Merchandise is shipped to the zone from the country where it is manufactured and is stored here until orders come in, at which point it is redistributed to customers.

Due to the proximity of the Panamá Canal, through which all freighters shipping goods between the east coast of the Americas and Asia and even Europe must pass, the Zona Libre is ideally located. Of course, Panamá's inexpensive labour and the quality of the financial and administrative services available here also play a role in the phenomenal development of this zone.

Surrounded by walls, the Zona Libre was created in 1948, and now employs 13,000 people and covers 300 ha. With over 1,600 firms, it is the second largest free zone in the world, after Hong Kong in size and volume of business, generating $4 billion a year in total. Because it is a duty-free zone, it at-

tracts numerous wholesale and retail buyers from around the world who place their orders here. The Zona Libre was initially restricted to one district of Colón, but now also encompasses another area on the outskirts of town, near the France Field Airport; the two zones are linked by a bridge. Given the ever-growing demand, the government is already contemplating extending the free zone to other areas.

While the offer may seem tempting, there are a number of hurdles to be overcome, both before and while you shop. First you must show your passport at the entrance. The guards may seem a trifle picky, but this formality should not be too much of a bother. Second, you cannot take your purchases with you; the next time you see them will be on the day you leave, at the airport. This of course is to avoid fraud and the entry of tax-free goods into the country.

Given all these difficulties, if you are shopping for minor purchases, it is much better to go to downtown Colón, where prices can be just as good – provided, of course, that you haggle! In some cases, 60% off the advertised price is possible. Despite these major discounts, however, note that in most cases, electronics bought here may be more expensive than those available in North America.

Fuerte San Lorenzo

Set amidst magnificent surroundings, Fuerte San Lorenzo was erected at the mouth of the Río Chagres in the 16th century, during the reign of King Philip II of Spain. At the time, the Río Chagres was a major maritime route used by the Spanish to transport precious goods from Ecuador and Peru to the Atlantic coast. After having reached the fort of San Lorenzo, the merchandise was then shipped to Portobelo and Cartagena, where other goods were loaded onto the ships and sent to Spain.

Despite being virtually impregnable, the fortress was attacked in January of 1671 and occupied by pirate Joseph Bradley, the right-hand man of sinister filibuster Henry Morgan. Bradley died during the siege, so Morgan decided to settle here for a while to strengthen his army. His goal was to attack Ciudad de Panamá via the river. In February of 1671, equipped with a fleet of about 30 ships, he set out to conquer the capital and, after an arduous

journey upstream and a short-lived battle, Morgan seized the city. After several days of pillaging, Morgan and his crew returned to Fort San Lorenzo, where, after a brief rest, they embarked for Jamaica. Morgan did not fail to live up to his notorious reputation and set fire to the fortress upon his departure, leaving nothing but ruins and desolation in his wake.

After having been fully rebuilt by the Spanish during a period of relative calm, the fort was stormed once again in 1740, this time by Sir Edward Vernon. Commissioned by Great Britain following the outbreak of the Anglo-Spanish war in 1739, Vernon was assigned to seize the enemy's colonial fortresses, among which were Portobelo and Fort San Lorenzo. After being destroyed by the English, the Spanish abandoned Fuerte San Lorenzo for good.

Today, besides an old gunpowder factory and rooms in which supplies were stored, you can see several old canons on site, some of which still boast various inscriptions bearing the effigy of the Spanish crown. After having enjoyed the unobstructed view of the sea and the river, take a visit to the trenches where, four centuries ago, soldiers were sent

Sensitivas

While strolling through the site of Fuerte San Lorenzo, you may notice interesting little plants on the ground. These are a kind of mimosa called *sensitivas* in Panamá. Touch them gently and see how quickly their leaves retract and even, if you persist, one of its branches coiling up its trunk! Out of respect for nature, do not pick the plants to take back home with you, because they have a great deal of trouble adapting to other climes.

Province of Colón

to defend the colony. Imagine the conditions in these trenches: the soldiers were isolated and surrounded by alien and hostile flora and fauna, at a time when people still believed in devils and demons. Both the fortress and the town Portobelo were listed as a UNESCO World Heritage Site in 1980.

Portobelo

Portobelo owes its existence to pirates. Indeed, it was after the destruction of the village of Nombre de Dios in 1596 by pirate Francis Drake that the Spanish built the Castillo San Felipe farther west, in a bay named Portobelo, in 1597. That same year, several other forts as well as a port and a church were also built, thus marking the official foundation of the village of Portobelo. Because of the deep waters surrounding it, Portobelo became a major port of trade; ships with provisions from Spain would come to unload their cargo, while others stocked with goods from South America would sail off for the mother country.

The port soon made the village prosper and, by 1668, no less than 400 families had settled permanently in Portobelo. Moreover, during the unloading of ships from Spain, which sometimes lasted several months, the village became the site of great *ferias* (fairs) and was literally overrun by swarms of merchants, officials and other distinguished people who settled here temporarily in makeshift lodgings (tents and wooden cabins). During these periods, the population of Portobelo could reach 8,000. Lots of precious metals were exchanged at these fairs, generating a great deal of trade for the

town. A customs house was built in 1630 so the authorities could collect royal duties on imports and exports. This influx of riches attracted marauding pirates of all nationalities and acts of piracy quickly multiplied. In 1668, the "invincible" Castillo San Felipe was stormed by pirate Henry Morgan, who destroyed the fort and plundered the village. Determined to defend the town, the authorities built four fortresses to fend off

various attacks – for a certain time, anyway.

At the start of the Anglo-Spanish war (1739-1748), Portobelo was captured by English Admiral Edward Vernon, and was returned to the Spanish after the war. Later on, renewed acts of piracy and, above all, the losses sustained from the war, led Spain to abandon Portobelo as a transhipment point for merchandise, and the village fell into decline.

Today, Portobelo is no more than a simple, quiet village with such a rich past that UNESCO listed it as a World Heritage Site in 1980. Its ruins make Portobelo a must to visit, and if you have the opportunity to go in the fall, do not miss the *Cristo Negro* festival, which takes place on the week of October 21st. The event features a parade of people dressed as Christ, and is very colourful indeed!

Old Canons at Portobelo

Among the ruins worth checking out are the remarkable remnants of the **Castillo Santiago de la Gloria** ★★★, located on the left-hand side of the road just before the last bend leading to the village. This fortress was the last one built in the area, between 1753 and 1760. Today, these fortified ramparts retain all their charm, with their 17 perfectly aligned canons pointing out to sea, and bear precious testimony to Spain's colonial power. This fort replaced the imposing Castillo San

Portobelo

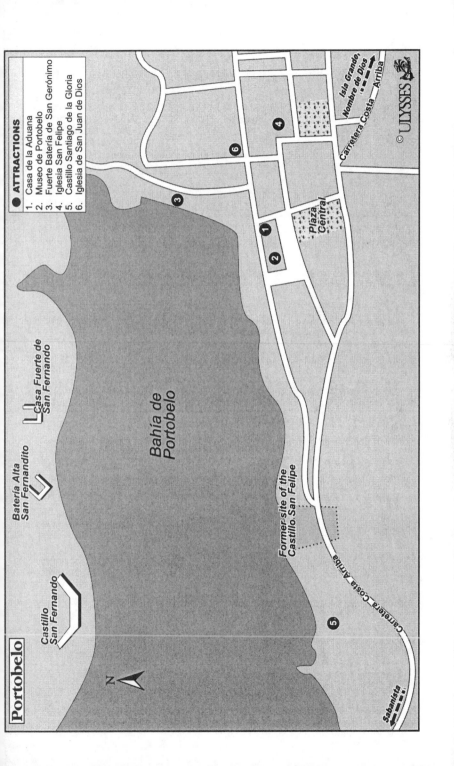

ATTRACTIONS

1. Casa de la Aduana
2. Museo de Portobelo
3. Fuerte Batería de San Gerónimo
4. Iglesia San Felipe
5. Castillo Santiago de la Gloria
6. Iglesia de San Juan de Dios

© ULYSSES

Castillo San Fernando

Batería Alta San Fernandito

Casa Fuerte de San Fernando

Bahía de Portobelo

Former site of the Castillo San Felipe

Carretera Costa Arriba

Sabanista

Plaza Central

Isla Grande, Nombre de Dios

Carretera Costa Arriba

N

Felipe, which was originally located a few metres away and was supposed to be impregnable. Unfortunately, nothing is left of the Castillo San Felipe today; the road to Portobelo was built over part of it.

Once in the heart of the village, you can't miss the **Casa de la Aduana** ★★, also known as the *Contaduría*, which once housed the royal tax offices. Taxes were imposed on all the goods that passed through the village. Built in 1630, damaged many times and entirely destroyed in 1744, the Casa de la Aduana was later rebuilt, then destroyed once again by an earthquake in 1882. It has now been remarkably restored and cuts a fine figure with its great archways facing the small central plaza. The *casa* also houses the **Museo de Portobelo** (*Tue to Sun 9am to 5pm*) with displays on the region's history including one on Spanish colonial military fortifications throughout the world.

Upon passing through the Casa de la Aduana's archways and reaching the other side of the building, you can see the vaulted entrance to the **Fuerte Batería de San Gerónimo** ★★★ on the right. Above it is a beautiful carved-stone coat of arms. Once on top of the fort, you will see several rather de-

crepit canons and a beautiful view of the bay. Erected in 1659, this fort was expanded between 1753 and 1758.

East of the central plaza is the **Iglesia San Felipe** ★. Built in 1814, its bell tower was added in 1945. Inside is the famous wooden statue known as *El Cristo Negro*, or the Black Christ. Legend has it that each time someone attempted to take the statue out of the village, the sea became turbulent, thus preventing any ship from sailing away with it. Many miracles have been attributed to the statue, and among the best known is one related to the cholera epidemic that ravaged the region in 1821. The inhabitants of Portobelo prayed to the Black Cross to spare them from this terrible ill, and their prayers were supposedly answered. Each year on October 21, a great procession is organized to commemorate this event and is attended by scores of pilgrims from across the country.

Behind the church of San Felipe also lie the ruins of the oldest church in the area, the **Iglesia de San Juan de Dios**, built in 1599, just a year after the official foundation of Portobelo. It also served as a hospital for victims of yellow fever.

Finally, there are also several ruins on the other side of the bay, notably the **Castillo de San Fernando**, the **Batería Alta San Fernandito** and the **Casa Fuerte de San Fernando**. However, because they are hard to reach and of limited interest, those with little time to spare need not bother visiting them.

Nombre de Dios

Although its name is steeped in history, Nombre de Dios has no ruins and little to offer tourists save for peace and quiet. Moreover, it has no hotels or restaurants worth mentioning, and the road leading here is in very bad condition, even virtually impassable on days with heavy rainfall.

Beaches

While there are many beaches in the province of Colón, most provide no services, are not supervised and are mostly located on private land. With the exception of those on Isla Grande, the only pleasant easily accessible beach on the way to Portobelo is **Playa Langosta**, a fine beach with many services. Very popular on weekends and during school holidays, the beach is located 17.2 km from

Sabanitas on the way to Portobelo.

Isla Grande

Located just off the mainland, Isla Grande boasts beautiful white-sand beaches, as well as wild and dense wilderness at the heart of the island. The island can be reached from the small village of La Guayra (see p176), where you can park your car for B/. 1 a day while staying on the island. The 5-min crossing also costs B/. 1. The island's main activites are tourism, fishing and growing coconuts – the best in country, according to the locals. Despite the presence of several hotels and restaurants, most of which are lined up along the only existing "road", these establishments offer a rather low level of comfort.

As elsewhere on the Atlantic coast, mosquitos are numerous and it is advised to bring insect repellent to make your stay more enjoyable. The island's southwest headland has larger beaches, some of which slope gently down to the sea. The northern part of Isla Grande, a short 15-min boat

ride away, is sparsely populated and has no tourist facilities beyond for a high-priced hotel complex. Moreover, the boat crossing, though pleasant, is rather pricey at B/. 10 for the return trip (from the south to the north of the island).

During carnival time, Isla Grande attracts scores of visitors for its folklore and *Congos* (see p39), famous lively and colourful dances. The island is also busy on weekends when it is literally overrun with locals, making it somewhat overcrowded and noisy. To really enjoy this spot, visit it during the week. Isla Grande will mostly please beach-goers.

Outdoor Activities

Diving

Portobelo

Divers Haven
2 km before Portobelo and left of the police station on the main road
☎/≈ **448-2003**
The Divers Haven is one of the few dive centres in the area to offer complete diving lessons and PADI certification (*B/. 300*). Diving lessons are available from B/. 50 (for 3 hours) and the friendly English-speaking team offers various scuba-diving excursions and rents out the necessary equipment. It costs around B/. 25 a day for full diving gear and B/. 5 for snorkelling gear.

Isla Grande

Diving School
on the main road running through the village, a little past the church when heading east
The affable owner of the Diving School offers an introductory diving course for B/. 40 (for 2 hours) as well as a 3-day package forB/.

Province of Colón

140, which includes 20 hours of theory classes and 3 ocean dives.

Accommodations

Colón

Hotel Washington
$$$
pb, hw, ≡, ℜ, ≈, tv
at the end of the Avenida del Frente
☎ *441-7133*
⌐ *441-7397*
This beautiful hotel with somewhat faded charm offers all the services one would expect from a major

hotel. Take the time to admire its monumental entrance and beautiful lobby.

Portobelo

Portobelo Divers Haven
$$
pb, ⊗/≡
2 km before Portobelo and to the left of the police station on the main road
☎/⌐ *448-2003*)
The Portobelo Divers Haven has recently built four *cabañas* with comfortable rooms and pretty, tiled bathrooms. The place is comfortable and, at press time, a restaurant was slated to be added to the newly opened bar.

Isla Grande

Sister of the Moon
$ dormitory
$$$
pb, ⊗, ≈, ℜ
on the southeasternmost tip of the island
Off a small, muddy and hard-to-reach road, the Sister of the Moon hotel sets guests up in wooden cliffside cabins. Despite being decorated with attractive colours and bamboo furnishings, the rooms lack comfort. Moreover, both the swimming pool and adjacent bar-restaurant are too small. Overall this hotel seems to

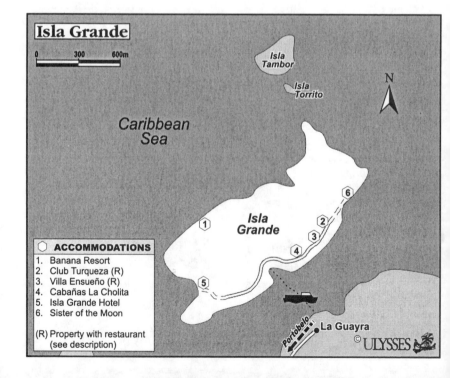

Isla Grande

Caribbean Sea

N

Isla Tambor

Isla Torrito

Isla Grande

ACCOMMODATIONS
1. Banana Resort
2. Club Turqueza (R)
3. Villa Ensueño (R)
4. Cabañas La Cholita
5. Isla Grande Hotel
6. Sister of the Moon

(R) Property with restaurant (see description)

Portobelo

La Guayra

© ULYSSES

suffer from a lack of maintenance, which is all the more unfortunate as the place has undeniable charm and offers beautiful views of the coast. The hotel offers budget travellers dorm-room accommodations at B/. 15 a night per person.

Cabañas La Cholita
$$
pb, ≡, #,
☎ *232-4561*
A small hotel composed of very rudimentary *cabañas* devoid of any particular charm.

Villa Ensueño
$$
pb, *hw*, ⊗/≡, ℜ
west of the free clinic
☎ *269-5819*
≈ *235-9917*
A favourite with Panamanian families, the Villa Ensueño hotel is quite a lively place. The rooms are in cottages surrounded by a lovely flowered garden, the whole located behind a large seafront restaurant. Though the rooms are air-conditioned, they provide rather rudimentary comfort, are poorly lit and lack privacy. Moreover, its concrete seafront facing the *Cristo del Mar* is rather unappealing. This place is ideal if you have children because the beach here is shallow and therefore safe for the young ones to swim in.

Club Turqueza
$$-$$$
ps, *hw*, ≈, ⊗, ℜ
west along the road skirting the coast and just past the Villa Ensueño
☎ *265-5044 ext. 10833*
Tue ☎ *639-2230*
Club Turqueza is second only to the Banana Resort. French owner Jean-Yves Ricard, who has been living on the island for quite some time, has recently built several motel-style units around a large swimming pool on a former palm grove.

The rooms are comfortable, well kept and sport a simple decor with white walls. For greater comfort, each bed has mosquito netting. Each unit has a small porch with a hammock, and there is an excellent restaurant (see p191) right nearby. Though the hotel is not right on the coast, the beaches are only a few hundred metres away and thus within easy walking distance. Various excursions are also available, including one on horseback around the Bay of Manzanillo. For the best deals, stay here on weekdays.

Hotel Isla Grande
$$$
pb, ⊗, ≡, *hw*
☎ *225-6722 (for reservations in Ciudad de Panamá)*
This hotel complex, which was being expanded during our

visit, offers shabby *cabañas* by a lovely beach well away from the village. There is also a restaurant that serves typical Panamanian fare, a bar, a ping-pong room and a pool room, which are all located in an old, less-than-engaging building.

Banana Resort
$$$$$
ps, *hw*, ≡, ≈, ℜ
Ave. Frederico Boyd, Edificio Parque Urrucá, PB, Apdo 6-7519, El Dorado, Panamá
☎ *263-9510*
☎ *263-9766*
≈ *264-7556*
gram@sinfo.net
Set up by a lovely little beach, in the northwestern part of the island, the Banana Resort has 16 large rooms in small cliffside cabins. The cabins' bright, white-and-yellow colour scheme contrasts marvelously with the many surrounding palm trees, banana trees and other vegetation. All the rooms have king-size beds and a large balcony with an ocean view. The decor, though refined, is relatively simple and even a tad kitsch. The restaurant is located in a circular beachside building that has a large swimming pool outside. All this is surrounded by a beautifully landscaped garden, which is delightful to relax in.

The price of a room (*B/. 60 to B/. 75 per person*) includes transportation from La Guayra, excursions to other beaches on the island, beach equipment (for games, etc.), breakfast and lunch or dinner. This isn't as great a deal as it sounds, as it only covers up to B/. 10 on meals, and most à-la-carte dishes are more expensive. Despite this, the Banana Resort is unquestionably the most appealing and comfortable hotel on the island.

Restaurants

Colón

Hotel Washington
$-$$
in the hotel of the same name, at the end of Avenida del Frente
☎ 441-7133
Here you have two options: a classic restaurant serving fine French cuisine in a welcoming atmosphere, or an unpretentious cafeteria where the fare is simple but good. Whatever your choice, you will be served with a smile. In addition to the restaurant, there is a bar and a gorgeous terrace with a pool facing the ocean.

Portobelo

Achar
$$
between the Iglesia San Felipe and the Casa de la Aduana in the centre of town
Those hungering for a bite to eat while visiting the ruins of Portobelo should head to Achar, a modest restaurant with a palm-thatched roof on a small square. The daily menu often features *corvina*, *cambodia* and *langostinas*.

La Torre
$$$
Tue to Fri 11am to 6pm, Sat and Sun 8am to 9pm
3 km from Portobelo
☎ 448-2039
On the right-hand side of the main road to Portobelo, the La Torre restaurant is aptly named indeed (*torre* means tower in Spanish). Located on the second floor of a modest bar and a little set back from the road, the restaurant, with its large palm-roofed dining room open on all four sides, does somewhat resemble a *mirador*. Enjoy Creole-style rice and beans or Colombian-style *empanadas* while seated hidden between the trees at one of the large wooden tables draped with tablecloths. Warm and smiling welcome in a Robin Hood-like setting!

Los Cañones
$$$
on the left-hand side of the Portobelo-bound road
Los Cañones is renowned for its fish and seafood specialties – such as octopus, *corvina*, shrimp and crab – which you can sample on its large terrace overlooking the bay.

Isla Grande

Villa Ensueño
$$
west of the free clinic
☎ 269-5819
Facing a concrete seafront and *Cristo del Mar* in the distance, the restaurant of the Villa Ensueño will please those who primarily enjoy socializing and nonstop bustle.

Whether you are seated in the shade on its large covered terrace or at one of the small seashell-encrusted concrete tables, the various simple and affordable Panamanian dishes are a real treat. Several vegetarian dishes are available on request every day. The restaurant also makes delicious tropical-fruit juices. After your meal, take a stroll through the establishment's flowered garden visited by numerous butterflies.

Club Turqueza
$$$
west along the road skirting the coast and just past the Villa Ensueño
☎ *265-5044 ext. 10833*
Tue ☎ *639-2230*
The restaurant at Club Turqueza is the best on the island and an absolute must. Jean-Yves Ricard, a Frenchman who has been calling Isla Grande home for some years now, serves

a refreshing mozzarella en carozza (tomato-and-mozzarella salad with basil leaves) as a starter, followed by a delicious seafood crepe. Also featured on the menu are various fish selections as well as a good coq au vin and, to accompany your meal, affordably priced Californian or Argentinian wines.

The dining room, a large covered terrace on a wooden dock, is most pleasant and offers a lovely view of the mainland. Despite the lack of decor, the owner has succeeded in giving the place an original style with hammocks suspended here and there and swings used as seats around the bar. A real must!

Province of Colón

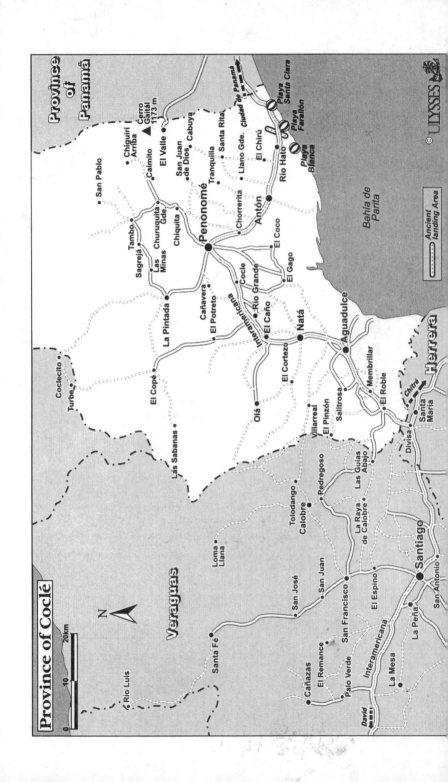

Province of Coclé

Province of Panamá

Province of Coclé

Veraguas

Herrera

0 40
0 20km

N

Río Luis
Cochecito
Turbe
Las Sabanas
El Copé
Santa Fé
Cañazas
El Remance
Palo Verde
San José
San Juan
San Francisco
El Espino
Loma Llana
Tolodango
Calobre
Pedregoso
La Raya de Calobre
Las Guías Abajo
Villarreal
El Pinzón
Saltrosa
Interamericana
La Mesa
La Peña
San Antonio
Santiago
Divisa
Santa María
Chitré
David
El Roble
Membrillar
Aguadulce
Natá
El Cortezo
Olá
El Caño
El Gago
El Coco
Río Grande
Cocle
El Potrero
Cañavera
La Pintada
Interamericana
Penonomé
Las Minas
Churuquita Gde.
Chiquita
Sagrejá
Tambo
San Pablo
Chiguirí Arriba
Caimito
El Valle
San Juan de Dios
Cabuya
Santa Rita
Tranquilla
Chorrerita
Antón
Llano Gde.
El Chirú
Río Hato
Cerro Gaital 1173 m
Ciudad de Panamá
Playa Santa Clara
Playa Farallón
Playa Blanca
Bahía de Parita

→ Ancient landing Area

© ULYSSES

The magnificent facade of Casco Viejo's cathedral – a must-see!
– *courtesy of IPAT*

The Callidrya frog shows off its beautiful blend of colours.
– *courtesy of IPAT*

The Central Provinces and the Azuero Peninsula

This region has a population of 547,000 and includes the provinces of Coclé, Herrera, Los Santos and Veraguas.

The pre-Columbian era saw significant development of the whole region, when it was under the control of Indigenous chiefs, some of whom (Natá, Urracá and Paris) went on to gain notoriety after the arrival of the Spanish because of their desperate resistance to the invaders. The provinces have a significant cultural heritage, both pre-Columbian and colonial. Each province possesses its own historical sites and its own sense of regionalism: Coclé with its El Caño archeological site, Herrera with its noteworthy museum, Los

Santos with its uniform museum at Guararé, and Veraguas with its fine Iglesia de San Francisco. What's more, regionalist sentiment is strong here, and even the attitudes of the inhabitants differ from one province to another.

The Azuero Peninsula is the veritable guardian of the tradi-

tions of the Hispanic era, and in keeping with this, carnival celebrations are the most traditional here. The carnival lasts four days, from Saturday to Shrove Tuesday (*martes de carnaval*), during which time all hotels are full and businesses are closed. In some cities, an equally festive *carnavalito* is held one week before. Take note that hotel prices can quadruple during carnival!

Careful preparations for the festival begin early, and the most prominent clothing designers create stunning costumes, always with due respect for tradition.

The Las Tablas carnival is the most celebrated carnival in Panamá. It is the occasion for a friendly competition between the Calle Ariba and Calle Abajo (High Road and Low Road). Each one names a queen and tries to produce the most spectacular costume, play the best music, etc.

The peninsula is now semi-arid. "Slash and burn" agriculture has eliminated every trace of its once luxuriant vegetation. The Sarigua desert, near Chitré, is the most extreme example of this. Today, stock farming is increasingly replacing crop farming, which is virtually disappearing. In fact, for several years now, because of the impoverishment of the land, many farmers have left the area for

the province of Darién, thus accelerating the depopulation of the central provinces. If the state of Panamá does not intervene to prevent these farmers from using the same methods in their new environment, there is a definite risk that in the near future a part of Darién will suffer a similar fate.

But this region is also one of mountains and is only just being discovered by tourists. A visit to the verdant little village of Chiguirí Ariba is a must. Visitors can now enjoy this magical spot while staying in the Posada Cerro la Vieja, amidst extraordinary wildlife and lush vegetation.

Finding Your Way Around

Note: the following schedules and rates are provided for reference only and are subject to change.

By Plane

As this guide goes to press, **Aeroperlas** is the only company that flies

to these provinces and only the cities of **Santiago** and **Chitré** are served.

Chitré

Ciudad de Panamá to Chitré
Departure: Mon to Fri 6:15am and 4pm;
Sat 7:20am and 4pm;
Sun 4pm
Travel Time: 30 min
Cost: B/. 30 one way

Chitré to Ciudad de Panamá
Departure: Mon 6:35am, 7:45am and 5:20pm;
Tue to Thu 7:45am and 5:20pm;
Fri 6;35am, 7:45am and 5pm;
Sat 8am and 5:20pm;
Sun 5:20pm

Santiago

Ciudad de Panamá to Santiago (stop-over at Chitré)
Departure: Mon to Thu 6:15am and 4pm;
Fri 6:15am and 3:30pm;
Sat and Sun 4pm
Travel Time: approx. 1 hour
Cost: B/ .55 one way

Santiago to Ciudad de Panamá (stop-over at Chitré)
Departure: Mon to Thu 7:25am and 4:55pm;
Fri 7:25am and 4:25pm;
Sat and Sun 4:55pm

Chitré
☎ *996-4021*
Santiago
☎ *998-0160*

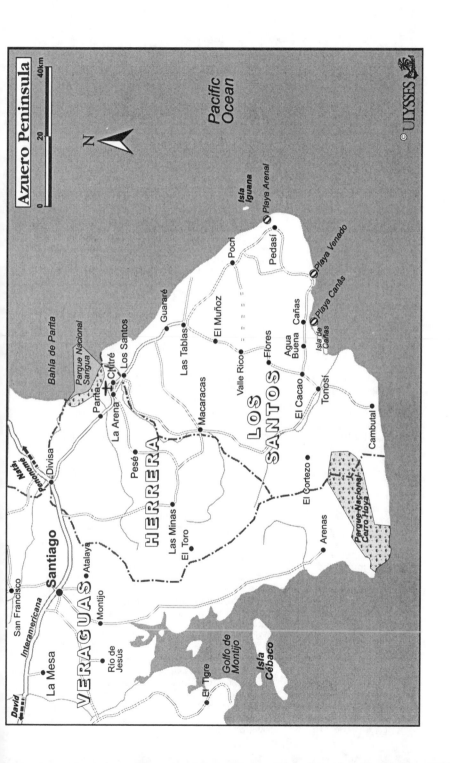

Azuero Peninsula

0   20   40km

N

Pacific Ocean

© ULYSSES

David

Interamericana

San Francisco

La Mesa

Santiago

VERAGUAS

Atalaya

Montijo

Río de Jesús

El Tigre

Golfo de Montijo

Isla Cébaco

Divisa

Chitré

Penonomé

Natá

Bahía de Parita

Parque Nacional Sarigua

Parita

La Arena

Pesé

HERRERA

Las Minas

El Toro

Macaracas

Las Tablas

Los Santos

Guararé

El Muñoz

Valle Rico

El Cacao

LOS SANTOS

Flores

Agua Buena

Tonosí

Cañas

Isla de Cañas

Playa Cañas

Poci

Pedasí

Isla Iguana

Playa Arenal

Playa Venado

El Cortezo

Arenas

Parque Nacional Cerro Hoya

Cambutal

By Car

The Interamericana runs across most of this region. The Azuero peninsula can be reached by heading south from Divisa.

To get to **Penonomé** from Ciudad de Panamá take the Interamericana westward. Penonomé is located 149 km from the capital, to the right of the intersection with the Interamericana. To reach **Natá**, continue westward until the next major intersection. The village is 31 km from Penonomé. When you get to the intersection, turn left (near the Véda restaurant) and continue straight ahead.

El Caño lies between Penonomé and Natá. To reach it from Penonomé, travel west on the Interamericana and take the turn-off to the left at the sign for the Parque Archeologico El Caño. This sign is 1.4 km beyond the metal bridge over Río Salobre. After the turn-off, continue for 2.5 km, then turn left and follow the signs. The 4 km road is only paved for 1 km; the rest is dirt and gravel, with many potholes, so watch out for the undercarriage of you car.

For the town of **Chitré**, take the Interamericana westward. Turn left at the Divisa intersection (34 km from Natá),

then follow the main highway for 37 km as its runs through the villages of **Parita** and **La Arena**.

To get to the *Parque Nacional Sarigua*, go through the small village of Parita to the intersection where a sign indicates the park, then take the road to the left. Continue on for several kilometres and, at the next intersection, turn left and drive for 1 km to the park entrance where the ANAM (INRENARE) station is located.

The villages of **Los Santos**, **Guararé** and **Las Tablas** lie on the main road heading south from Divisa. They are located 47 km, 69 km and 75 km, respectively, from Divisa.

Santiago lies 69 km west of Natá. To get downtown, turn left on the Interamericana at the main intersection and go straight ahead to the end of the road. Then turn right, and continue to the central plaza, where you will find the church.

For **San Francisco**, turn left on the Interamaricana at the Santiago intersection, and keep going on the main road for 18 km.

To reach **Chiguirí Ariba** (*Posada Cerro la Vieja*), go to Penonomé first. From there, turn right on the road after the Hotel Dos Continentes, towards Churuquita. A

20-km drive through a lovely tropical landscape takes you to Sofres, after which point the road is no longer paved and is in poor condition for the remaining 9 km to the Posada.

By Bus

Buses heading to destinations west of the capital depart from the bus station on Calle Curundú (also called Calle Ascanio Villalaz and Via La Amistad), in the Curundú district.

Note: a new bus station is under construction near the Albrook Airport and, if all goes according to plan, all bus services should be transferred there by the year 2000.

To get to Chiguirí Arriba from the capital you have to go to **Penonomé** first. Departures take place every half hour (*approximately B/. 4*). Get off at the Penonomé bus stop on the Interamericana. From there, it is a 10-min walk to the bus stop next to the Mercado Municipal in the centre of town. The bus to Chiguirí Arriba departs from there.

To get to **Natá** from the capital, take any bus (except an express bus) leaving for Citré or Santiago and tell the driver where you are going. No bus goes directly to the village centre so to get there you must take a taxi from the bus stop on the Interamericana. This is also the case for the **El Cano** archaeological site.

Many buses go to **Chitré** (*approximately B/. 8*), by way of **Parita** and **La Arena**. Buses for **Los Santos**, **Guararé** and **Las Tablas**, as well as other destinations on the peninsula, leave from the Terminal de Transportes de Herrera, situated on the Via Circunvalación (sometimes called Roberto Ramírez de Diego or else, Calle 19 de Octubre!).

The town of **Santiago** can be reached by bus several times a day (*approximately B/. 8*). To get to the small village of **San Francisco**, first go to Santiago, then take a bus (30-min ride) to the centre of town.

Practical Information

Telecommunications (Correos y Telégrafos)

Chitré
Calle Belardino Urriola

Santiago
Calle 8, two streets west of the intersection with the Interamericana

Tourist Information

Santiago

IPAT:
Avenida Central, Plaza Palermo

David

IPAT:
Central Plaza;
to the left of the church, just under the Pazin store;
first floor of the Galerma building;
Suite 4

Exploring

The Province of Coclé

This was one of the first regions to be colonized after the capital. Many of the area's indigenous people were assimilated by the colonists. Others chose to flee to the more westerly provinces.

Today, in the mountainous regions there are still small, isolated indigenous communities cut off from all contact with "civilization". The province of Coclé is also the largest agricultural area nearest the capital. It produces mostly rice, corn, sugar cane and citrus fruit.

Coclé is also famous for its crafts, among them the famous Panamá hat (see p206) or to be more precise, *montuno*, a hat made from palm fronds. Because it is sometimes available in two colours (straw and black), it is commonly called *sombrero pintado*, or black and white hat.

Penonomé

With over 60,000 inhabitants, this pleasant business town is worth a short visit, as much for the charm of its small central plaza and its church as for its lively shopping streets. Take a walk in the little park in front of the church, where you will find a handsome statue of Simón Bolívar. In addition to its colonial façade, the church has a lovely pulpit made of carved wood.

The town was founded in 1581 and according to legend, was named after an Amerindian called Nomé, who, having been expelled from his land by the Spaniards, died of homesickness (*Peno* means sadness).

The city is known as a marketing centre for arts and crafts. On the left side of the Interamericana highway going west, a little before the turn-off for Penonomé, is the **Mercado de Artesanías**.

The market, set up in little cottages with pretty tile roofs, displays a great variety of interesting objects made in the region.

The **Museo de Historia y Tradición Penonomeña** *(B/. 0.50; Tue to Sat 9am to 12:30pm and 1:30pm to 4pm, Sun 9:30am to 1pm; Calle Simón Quiroz near Parque Rubén Darío Carles, ☎ 997-8494)* offers visitors an opportunity to familiarize themselves with the history of the region. Located in a house built at the beginning of the century, the exhibit features objects from dif-

ferent periods, ranging from 10,000 BC to AD 1520 all displayed in chronological order. You will notice how the forms became much more complex over time, and learn about the evolution of ceramic painting in the years leading up to the arrival of the Spanish. A lovely chandelier made of hammered and embossed silver, depicting a unicorn, can also be seen, as well as a beautiful silver collection, both testimony to the colonial presence. Several of the objects come from the Iglesia San

Juan Bautista in Penonomé.

Chiguirí Ariba

This whole mountainous region to the north of Penonomé is a pleasant area to explore. The higher altitude means cooler temperatures and fewer mosquitoes, and there are extraordinary landscapes to behold. The fauna and flora are as fascinating as the culture and traditions of the villagers.

The Panama Hat or "Montuno"

Who is not familiar with the famous "Panama" hat? Contrary to what one might think, this hat did not originate in Panamá, but in Ecuador, in the Montecristi region, to be precise, where they are made by numerous craftspeople. The name comes from the fact that many workers wore these hats as protection from the sun and rain during the construction of the canal. Ironically, many Panamánian men, particularly in the

cities of the Azuero peninsula, proudly sport either of another two kinds of *montuno* hats which are mostly made in the villages of Ocú and La Pintada. The most popular model is the *ocueno* (made mainly in Ocú) which has only one narrow black line as decoration and its brim is turned up. The other model, called the *pintado* (made in the village of La Pintada), is decorated with many black motifs and its brim is straight. Both hats are made from the white

fibres of the palm tree, and the dark motifs come from the same material, dyed with a special ingredient that is a jealously guarded secret. The braided cord attached to the hat is exclusive to the little village of Ocú. This cord can be black or another colour and is meticulously worked.

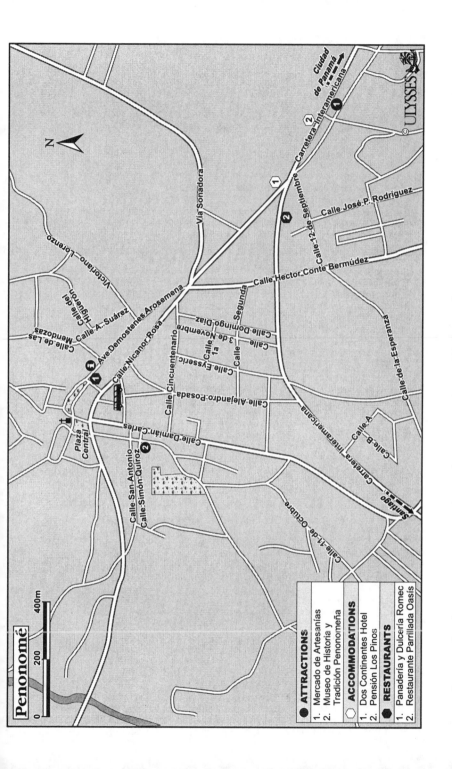

Penonomé

Scale: 0 — 200 — 400m

N

ULYSSES

ATTRACTIONS
1. Mercado de Artesanías
2. Museo de Historia y Tradición Penonomeña

ACCOMMODATIONS
1. Dos Continentes Hotel
2. Pensión Los Pinos

RESTAURANTS
1. Panadería y Dulcería Romec
2. Restaurante Parrillada Oasis

Carretera Interamericana → Ciudad de Panamá
Via Sonadora
Victoriano Lorenzo
Calle del Higuerón
Calle A. Suárez
Calle de las Mendozas
Ave. Demostenes Arosemena
Calle Nicanor Rosa
Calle Cincuentenario
Calle Alejandro Posada
Calle Eysseric
Calle 1a
Calle 3 de Noviembre
Calle Domingo Díaz
Calle Segunda
Calle Hector Conte Bermúdez
Calle 12 de Septiembre
Calle José P. Rodriguez
Calle Damián Carles
Calle San Antonio
Calle Simón Quiroz
Calle 11 de Octubre
Carretera Interamericana
Santiago
Calle B
Calle A
Calle de la Esperanza
Plaza Central

Coffee beans, still enveloped in their shells, drying in the sun, oriole (*oropéndolas*) nests hanging from the trees, unripened, flat guavas, and all sorts of curiosities await, sure to astound any urban dweller. Small thatched-roof houses scattered about in the forest are a reminder of the presence of local peasants, who by "cultivating" this forest, are able to support themselves without harming the environment. This region is actually very sparsely populated. The thatched roofs of the peasants' houses last about five years. The frame is made of wood, and the peasants use vines (*bejucos*) to attach the palms.

In the summer, winds can become so strong that the clouds fly by at an amazing speed: you'll feel like you've been dropped into a movie, and someone has pressed the fast-forward button!

If you decide to stay in Chiguirí Ariba, you will most probably lodge at the Posada Cerro la Vieja (see p211), situated 450 m below sea level and some 30km from Penonomé where the staff can suggest various excursions on foot or on horseback, guided by residents of the neighbouring village of Tabridal. Do not miss this opportunity, as the locals are the only ones who can truly reveal the richness of the Chiguirí Ariba's plant and wildlife. Guide services are included in the packages offered at the Posada, but it is nonetheless customary to give your guide a tip (*about B/. 3 for a three-hour tour for one or two people*).

Among the different possibilities for excursions in the area, we especially recommend a trip to **El Valle** (see p 153) or **El Congal**. On clear days both oceans are visible from the latter. There are also some lovely waterfalls, named in honour of Chorro Antolino, an Ameridian chief. You can also go swimming. There are **petroglyphs** (drawings or carvings on rock) nearby but getting to them requires good walking shoes and long trousers as there are many thistles on the path.

El Caño

El Caño (*B/. 1; Tue to Sat 9am to 12pm and 12:30pm to 4pm. Sun 9am to 1pm*) is one of the few pre-Colombian archeological sites in Panamá that is both well preserved and easily accessible. Here you can admire stone steles pointing skyward. Little is known about this ancient construction, which is now considered to have been some sort of game. On a mound a little farther, a deep hole has been dug into the ground, where tombs containing the remains of a *cacique* (Amerindian chief) and his family can be seen. According to archaeologists, the remains and the pieces of pottery and other objects found next to them are about 1,500 years old. By examining the objects found in each of the tombs, ethnologists have determined that a sociopolitical stratification existed in this society. A small museum adjoining the site displays some of the items found here.

Natá

For a long time, Natá, along with Panamá Viejo, was one of the main towns in the country. The village was named after the Amerindian chief who controlled the region before the Spaniards arrived. In 1515, Gaspar de Espinosa began settling these territories by setting up a military station in the region. Later, in 1522, governor Pedro Arias Dávila officially founded the village of Natá de los Caballeros. A great many merchants were soon attracted by the garrison; they settled here and made the town prosperous.

Now a peaceful little village, Natá is home to the oldest **colonial church** ★ in the country still in use. The building, which was promoted to the rank of a basilica and classifed as a historical monument in 1941, has a fine colonial façade and a remarkable interior. The altar of the Virgin, on the right, is especially interesting because of its two columns with sculpted fruit and leaves and two feathered serpents. This unusual decoration clearly shows the influence of Amerindian culture. Another curiosity is the painting of the Holy Trinity. Located to the right of the altar to the Virgin, this painting was executed in 1758 by the Ecuadorian artist José Samaniego. For a long time it could not be displayed because it was deemed inconsistent with Church dogma. The representation of the Trinity as three persons who all look like Christ was contrary to Church canons. The fine interior of the church, has been recently renovated and is complemented nicely by the carved wooden pulpit and the wooden pillars.

The village of Natá also features a number of well-preserved colonial houses.

The Colonial Church in Nata

The Province of Herrera

Parita

The **Iglesia de Santo Domingo de Guzmán** ★★, in the middle of the village of Parita, is worth a visit. While its exterior appears relatively simple, it boasts magnificent altars and an interestingly decorated pulpit. The interior, made of wood, is richly and harmoniously decorated. The three wooden altars date from the 18th century. The central altar, supported by two serpents, reflects an Amerindian influence. The side altars stand on columns with plant motifs, such as leaves, grapes and other fruits.

The beautiful, churrigueresco pulpit is also worth examining.

A door at the right of the choir gives access to a small museum of colonial religious art, where some fine pieces of silver are displayed. If the church s closed, the village *padre* can let you in; his office is on the right side of the street facing the church.

La Arena

This village is known above all for its many craft shops. Among the items offered at very good prices are a vast selection of pottery, highly decorative papier maché masks (used during festivities and religious processions), fabric with traditional motifs and much more. Most of the shops are located along the main street.

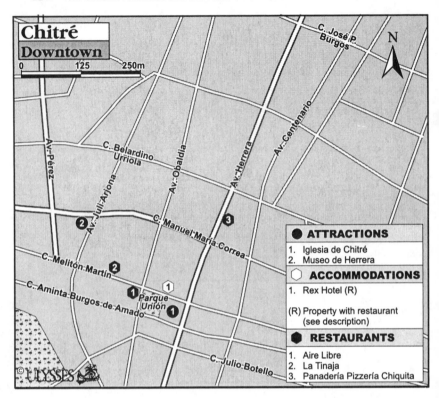

Chitré
Downtown
0   125   250m

C. José P. Burgos
N

Av. Pérez
C. Belardino Urriola
Av. Juli Arjona
Av. Obaldia
Av. Herrera
Av. Centenario
C. Manuel María Correa
C. Meliton Martin
C. Aminta Burgos de Amado
Parque Unión
C. Julio Botello

© ULYSSES

● ATTRACTIONS

1. Iglesia de Chitré
2. Museo de Herrera

◯ ACCOMMODATIONS

1. Rex Hotel (R)

(R) Property with restaurant
    (see description)

⬢ RESTAURANTS

1. Aire Libre
2. La Tinaja
3. Panadería Pizzería Chiquita

★

Chitré

This pleasant town has a fine little church and a very interesting museum that is worth a thorough visit. Besides its many bargain-filled stores, it has a small central plaza, which is a good place to unwind at the end of the day. Chitré is certainly worth a visit.

The **Iglesia de Chitré** (*beside the central plaza or Parque unión*) doesn't look like much on the outside, but is worth a peak inside for its rich and harmonious wooden decor. Also take a look at its gilded altar and mahogany vault.

Museo de Herrera ★★★ (*B/. 1; Tue to Sat 8:30am to 12:30pm and 1:30pm to 4pm, Sun 9am to noon; Calle Manuel Maria Correa y Avenida Julio Arjona, ☎ 996-0077)* A very interesting museum located in the centre of Chitré, traces the entire archaeological history of the central region of the isthmus. It is installed in a fine, stylish house, once a bourgeois home and later a post office.

Starting at the entrance, explanatory panels (only in Spanish but highly visual) guide visitors through the exhibition. Prior to the arrival of the Spanish, three distinct types of art developed on different part of the isthmus. You can admire various objects dating from prehistory until the 17th century, found at archaeological sites located in the central region of the country. In addition to arrow tips from 8,000 to 10,000 BC, vases and ancient pieces of pottery, the museum also has some fine reproductions of pre-Columbian gold jewellery called *huacas*. The original pieces are exhibited in the capital (see Reina Torres de Araúz anthropological museum) (see p92). The final item in the first exhibition hall is a life-sized reproduction of the grave of an Amerindian chief, with a text containing notes made in 1519 by Gaspar de Espinosa at the time of the burial.

The second hall, one floor up, covers the history of the province since its creation. Part of the exhibition is dedicated to the founders of the region, while another contains traditional costumes and lace.

To take another route back to the Interamericana from Chitré, use the road that goes through Las Minas.

A mixture of mountain roads and pastoral plains, this route offers lovely views but no cultural sights, and will thus appeal mostly to those who appreciate the countryside above all. It is important to note, however, that this alternative route is some 47 km longer; and because the road is winding, travel is slow. To get to the road, drive toward Pesé. Once there, a little past the police station (on your left) you will come to a stop. Turn right then immediately left to get back on the road to Los Pozos.

Once there, continue to Las Minas and then on to the Interamericana.

The Province of Los Santos

Los Santos

A lovely group of old gabled houses clustered around the village park and on the road leading to it, about 400 m on the right before the church, can be admired in this quiet little town founded in 1557. The colonial church of **San Atanacio** ★ is worth seeing for its lovely rococo reredos in red and gold (take a look at the centre of the vault as well). Los Santos can also boast that the call to arms against the Spaniards, the "Cry of Los Santos", which culminated in the independence of the country, was sent out from here. The Museo de la Nacionalidad explains the various stages of independence.

Los Santos is also known for its celebration of the festival of Corpus Christi, when a religious procession is held, which features a struggle between the *diablico sucio* (dirty devil) and the *diablico blanco* (white devil), symbolic of the struggle between good and evil. The feathers stuck on some of the papier

maché masks reflect an Amerindian influence. The procession is held every year in June.

Museo de la Nacionalidad ★ ★ *(B/. 1; Tue to Sat 9am to noon and 1pm to 4:30pm; Sun 9am to 1pm; Calle José Vallarino, near the church, ☎ 996-8192)* Various objects and documents are on view at this museum, which traces the history of the region from colonial days to independence and its attachment to New Granada. Among other things, there is a map illustrating the conquest of the country, a war order against the Spaniards signed by Simón Bolívar himself, items that belonged to the conquistadors, and a copy of the Declaration of Independence.

The museum has been set up in a former house built in the style of a Spanish hacienda, and is decorated with period furniture. To the immediate left of the entrance is a reconstruction of the Council Chamber where the Declaration of Independence was signed. The fine chandelier hanging there is from the colonial church at Cañazas, in Veraguas. Behind the museum is a lovely garden providing an interesting view of the house and the bell tower of the church.

Central Provinces and Azuero Peninsula

La Pollera

This traditional costume is worn by women during major festivities or for the annual festival that takes place every September in the village of Guararé. It consists of a blouse and a long skirt, both fringed. Generally, these are white with a lot of colourful embroidery. A number of accessories go with this costume. The hair is decorated with golden combs, *trembleques* (tremblers), and many *cadenas* (golden or gilded chains) engraved with the national emblem, the fish. The *trembleques* are finely worked and are made of many pearls, beads and sometimes fish scales, among other things. Some of the pearls are hooked on very thin supports, so that they tremble when the *empollerada* begins to dance – hence the name *trembleques*. A number of barrettes are placed in the hair, creating the effect of a lovely bouquet. Very often these barrettes are in the form of

flowers or insects. Panamanian flora and fauna are always represented on national costumes or crafts. This is not surprising considering the rich natural beauty to which inhabitants of the isthmus are constantly exposed. Panamanians take genuine pride in the beauty and many details that go into the design of the *pollera*, and consider it a veritable national costume. In contrast, the men escorting the *empolleradas* dress very simply: trousers, a linen shirt, and the famous straw hat, a symbol of virility.

There are doubts as to the origin of the *pollera*; some claim that it began with the gypsies. The dress was originally much simpler, and was apparently worn by the maids who accompanied affluent ladies settling in the new colony. Later, merchant-class women began to wear the dresses themselves, having first embellished them with all sorts of decorations.

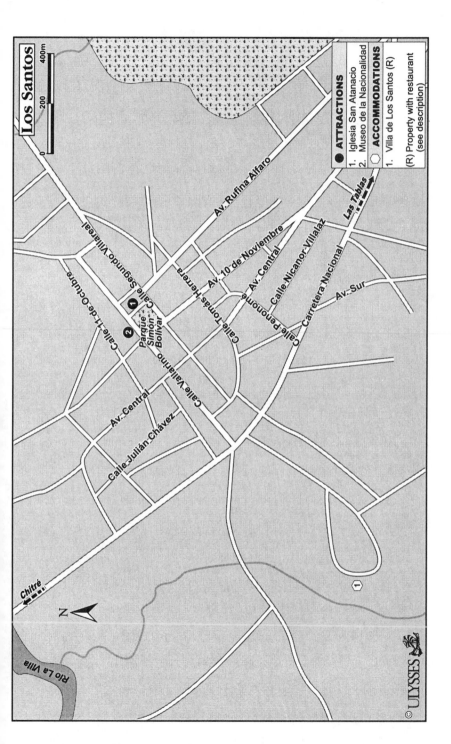

Los Santos

0   200   400m

ATTRACTIONS
1. Iglesia San Atanacio
2. Museo de la Nacionalidad

ACCOMMODATIONS
1. Villa de Los Santos (R)

(R) Property with restaurant
(see description)

Av. Rufina Alfaro

Calle Segundo Villareal

Calle 14 de Octubre

Av. 10 de Noviembre

Calle Tomás Herrera

Av. Central

Calle Pennomé

Calle Nicanor Villalaz

Av. Central

Carretera Nacional

Av. Sur

Parque
Simón
Bolívar

Calle Vallarino

Calle Julián Chávez

Las Tablas

Chitré

N

Río La Villa

© ULYSSES

Guararé

Guararé is known mainly for its costume museum. It is a charming village so quiet that it has an other-worldly feel to it.

Every September 24, however, the village comes out of its isolation and quietude to celebrate the Festival Nacional de la Mejorana, where the best singers in the province are chosen. A parade of decorated chariots drawn by oxen makes its way through the village. On top of the floats, Panamanian girls wearing their best *polleras* sit enthroned, vying for the title of the most beautiful *empollerada* in the parade. A variety of folk dances are executed as well. Besides the *pollera*, there is also the *montuna* for women and the *montuno* for men. These less ornate costumes originated in Los Santos, but are worn all over the peninsula. They are usually worn by the less privileged, as alternatives to the *pollera*, which is very expensive (a simple *pollera*, without accessories can cost up to B/. 4,000). The *montuna/o* are not without their charms, however. The composition of the costume can vary greatly from one region to another, and even from one village to another. In the village of Ocú, for instance, women wear hats. Sometimes a *montuna* is worn with a long frilly shawl. Generally, though, the *montuna* consists of two pieces of clothing: a gathered blouse and long skirt in warm colours. There are variations of the *montuno* as well. This costume consists of a shirt in coarse linen cloth (simply embroidered), leather sandals with laces (called *cutarras*), a matching small pouch carried over the shoulder, and the indispensable hat. Although traditional *montunos* include knee-length shorts, long pants are worn in some regions. These clothes were originally worn every day, but have become rarer and now can only be seen at traditional festivals or in small, isolated country villages.

Casa Museo Manuel F. Zárate ★★★

(B/. 1; Tue to Sat 8am to noon and 1pm to 4pm, Sun 8am to noon). This museum is devoted to folk costumes, and contains an impressive collection of masks (representing heads of animals or demons), dresses, ornaments, musical instruments, and, of course, the famous *pollera*, the Panamanian national costume, and its accessories. There is also the famous costume of the *diablico sucio* (see p203) used in various religious festivals.

Las Tablas

The town of Las Tablas is famous for its exceptionally lively carnival. It is here, furthermore, that the finest *polleras* in the country are made, as well as the jewels and decorations worn with this dress. The town's church, the **Iglesia de Santa Librada ★**, dates from 1789, and its gilded reredos is worth a look. It is decorated with angel heads, some of which, curiously enough, have moustaches! Another strange item – a crucified virgin – is located to the right of the entrance. The village also has a history museum.

Museo Belisario Porras

(B/. 0.75, Tue to Sat 9am to 12:30 and 2pm to 4pm; Sun 9am to noon; Avenida Belisario Porras, across from the Parque Central; ☎ 994-6326) This museum is dedicated to Belisario Porras, three-time president of the republic (1912-1924) born in Las Tablas. Porras studied in Colombia and Belgium, and during his career served successively as ambassador to the United States, France, Great Britain and Italy. During his terms, he contributed to the creation of a law school in the capital (the ancestor of the present university) and instituted the state register. He also faced a short territorial war with Costa Rica in 1921.

The many decorations awarded him by foreign countries such as France and Belgium are on display. Unfortunately, the museum does not provide enough historical background on the objects exhibited.

The Province of Veraguas

Veraguas is the only province in the country with access to both coasts, hence its name: *ver-aguas* means "to see the waters". This province consists predominantly of large-scale farming operations and pastures. There are also some (unprofitable) gold mines and some saltworks. Outside of San Francisco, Veraguas has little in the way of attractions or services for tourists. For most tourists, it is simply a place to pass through on the way to the province of Chiriquí. A journey across this province via the Interamericana will be especially appreciated by people who enjoy dry (particularly in the summer), hilly landscapes.

Santiago

While Santiago is the capital of the province, it is not a very pleasant or interesting place to visit, particularly as a great many of its hotels and motels are located on the Interamericana rather than in the centre of the city. Santiago is more of a city to pass through. However, if you do choose to pass here, you should not miss an opportunity to visit the **Escuela Normal Juan Demóstenes Arosemena ★★★** in order to admire the façade of the main building, a veritable work of art in the Baroque style. This school was founded in 1938 by the President of the Republic. It was for some time one of the most important schools in the country, and many Panamánians completed a portion of their studies here. Also, Santiago is situated about halfway between David and Ciudad de Panamá, making it a convenient place to rest a while, or even stay the night.

San Francisco

This small village has a magnificent church and a lovely waterfall tumbling into a natural pool. The road to the village is a pleasant one. At 12.3 km from the Interamericana a narrow suspension bridge built in 1925 adds a little bit of adventure to the trip.

Iglesia de San Francisco de la Montaña ★★★ probably has one of the most beautiful and harmonious interiors in the country. The altar is made mostly of wood, and is a veritable jewel of the colonial period. With many details that show an Amerindian influence, the altar has some remarkable decorations. Study the fruit and vegetable motifs (incorporating pineapples, corn and other items) on the columns and the rich decoration of the reredos, where the dominant colours are red and gold. Very beautiful silver *adornos* (ornaments) on either side of the altar embellish the overall arrangement even more. The unusual base of the altar rests on a creature that is half animal and half human.

The two side-altars are admirably crafted, contain a multitude of small details, and blend in perfectly with the high altar. The pulpit is also worth a close look. The figure supporting it bears pronounced Amerindian traits. The baptismal fonts at the right of the main entrance date from 1727, when the church was built. The bell tower is also accessible. Not only is there a fine view from the top, but visitors can also admire three old bells from the colonial period, each of which has a different tone. The outside walls of the church are made of a mixture of brick and stone, and, something quite rare in Panamá, the tower serves as an entrance.

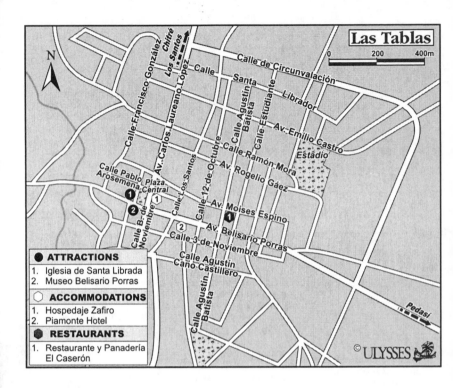

Las Tablas

Calle de Circunvalación

Chitré
Los Santos

Calle

Santa
Librador

Calle Francisco González
Calle Carlos Laureano López

Calle Agustín Batista
Calle Estudiante
Av. Emilio Castro

Estádio

Calle Ramón Mora
Av. Rogelio Gáez

Calle Pablo Arosemena
Plaza Central

Calle B- de Noviembre
Calle los Santos
Calle 12-de-Octubre

Av. Moises Espino
Av. Belisario Porras

Calle 3-de-Noviembre

Calle Agustín Cano-Castillero

Calle Agustín Batista

Pedasí

0   200   400m

● ATTRACTIONS
1. Iglesia de Santa Librada
2. Museo Belisario Porras

⬡ ACCOMMODATIONS
1. Hospedaje Zafiro
2. Piamonte Hotel

● RESTAURANTS
1. Restaurante y Panadería El Caserón

© ULYSSES

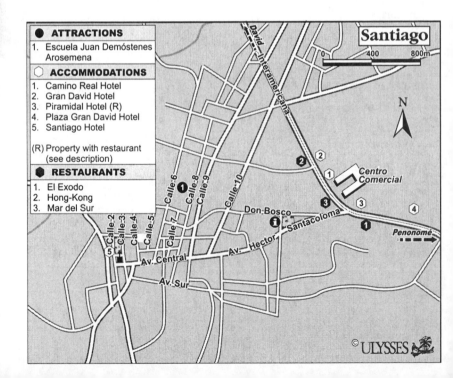

Santiago

David-Interamericana

Centro Comercial

Penonomé

0   400   800m

● ATTRACTIONS
1. Escuela Juan Demóstenes Arosemena

⬡ ACCOMMODATIONS
1. Camino Real Hotel
2. Gran David Hotel
3. Piramidal Hotel (R)
4. Plaza Gran David Hotel
5. Santiago Hotel

(R) Property with restaurant (see description)

● RESTAURANTS
1. El Exodo
2. Hong-Kong
3. Mar del Sur

Calle-2
Calle-3
Calle-4
Calle-5
Calle 6
Calle-7
Calle-8
Calle-9
Calle-10

Don-Bosco
Santacoloma

Av. Hector

Av. Central

Av. Sur

© ULYSSES

The **Balneario El Salto**, a small, natural freshwater basin is formed by a waterfall. People come to bathe here, since the water is locally reputed to have curative powers. You can get to it by turning right after the church, then taking an immediate left. Go down the hill and turn right after the baseball diamond.

Beaches

Province of Los Santos

The beaches described below are all located in a loop running from Las Tablas to El Cacao through El Arenal, then back to Las Tablas through the mountains.

The road from Las Tablas to Playa El Arenal runs through fairly dry countryside with small hills and is in quite good shape. The main activity in this region is stock breeding. Past the village of Pocri on the right side of the road, there is a small cemetery. The tombstones are built in the shape of miniature chapels and are painted in pastel colours from sky blue to candy pink. To get to the beach, take the first road to the left after entering the village of El Arenal, just before the Accel ser-vice station and after Hotel Residencial Pedasí. The beach is at the end of the road, 3 km farther (be careful not to get stuck in the sand at the end of the road).

Playa El Arenal

Playa El Arenal is a large white-sand beach that seems to stretch out endlessly. Except for a few little crabs wandering here and there, it is empty. The only shady place is a small open cabin at the edge of the beach, as there are no trees. In the distance, you can see the Isla Iguana wildlife reserve. There are no services on the beach, but supplies may be purchased from the village grocer, on the main road through El Arenal. There are also two small restaurants. The beach is not supervised, so swimmers are advised to be cautious.

Playa Venado

For those who enjoy surfing and big waves, Playa Venado is a dream spot. Thrill-seekers will not be disappointed. The beach is not supervised, however, so be careful, and do not venture too far out. The less adventurous can enjoy long walks on the vast sandy beaches, or just soak up the sun.

To get to Playa Venado from Pedasí, follow the same main road west, which gradually becomes greener and more winding. The countryside is characterized by small hills, often topped by palm trees. Along the road, you will likely come across many people on horseback sporting the ever-present little straw hats. The stretch of road from Pedasí to Playa Venado is not in good condition, and the many potholes will limit your speed to 40 km/h.

Playa Cañas

Playa Cañas is not really a beach for swimming, but rather a lagoon in whose waters many trees and shrubs grow, giving it a certain charm. This spot is part of a nature reserve, and if you enjoy ornithology you will love it. Many birds, mostly waders, live here.

To reach Playa Cañas, get back on the main road leading to Tonosí. On the road, 4.5 km after Playa Venado and on the way downhill, there is a very fine view of Isla Cañas. Once you have entered the village of Cañas, turn left at the main intersection, and carry on for 1.6 km, at which point you will see the beach on your left.

El Cacao to Las Tablas

From Playa Cañas to El Cacao the road is very bad, riddled with potholes. Along the side of the road, many birds may be seen, including, occasionally, some raptors. At El Cacao the main road divides: to the right is the road to Las Tablas and to the left the road to Tonosí. The road from El Cacao to Las Tablas is good, but from Flores to El Munio it is particularly winding. It passes through some beautiful mountainous regions, making for a lovely drive.

There is another way to drive up the peninsula to Los Santos. At El Cacao, head toward Tonosí and then to Macaracas.

Those in need of sustenance before heading north may want to stop for a drink or a snack (though the choice is very limited) at Tonosí's Restaurante Linda.

Parks

Province of Herrera

Parque Nacional Sarigua

Visitors will certainly be surprised to dis-

cover this park, where the word arid is no exaggeration. This veritable desert is the sad result of intensive deforestation practised by farmers during the first half of the 20th century. This destroyed forever a once luxuriant flora. More than 8,000 ha were transformed into an arid zone where only a few scrawny bushes grow, and no less than 4,500 ha are today a semidesert. Scientists estimate the desert's progression at one metre per year. Even though the average temperature in the park zone is about 27°C, readings of 41°C are not infrequent. Also, during the dry period, January to May, violent winds, sometimes reaching 100 km/h, sweep up great quantities of sand, thus shifting millions of cubic metres per year.

In the 1940s, the discovery of human bones led to the conclusion that the region had been inhabited about 11,000 years ago by a sizeable fishing community. To date, this is the earliest proof of human presence in the country. Apart from numerous shards of pottery, several tombs containing many precious objects were discovered, the most impressive number of pre-Colombian objects ever found in Panamá. A small portion of these has been brought to the Museo

Antropológico Reina Torres de Araúz (see p92). Unfortunately, only a few of the less important pieces of pottery are exhibited at the ANAM station (☎ *966-8216*). No visible trace of this ancient community exists on the site.

Province of Los Santos

Refugio de Vida Silvestre Isla de Cañas

The Refugio de Vida Silvestre Isla de Cañas has been classified by the ANAM as a protected area since 1947. Located at the tip of the Azuero peninsula, this island reserve, about 14km long and partially covered by mangroves, is one of the favourite spawning grounds of marine turtles. There are eight different kinds of marine turtles in the world, four of which can be observed here (see p 264).

Although there is neither electricity nor running water on the island, the Cooperativa Isleños Unidos does have primitive (*Bl. 5*) cabins and offers a very simple snack-bar service to visitors. This is a well-known attraction for those who are interested in turtles. To reach the island from Playa Venado, proceed west in the direction of El Cacao. After the village of Cañas, a few kilometres to the west, a sign on the right side of the highway indicates the small road to Isla de Cañas. This road, accessible by car, leads to the coast where you must take a boat to the island. However, before departing, make sure of the availability of transportation and lodging by reserving your cabin in advance at the Comunidad de la Isla de Cañas (☎ 995-8002) or at ANAM (☎ 994-7313). Guides will welcome you and in their company you will be able to observe the night work of the marine turtles during spawning season.

Outdoor Activities

Hiking

Chiguirí Ariba is an ideal base for travellers looking to do some hiking. What better way to discover the wonders of the tropical forest, and at the same time keep fit? Be careful, however, as the trails are rarely marked. Also, unless you plan on heading far from the villages, it is a good idea to enlist the services of a guide who can provide all sorts of information on the

flora and fauna of the region... and will give you a chance to practise your Spanish. As a general rule, the guides are from Tabidal, a small neighbouring village. They can take you to a waterfall called Salto el Chorro Antolino, fed by the Río Tabidal. From there, another excursion along the *río* to admire the petroglyphs will be suggested. For the latter excursion, however, be sure to wear good walking shoes and trousers, as there are many thistles along the path.

Horseback Riding

If you are staying at the Posada Cerro la Vieja (see p 211), in **Chiguirí Ariba**, the staff can suggest various guided trail rides. It is possible to get to El Valle by horse, but you'll have to get up early and prepare yourself for a full day of riding. The horse will cost about B/. 12 for three hours. Take note that the trip takes the same amount of time on foot as on horseback. Guide services are included in the packages offered by the Posada, but it is nonetheless customary to give the guide a small tip (usually about B/. 3 for three hours for one or two people).

Accommodations

Province of Coclé

Penonomé

Los Pinos
$
pb, hw, ≡ or ⊗
on the right side of the Interamericana, just before Penonomé when coming from Ciudad de Panamá
☎ 997-9518
This small hostelry offer 11 basic rooms.

Dos Continentes
$$
pb, hw, ≡, ≈, ℜ
at the entrance to town when coming from Ciudad de Panamá, Apdo 54, Penonomé, Coclé
☎ 997-9325
= 997-9390
This simple, non-descript hotel is advantageously located at the entrance to town.

Chiguirí Ariba

Posada Cerro la Vieja
$$$-$$$$,
pb, hw, ⊗, ℜ
Apartado 543-9A, Chiguirí Ariba, Panamá, Calle 51, Casa 24, local 4
☎ 983-8900
in Ciudad de Panamá
☎ 223-4553
= 264-4960

www.posadacerrolavieja.com
info@posadacerrolavieja.com

Considering its isolation, the packages at the Posada Cerro la Vieja are a good idea:

Central Provinces and Azuero Peninsula

B/. 56 per person for one night's lodging and three meals or B/. 96 per person for two nights, six meals.

This establishment is certainly one of the most interesting additions to the Panamanian tourist industry in recent years. You'll feel a million miles away here, in the middle of an extraordinary landscape, surrounded by mountains blanketed by a tropical forest. And in a sense, you are: a generator supplies the electricity, a pump brings the water, and the radio is the only connection with the outside world. These instruments then break down one by one, adding to the sense of adventure.

Rooms are simple but comfortable. Groups of 4 to 10 people may want to stay in one of the two adjoining *cabañas*, set atop a hillock and offering a beautiful view; a number of hammocks hang in its large terrasse beside the main building. One of the advantages of lodging at the Posada is that meals are eaten around large round tables, where you will surely encounter Panamanians and other travellers intrigued by the natural surroundings.

Province of Herrera

Chitré

Hotel Rex
$$
pb, bw, ≡, ℜ, tv, #
facing the central park or Parque Unión
☎ 996-4310
☎ 996-2408
⊷ 996-4310
(we suggest you call beforehand)
This hotel lacks luxury but offers good value for the price. It also offers the advantage of being located in the heart of downtown. The third story has a beautiful terrace with a view of the central plaza and the church. The newer back rooms are brighter and quieter and offer a pleasant, but slightly kitschy decor. The staff is welcoming and helpful.

Hotel Hong Kong
$$
pb, bw, ≡, ℜ, tv, #
on the right side of the main road from Chitré to Los Santos, just before the intersection with Via Circunvalación
☎ 996-4483
⊷ 996-5229
This is a very pleasant hotel with an interesting Chinese decor. The rooms are comfortable and very well maintained. There are plans for a pool, which should make the place even more appealing. Very good value.

Hotel Versalles
$$
pb, bw, ≡, tv, ≈
Paseo Enrique Geenzier, Apdo 298, Chitré
☎ 996-4422
☎ 996-4563
⊷ 996-2090
bversall@pan.gbn.net
With its large, lacklustre concrete façade, the Hotel Versalles appears at first glance to be rather lacking in charm. However, the interior is attractively decorated and exhibits various objects crafted by artisans, including many reproductions of pre-Colombian pottery displayed in original ways.

The rooms are modern, clean and comfortable and look out onto the pool. A large garden and lawn complement the arrangement. A parking area with attendant is available to guests. Although the hotel is located a short distance from the downtown area, it offers the best value for money in the city.

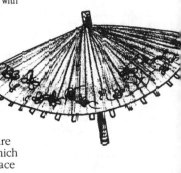

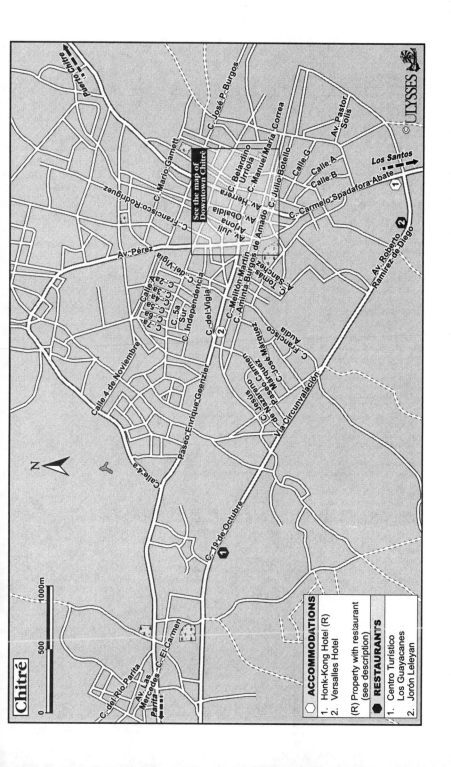

Chitré

Province of Los Santos

Hotel La Villa de Los Santos
$
pb, hw, ≡, ≈, ℜ, *tv,* #
on the road from Chitré to Los Santos. As you leave Chitré on the way to Los Santos after passing the Río La Villa, turn right at the third intersection, just after the Delta station (where there are signs for the Restaurante Las Palmeras). Follow the main road and at the obelisk, take the road on the left. The hotel is a little farther on
☎ *966-9321*
⊷ *996-8201*
While called a hotel, the two rows of accommodation at La Villa de Los Santos more closely resemble a motel. The rooms are dingy and not very comfortable, nor is the soundproofing the best; ask to be put beside an unoccupied room. A more recently constructed third wing, next to the pool, is more comfortable. This hotel's major asset is its swimming pool, surrounded by palm trees and greenery. Swimming here is a real pleasure. Non-guests may also use the pool for B/. 2. The hotel also has a small bar and a restaurant.

Guararé

Residencial La Mejorana
$$
pb, hw, tv, ≡
on the Carretera Nacional, on the right side of the highway to Las Tablas
☎ *994-5794*
⊷ *994-5796*
On the main highway between Los Santos and Las Tablas, the La Mejorana offers clean, attractive rooms. Although the building is quite modern, the owner has created a warm atmosphere by choosing tasteful wooden furniture. Unfortunately, most of the rooms, while equipped with all of the necessary comforts, are fairly small. This establishment offers good quality for the price.

Las Tablas

Hotel Piamonte
$$
pb, hw, ≡
in Las Tablas, Avenida Belisario Porras
☎ *994-6372*
Located right in the centre of Las Tablas, the Hotel Piamonte is the most comfortable place in town.

Hospedaje Zafiro
$
pb, hw, ≡
corner Belariso Porras, first floor
☎/⊷ *994-8200*
This small guesthouse located on the second floor of a corner building has a dozen or so rooms that do not afford the greatest comfort, but are well cared for. Tiles form the basis of the décor and are employed everywhere. The advantage of this establishment is its central location facing Parque 8 de Noviembre and the largest church in the city, the Iglesia Santa Librada. If possible, rent one of the rooms facing the rear in order to avoid the noise from the numerous businesses on the main floor of the building.

Pedasí

Pension Moscoso
$
Avenida Centrale in Pedasí, on the left side of the main road through the village
☎ *995-2203*
The Pension Moscoso is a small boarding house run by the owner. It is charming and clean, though the rooms lack privacy.

Hotel Residecial Pedasí
$$
pb, ≡, ℜ
at the entrance to the village on the road to Las Tablas
☎ *995-2322*
Decidedly less charming than the Pensión Moscoso, the Hotel Residencial Pedasí is an alternative should the

small guest house have no vacancies.

Playa Venado

Those who wish to stay on the beach will have to settle for primitive cabins (five in all) with a corner for the shower and toilets. Lacking a sign, but known as **El Jorón** (*$*), these rooms are not equipped with air-conditioning or mosquito netting. Although a generator provides electricity, power failures are not unheard of. As the number of *cabañas* is limited and reservations are impossible, it is best to avoid weekends. This place is suitable only for those with a spirit of adventure!

Province of Veraguas

Downtown Santiago

Hotel Santiago
$
pb, hw, ≡
Calle 2, on the street behind Santiago's church
☎ *998-4824*
The Hotel Santiago is located in a very pretty little house with colonial charm, made all the more attractive by a small interior courtyard. Unfortunately, the rooms are not that comfortable.

From Divisa to Santiago along the Interamericana

Gran David
$$
pb, hw, ≡, ≈, ℜ, *tv,* #
on the Interamericana just before the intersection for Santiago
☎ *998-2622*
☎ *998-4510*
⇄ *998-1866*
A fine, tastefully decorated establishment, the Hotel Gran David has a pleasant pool, and offers very good value for your money. If you are looking for quiet, however, avoid this hotel, since there is a constant stream of guests coming in and out. The hotel is quite large and accommodates many families. Its cafeteria (*$*) should only be used as a last resort. There is no set menu, no wine, and only a limited choice of dishes. Furthermore, the staff is not very welcoming.

Plaza Gran David
$$
pb, hw, ≡, ≈, ℜ, *tv,* #
on the right side of the Interamericana highway heading west, just before the turn-off for Santiago
☎ *998-3433*
⇄ *998-5411*
This hotel-motel is recommended above all for its quiet setting and large pool. The decoration is rather dubious. You can park your car next to your room.

Hotel Piramidal
$$
pb, hw, ≡, ≈, ℜ, *tv,* #
on the right side of the Interamericana heading west, shortly before the turn-off for Santiago
☎ *998-3123*
⇄ *998-5411*
Despite its interesting architecture and comfortable rooms, this hotel lacks charm. There is a garage in front of the entrance, and the many trucks that use it make a lot of noise.

Camino Real
$$
pb, hw, ≡, *tv,* ℜ
via Interamericana
☎ *958-7950*
☎ *958-7951*
⇄ *958-7954*
The Hotel Camino Real offers rooms that are not very charming, but comfortable nevertheless. As well as being reasonably priced, this hotel has the advantage of being next to Santiago's new commercial centre.

Restaurants

On the Interamericana

Rincón Los Camisones
$
on the Interamericana, 11.7 km from San Carlos on the right when going toward Santiago
Set on a small hill overlooking the Interamericana, this cute outdoor restaurant

Central Provinces and Azuero Peninsula

boasts a fine view. It serves classic Panamanian meals with no great surprises. The restaurant is not very easy to see from the road, so watch for signs advertising the place.

Province of Coclé

Penonomé

Panaderia y Dulceria Romec
$
near the central plaza in Penonomé, on the street to the right of the church, near the corner, facing the post office
Good pastries and coffee, fruit juice and *chicha* are available at this pleasant place, which has a little terrace and a friendly staff.

Parrillada Oasis
$
to the left of the road, after the turn-off to the city, on the way from Ciudad de Panamá
This restaurant serves pizza and Panamanian cuisine in a pleasant, traditionally decorated setting.

Chiguirí Ariba

Posada Cerro la Vieja
$$
☎ 997-8191
☎ 223-4553
The Posada Cerro la Vieja offers package deals including accommodation and food, but you can also just eat here if you are only passing through. Meals are taken at round tables large enough for about a dozen people, making

it easy to meet other nature-lovers, often Panamanians. The meals are served buffet-style, and when there are fewer patrons, only one dish is prepared. A salad, potatoes or rice, plantain and dessert are the usual accompaniments. Considering the out-of-the-way location, you will eat quite well.

Natá

Vega
$
on the Interamericana, to the left, at the intersection for Natá
The Vega is a small, ordinary restaurant with a simple, standard menu.

Province of Herrera

Chitré

Aire Libre
$
Av. Obaldia, across from Parque Unión
In a room with minimalist décor that opens onto the street, the little Aire Libre restaurant serves various simple Panamánian-style rice dishes. This place is ideal for tourists seeking simple, inexpensive fare.

La Tinaja
$
Calle Meliton Martin, a little beyond the Rex Hotel, on the way toward the Herrera Museum
Decorated with arcades, this tiny unpretentious restaurant has a great atmosphere,

except for the omnipresent, blaring television. The staff is very friendly and welcoming. Open early in the morning and in the afternoon (closed at night). Good family cooking at very reasonable prices (*main dishes with soup B/. 3*). To take advantage of this bargain you should arrive early, as lunch in Chitré begins at 11am. After that, the choice is very limited.

Panadería-Pizzería Chiquita
$
Av. Herrera
If a good pizza is what you crave, the place to go is the Panadería-Pizzería Chiquita. In its large open dining room you can order an excellent pizza with your choice of toppings, and choose from a vast assortment of desserts. Ice cream is sold here. This establishment is very popular with the young locals, and even if its only décor is the street scene outside, it is still attractive.

Jorón Leleyán
$
on the road from Chitré to Los Santos, just before the intersection of Via Circunvalación. Turn right after the Hotel Hong Kong restaurant and keep going 0.5 km; on the right side
This open-air bar and nightclub, with its palm roof, serves copious meals and beverages at ridiculously inexpensive prices (*B/. 0.45 for a beer*). The choice, however, is limited. This is a good place for

listening to popular music. Open late afternoons only.

Hong Kong
$$

on the right of the main road from Chitré to Los Santos, just before the intersection of Via Circunvalación

☎ 996-4483

The Hong Kong is a beautiful elaborately decorated Chinese restaurant. It offers a varied menu at affordable prices, and the staff are very welcoming. Breakfast served from 7am.

Centro Turístico Los Guayacanes
$$$

via de Circunvalación on the right side of the road to Los Santos

☎ 996-9758

Although outside the downtown area of Chitré on the Via de Circunvalación, the brand new Centro Turístico Los Guayacanes is worth the extra effort due to its beautiful surroundings. Perched on a hill, the restaurant of this mini tourist complex has a pleasant view of the surrounding countryside. Guests can choose either the large open-air dining room protected from the sun by a tile roof, or the indoor dining room. This room is more formal and has air-conditioning, but lacks the view. In either case, the menu offers many Panamánian dishes as well as some classics of international cuisine. For visitors seeking a

refreshing dip before their meal, the swimming pool (*B/. 2*) with locker room and showers is available in the lower part of the complex.

Restaurante El Mesón
$$$

facing Parque Unión, inside the Rex Hotel, behind the cafeteria

☎ 996-4310
☎ 996-2408

The Restaurante El Mesón specializes in seafood. The friendly staff and tasteful decor make this a pleasant spot to eat. You can enjoy such dishes as *Longorones, langostinas a la criolla o al ajilloa* (scampi with tomatoes, onions and pepper, or garlic), *camarones* (shrimp), and *corvina*. Lighter meals are available in the cafeteria, in the front of the restaurant, where you can also enjoy fresh fruit for breakfast, a rarity in Panamá.

Province of Los Santos

Los Santos

Las Palmeras
$

in the Villa de Los Santos Hotel; see "Accommodations" section above

The Restaurante Las Palmeras is a small open restaurant with a view of the garden and the pool. At night, the interior is poorly lit. The simple cuisine is Panamanian and the choice is limited.

Las Tablas

Restaurante y Panadería El Caserón
$$

every day 8am to 9pm
corner Av. Moisés Espino and Augustin Batista

☎ 994-6066

With its charming terrace on the street corner of a picturesque district, the Restaurante y Panadería El Caserón is the right choice for those who like quiet, authentic atmosphere. The extensive menu will satisfy those who appreciate the typical cuisine of the country, as well as those who prefer more classic offerings. The warm welcome by the owners makes up for the particularly slow service.

Pedasí

Pedasí
$

Carretera Principal, at the entrance to the village on the road to Las Tablas

☎ 995-2322

At the modest Hotel Residencia Pedasí, you will find reasonably priced food, but the choice is limited.

From Playa Arenal to Playa Venado

Shortly after crossing the Río Oria, you will see a small sign that says *Pepsi Nancy* on your left. By heading up the little road, you will reach a house whose occupants sell drinks and pastries.

Central Provinces and Azuero Peninsula

Although very modest, the place makes for a pleasant little stop on this otherwise not very relaxing road. The view of the sea from here is beautiful. Welcoming staff. Breakfast served starting at 7am.

Playa Venado

El Jorón
$
Right on the beach near the little cabins, El Jorón is a simple open-air restaurant. There are no signs, but it is known as El Jorón. A few balboas (*approximately B/. 2 to B/. 3*) will buy a plate of fish and rice or *patacones*. Simple but nourishing!

The Province of Veraguas

From Divisa to Santiago on the Interamericana

Piramidal
$
turn right on the Interamericana, head west; just before the intersection for the town, beside the hotel of the same name
☎ *998-3123*
Large self-service cafeteria serving a number of traditional meals: chicken, *corvina*, beef... This may not be the most attractive place, but the meals are cheap and the choice is good.

Restaurante Hong Kong
$
facing the Hotel Gran David on the Interamericana
The Hong Kong is an unpretentious place that serves a small selection of light meals. The tv is always on.

Restaurante Hotel Plaza Gran David
$
take a right on the Interamericana and head west; just before the turn off for Santiago
The restaurant in the Hotel Plaza Gran David serves traditional, family cuisine with no surprises.

Mar del Sur
$$$
on the left side of the Interamericana going west, just across from the shopping centre
On a par with the original restaurant in David, the Restaurante Mar del Sur prepares authentic Peruvian dishes such as *papas a la huancaína* and *almejas a la sureña*. Excellent Chilean and Argentinean wines are available. Prices are reasonable for the quality offered.

Downtown Santiago

Pasteleria Abeja
$
Calle Estudiante and Avenida C, two streets west of the intersection for Santiago
This pastry shop is worth a visit for its vast choice and low prices. The brightly coloured cakes are a big part of the decor!

Entertainment

Province of Herrera

Chitré

On the Vía Circunvalación, so not quite centrally located, the brand new **Centro Turístico Los Guayacanes** (*Vía de Circunvalación, on the right side of the road to Los Santos,* ☎ 996-9758) has two bars, a nightclub and a restaurant in a building set on a rise. If you arrive before sunset, you can enjoy a lovely view of the surrounding countryside. Atmosphere and Panamánian music guaranteed!

Shopping

Province of Herrera

Chitré

Downtown Chitré is an excellent place to shop. You can find almost everything you need at very reasonable prices (*pants for B/. 8.95, jeans for B/. 12.95, shirts for B/. 7, T-shirts for B/. 4*). But be careful, the quality of the clothes is not always up to par.

Discoteca Angelina
near the church and the central plaza
This is an excellent place to buy records, tapes and CDs of local music. The owner will be pleased to introduce you to the various styles of Latin and Central American music and answer your questions about the area too.

Province of Los Santos

Las Tablas

Talabarteria Gonzalez
downtown, on Calle Pablo Arosemena about 100 m from the central plaza, on the left
This small store sells a number of leather articles, including belts. Leather chairs are made here, as are very fine saddles at incredibly low prices – perfect for riding fans.

On the Interamericana, toward La Peña

Mercado Artesenal Veraga La Peña
Mon to Fri 7am to 4pm, Sat 7am to noon
6.4 km from the turn-off for San Francisco, on the left of the road A stop in this little co-operative is a must, to admire the fine reproductions of pre-Columbian pottery and figurines. You can also buy quality leather goods (sandals, belts, and so on). Stop in at the workshop to observe the highly-skilled, craftsmen and learn some of the secrets of their trade.

Province of Coclé

Penonomé

Penonomé is famous for the crafts produced in the area.

Carnival Mask from Los Santos

There is a vast choice of beautiful items at the **Mercado de Artesanías** (*left side of the Interamericana west, just a little before the turn-off for Penonomé*)

Province of Veraguas

Santiago

For ultra-keen shoppers, a trip to the new **Centro Comercial** (*on the Interamericana, just before the turn-off for the road to the downtown area*) is essential to your visit.
Everything is available here: footwear, clothing, electronic equipment, records, groceries, etc. However, do not expect competitive prices or original objects; this complex is just like those in any so-called "civilized" country.

Province of Chiriquí

I n the Guaymíe language, Chiriquí means "Valley of the Moon".

With the Volcán Barú and Parque Internacional La Amistad, this region (with more than 370,000 inhabitants) is not only the highest in the country, but also the one with the most varied landscape. Chiriquí has vistas to suit every taste, from verdant mountains and white sandy beaches to trails bordered with wild flowers. With an excellent climate, which is usually in the 20-degree range, agriculture is a major and diverse activity. For example, at higher altitudes you can enjoy the province's cheeses, its excellent coffee and its oranges (reputed to be the best in the country), while in the lower regions, banana groves and sugar cane fields offer an ideal treat for anyone craving more exotic flavours. The main attraction of this province, however, is still hiking, as the

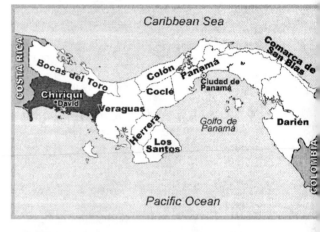

cool climate is perfect for it. Whether it's a climb up Volcán Barú (3,475 m), for an expedition in the tropical forest in search of the quetzal, or a simple walk across the flowered valleys along little streams, nature-lovers will find a wide selection of hikes here. Along with Bocas del Toro, the province of Chiriquí is also one of the rare regions in the western part of the country where there is a large population of the people native to this land, the

Guaymíes.

The Mama Chi Movement

Facing increasing expropriation of their land, the Ngobes (see p34) began to form several opposition movements in the 1960s, most of which leant heavily towards messianism. To understand the attraction to such an idealistic defiance, one must look back to the turn of the century, a time when immigrant farmers and, more specifically, the

United Fruit Company settled on land inhabited by the Ngobe people. The employment of seasonal workers by the land owners and large banana plantations greatly upset the Amerindian ways of life. Traditionally, work was distributed by the elders and was performed according to community needs. The sudden apparition of personal wealth created a new, more individualistic lifestyle and focused on needs that had previously been unknown. The schooled younger generation began to question the power of leaders and religious authorities. It no longer wanted to follow in the footsteps of its ancestors. It is in reaction to this upheaval that many small political groups begin advocating the refusal to work for *latinos*, seclusion and the return to more traditional ways.

In 1960, the Chiriqui Land Company employed nearly 5,000 Ngobe-Bugle workers in its banana plantations throughout the province of Bocas del Toro. The same year, a widespread strike erupted and, after a long and difficult walk-out, over 1,700 workers were fired, most of whom had little choice but to return to their community. It is in the midst of this bleak context that Mama Chi appeared. Delia Bejerano, then in her 20s, lived with her small daughter on one of the plantations owned by the company. In September 1962, she claimed that she suddenly saw a man and a woman clad in white descend from the heavens on what appeared to be a motorcycle. As they touched the earth, the ground shook violently and two nearby hillocks noisily crumbled. At this point, she fainted.

When she awoke, the strangers were in her house. They told her that they lived in the sky and that the father of the sky had sent them down to earth for the first time to ask her for a sack of earth for God. The strangers also asked the woman to gather together the Sukias and Ngobes every two years to welcome God. Further commandments included banning the *clarida*, *balsería* and *chichería* and having the Ngobes gather regularly to pray in chapels over the next five years. Work had to be reduced to five days a week so that weekends could be dedicated to the worship of God.

Should these commandments not be heeded, it was said that life on earth would be destroyed. Finally, Delia Bejerano was handed an encrypted message that was to be transcribed by the faithful; non-indigenous peoples were not to set eyes upon the sacred inscriptions that would be revealed in the near future. This story is the basis of the Mama Chi (Delia Bejerano) movement. In the native tongue of the Ngobes, Mama Chi means "little mother", while Mama Kri means "big mother", the name given to the Virgin Mary. The number of followers has never been known, but it seems that this is one of the most significant Ngobe opposition movements ever to exist.

Mama Chi succumbed to illness on September 14, 1964 without seeing the re-unification of her people. Her daughter, the Niña Chi, was to inherit the divine mission when she came of age. In the meantime, Sandalio Moreno was mandated by Mama Chi to pursue the goals of the movement. In April 1965, given his more political nature, Moreno organized a meeting of nearly 4,000 Ngobes (an indication of the size of the Mama Chi movement) at which time a vote was passed declaring a free Ngobe republic. Soon after the creation of the Ngobe Republic, Sandalio became president and a constitution and flag were adopted based on the commandments given to Mama Chi.

However, the Panamanian government was quick to react and within the year sent troops under Omar Torrijos Herrera. To avoid a war, the president of the short-lived republic signed a treaty with Torrijos. This significant event marked the downfall of the Mama Chi movement and its subsequent split into various factions.

Nowadays, faithful followers of the prophetic vision of Mama Chi include the Sukias in the San Felix sector. Niña Chi is rumoured to live among them, adulated by her followers and completely isolated from non-indians with whom it is strictly forbidden to have any contact. Some say that the movement, now called *Mama, Tadta y Niña Chi* (father, mother and little girl), represents nearly a quarter of the Ngobe population. Although the Mama Chi movement failed to accomplish many of its goals, it did succeed in reuniting the Ngobes and teaching them the importance of political unity in order to claim what is their's by right, their ancestral land.

Finding Your Way Around

By Car

To drive to **Playa Las Lajas**, turn left at the intersection of the road to San Félix and the Interamericana. Stay on the main road for the next 3 km then turn left at the intersection. Keep going for 9.2 km, and the beach is at the end of the road.

To get to **David** from Ciudad de Panamá, take the Interamericana west, and 438 km farther along, at the intersection for Boquete, take the main road located on the left. This road will take you directly to the heart of the town.

To reach **Boquete** from the Interamericana highway, turn right at the intersection for David. Keep going north for 14.4 km until the next major intersection. Now take the road to the right (there is a sign for Boquete) and again keep going north. Boquete is 35 km from the Interamericana. There is also another way to reach the village: take the same road, but at 33.5 km on the Interamericana, turn off on to the road to the right of the main road, where a sign points you to Boquete. This is the less spectacular road. It runs along the Río Caldera and ends in the central plaza of the village.

To reach **Caldera** from the Interamericana, take the road to Boquete for about 30 km. The intersection for Caldera is on the

Province of Chiriquí

right-hand side of the road.

To get to the **Carta Vieja** rum distillery in Alanje, from David, take the Interamericana west, and 21 km farther along, follow the main road located on the left. The entrance to the distillery is about 4 km beyond, on the left of the road.

To drive to **Cerro Punta** and **Volcán**, turn right off the Interamericana at the exit for La Concepción. This turn off is about 24.2 km west of the one for Boquete and David. Now drive north along the main road until you get to Volcán. You can also follow the signs for the Bambito Hotel, which is on the same road. To get to Cerro Punta, turn left at the end of the village of Volcán and follow the signs. The road to Cerro Punta is very pleasant and at times runs along the Río Chiriquí Viejo.

Note: the following schedules and rates are provided for reference only and are subject to change.

By Plane

David

The **Enrique Malek airport** (see below) in David is the only airport in the province. It is situated 3 km from David. To get there by car, drive south on Avenida 3 de Noviembre. As no bus service is provided between the airport and downtown, a taxi is the only option (approximately B/. 2). A small cafeteria on the second floor of the building offers a limited choice of drinks and snacks.

Mapiex-Aero and **Aeroperlas** are the only two airlines that currently service this destination from the capital.

Mapiex-Aero

Ciudad de Panamá to David
Departure: Mon to Fri 6:30am, 9:15am, 4pm; Sat and Sun 7am, 4pm
Travel Time: 1 hour
Cost: B/. 55 one way

David to Ciudad de Panamá
Departure: Mon to Fri 7:45am, 10:30am and 5:15pm;
Sat and Sun 8:15am and 5:15pm

David (Enrique Malek Airport)
☎ *721-0841*
☎ *721-0842*
☎ *721-0843*

Aeroperlas

Ciudad de Panamá to David
Departure: Mon to Thurs 6:30am, 9:45am and 4pm;
Fri 6:30am, 9:45am, 1pm and 4pm;
Sat 7am, 10:30am, 4pm;
Sun 8am and 4pm
Travel Time: 1 hour
Cost: B/. 55 one way

David to the Ciudad de Panamá
Departure: Mon to Thurs 7am, 11:15am, 5pm, 5:30pm;
Fri 7am, 11:15am, 2:30pm, 5pm and 5:30pm;
Sat 8:30am and 5pm;
Sun 9:30am, 5pm and 5:30pm.

David to San José (Costa Rica)
Departure: Mon to Fri 8:15am
Travel Time: 2 hours
Cost: B/. 85 one way

David (Enrique Malek Airport)
☎ *721-1195*
☎ *721-1230*

By Bus

David

Ciudad de Panamá to David (or any other westbound destination)
Departure: every hour between 7am and 6pm from the bus station on Calle Curundú (also called Calle Ascanio Villalaz or Vía La Amistad) in the Curundú section of town
Cost: B/. 11 one way by regular bus;
B/. 15 one way by express bus

Some buses drive directly to David, while others stop frequently along the way. Thus, depending on the bus, the length of the trip may vary between 5 and 7 hours.

Note: a new bus station is under construction near the Albrook Air

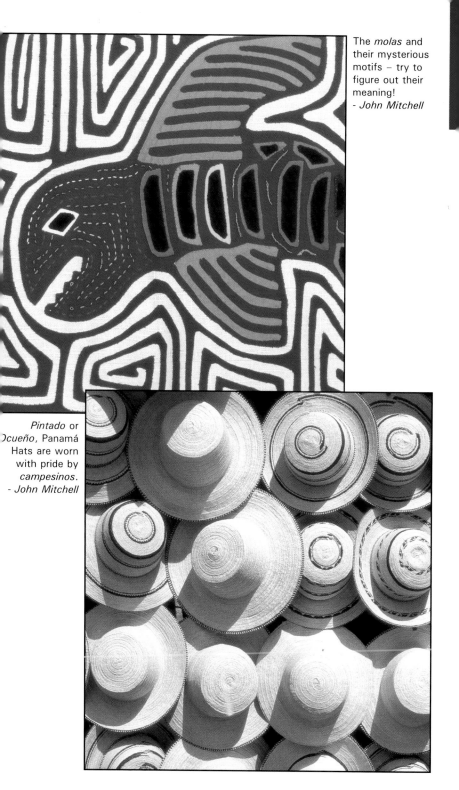

The *molas* and their mysterious motifs – try to figure out their meaning!
- *John Mitchell*

Pintado or *Ocueño*, Panamá Hats are worn with pride by *campesinos*.
- *John Mitchell*

The Iglesia de Natá, a splendid example of the colonial style in all its simplicity.
- *John Mitchell*

The ruins of Portobelo, a UNESCO World Heritage Site.
- *John Mitchell*

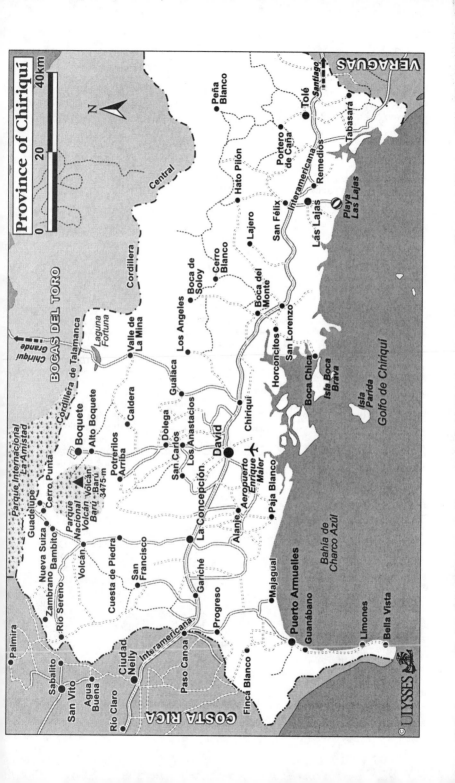

port and, if all goes according to plan, all bus services should be transferred there by the year 2000.

Other Destinations

Buses to **Chiriquí, Boquete, Cerro Punta, Playa Las Lajas, Puerto Armuelles** and other areas in the province leave from the terminal in David as there is no bus service from the capital. In most cases, buses to small villages are fairly old and uncomfortable, and stop frequently. This, combined with the poor state of the roads, makes even short trips seem like an eternity. For instance, getting to Boquete – only 37 km away from David – takes between 60 and 90 min. Generally speaking, most regional buses travel at 30 km/h and since the sun begins to set at 6:30pm in Panamá, itineraries should be planned accordingly. The following are a few examples of travel times and rates to some of the most popular destinations in the province:

David Terminal de Transporte Paseo Estudiante

Boquete
Travel Time: 1 hour to 1 hour 30 min
Cost: B/. 2 one way

Cerro Punta
Travel Time: 2 hours 30min
Cost: B/. 3 one way

Volcán
Travel Time: 2 hours
Cost: B/. 2.50 one way

Puerto Armuelles
Travel Time: 2 hours 45 min
Cost: B/. 3.50 one way

San José (Costa Rica)

See "Practical Information" p 41

Practical Information

Post Office

David
Calle C Norte 3/4 and Avenida Bolívar

ANAM (INRENARE)

David
Via Aeropuerto
☎ 775-7840
☎ 774-6671
≈ 775-3163

IPAT (tourist office)

David
to the left of the church, on the first floor of the Galherma building (office #4)
☎ 775-4120

Paso Canoa
next to the border station

Boquete
on the right side of the road heading to Boquete, just before the descent leading to the village

Exchange Office

David
Banco Exterior, one block south of the central park (across from the church on the right side), at the corner of Avenida 4 Este The bank also accepts traveller's cheques

Exploring

Chirquí

The only points of interest in this small rural village close to the Interamericana, are that it is en route to Chiriquí Grande (in the Province of Bocas del Toro), and that it is here that one can witness cock fights.

With this in mind, on entering the village, you will notice a green wooden building on the right with a sign reading *Club Galisticó*. This is an indication to visitors that under its roof, cock fights take place.

This lovely village on the road to Chiriquí Grande is exactly 18 km from the Interamericana and is composed of small, attractively adorned rustic houses. Adding

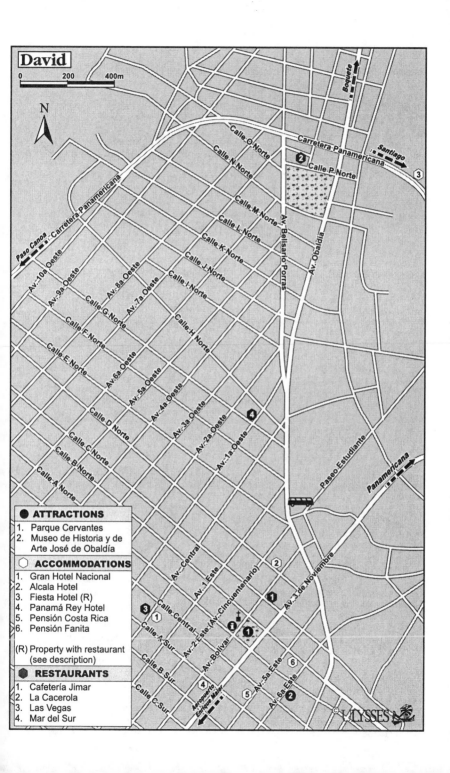

David

0   200   400m

N

Calle O Norte
Calle N Norte
Carretera Panamericana
Santiago
Calle P Norte
Calle M Norte
Calle L Norte
Calle K Norte
Calle J Norte
Calle I Norte
Calle H Norte
Calle G Norte
Calle F Norte
Calle E Norte

Paso Canoa
Carretera Panamericana

Av. 10a Oeste
Av. 9a Oeste
Av. 8a Oeste
Av. 7a Oeste
Av. 6a Oeste
Av. 5a Oeste
Av. 4a Oeste
Av. 3a Oeste
Av. 2a Oeste
Av. 1a Oeste

Av. Belisario Porras
Av. Obaldía

Boquete

Calle D Norte
Calle C Norte
Calle B Norte
Calle A Norte

Paseo Estudiante
Panamericana

❹

Av. Central
Av. 1 Este
Av. 2 Este (Av. Cincuentenario)
Calle Central
Calle A Sur
Calle B Sur
Calle C Sur

Av. Bolívar
Av. 3 de Noviembre
Av. 5a Este
Av. 6a Este

❷

❸ ①
① ❶
① ❶

⑥
⑤
❷

Aeropuerto
Enrique Malel

● ATTRACTIONS
1. Parque Cervantes
2. Museo de Historia y de
   Arte José de Obaldía

○ ACCOMMODATIONS
1. Gran Hotel Nacional
2. Alcala Hotel
3. Fiesta Hotel (R)
4. Panamá Rey Hotel
5. Pensión Costa Rica
6. Pensión Fanita

(R) Property with restaurant
    (see description)

● RESTAURANTS
1. Cafetería Jimar
2. La Cacerola
3. Las Vegas
4. Mar del Sur

©ULYSSES

to the country atmosphere, a number of villagers travel on horseback. Chirquí is a pleasant little stop on the way to the Caribbean!

David

David (pop. 110,000) is far from being an architecturally outstanding city, and its general appearance leaves much to be desired. However, you should not miss a chance to visit the city's interesting history museum, as well as its many restaurants and boutiques.

This is the only large city in the province, and consequently its active ambience is worth experiencing. Many buses leave from David, carrying passengers to Ciudad de Panamá or San José (Costa Rica), and making this a busy place. As well, **Parque Cervantes**, the true heart of the village, is a good vantage point for observing the constant comings and goings of shopkeepers, travellers and school children, all in a typical Panamanian ambiance. David is also a good city for shopping, with reasonable prices and a good selection. Besides the usual purchases (clothing, music, shoes, etc.), various handicrafts, including beautiful *molas* at good prices (*B/. 10 to B/. 15*) are sold in Parque Cervantes.

Museo de Historia y de Arte José de Obaldía ★★★ (*B/. 1; Tue to Sat 8:30am to 4:30pm; Avenida 8A Este, between Calle A Norte and Calle Central,* ☎ 775-7839) This museum has been set up in a large turn-of-the-century bourgeois house, once the home of the Obaldías, a famous political family. Don José de Obaldía Orajuela was the founder of the province of Chiriquí and his son was the second president of the country.

Various objects and documents dealing with the Spanish colonization can be found in the entrance hall. Take note of the map in the lobby, which describes the history of piracy along the isthmus. You can also see military equipment like stirrups and swords, which once belonged to the *conquistadores*. In many respects, however, the room on the right is more interesting, where pre-Columbian objects, some of which date back to 500 B.C., are on display, along with several large funeral urns. In the past, people who had died were exhumed some years after they had been buried, and their bones placed in these urns.

A glass case at the end of the hall contains some very interesting pieces of pottery. They have been well preserved and are handsomely decorated with figures of reptiles and humans. There are also some jade jewels and primitive utensils on view. The room to the left of the entrance is devoted to religious art; the objects exhibited illustrate well the influence of the Spanish church during colonization. Especially striking is the sadness depicted in the figures – a reflection of the humility and sacrifice that are considered moral virtues in the eyes of the church.

There are four rooms on the second floor. In the first, several documents related to the Obaldía family, and a number of papers relating to the foundation of the Republic of Panamá, including a copy of the treaty declaring the isthmus independent from Colombia, are exhibited. The other rooms are reconstructions of rooms in the Obaldía family residence, with period furniture and accessories. There are also old photographs of the building of the canal.

Dolega

Located on the road to Boquete, about 13 km from the Interamericana, the village of Dolega is worth a short stop. Admire the inside of its small church, with a lovely altar in detailed wood and gold.

Boquete

Inhabited since 1880 by local peasants as well as immigrants from various countries such as Switzerland, Germany, the former Yugoslavia and even the United States, Boquete is undoubtedly the most pleasant area in the province and, at only 40 km from David, a favorite vacation spot for many Panamanians. Perched at an altitude of 1,600 m and averaging ideal temperatures of 20 °C throughout the year, this village features idyllic scenery composed of superb mountains, the tumultuous Río Caldera, and flower-bordered roads. You will see primroses, lilies, impatients, carnations, roses and a bounty of other types.

Boquete has made quite a reputation with these flowers and they have become an important part of the local economy. Every year, during the third week of January, the **Feria de Las Flores y del Café** takes place, a competition to determine which villager has the best garden. Those visting the region during this period will be struck by the veritable orgy of colour. Besides flowers, Boquete is equally

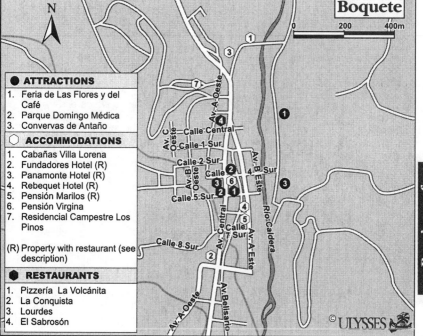

Boquete

0   200   400m

● **ATTRACTIONS**
1. Feria de Las Flores y del Café
2. Parque Domingo Médica
3. Conservas de Antaño

○ **ACCOMMODATIONS**
1. Cabañas Villa Lorena
2. Fundadores Hotel (R)
3. Panamonte Hotel (R)
4. Rebequet Hotel (R)
5. Pensión Marilos (R)
6. Pensión Virgina
7. Residencial Campestre Los Pinos

(R) Property with restaurant (see description)

● **RESTAURANTS**
1. Pizzería La Volcánita
2. La Conquista
3. Lourdes
4. El Sabrosón

© ULYSSES

Province of Chiriquí

known for its exceptional coffee. Three major types of coffee are grown in the area, including the famous Arabica. Many Guaymíes from Tolé and the nearby mountains flock to the area during the coffee-bean harvesting season for seasonal work. And last, but certainly not least, the region of Boquete is renowned as one of the best places to observe exotic birds, such as the celebrated quetzal. According to ornithologists, the optimum time to observe this rare bird is in April or May.

In the village, commonly known as Bajo Boquete, there is not much to see but a stroll on the main bridge near

the Parque Central offers a lovely view of the river and the region. Every weekend, the **Parque Central** or **Parque Domingo Médica** becomes a market where Guaymíes come to sell their products, stock up on supplies in the village and socialize with friends and family. Once the day's trading is done, the evening becomes particularly festive and the women

don their traditional dresses. On very rare occasions here, just like in many other places around the world, an afternoon might end in a collective drinking bout that degenerates into a heated quarrel.

For an educational introduction to the coffee-making process, visit the **Finca Café Ruiz** (*Avenida Central, past the centre of the village on the right side of the road leading to Los Cabezos,* ☎ *720-1000* or *720-1392,* ≈ *720-1292*). This small but already famous enterprise reaps the fruits of the coffee tree and lovingly transforms them into aromatic coffee beans.

Coffee Branch

A free tour (in Spanish, English and German) can be reserved by calling ahead of time. Visit early in the morning as this is the busiest time of the day, and, during the harvest period (from November to March), employees can be seen at work in the plantation. The

brightly coloured dresses of the Guyamíe women outlined by the green coffee trees make for a picture-perfect sight. Those for whom coffee drinking is a religious experience should not miss this informative visit which also provides an opportunity to purchase various products made on site (see p 251).

Gardeners, as well as those who merely admire gardens, will love **Mi Jardín es su Jardín** (*Avenida Central, 50 m after the Finca Café Ruiz*), located within a large estate. Flowers, fruit trees, a colourful fishpond and a small chapel make up this bewitching garden, located next to a residence which is as lovely as the setting. Although this is private property, the owners allow visitors onto the grounds provided, of course, that they respect the environment.

The secrets of making mango jam are revealed during a tour of the **Conservas de Antaño** (*from the Parque Domingo Médica, cross the bridge and follow the road to the right for 100 m,* ☎ *720-1539*). A variety of other jams simmering in large cooking pots can also be sampled.

Taking a walk through the village in the evening, on the little flowered paths, your senses will be awakened by the smell of numerous flowers. To fully appreciate the beauty of the area, two tours are suggested on p 231.

Alto Boquete

Those who appreciate sweeping vistas will not want to miss the panoramic view of the town of Bajo Boquete and the Río Caldera from the **Mirador de la Virgen de la Gruta ★★** (*on the right side of the main road to Bajo Boquete, just before it curves and descends to Boquete*). Ideal for excellent photos so have your camera ready.

Boquete and Surroundings

As you leave **Boquete**, either by car or on foot, there are two interesting loop-shaped tours you can try; both start at the Hotel Panamonte (see p 232).

Tour No. 1

After crossing the little bridge at the end, and to the right, of the road in front of the Hotel Panamonte, continue by following the main road. Immediately after crossing the Río Palo Alto, you will notice a profusion of different flowers along the side of the road. A few kilometres further on, the road crosses the Río Alto again, and later, the Río Pianista; both rivers join the Río Caldera, which runs through the village of Boquete, farther on. All along the route, white and orange lilies, impatiens, and many other flowers join the surrounding mountains to constitute the main tourist attraction. Although this tour should present no problem, as the road is in satisfactory condition, it is strongly advised to drive it only during the dry season.

Tour No. 2

This is the more spectacular of the two tours, with gorgeous vistas overlooking the mountains. Although the road is resurfaced in parts, in others, potholes remain. While it is possible to make the journey in a regular vehicle, if you can afford it, it is more comfortable to travel in a 4WD vehicle. Whatever vehicle you use, make sure to do the tour only when the weather is clear, and in the dry season. Count on an average speed of 10 to 20 km/h, or about one hour to complete the circuit. On foot, it will take a full day.

Shortly after starting the tour, you will see a rare geological formation on the left of the road, a hexagonal basalt flow. The rock has formed into a surprisingly regular shape, perpendicular to the rock. Nature is showing off its sculpting talents! These formations are visible from two places on the tour. Continue alongside a beautiful river, which will lead you through a village to an imposing waterfall (about 20 m high), also worth a stop. Following along the same road, you will zig-zag your way into a steep valley, and the many impressive vistas are all worth stopping at.

A massive, almost oppressive wall of rock, covered with immense trees, stands in between the road and the river. It is easy to grasp the insignificance of humans in the whole scheme of nature in a place like this. As well, all along the route, you will see Guaymíe dwellings. Farther along in the valley, the road turns back on itself, and climbs abruptly to the top of the rock wall. At the summit, the tour continues through *fincas* (coffee plantations) where the deep green of the leaves are the crowning glory of the countryside. From December through April, Guaymíes pick coffee on the plantations. With wicker baskets strapped to their waists

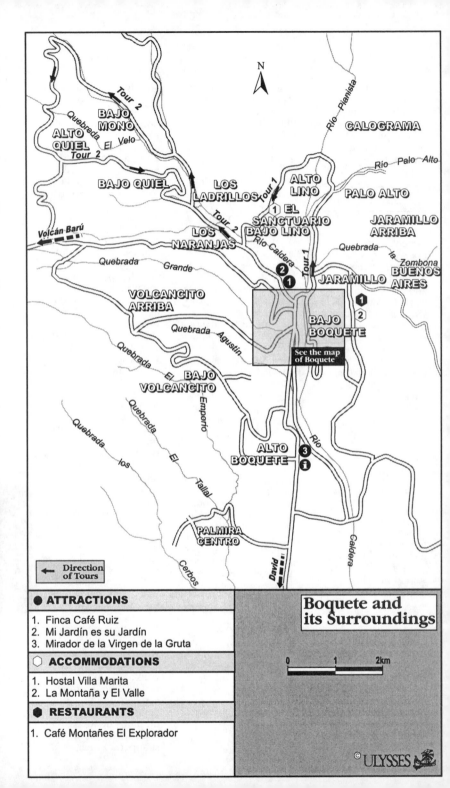

N

Tour 2

BAJO
MONO

ALTO
QUIEL
Tour 2

Quebrada

El Velo

BAJO QUIEL

LOS
LADRILLOS

Tour 1

ALTO
LINO

Río — Pianista

CALOGRAMA

Río — Palo — Alto

PALO ALTO

Volcán Barú

Tour 2

LOS
NARANJAS

EL
SANCTUARIO
BAJO LINO

Río Caldera

Tour 1

JARAMILLO
ARRIBA

Quebrada   la

Zombona
BUENOS
AIRES

Quebrada   Grande

VOLCANCITO
ARRIBA

Quebrada   Agustín

BAJO
VOLCANCITO

Quebrada

El

Quebrada

los

Emporio

El

Tallal

Quebrada

2
1

JARAMILLO

1
2

BAJO
BOQUETE

See the map
of Boquete

Río

ALTO
BOQUETE

3
1

PALMIRA
CENTRO

Cerbos

David

Caldera

→ Direction
of Tours

● ATTRACTIONS

1. Finca Café Ruiz
2. Mi Jardín es su Jardín
3. Mirador de la Virgen de la Gruta

◯ ACCOMMODATIONS

1. Hostal Villa Marita
2. La Montaña y El Valle

⬣ RESTAURANTS

1. Café Montañes El Explorador

Boquete and
its Surroundings

0   1   2km

© ULYSSES

for collecting the harvest, the average worker receives B/. 1 and B/. 2 for every 4-kg basket of beans picked. A worker can pick between 5 and 20 baskets per day. Following the road, you will come back toward Boquete along a grandiose slope.

Alanje

Located between the cities of David and La Concepción, Alanje is best known in the region for its production of rum from sugar cane, apparently one of the best in the world! Although the village is not that spectacular, do not miss the chance to visit the **Carta Vieja rum distillery** ★ (*free admission; Mon to Fri 7:30am to noon and 12:30pm to 4pm*), where a guide will explain the various steps in the production of rum. You can see the fermentation tanks, where the cane juice is kept, and follow the different distillation processes. Depending on its intended use, the percentage of alcohol varies: 80% to 95% for the production of gin; 40% for regular rum, destined for use in most bars. The quality of taste is influenced by many factors, including the container (here vats are made of white birch from Canada), as well as the length of storage time, which can be as long as six or eight years. Outside the warehouses, two old

stills (one of which was imported from Italy) hark back to earlier times; a small room next to the offices commemorates the glorious past of the distillery (active since 1915) in a series of photographs. Count on 30 to 60 min for the tour. In addition to the educational benefits of this excursion, the road leading out passes through very pleasant sugar cane fields. The only regrettable part is that the distillery does not have a sales counter for visitors, and it is impossible to buy products on-site.

From La Concepción to Volcán

Mirador AlanHer (*B/. 0.25; from the Interamericana, drive 15.9 km on the road to Volcán, the mirador is on the left side of the road*) On the way to Volcán and Cerro Punta, stop at the Mirador AlanHer to enjoy the picturesque, verdant landscape and, should the urge arise, taste one of the local specialties. With a little patience, some of the many birds that inhabit the area might be spotted.

Volcán

Higher up in the mountains and more European in appearance than Boquete, Volcán is a small village with

little to offer beyond a few hotels and restaurants. From here it is possible to scale the Volcán Barú and descend to Boquete. However, the hike from Volcán to the summit is quite difficult and takes between 8 and 10 hours. Because the path is unmarked, a guide is essential. Volcán is thus more of a stopping point between Cerro Punta and the Parque Internacional La Amistad.

Cerro Punta

The little village of Cerro Punta, which is not really extraordinary in itself, is definitely worth a visit for the beautiful mountain scenery surrounding it. Like Boquete, it is ideal for people seeking cooler weather and for hikers. In the area called Bella Vista, hiking trails lead over steep hills, some of which are cultivated. The growing of vegetables is a central activity in the surrounding region. If you like fresh produce, this is a good place to buy straight from the producer. Guaymíes work the land in the region for farmers, some of whom immigrated from Europe long ago. Families with origins in such faraway lands as Yugoslavia, Germany or Switzerland are common. The style of the

Province of Chiriquí

small houses and the immediate environment create an impression that one is no longer in a tropical country but in Europe.

Agriculture is taking a toll on the mountain forests of Panamá. Clearing land for farming not only destroys the trees but encourages erosion; this in turn does additional damage to the forests.

Guadelupe

This enjoyable small town is known for its flowers (*after passing through Cerro Punta, continue straight on the main road until Guadelupe*). Those who are fascinated by orchids should visit the **Finca Dracula** ★ (*B/. 5;* ☎ *771-2223*) where Andrés Maduro lovingly and patiently tends to over 1, 200 species of orchids in a fairy-tale garden. The rather strange name of the garden owes its origins to the hundred *Telipogon vampirus* orchids he found already growing on site at the time he purchased the land. A tour of the grounds lasts an

hour and a half, and is conducted in groups of six or less. Biologists or orchid specialists provide comprehensive explanations in English or Spanish.

In the town itself, make a quick stop at the **Los Quetzales Hotel** (see p245), the only tourist lodgings in the park. Budget permitting, this is an experience not to be missed. Those who are just passing through can enjoy a good meal in its charming restaurant (see p249).

Puerto Armuelles

Puerto Armuelles (pop. 40,000 inhab) is the second largest city in the province and has no extraordinary sites unless you have a keen interest in banana plantations. Immense private plantations called *fincas*, owned in the majority by the Chiriquí Land Company, extend from the borders of the city beyond sight.

The only attractions worth mentioning are the immense deserted beaches that embellish the nearby coastline.

Banana Flower

Unfortunately no services are available so food and drink must be brought in. Those interested in oil tankers can drive along an unpaved road to the installations of the Petroterminal de Panamá, about 6 km south of Puerto Armuelles on the Península Burica. Visitors can watch gigantic tankers as they pour their precious cargo into a pipeline that links the Pacific and Atlantic coasts.

Parks

Parque Internacional La Amistad

In 1974, the first conference dedicated to the conservation of natural and cultural resources in Central America passed a resolution to create, for the first time ever, a park involving two sovereign countries, Costa Rica and Panamá. The resulting Parque Internacional La Amistad was to extend along the Talamanca mountain range that borders both countries. To endorse this historical agreement, the two countries began a cooperative project in 1979 to ensure the protection of the area and, in 1982, signed a treaty in which they agreed to define the respective zones covered by previous agreements. During the same year, an area of 193,929 ha was defined in Costa Rica; however, it was not until 1986 that Panamá alloted 207,000 ha to this project. Soon after its creation, the Costa Rican park was declared, along with 14 neighboring zones, a UN Biosphere Reserve (248,337 ha) and a year later, in 1983, a World Heritage Site. It was not until 1990 however, that UNESCO listed the Panamanian park as a World Heritage Site. It has yet to be classified as a Biosphere Reserve in this country, nevertheless there are plans in the works to add five protected zones to it, including the Volcán Barú national park, extending this zone to close to 4,000 km^2. The La Amistad Biosphere Reserve would thus encompass over 10,000 km^2, making it the largest protected area in Central America.

In Panamá alone, many summits exceed 3,000 m, the highest being the Barú volcano, at an altitude of 3,475 m. With temperatures ranging between 15°C and 24°C and annual precipitation between 2,500 and 5,000 mm, this is one of the most humid regions in the country. This immense wilderness encompasses seven of the existing 13 life zones of the Panamanian isthmus. It is thus a very bountiful region, rich in flora and fauna, where vegetation changes with altitude. Among the numerous wild animals that live here are a number of endangered species, possibly the most impressive of which are the jaguar, tapir, white-tailed deer and the famous quetzal. Studies reveal that over 1,000 species of mammals, 60 kinds of reptiles, 100 types of amphibians and 400 varieties of birds inhabit the park. Current estimates show that the park is home to 60% of all vertebrates and invertebrates in Panamá. The sheer size of the territory allows big cats such as jaguars, pumas and ocelots to hunt and reproduce without being disturbed. Jaguars, for instance, which weigh up to 150 kg, require hundreds of hectares of land to roam and to hunt agoutis, peccaries and deer.

Though the park is actually located in the neighbouring province of Bocas del Toro, access to the park is easier from the province of Chiriquí. And although part of the access road can

Quetzal

in fact be driven in an ordinary car, a 4WD vehicle is preferable for the few kilometres leading up to the entrance, only passable during the dry season.

Once inside the park itself, there are no driveable roads (except on the Costa Rica side) and the only way to get around is on hiking trails. To get to the entrance in the village of Cerro Punta, turn left at the main intersection of the village, and keep following the signs. The entrance to the park is 6.8 km farther on, and the road is beautiful. As you get closer to the park, the vegetation becomes more dense, almost engulfing the road. People here seem rather insignificant and at the complete mercy of nature. This route up to the entrance of the park is a pleasant trip for those who want to

Province of Chiriquí

admire the extraordinary natural beauty of the park close up, without actually venturing on an expedition.

The park currently does not have many marked paths or tourist facilities. Nonetheless it is a magical place where hardy adventurers, accompanied by guides accustomed to long hikes through dense and humid tropical forests, can scale mountains and observe many animals that are hard to spot in other parts of the country. Bird watchers will also find it an exceptional observation ground, off the beaten track, where the chances of sighting the famous quetzal are excellent.

To fully appreciate the park's bountiful nature, newcomers are urged to use the services of local tour agencies who work with ecologists. Furthermore, because of the park's immense territory, it is inadvisable to venture out alone.

Before entering the park, you must obtain authorization from INRENARE. While there is no official system in place for keeping track of visitors, it is **strongly** recommended that you get the proper permit. To obtain authorization or further information, contact ANAM (INRENARE), in the capital (see p72) or at its local office in David (see p226).

Parque Nacional del Volcán Barú

Next to the Parque Internacional La Amistad, the Parque Nacional del Volcán Barú covers over 14,000 ha of land.

Rising to 3,475 m above sea level, it is home to the

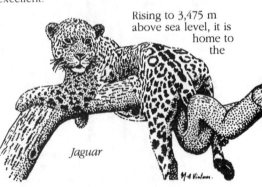

Jaguar

highest peak in Panamá. Like its neighbour, this park fosters extremely varied vegetation, which changes with altitude. At low altitudes, there is a prevalence of species common to the tropical rain forest, notably very large oaks, which give way, with rising altitude, to

much scrawnier trees. Above 1,800 m, the vegetation progressively recedes and, in its place, more and more volcanic rocks and shrubbery. Temperatures at the summit can change rapidly, often plummeting within minutes from 16°C to below 10°C when clouds move in.

To enjoy a clear view of the two largest oceans on the planet, the Pacific and the Atlantic, it is best to reach the summit at the crack of dawn. Unfortunately being the highest peak in the country also means that it plays an important role in telecommunications, and antennae and radars somewhat deform the landscape. Be that as it may, the park is reputed to be one of the easiest places to sight the quetzal (provided you have a good guide).

From May to December, hiking to the mountaintop is inadvisable because of the heavy rains which turn paths into mud slides.

Beaches

Playa Las Lajas

This immense beach lies 12.2 km from the

Interamericana. It is just the place for people who like long walks along quiet shorelines. Those who wish to swim should be very careful as the waves are violent and sharks reputedly visit this area. The fine white sand of Playa Las Lajas is bordered by luxuriant vegetation. There is no accommodation available on site, but the **Gran Club** does provide a few rudimentary services (snacks, drinks, showers...). To get something to eat before heading to the beach, stop at the cafeteria at the intersection of the road to Las Lajas, just to the right of the Interamericana. Most of the time, there is also a merchant who sells the excellent oranges grown in the region, as well as *pipas* (coconuts).

Outdoor Activities

Hiking

Volcán Barú

The hike up the Volcán Barú is for people in good physical condition who mountain climb on a regular basis. Two trails wind

their way up the volcano. The first trail starts from the main road in Boquete and takes about four to five hours. The second starts in Cerro Punta and requires up to eight hours of hiking. As the entrance to the park from Cerro Punta is along the road to Volcán, the most convenient starting point is Boquete. To get there, go north on the main road through the village and turn left on the first street after the church. After 10 km or so on a fairly good road, continue on foot or 4WD as the road starts looking more and more like a battlefield. Those who choose to drive should not do so alone as there is a good chance of having an accident. It is best to hire a local guide who is accustomed to driving on such roads.

Should you decide to climb the volcano on foot, the following advice will help you reach your destination more easily:

Because clouds move in quickly during the morning, it is best to reach the summit at day break to get a clear view of the coast or, if you're lucky, both coasts. To do so, you should hike by night starting at around 1am.

To save your energy for the lengthy climb to the summit, have a taxi drop you off at the park entrance. From

this point, the hike is a good 10 km, which should take some four to five hours.

Bring warm clothes as temperatures at the summit can be very low.

Do not hike alone at night. Bring a reliable flashlight, food and plenty to drink.

Do not forget that in order to enter the park you must have acquired authorization beforehand from ANAM (INRENARE). While this formality is not always observed or supervised, it is still necessary to ensure that flora, fauna and tourists are protected. Both the authorization and additional information on the park are available in the capital (see p72) and at the local ANAM (INRENARE) office at David (see p226).

Expediciones Tierras Altas
☎ *720-1342*

Those who prefer to be accompanied by a guide can contact Enrique Boutet or his brother, both of whom have been operating the tour company *Expediciones Tierras Altas* for several years now. The Boutet brothers know the region like the backs of their hands and offer a range of walking tours in addition to expeditions to the top of the volcano (*about B/. 50 à 75 per person depending on the services provided*).

Río Monte Ecological Tours
☎ *720-1536*
⇌ *720-1324*
Another local company, Río Monte Ecological Tours, affiliated with the Panamonte Hotel, also organizes excursions to the summit of the volcano that include breakfast at the hotel, transportation, a snack, the rental of binoculars as well as the services of a nature guide. B/. 75 per person (price based on the participation of two people).

From Cerro Punta to Boquete

Los Quetzales
Guadelupe, Apdo 55-0039
☎ *771-2182*
⇌ *771-2226*
www.LosQuetzales.com,
carlos@losquetzales.com
If a hike from Cerro Punta to Boquete sounds appealing, contact Los Quetzales. Two local guides accompany hikers beyond the Volcán Barú, where there is extraordinary flora to see (see p 237). The expedition lasts between six and eight hours and is meant for people in top physical shape who are accustomed to long hikes. Expect to pay about B/. 40 per person (this includes a picnic and return transportation the next day to Cerro Punta or Guadelupe). Because of the length of the hike and the return on the following day, hikers should plan to stay overnight in

Boquete. A similar tour is available on horseback.

Bird-watching

Boquete

Río Monte Ecological Tours
☎ *720-1536*
⇌ *720-1324*
For people who are especially interested in quetzals, Río Monte Ecological Tours, affiliated with the Hotel Panamonte, offers a very interesting guided tour through the tropical rainforest of Colograma, reputed to be frequented by families of quetzals as well as toucans and other exotic birds.

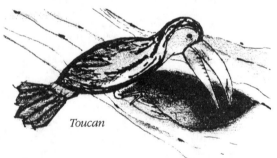
Toucan

During the excursion, you will also have the chance to spot small mammals as well as an incredible number of plants and flowers, especially orchids. The tour lasts approximately five hours, and costs B/. 75 (two or more people), including transportation, a naturalist guide, picnic,

and rental of binoculars. Although the cost might seem a little steep, the package is a good idea because the guides are extremely knowledgable about the region and are familiar with bird-watching. With an experienced guide, you will have more of a chance to spot a quetzal, a bird that is both rare and difficult to see because of its camouflage. According to ornithologists, the best time to observe a quetzal is in April and May. For people staying in the capital, various ecotourism agencies offer packages departing from Ciudad de Panamá
(see the "Hiking" section in that chapter)
(see p100, 157).

Expediciones Tierras Altas
in Bajo-Boquete
☎ *720-1342*
The two Boutet brothers of Expediciones Tierras Altas are also very familiar with the region and provide, in addition to outings in search of the elusive quetzal (*about B/. 50 to*

75 per person depending on the services provided), a host of other outdoor activities in the area.

David

Agencia de Viajes 4 Tours
Vía Belisario Porras, Apdo 12, David
☎ 775-1397
☎ 775-4282
✆ 775-4652
Those staying in David who are interested in this type of excursion, should contact the Agencia de Viajes 4 Tours, which offers a variety of package deals. As tour agencies abound in the region, do not hesitate to shop around and bargain for a better price.

Los Quetzales
Guadelupe, Apdo 55-0039
☎ 771-2182
✆ 771-2226
www.LosQuetzales.com,
carlos@losquetzales.com
With its evocative name, Los Quetzales is yet another specialized agency which offers numerous expeditions in the Parque Internacional La Amistad as well as very unique accommodations. Fifteen different hikes are available, ranging in length from 30 min to 4 hours and priced accordingly. A Guaymíe guide will point out many varieties of birds during a walk through the park. Approximately one hundred different bird species have been identified by the Audubon Society and

Smithsonian Institute, both of which still conduct regular surveys in the park.

Swimming

From David to Boquete

Two "refreshing" stops on the way to Boquete allow swimming enthusiasts to dive into one of the many *ríos* that irrigate the region. Swimming is free of charge at the **Balneario Majagua** (*4 km from the intersection with the Interamericana*) located on the right side of the main road to Boquete. This delightful site features a small waterfall cascading into a freshwater pool. There is parking right in front of the swimming hole as well as a restaurant-bar that serves basic meals. If it is too crowded, continue a few kilometers north to the **Balneario La Cascada** (*B/. 50; swimming from 9am to 5:30pm; 8.9 km from the intersection with the Interamericana, on the right side of the road to Boquete*), another swimming hole with a much mightier waterfall. The setting is just as enjoyable but there is a fee for most services. There is also a parking lot and a small restaurant. As both these freshwater basins are fed by rivers, it is important to follow

certain hygiene precautions (see "Warning") (see p 51).

La Concepción

Parque Recreativo Borinquito
B/. 1, children B/. 0.75; 11am to 10pm
at the end of the Avenida Centenario
☎ 770-4625
Children and adults alike will enjoy the olympic-sized pool and tennis courts at the Parque Recreativo Borinquito in Solano. Also, guides will accompany visitors free of charge on walks along a series of paths lined with signs.

Gariché

Nine km from the city of Concepción en route to the Costa Rican border, the Interamericana crosses the Río Gariché, which originates in the Cordillera de Talamanca. Many *Chiricano* families enjoy swimming in the river's calm, shallow waters. Right after the bridge, turn right off the main road onto a dirt road. This leads to a parking lot (free) and the **Balneario Restaurante Camino al Cielo** (see p249) where there is a restaurant overlooking the *río,* and changing rooms for visitors. Stairs lead down to the shore of the river, which is a good place for a swim. On weekends and holidays, this becomes a very popular picnicking spot for

Panamanians. To avoid any unpleasant surprises, do not leave anything of value in a parked car.

Rafting

The Río Chiriquí originates in the Cordillera Central and, after flowing into the Lago Fortuna, which is formed by a dam, continues another 100 km or so to the Pacific Ocean. Once a powerful river now controlled by human hands, the Río Chiriquí regains its original force with the Río Estí, which runs into it a few kilometers after the small village of Ricón. The harnessed flow of the Río Chiriquí makes it one of the only rivers on which whitewater rafting excursions are available all year long.

Two groups that organize rafting outings for beginners as well as more experienced thrill seekers:
Panamá River Rafting
☎ 774-1236

Chiriquí River Rafting
Apdo 1686, Balboa, Ancón
☎ 236-5218
✆ 236-5217
hsanchez@panama.c-com.net

Participants travel from the capital or David to the small town of Gualaca before reaching the Río Chiriquí a little further on. The

ride down the river lasts between two and four hours depending on the level of difficulty. Prices vary between B/. 75 and B/. 210 according to the chosen option (with or without accommodations) and the number of participants. Excursions include one or more meals as well as the services of one or more guides.

Fishing and Diving

Isla Parida

The largest of a group of 20 islands, Isla Parida is a fishing and scuba-diving paradise located about a two-hour boat ride from David's port, Puerto Pedregal.

Sharon and Dave Simpson
☎ 774-8166
*paridas@chiriqui.com,
chiriqui.com/lasparidas*
A Canadian couple living on the island, Sharon and Dave Simpson, offer diving excursions to the crystal-clear waters of such destinations as the Islas Ladrones, 16 km southwest of the island of Parida. Fishing enthusiasts, for their part, cast their lines into waters teeming with tuna, marlin and other fish.

Accommodations

David

Pensión Fanita
$
sb, ℜ
Corner of Calle B Norte and Avenida 5 Este, two streets southeast of the Plaza
☎ 775-3718
The noisy and very basic rooms at the Pensión Fanita have rickety floors but, for B/. 6 a night, who can complain? Only to be considered by those whose budget is in serious need of a break.

Pensión Costa Rica
$
pb/sb, ⊗
Corner of Avenida 5 Este and Calle A Sur
☎ 775-1241
In the same category, the Pensión Costa Rica has a charming façade and rooms which are a little more comfortable but pretty rustic all the same. Prices are low and range from B/. 6 to 12 depending on whether the bathroom is shared or private. Its proximity to a bus station makes it fairly noisy. Friendly welcome.

The Hotel Panamá Rey
$
pb, hw, ≡, #
Avenida Bolívar
☎ 775-0253
The Avenida Bolívar is a large, moderately

comfortable hotel with haphazard decor. The street is fairly quiet compared to others in the area, but the staff is somewhat unaccommodating.

Hotel Fiesta
$$
pb, hw, ≡, ≈, tv, ℜ, #
on the right side of the Interamericana heading west, at the intersection with the road to Boquete
☎ 775-5453
☎ 775-5454/55/57
≓ 774-4584
Situated on the Interamericana, the motel-like Hotel Fiesta has 59 simple but tastefully decorated rooms set around a large pool and garden. Choose a room at the back so as not to be bothered by the noise of the nearby road. During the week, breakfast is served starting at 6:30am, ideal for early expeditions. On sweltering days, its pool is much appreciated. Good quality for the price.

Hotel Alcala
$$
pb, hw, tv, ℜ
Avenida 3 Este and Calle D Norte
☎ 774-9018
☎ 774-9019
≓ 774-9021
Situated close to downtown David, the Hotel Alcala has 54 comfortable and simply decorated rooms. Its proximity to many busy commercial streets, the bus station and the *mercado público* will please travellers who enjoy lively areas.

Another advantage is its private, guarded parking lot.

Gran Hotel Nacional
$$
pb, ≡, ≈
corner of Calle Central and Calle Primera, Apartado 37-B
☎ 775-2222
☎ 775-2221
≓ 775-7729
Located in the heart of a large Spanish-style villa, the Gran Hotel Nacional has 75 acceptably comfortable, well-kept rooms, but the decor is simple and lacks charm. Its location in the heart of the city, as well as its moderate prices, nevertheless make it one of the best places in downtown.

From David to Boquete

Cabañas La Cascada
$
pb, ℜ, #
on the right side of the road leading to Boquete, 8.9 km from the Interamericana
☎ 776-0011
These small, barely comfortable cabaña-style rooms are situated in lovely leafy surroundings. The setting is enhanced by a waterfall plunging into a small basin. The number of *cabañas* is restricted so it is best to reserve in advance, especially on weekends. Expect to pay B/. 11 per night for a double room.

Boquete

Hotel Rebequet
$
pb, hw
take the main street in the village and turn right on the second street after the Texaco station, there is a small sign for the hotel
☎ 720-1365
Small family hotel, clean, and fairly comfortable. A pleasant indoor garden adds to the setting.

Pensión Marilos
$
follow the signs for the hotel Rebequet on the main street of the village; the boarding house is directly in front of the hotel
☎ 720-1380
This unpretentious little boarding house provides a pleasant family setting. Good breakfasts for B/. 2.

The Hotel Fundadores
$
pb, hw
to the left of the main road at the entrance to town
☎ 720-1298
This simple hotel offers very basic rooms, located in a lovely setting. The rooms face a garden through which a pretty river flows, and some rooms offer views of the surrounding mountains.

The Pensión Virginia
$-$$
pb, hw, ℜ
on the central plaza
☎ 720-1260
The Pensión provides either ordinary or more luxurious rooms, depending on the price.

Province of Chiriquí

The owner's daughter is very kind, and speaks English (she lived in the U.S. for a long time). The place is well kept up and the interior is enhanced by a small garden. You will be received warmly.

Cabañas Villa Lorena
$$
pb, hw
Calle 11 de Abril
☎ *720-1848*
A stone's throw from the Panamonte Hotel, right next to the bridge over the Río Caldera, the Cabañas Villa Lorena are three small cabins set in an attractively landscaped garden facing the Río Caldera. The cabins are connected to the owners' residence but set back slightly from each other. The small but comfortable rooms provide a peaceful stay accompanied by the sounds of birds and the nearby river. Renting a cabin costs about B/. 35 per day.

Residencial Campestre Los Piños
$$$
pb, hw, tv, K
Avenida Central, Apdo 275, Boquete, on the left side of the road heading to Los Naranjos
☎ *775-1521*
⌨ *774-6536*
Perched on a small hill, the Residencial Campestre Los Pinos is a new building whose modern appearance clashes somewhat with its surroundings. It includes five modern, fully furnished

two-storey apartments. Each apartment contains a fully-equipped kitchenette, a small dining room and living room, and guest rooms on the upper floor. The decor, although basic, is tasteful and each apartment features a small balcony affording a "plunging" view of the village of Boquete far below. Although the site is somewhat lacking in charm, the garden and lovely country scenery will remind you that you are indeed in exotic territory. Good quality for the price for small (or large) families.

The Hotel Panamonte
$$$-$$$$
pb, hw, ℜ, #
at the edge of town, turn right at the intersection and head toward the small bridge which crosses the river
☎ *720-1327*
⌨ *720-1324*
The Hotel Panamonte is a charming hotel composed of two pretty wooden houses facing each other. The main house, painted blue, is very tastefully decorated with a lovely entrance hall where a collection of old objects testifying to the European roots of the owners are displayed. A spacious and elegant dining room, which also serves as a restaurant, is located to

the right of the hall. In the left wing, at the back, is a lounge equipped with a bar and a pool room, making a pleasant ensemble. At the beginning of the evening, you can relax in comfortable armchairs and warm up near the fire, since the air at this altitude can get quite chilly after nightfall. The rooms are all very comfortable, spread out on the first floor around a magnificent garden which is home to hundreds of different species of plants. At the back of the garden, small *cabañas* with porches and kitchenettes have been set up harmoniously.

The second house, just as charming as the first, has a large apartment which can house from six to eight people (*B/. 94*), as well as several individual rooms (*from B/. 45*), all decorated in the English style complete with hardwood floors. A warm welcome tops off this enchanting spot. At the reception, guests can gather information on the region, or sign up for numerous hikes organized by the hotel (see p238). As this spot is well-known for its beauty and the high quality of the service, it is highly recommended you reserve well in advance.

Jamarillo Arriba Sector

La Montaña y El Valle
$$$
pb, hw, K
Apdo 4-014, Jamarillo Arriba, Boquete
☎/≈ **720-2211**
montana@chiriqui.com,
www.ncal.verio.com/~ptpub
/montana

For those in search of some peace and quiet, La Montaña y El Valle is the ideal location. It features three hillside cabins surrounded by greenery and located on a vast property where orange and coffee trees grow alongside wild vegetation. Paths allow guests to roam about and get a full appreciation of the local flora and fauna.

Each cabin includes a large living room with a view of the mountains on the horizon, dining room, guest room with top-quality mattress, and a fully-equipped kitchen complete with dishes, oven and microwave. As for the decor, the Canadian owners were inspired by local Panamanian handicrafts. Leaving nothing to chance, even a parking space has been included beside each dwelling. And, miracle of miracles, smoking is forbidden in the cabins. As for meals, the health conscious will delight in such creative dishes as the tasty country-style moussaka, pre-

pared by Barry Robins and Jane Walker. Meat lovers, for their part, can savour the likes of a tender garlic-seasoned beef filet with mustard sauce. Delicious cookies, cakes and other temptations are served at the end of the meal. It's a shame that such delicious meals are reserved for hotel guests only! Prices range from B/. 6 to B/. 9 per dish. For a change of pace, visit the library and pick up one of the more than a thousand English and Spanish books available to guests.

El Santuario Sector

Hostal Villa Marita
$$
pb, hw
2 km north of the centre of Boquete, in the El Santuario sector, Apdo 4077, Boquete
☎/≈ **720-1309**
chevita@chiriqui.com

Imagine a cluster of seven small *cabañas*, set in the middle of a well-kept garden, painted in bright hues of ochre and adorned, to the great pride of their owners, with French windows. Such dwellings are found at the Hostal Villa Marita. Each cabin is warmly decorated in wood and includes comfortable double guest rooms as well as a small, fully-equipped kitchen in which one`s favorite meals can be prepared. The far-reaching view from each cabin, with the Volcán Barú as a backdrop, serves as a

reminder that the "rooftop" of Panamá is only 2,000 m above.

Volcán

Cabañas Reinas
$
pb, hw, K, #
29.5 km from the Interamericana, at the village, turn left at the sign, the cabañas are 400 m from the main street
☎ **771-4338**

These small well-equipped cabins can accommodate anywhere from 2 to 12 guests. They are attractively decorated and are surrounded by an extensive garden. This is a good place for an extended stay.

Motel California
$-$$
pb, hw
on the left side of the main street, 200 m after the intersection to Cerro Punta
☎ **771-4272**

Guests can choose from amongst 20 rooms at the Motel California. The interior is basic but clean and the owner, originally from central Europe, greets his customers with a smile. Some of the *cabañas* include several beds and are perfect for groups.

Hotel Dos Ríos
$$
pb, hw
on the left side of the main road which crosses the village, 2 km after the intersection to Cerro Punta
☎ **771-4271**

One of the more enjoyable hotels in Volcán is the Hotel Dos Ríos.

Province of Chiriquí

Ten dwellings face a lovely garden and meandering brook framed by the surrounding mountains. Rooms are fairly comfortable, decorated simply, and kept immaculate.

From Volcán to Cerro Punta

The Cabañas Kucikas
$$$
pb, hw, K
on the left of the road from Cerro Punta to Volcán, pay attention as there is no sign advertising the cabañas on the road
☎/⇄ *771-4245*
☎/⇄ *269-0623*
The Cabañas Kucikas are located 6.8 km from Volcán on the shores of the picturesque Río Chiriquí Viejo which flows in full force all year long. It is here that Anthony and Gladys Kucikas built 18 very charming cabins, some of which can accommodate up to 10 people.

All the cabañas are fully furnished and the decor, if outdated, is pleasant with its prevalence of wood. A fully-equipped kitchen and small dining room occupy the first floor of each cabin whereas one or more rooms make up the top floor. There is enough space between cabins for privacy and a large lawn with swing-sets allows children of all ages to play to their heart's content. This location is perfect for peaceful stays where the only sound is the soft murmur of the river. Good quality for the price.

Cabañas Fistonich
$$
pb, hw, K
a few kilometers after the Bambito Hotel and Bambito Camping Resort; on the left side of the road leading to Cerro Punta, right after a bend, there is a small sign indicating "cabañas"; at this point, cross the wooden bridge and take the road on the right which passes by a farm and leads to the owners' residence; Nueva Suiza sector
☎ *771-2115*
☎ *774-8663*
If staying on a farm is appealing, visit the Cabañas Fistonich. Each of the several small cabins contains one or more guest rooms, a fully-equipped kitchen and a small living room. Since most cabins are right on the property, guests can watch the owners performing their daily farm chores. Crops can be purchased right on the farm, providing a steady supply of fresh and delicious produce for every meal. The cabins are not very stylish and are starting to show their age but the site has a certain charm and is rather picturesque. For those preferring a little more privacy, a cabin rests beyond the little ravine separating the property from the main road. Outdoor living at a reasonable price!

Hotel Bambito
$$$$
pb, hw, ≡, ≈, ℜ, ⊖, ◌, *tv*
on the right heading toward Cerro Punta, approximately 7 km from the centre of Volcán, Apdo 1753, Zona 1, District Bugaba
☎ *771-4265*
⇄ *771-4207*
bambito@chiriqui.com,
www.chiriqui.com/bambito/
Nestled against a lush green backdrop, the Hotel Bambito is not only the most luxurious hotel in the province but also a true haven of peace. The hotel's 46 rooms face beautiful gardens and waterfalls set against the backdrop of a dense forest. Rooms are equally elegant, sometimes even featuring freshly cut flowers. The hotel prides itself in offering all that a traveller in search of comfort might require: tennis court, swimming pools, sauna, gym, bar, night club and, of course, restaurant. Guests can borrow bicycles or go horseback riding.

Ecological excursions are also available. Expensive but oh! so very comfortable.

Bambito Camping Resort
$$$$
pb, hw, tv, ≈, ℜ
on the left side of the road to Cerro Punta, a few kilometers after the Hotel Bambito and immediately after a bridge
☎ 774-4282
☎ 265-5103
⇒ 264-3972
info@bambito-forest-resort.com
bambito-forest-resort.com
Not to be confused with the Hotel Bambito (described above), the Bambito Camping Resort is a new tourist facility composed of a large campground and a few cabins called Royal Suites and Junior Suites. During our visit, the garden around the cabins was still being landscaped and the small swimming pool seemed temporarily unusable.

Suites are spacious and feature, in addition to one or more large guest rooms, a small living room at the entrance. The woody interior lends a rustic and cozy note to the ambiance. Unfortunately, due to the high price, this option would only be worthwhile for groups. As for the campground, prices seemed excessive even though breakfast and equipment rental were included. However, do not hesitate to bargain as the owners are sometimes willing to reduce prices consider-

ably, except on weekends and holidays.

Cerro Punta

The Pensíon La Primavera
$
pb, hw
0.2 km from the main intersection of Cerro Punta, just past the highway
A great choice for budget travellers. It is clean but rudimentary. Between B/. 12 and 15 per night.

The Hotel Cerro Punta
$$
pb, hw, tv, ℜ
on the left side of the main road to Cerro Punta, just before entering the village
☎/⇒ 771-2020
The Hotel Cerro Punta is a pleasant alpine style restaurant (see p249 with a recently added 10-room wing. Although set in a row like a motel and decorated in a somewhat outdated style, the rooms are pleasant and comfortable.

Unfortunately, no windows face the front, thus hiding the exquisite view of the lush green valley capped by magnificent mountains. Those not in need of privacy can enjoy the view by sitting out awhile on the common veranda that links all the rooms. Good quality for the price and very friendly welcome.

Guadelupe

Los Quetzales
$$-$$$$
pb, hw, ℜ, △, ☉
after reaching the end of Guadelupe, turn right at the intersection; the hotel is situated on the left side of the road, Apdo 55-0039
☎ 771-2182
☎ 232-6568
⇒ 771-2226
⇒ 252-2384
www.LosQuetzales.com,
carlos@losquetzales.com
Who hasn't dreamt of staying in the middle of the jungle in total comfort? If this possibility sounds tempting, try one of the lodging options offered by Los Quetzales, located in the small town of Guadelupe. The first is a brand new wooden, alpine-style hotel built at the entrance to the Parque Internacional La Amistad. The 10 rooms are simply furnished but comfortable, and there is also a fine restaurant as well as a bakery. Moreover, a sauna and a spa have been set up next to the river as well as a room with a ping-pong table.

A playground and animal farm keep children busy and give parents a break. For something to do on rainy days, wood sculpting classes are offered as well as cooking classes for the less artistically inclined. Those who crave news from home despite all of these activities can take advantage of an

Province of Chiriquí

Internet service, which is available for B/. 5 an hour.

The second option, **La Amistad**, is more expensive (*about B/. 99 to rent a chalet for 4 people*) but extraordinary. There are three cabins for rent in the heart of Parque Internacional La Amistad. Each dwelling is completely secluded and nestled deep in the forest. Getting there involves a half-hour hike with a guide from Los Quetzales or being driven part of the way in a 4WD vehicle (*free transportation*).

Two of the dwellings are on the mountainside and include kitchen, living room and fireplace, guest rooms and observation deck, on two storeys. The hotel provides a daily catering service for those who do not want to cook. The third cabin is located below a river and has two separate floors each of which can accommodate up to six people (*B/. 55 per storey*).

Each storey has two guest rooms, living room, dining room with fireplace, kitchen and bathroom. Because the cabins are located in a national park, strict rules must be followed. For example, it is forbidden to smoke, bring a radio, pick plants, capture insects or animals and all non-biodegradable waste must be carried out upon departure.

Those who can afford it should not miss this unique experience especially since it also includes various guided excursions at no extra charge.

Restaurants

David

La Cacerola
$
corner of Avenida Francisco Clark and Calle P Norte, to the right of the shopping centre Super Baru, turn left on the main road to David, just after the intersection with the Interamericana and Boquete
This restaurant-cafeteria serves different dishes (vegetables, rice with vegetables, beef tongue, chicken, etc.) at unparalleled prices. Expect to pay B/. 2.5 for a meal – a real deal!

Restaurante y Cafeteria Jimar
$
Avenida Bolivar and Calle C Norte
The Restaurante y Cafeteria is a bustling place that is particularly popular with students attracted by the inexpensive prices. The large windows give the restaurant an open feeling even when all the tables are taken. A complete lunch can be had for B/. 2.

While the menu is predictable for the most part (chicken, *corvina*, shrimp...), a few less common dishes are available, including smoked meat with tomato and onion and *tortas* (a kind of Spanish tortilla made with eggs, similar to an omelette). While this is a good place for travellers who are watching their pennies, the food is average.

Restaurante Hotel Fiesta
$$
at the intersection for David and Boquete, on the right of the Interamericana
☎ 775-5454
☎ 775-5453
The Restaurante Hotel Fiesta is a large restaurant with appealing colonial decor. A wide variety of dishes, both Panamanian and French, are offered at reasonable prices.

Las Vegas
$$
11am to 3pm and 6pm to 11pm, pastries from 7am
corner of Avenida Central and Calle Primera, facing the Hotel Nacional
Whether for a generous breakfast, a delicious plate of fresh pasta, a pizza or just a simple pastry and coffee, the café-restaurant Las Vegas is a very pleasant place. A small patio filled with flowers is a great complement to this unpretentious spot, whose clientele is mostly local.

Mar del Sur
$$$

*every day 11am to 3pm
and 6pm to 11pm*
Calle H Norte and Avenida 1
Oeste, on the right side of the
main road to David, behind the
Supermercado La Fe de
Dolequita
☎ *775-0856*
If you would like some
delicious South Amer-
ican cuisine, be sure to
try the Mar del Sur,
where authentic Peru-
vian dishes make up
the menu, including
*Papas a la huancaína,
Almejas a la Sureña*
(southern-style soft-
shelled clams), or
Mariscos Salteados (sea-
food sautéed with on-
ions, tomatoes and
garlic).

For customers who
want meat, a *filete a la
pimienta verde* or *al
curry* would be a good
choice. To go with
your meal, excellent
Chilean and Argentin-
ean wines are available
at reasonable prices.
Finally, for a lovely
finish, try the *Suspiros
de Lima*, the house des-
sert. The atmosphere is
pleasant and the decor
welcoming. A good
price/quality ratio.

From David to
Boquete

The Restaurante Bar
Bonjour
$

on the left side of the road to
Boquete just after it crosses the
Interamericana
The Restaurante Bar
Bonjour is a large
open-air restaurant that

offers a range of dishes
(including pizza,
chicken, shrimp, ham-
burgers and rice).
While close to the
road, it is in a nice area
and is surrounded by
tropical plants. This is
also a good place to
stop for a drink.

Bar y Restaurante La
Cascada
$

8.9 km from the
Interamericana on the right
side of the road leading to
Boquete
Typical, inexpensive
Panamanian fare served
in an open-air restau-
rant under a palm-
thatched roof, next to a
water fountain. A plate
of chicken will set you
back B/. 5.

Boquete

Volcánita
$

on the right side of the road
through town, just before the
central plaza
For a good selection of
pizzas, head to the tiny
PizzeriaVolcánita res-
taurant, where you will
be warmly welcomed.

Restaurante El Sabrosón
$

Calle 1 Sur and Avenida Central
The restaurant El
Sabrosón prepares
typical Panamanian
fare with the ubiqui-
tous beans, rice and
platanas fritas. No big
surprises but for B/. 2 a
meal what more could
you ask for?

Restaurante Lourdes
$

overlooking the main street, on
the left side, just before the
central plaza
The Restaurante
Lourdes is an unpreten-
tious, simply decorated
place that serves home-
style Panamanian food.
For some reason, it is
renowned for its french
fries.

Café Montañés El
Explorador
$

9am to 6pm
head past the bridge near the
Panamonte hotel and follow the
main road to the left; continue
for another km and take the
road branching off to the right;
continue straight for 3 km, and
turn right just after the basket-
ball court. The restaurant is
1.5 km beyond on the left side of
the road
This charming restau-
rant is located at an
altitude of 1,200 m, and
has a spectacular view.
The menu includes
mostly traditional Pana-
manian dishes, such as
sancocho de gallina (a
rich chicken soup) and
corn tortillas. While the
road to the restaurant is
in rough shape, partic-
ularly the last section,
the trip is worth it for
the exceptional sur-
roundings. Friendly
staff.

Conquista
$$

on the left side of the road
facing the Pizzeria la Volcanita
The Conquista restau-
rant prepares a variety
of simple, family-style
dishes for around
B/. 15.

Fundadores
$$
on the left, at the start of the main road going through the village
☎ *720-1298*
The restaurant in the Fundadores hotel is worth a mention for its lovely surroundings. There are two levels; the room on the first floor offers an interesting view of a pretty flowered garden and a river which, surprisingly, runs right under the building. Sculptures of exotic birds made from painted car tires (who would have thought...) are another delightful detail.

Finally, the owner adds her own personal touch with fresh flowers on every table. A complete menu of Panamanian cuisine is offered for B/. 15, and good breakfasts are served for as little as B/. 4. For smaller appetites, spaghetti or *arroz con camarones* (rice with shrimp) at B/. 4 are perfect. Friendly staff.

🌴Panamonte
$$$
at the edge of town, turn right at the intersection and head toward the small bridge which crosses the river
☎ *720-1327*
The Restaurante Hotel Panamonte is located in an attractive and charming hotel. The menu is varied and the high quality food is very well prepared. Dishes include filet mignon, excellent corn soup, *pernil de porco*

and scampi. The desserts are simple but also very good (try the home-made flan). A very tasty cocktail made with fresh orange juice is a good way to start your meal. Breakfasts are big and inexpensive, the staff efficient and friendly. One little drawback, the selection is limited and there are no menus as such. The staff, however, will gladly describe the different dishes available and they did promise us a menu was on the way! Very good value for money.

From La Concepción to Volcán

Mirador AlanHer
$
take the road to Volcán from the Interamericana, the Mirador is 15.9 km farther, on the left side of the road
This modest restaurant at the bottom of a *mirador* serves very good light meals. Try the *queso deretido* (cheese on the grill) or the *batidos* (a kind of *chicha*). There is also a good selection of cheeses and yoghurts. This is perfect place to stop on the way to Volcán.

Restaurante La Cabaña
$
open from 7am to 6pm
north of Cuesta di Piedra, 18.8 km from the Interamericana toward Volcán
A pleasant little restaurant with a lovely

garden and a nice view. Simple, unpretentious local dishes.

From Volcán to Cerro Punta

Bambito
$$$
turn right onto the highway on the way to Cerro Punta, about 7km from the centre of Volcán
☎ *771-4265*
Very pleasant restaurant in a charming location with a view of artificial waterfalls. Varied and refined menu, composed of Panamanian and French cuisine. Good quality for the price, with amenable staff and services.

La Campagnola
$$$
to the left of the road leading to Cerro Punta, a few kilometers after the Bambito Hotel and immediately after a bridge
☎ *774-4282*
☎ *265-5103*
Part of the Bambito Camping Resort, the La Campagnola restaurant offers an extensive Italian menu featuring mostly pasta dishes. A considerable wine list is also offered but prices are prohibitive. The two wood-panelled dining rooms are cozy and offer an attractive view of the gardens. The house also prepares meat and fish dishes for those not in the mood for pasta. Nice decor but a little expensive.

Cerro Punta

Cerro Punta
$$
on the left of the main road, at
the entrance to the village
☎ *771-2020*
Located in a lovely
setting, with a very
good view of the
mountains, this restau-
rant serves traditional
local cuisine at afford-
able prices. Friendly
staff.

Guadelupe

🦐Los Quetzales
$$
at the end of Guadelupe, turn
right at the intersection, the
hotel is situated on the left side
of the road
☎ *771-2182*
☎ *232-6568*
On the second storey
of the hotel of the
same name, the Los
Quetzales restaurant
serves pizza and Pana-
manian dishes at low
prices. However, the
pride of the house is its
farmed trout served
with fresh vegetables
grown locally without
the use of chemical
fertilizers. Its large
wood-panelled dining
room complete with
fireplace is particularly
enjoyable and warm.
After a meal the com-
fortable sofas in the
cozy bar beside the
restaurant are the per-
fect place to sip a
digestif. Finally, visit the
bakery on the first floor
and stock up on nu-
merous goodies for
upcoming excursions.

Definitely an address to
remember.

Gariché

**Balneario Restaurante
Camino al Cielo**
9 km from the town of
Concepción, en route to the
Costa Rican border, the
Interamericana crosses the Río
Gariché which flows from the
Cordillera de Talamanca
The small Balneario
Restaurante Camino al
Cielo overlooks the *río*.
Choice is very limited,
and one must not
expect a gastronomical
experience, but as little
as B/. 4 will buy a
typical Panamanian
meal. To get there,
soon after the bridge
over the river, turn
right off the main road
onto a dirt road. This
leads to the restaurant's
parking lot (free). To
avoid any unpleasant
surprises, do not leave
anything in a parked
car.

Entertainment

From David to La Concepción

Disco Metropoli
Mon to Sat from 10:30pm
Located less than 3 km from the
intersection for David and
Boquete
The Disco Metropoli is
one of the places for
hip young people from
David to see and be
seen. Latin-American
and English music.

Ambiance and "cruis-
ing" guaranteed!

Jorón las Totumas
every day from 11am
on the right of the
Interamericana, 5 km after the
exit for David and Boquete
Located on the edge of
the Interamericana, the
Jorón las Totumas is a
huge restaurant-club,
where you can relax
and have a drink under
the *bohío* into the wee
hours. It's a good meet-
ing place for young
people who come to
dance. There's always a
fun atmosphere, and
you can order simple
little dishes at very
respectable prices:
arroz con camarones
(rice with shrimp) is
available for B/. 4. The
staff is friendly, and as
long as you like plenty
of action, this is a great
place.

Zebede Disco
Mon to Sat
on the left side of the main road
leading to Boquete, 700 m from
the intersection with the
Interamericana, also called El
Jorón del Amor (!)
Also close to the
Interamericana, the
Zebede Disco attracts
mainly couples after
10:30pm. The dance
floor is surrounded by
many tables, where
you can drink or order
a meal (*expect to pay
about B/. 10*). Latin-
American music.

Shopping

Along the Interamericana

Once you have entered the province of Chiriquí on the Interamericana and passed the large intersection which leads to Tolé but is not marked, the side of the highway is dotted with small shops with palm roofs selling Amerindian arts and crafts. **Jewellery**, such as *chaquiras* (necklaces), bracelets and earrings, as well as **clothing**, including colourful dresses are available here. Most items are made by the Guaymíes. A reduction of about 10% is possible if you bargain.

David

David is a pretty good place to do your shopping since the prices are reasonable and the selection is varied. Other than the usual purchases (clothes, music, shoes, etc.), you can find various handicrafts in the central plaza, including very beautiful *molas* which are not too expensive (*B/. 12 to B/. 15*).

Boquete

Café Ruiz
Avenida Central, past the centre of the village on the right side of the road to Alto Lino
☎ *720-1000*
☎ *720-1392*
⇄ *720-1292*
After an educational introduction to coffee making, buy some of the country's finest coffee at the Café Ruiz. Regular, amaretto, chocolate or hazelnut flavored coffees are available.

Conservas de Antaño
from the Parque Domingo Médica, cross the bridge and drive 100 m on the street to the right
☎ *720-1539*
After having discovered (and tasted) all the secrets of jam-making at the Conservas de Antaño, it is highly unlikely that you will leave empty-handed. Pick up some mango jam for future breakfasts (providing there's some left!). Delicious!

On weekends in the village of Boquete, **Place Centrale** in the centre of town is transformed into a morning market, where the Guaymíes come to sell their arts and crafts.

Along the Interamericana to Volcán

Arte Cruz
on main road leading to Volcán, the workshop is on the left side of the road going up the hill, 26.2 km from the Interamericana
The Arte Cruz is a small studio that sells wood sculptures and engraved glass. José Cruz Gonzalez, the artist, will be happy to show you around. Some pieces are for sale and you can special order from Gonzalez who is very proud of his work; he'll even show you an album of his nicest pieces, some of which have taken first prize in contests. José Cruz Gonzalez, who studied in Italy, has sold pieces to buyers from the United States, Europe, and South Africa. He can even engrave a beautiful landscape in glass for you on the spot. A worthwhile stop.

From Volcán to Cerro Punta

Stalls sell fresh fruit all along the road to Cerro Punta just after the Hotel Bambito. Great for a picnic.

Province of Bocas del Toro

The Province of Bocas del Toro is aptly named the province of "green gold".

Covered by exuberant vegetation, it contains almost all of the vast Parque Internacional La Amistad, one of the largest protected zones in Central America. In spite of being the site of a landing by Christopher Colombus in 1502, the Spanish colonists ignored this region because of its remote location and it remained totally undeveloped for two centuries.

Except for indigenous peoples (see p34), the temporary presence of English pirates and a small Huguenot community in the 18th century, it was only at the beginning of the 19th century that the first permanent settlers were established. The little town of Bocas del Toro came into being in

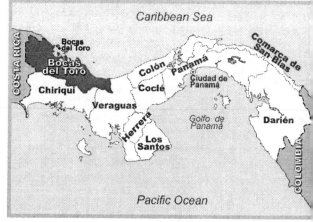

1826. Populated by landowners and former slaves from the islands of San Andrés and Providencia, it started out more like a campsite than a town. Many adventurers and merchants stopped here while hunting sea turtles, very much in demand at the time. With the subsequent arrival of people from Jamaica, the place became a little town. Cacao cultivation, lumbering, gathering coconuts

and fishing were the principle economic activities on the island. However, the intensive cultivation of bananas is the main reason for the development of Bocas del Toro. In 1899 the famous United Fruit Company set up its head office here and, in only a few years' time, transformed the modest city into one of the country's largest areas of available employment. In addition to the Amerindian populations (notably Guyamíes), many former workers at the then bankrupt canal (mainly black people from the Antilles) came here in an effort to improve their circumstances. This created significant traffic between Colón and Bocas del Toro. When the Republic of Panamá was created in 1903, it was one of the most influential regions, and the third largest commercially. During this era there were even several foreign consulates operating in the little city on behalf of France, Great Britain, Germany and the United States.

Unfortunately for the fledgling metropolis, prosperity was to be short-lived. During the 1920s, diseases affecting the banana crop caused the ruin of the city. United Fruit transferred its head office, first to Changuinola, and subsequently to Puerto Armuelles in the neighbouring province of Chiriquí. This left the entire region destitute, and Bocas del Toro and its province have gradually regressed to

their original state of isolation.

Today, with only modest cities like Chiriquí Grande, Changuinola, Almirante and Bocas del Toro, this large province is sparsely populated, and many of its Guyamíes inhabitants are scattered in innumerable isolated communities. Since the establishment of a road between Chiriquí Grande and the Pan-American Highway, the economy has been mainly based on the transport of merchandise from neighbouring Costa Rica to the port city, Almirante.

Among other sources of revenue, an oil pipeline that runs from north to south through the country is used for transporting various products from one ocean to the other. Also, for several years now, the cultivation of bananas has resumed in the region of Changuinola, although on a more modest scale than formerly. It figures as an important economic factor.

As far as tourism is concerned, like

Darién, it is still among the least developed provinces, but it seems to be ready to take up the challenge and become fully involved.

The new hotels and restaurants that have established themselves in the little town of Bocas del Toro, while few in number, indicate a trend in this direction. The island on which it is located, Isla Colón, marks the start of the Archipiélago de Bocas del Toro, which contains the only marine park in the country, at Isla Bastimentos. Well known for the beauty of its ocean floor and the richness of its coral, the archipelago is the principal attraction in the province. If diving and the underwater world are particularly interesting to you, make sure to visit the area.

Finding accommodation on this beautiful island is difficult. At press time, a project to create a veritable floating vacation village was in the works. Called "**Les Robinsons**" (*information: Laval@iname.com, www.robinsons-sa.com*), the complex will consist of 60 houses, each on a 70 m² area of land, with all the services of a room in a luxury hotel. It will be built on the open sea, a good distance from the shore.

As for the other important object of curiosity in the region, the Parque Internacional La Amistad, its main entrance is in the neighbouring province of Chiriquí, so it can be explored without passing through Bocas del Toro. The province has enough unique aspects to be charming on its own. Since many of the inhabitants are of either Caribbean or Indigenous descent, both the form of housing and the language spoken here are different from those in other parts of the country. English is more widespread here and in addition to its being spoken with strong Creole intonations, it is enriched by many Spanish, and, sometimes, Guyamíes, terms. To add to the linguistic potpourri, in an attempt to Hispanicize the remote province, former authorities renamed, or simply translated, many

of the place names. Do not be surprised to find two names for the same island or beach, with *cay* transformed into *cayo*, or sometimes even, *isla*.

Finding Your Way Around

By Car

To get to **Chiriquí Grande** when driving west on the Interamericana, turn right at the intersection 85 km past Tolé. If you are coming from David, that is, driving east, the intersection is about 10 km away, on the left side of the Interamericana, just after the bridge over the Río Chiriquí. There is a service station at Chiriquí Grande, on the left at the end of the main road through the village.

To get to **Bocas del Toro** by car, the only way is to go first to Chiriquí Grande, and from there, to take a ferry to Isla Colón. Since the island is quite small and easy to see by bicycle, there is little point in travellers going by car.

At Chiriquí Grande proper, the **Expreso Taxi 25** and **Dela-Tours** (see p254) transportation

companies will keep your vehicle for the modest sum of B/1.50 to B/. 2 per day.

To get to **Parque Internacional La Amistad** see the "Province of Chiriquí" chapter (see p221, 240).

Note: the following schedules and rates are provided for reference only and are subject to change.

By Plane

For Bocas del Toro and Almirante, the best way is by plane, since it is not only the fastest way to get there, but also the most comfortable.

Bocas del Toro and Changuinola

Mapiex-Aero and **Aeroperlas** are the only companies currently serving these destinations. Flights are available from the capital or from David.

Mapiex-Aero

Ciudad de Panamá to Bocas del Toro
Departure: daily at noon
Travel time: 1 hour
Cost: B/. 48 one way

At press time, the company was planning to create a link between David and Bocas del Toro with a stop in Changuinola. Flight time: 30 min., cost: B/. 24, one way.

Bocas del Toro

Bocas del Toro
☎ *757-9841*
⇆ *757-9842*

David (Enrique Malek Airport)
☎ *721-0841*
☎ *721-0842*
⇆ *721-0843*

Aeroperlas

Ciudad de Panamá to Bocas del Toro (stop-over in Changuinola)
Departure: Mon to Thu 6:45am;
Fri 6:45am and 1:45pm;
Sat 7am;
Sun 3pm (non-stop)
Travel time: 1 hour 15 min
Cost: B/. 51

David to Bocas del Toro (stop-over in Changuinola)
Departure: Mon 7:45am;
Tue to Thu 7:25am;
Fri 7:25am and 4:15pm
Travel time: 50 min
Cost: B/. 24

Bocas del Toro
☎ 757-9341

David (Enrique Malek airport)
☎ *721-1195*
☎ *721-1230*

By Boat

Bocas del Toro and Almirante

The ever-increasing stream of tourists heading to Bocas del Toro has given rise to growing numbers of private operators in the little port of Chiriquí Grande who offer to take visitors to the islands for a few dollars. Unfortu-nately, given the irregularity of these activities, there is practically no control over the boats, and although the traveller may be attracted by the competitive prices, too often they are offered at the expense of safety. Under the circumstances it is far better to pay a few dollars more to a duly licensed company that is subject to regular inspections.

Among these, there are two businesses that have been operating for some time, **Expreso Taxi 25** (☎ 757-9691) and **Dela-Tours** (☎ 757-9172 or 758-3117). Both make regular crossings to Almirante, stopping in Bocas del Toro when there are enough passengers to justify making the trip. Although there are departures hourly (*7am to 5pm*), the schedule is subject to changes (depending on ocean conditions, the number of passengers, vacation times and national holidays) so it is best to call ahead before venturing to Chiriquí Grande. Ferries depart from the main wharf near the gas station. It takes about 45 min to go to Bocas del Toro (*cost one way: B/. 8*). The trip to Almirante takes 1 hr to 1 hr 15 min (*cost one way: B/. 10*).

Boca del Drago and the Islands of the Archipelago

Many outfits offer transportation to the islands in the archipelago. Since almost none of the islands have hotels or restaurants, most of these excursions are round-trip. Addresses for these enterprises and advice about exploring the islands is found in the "Outdoor Activities" section of this chapter.

Chiriquí Grande

From Bocas del Toro, **Expreso Taxi 25** leaves from the wharf off Calle 1 at the intersection with Calle 3 (see below for times and rates). Crossings via **Dela Tours** leave from the little dock just beside Le Pirate restaurant (Calle 3).

By Bus

Chiriquí Grande

There is regular bus service between David and Chiriquí Grande; the bus stop in David is on Paseo Estudiante and the fare is about B/. 6. The trip takes approximately three hours.

Boca del Drago

While there is bus service of a sort between Bocas del Toro and Boca del Drago, on the northeastern part of the

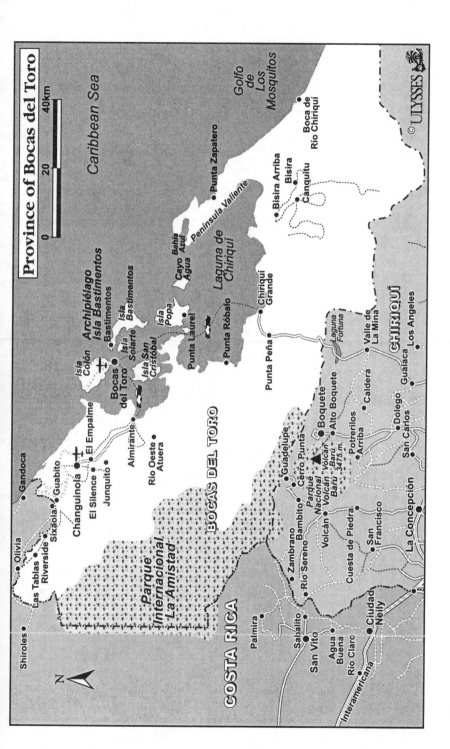

island, it serves mainly as transport for local workers as the need arises. The trip takes about 45 min (*B/. 2.50 one way*) and you can be let off at the grotto. However the trip back from either destination only takes place late in the day when there are sufficient passengers to make the trip worthwhile, so this mode of transport is more adventurous than practical.

Unfortunately, apart from cycling or walking, the taxi is the only reliable way to get to Boca del Drago, and it costs B/. 25 round trip. It is best to round up a large group of friends to split the fare, which is somewhat expensive since the distance travelled is only 15 km!

By Train

While there is a railway line between Almirante and Changuinola, and another to Guabito, they are for transporting merchandise (mainly bananas). Since the trains offer no amenities for passengers, the owners, **Chiriquí Land Company** (☎ *758-8414*), are reluctant to let non-personnel aboard.

To Get to Costa Rica

There are two ways to reach **Sixaola (Costa Rica)**: either directly to Sixaola, through Almirante, or via Bocas del Toro on Isla Colón. The second route is more interesting, as you will spend your time on beautiful and exotic Isla Colón rather than the less interesting town of Almirante. By leaving early in the morning from Chiriquí Grande, you can spend a day and evening exploring Isla Colón before setting off for Almirante first thing the next day.

From there, there are two ways to continue your travels: by bus or by train. The bus is the more comfortable and dependable way to go. Take the bus to Changuinola and transfer to the bus bound for Guabito. Guabito is connected to the village of Sixaola by a bridge over the Río Sixaola (which flows along the border of Costa Rica and Panamá).

There is a one hour time difference between Panamá and Costa Rica. Remember to put your watch back an hour when you arrive in Sixaola.

Practical Information

Bocas del Toro

IPAT Tourist Bureau

On the main street of Bocas del Toro inside a little house on stilts, the tourist bureau provides all the necessary information for a pleasant stay. Entry to the office is by way of a narrow wooden gangway, and is therefore not recommended for people who suffer from vertigo! Fortunately, during our visit a new, more accessible office was under construction on Calle 1. In the near future it will house both the IPAT and ANAM offices.

IPAT
Mon to Fri
Calle 3
☎/⇆ *757-9642*

ANAM (INRENARE)

Vistors to the national parks, including Parque Marino de la Isla Bastimentos, must obtain authorisation from ANAM. As a general rule, local agencies do not include the cost of the permit in the excursion rate. Would-be visitors must go to the ANAM office to obtain it.

ANAM
Calle 1
☎ *757-9244*

Bank

Banco Nacional de Panamá
Avenida F, between Calle 1 and
Calle 2

Telecommunications

There is a public tele-
phone next to the
Parque Simón Bolívar
(Parque Central) on
Calle 3.

Exploring

From Chiriquí to Chiriquí Grande

The road leading from
the Interamericana to
Chiriquí Grande makes
for an especially fasci-
nating trip. While
crossing the Talamanca
Cordillera, which is
covered in thick jungle,
the landscape is dotted
with the typical dwell-
ings of the Guaymíes.
As well, the landscape
varies the whole way
not only depending on
the altitude, but also
depending on which
side of the road you
are on. On the Pacific
side, the scenery is
made up of plains
dotted with hills and
mountains covered
with rich green vegeta-
tion here, and scorched
brown there, while the
Atlantic side is blan-

keted by a veritable
jungle of tropical vege-
tation. The vegetation
becomes particularly
distinct in the Reserva
Forestal La Fortuna.
The entire length of the
route is attractive, and
a number of dramatic
views provide memora-
ble highlights. The
return trip can easily be
made in a day from
David or Boquete. The
distances mentioned in
the following descrip-
tions correspond to
distances from the
Interamericana high-
way.

The first stop at the
30,9 km mark allows
you to admire a beauti-
ful view of the plains
and the hills beyond;
clouds seem to have
been carefully placed
above to make a
picture-perfect land-
scape.

At 32.4 km and 34.5
km, there are two rudi-
mentary rest stops on
the left that have lovely
views of the Pacific
Ocean and, farther off
in the distance, the
islands of Boca Brava
and Parida.

At the 45.7 km mark, a
small, refreshing stop is
perfect for admiring a
charming waterfall on
the left side of the
road.

At 47.9 km, just after
the entrance to a ceme-
tery, the road turns left.
From here, there is a
good view of an artifi-
cial lake, Lago Fortuna,
the by-product of a
hydroelectric dam. The

one-lane bridge over
the lake is a great spot
for beautiful vistas. A
little further on, on the
left side of the road, a
section of the oil pipe-
line taking the oil from
Puerto Armuelles (on
the Pacific coast) to the
Atlantic coast is easy to
spot.

At 52.8 km, on the left
side of the road, an-
other more impressive
waterfall spills down
(about 10 m high).

At 56 km, you can stop
briefly to see the conti-
nental divide for the
country's water. From
this point on, rivers
flow toward the Atlan-
tic. This is also the
location of the border
between the provinces
of Chiriquí and Bocas
del Toro.

There is another water-
fall at 58.7 km, on the
right-hand side of the
road. Just after it, you
will see the occasional
traditional Guaymíe
houses, balancing on
high stilts. 10 km
ahead, the road passes
through the little Amer-
indian village of Malí.

Chiriquí Grande

A small port city where
travellers and merchan-
dise pass through,
Chiriquí Grande is not
really an attractive
place. It is nonetheless
striking and worth a
brief visit. A walkway
along the sea provides
a good view of residen-
tial architecture typical
of the region and char-

Bocas del Toro

acteristic of houses on the Caribbean coast. To do this, turn right at the end of the main street in the village, walk to a small bridge, which you must cross to keep going straight. You'll soon find yourself on a winding street past small houses up on stilts, with children playing around them. The mood of this place combined with the richness of the surrounding vegetation, are enough to set travellers dreaming. Canoes paddled by the Amerindians add to the wonder of this isolated corner of the world. It's magical!

Isla Colón

Aside from the airport in Changuinola on the mainland, the 60-km² Isla Colón has the only one in the province, thus it is the main gateway to the archipelago and the national marine park at Bastimentos Island. Almost deserted, it has a total of two roads and only one of them is partially paved. Because Bocas del Toro is the only "city" on Isla Colón, it is a required stop, as far as accommodations and restaurants are concerned. With the exception of some beautiful isolated beaches (see "Beaches" section) (see p260), the island's only tourist attraction is a spot called **La Gruta** (also named Sanctuario Natural de Nuestra

Señora de la Gruta), located in the middle of the island. This grotto contains a statuette of the Virgin that is an object of annual pilgrimages. It is also home to a colony of bats, numbering in the hundreds and very easily observable. Unless you are on the way to the beach at Boca del Drago (the road passes nearby), or wish to make a pilgrimage, the trip is not worth the 5 km on a miserable dirt road, which is frequently transformed into a series of mud holes after a rainfall.

Bocas del Toro

Founded in 1826 by immigrants from the islands of San Andrés and Providencia (see introduction to chapter) (see p251), the little town of Bocas del Toro has certainly seen better days. Aside from being abandoned by the United Fruit Company, the town has faced several fires (1904, 1907, 1918 and 1929) and two terrible tornadoes: one in 1964 that destroyed its cathedral (circa 1897), and another in 1975. To top it off, an earthquake damaged the airplane landing strip and several buildings in 1991. It comes as no surprise that there are few surviving historic buildings... just some fine examples of Caribbean-style wooden houses that too few residents seem

motivated to restore. Nevertheless, it is a required stop since it is the only town in the province that offers any significant choice of hotels and restaurants. Most of these establishments are on Calle 3, which is the town's de facto "Calle Central" and one of the rare paved roads. The park in the town centre is lovely, but badly neglected. It would also be helpful if the information kiosque of the Caribaro Association in the middle of the park, which seems to contain valuable information about the flora and fauna of the region, were repaired so that tourists could find out more about the area's resources.

As things stand, having a pleasant stay in Bocas del Toro is limited to visiting the islands of the archipelago, or the nearby beaches, and spending the evening at one of the town's restaurants. Anyone passing through in September should make sure to catch the "Feria del Mar", a large fair with displays of crafts and local products, followed by enthusiastic celebrations. Finally, an amusing detail: fans of antique vehicles should stop by the firehouse (Calle 1 and Avenida G) to admire the remarkable model of a fire engine which has long been the pride and joy of the inhabitants.

The Phantom Fleet

Perhaps you have noticed the many vessels flying the Panamanian flag. In fact, the Panamanian fleet is the biggest in the world after Liberia's. Don't be fooled, however, because few of these ships actually belong to Panamanian companies. Rather, Panamá, like Liberia, offers foreign companies licenses to operate their vessels on advantageous terms. For example, Panamá charges vessels flying the Panamanian flag less to pass through the canal. Some say it is a flag of convenience in reference to the more lax restrictions invoked by Panamá and Liberia. This phantom fleet generates more than $120 million US per year for Panamá, or 3% of the GNP.

This fleet may expand considerably in the coming years, since the regulation restricting American vessels from registering anywhere but in the United States is about to be lifted.

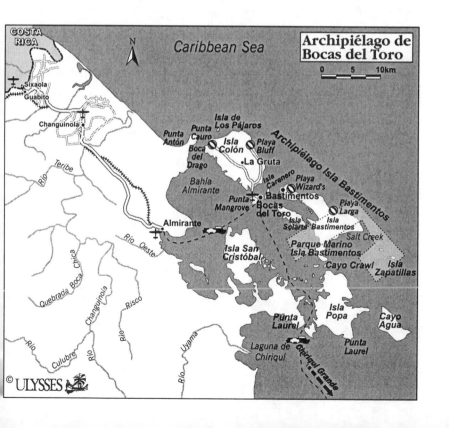

Isla Carenero

Across from the town of Bocas del Toro, Isla Carenero has no specific attraction except for a few tourist restaurants. If you decide to have breakfast here, take a stroll through the neighbouring village. Just follow the shore to the left of the landing stage to the little concrete path that winds through the locality. This will plunge you into the daily life of the inhabitants of Carenero and let you see their little houses on stilts, which are so typical of the archipelago. It seems miraculous that some of them are still standing!

Isla de Los Pájaros, or Swan Cay

This tiny island, better described as a large rock, is a bird sanctuary, and is mainly of interest to birders. Although landing on the island is strictly forbidden, numerous so-called "guides" will offer a little tour on the island itself. To avoid disturbing the nesting process, refuse any such offer and enjoy the beauty of the site from a boat.

Isla Solarte, or Cay Nancy

A mere 2 km from Isla Colón, this island's history began when, hard on the heels of its establishment at Bocas del Toro, United Fruit decided to erect housing facilities for members of its staff who had caught malaria. Over the years, the 16 buildings of Hospital Point, as the company named it, became the largest hospital in the province. When the banana plantations were destroyed by disease, the company completely dismantled the hospital before leaving the area, around 1920. Although some agencies in Bocas suggest excursions to the island, there is really nothing left to see except for a few structures overgrown with vegetation.

Isla San Cristóbal

As is the case with many of the islands in the archipelago, the waters surrounding Isla San Cristóbal are rich in marine wildlife. The northern part of the island, with its vast stands of mangrove, is habitat for many dolphins that may be observed there. A lighthouse stands at the northernmost point of the island to guide ships through the passage on their way to Almirante, where they take on large cargoes of bananas destined for America or Europe. San Cristóbal is also the name of a Guyamíes village, which is visited by some tour groups.

Almirante and Changuinola

Although these two little towns have a few modest hotels and restaurants, they are well off the beaten path. And rightly so! Almirante is just a simple port with shabby houses; and Changuinola is really only a centre of banana cultivation surrounded by plantations as far as the eye can see. Except for people taking the land route to Costa Rica, and those who are fascinated by the technical aspects of growing bananas, Changuinola has nothing to offer tourists.

Beaches

As is unfortunately the case on many of the beaches on the archi-

pelago, nasty insects seem to show particular delight in biting new arrivals. To take full advantage of the province's beautiful beaches, come prepared with ample supplies of insect repellent.

Isla Colón

Playa El Istmito

This popular, modest beach is not one of the prettiest, but it has the advantages of relative safety and being located directly outside the little town of Bocas.

Playa Bluff

Swimming is dangerous here because of the violent waves; it is best for surf boarding and hiking.

A 3-km stretch of shoreline swept by violent waves, Playa Bluff is a great place for long, solitary walks. From June to September, many sea turtles, especially leatherbacks, come up onto the beaches at night to lay their eggs. Since this is an endangered species, visitors during this season must follow certain rules. Those who wish to witness this event can do so though the auspices of ANAM (INRENARE) or Ancon Expeditions of Bocas del Toro which offer guided tours here at night. If this subject fascinates you, make

sure you visit the Biblioteca Pública de Bocas (Calle 3), where the Caribaro association can inform you about the lifestyles of these marvelous reptiles.

Boca del Drago

Opposite Bocas del Toro, on the northwest side of the island is the bay called **Boca del Drago** and the beach of the same name. This is one of the loveliest beaches on the island. As long as a few precautionary rules are followed, beginners can safely swim in the limpid waters and stretch out to tan on the attractive, light-coloured sand. The only drawback is that, apart from some cabañas that have been turned into a hotel, and a modest, unidentified little restaurant, there are no services available. One has to bring all the essentials for having a pleasant time.

Parks

Parque Marino de la Isla Bastimentos

With its rich underwater fauna and gigantic beaches that are visited by as many as four species of sea turtles, Parque Marino de la Isla Bastimentos is unique. The island

section represents only one tenth of the park's 13,235-ha area; the remaining 11,600 ha consist of stretches of water where red and white mangroves and coral are readily observable. On the northern part of the island is **Long Beach**, or **Playa Larga**, a vast expanse of spectacular natural beauty made hard to get to by the violent waves that crash against it. A large number of sea turtles (see box p 263) come here each year to lay their eggs. Just a few kilometres inland from Long Beach, a large lake serves as a refuge for fresh water turtles as well as numerous other reptiles, including crocodiles.

The park is also home to a venomous frog, *dendrobates pumilio*, whose skin secretes a toxic substance. Its skin shows a wide palette of colours ranging from vivid scarlet and bright orange to acid green. In spite of its brilliant colouring and the fact that it is present on other islands, it is rarely observed. On the eastern

Sea Turtles

There are eight different kinds of sea turtles that belong to seven distinct species. Sea turtles, along with land and fresh water turtles, belong to the *chelonidae* order and are reptiles. Unfortunately, all species of sea turtles are in danger of extinction, but measures have been adopted both nationally and internationally (creation of nature reserves, protection programs, establishment of reproduction facilities, etc.) to protect these animals.

Physically, these strange creatures have very limited vision when out of water, but this is compensated for by their keen sense of smell and acute hearing. Mostly carnivorous, they have no teeth so they grind up fish, shellfish and crustaceans with their powerful jaws. Their rate of growth is particularly slow, and some claim that certain species can live more than 100 years! Given the limited number of species, the size and consequent weight of sea turtles varies surprisingly. Some weigh a mere 35 kilograms, while others can weigh up to a ton. Part of the latter group, the colossal leatherback turtle is not only the largest, it is also the only species of turtle able to withstand water temperatures under 4°C. For this reason it is found in all of the oceans on the planet. On last fact about the leatherback: it is the only marine turtle species without a hard shell; its skin is tough and thick, but nevertheless supple.

By far the most fascinating aspect of these reptiles, however, is their method of reproduction. They travel hundreds, perhaps even thousands of kilometres to lay their eggs on the beach where they were born! On the Pacific coast, eggs are laid between the months of October and March. On the Atlantic coast, egg-laying season is between April and August. Various studies are trying to explain this strange migration. For example, as mating season approaches and both male and female sea turtles set out for the original nest site. How do they get there? To date, only a few hypotheses have been put forward. Among these, the theory that the animals detect magnetic fields is the only one that is widely accepted by scientists. Also, why do sea turtles return to the precise place of birth and ignore other beaches with identical conditions that are sometimes right nearby? Although scientists have no exact answers to these questions, they suspect that genetics is involved: turtles have used the same ideal nesting sites over centuries, and this information has been recorded in the genetic memory of the animals.

The egg-laying itself is astonishing. While most of the species lay their eggs individually, two turtle species, the Atlantic Ridley and the Green Turtle (in the Pacific), lay their eggs in large groups. This is called the *arribada*, in which all the turtles land on the beaches at the same time, creating a surreal spectacle. In 1942, at Ranch Nuevo, Mexico, 40,000 Atlantic Ridley turtles came ashore in a single night. Sadly, hardly 50 years later, only 1,500 turtles were counted there. The question is: can these animals survive without human intervention? Facing the danger of their variety diminishing, at least, sea turtles seem to have found an answer: having mated with several males, the female stores their sperm and fertilizes her eggs with the semen from the different males, creating a larger gene pool.

Generally, most females lay eggs twice during egg-laying season and at two-to three-year at intervals. After digging a relatively deep pit in the sand, each turtle deposits 50 to 120 eggs, depending on the species. As they are being laid, the eggs are soft and are coated with a gelatinous substance to prevent them from breaking as they fall into the pit. The temperature inside the pit determines the length of the incubation period: on the average, 60 days. At the end of the incubation period, the baby turtle uses an excrescence on its jaw to break out of its shell; this natural tool disappears shortly after birth. Like egg laying, hatching (usually in a group) also takes place at night or, occasionally, on rainy days. Once out of their shells, the young turtles face life's first challenge: they must reach the ocean before becoming dehydrated. Guided to the water by the shimmering reflection of moonlight on the surface of the ocean, they may be misdirected by lights from houses or hotels along the beach. Many baby turtles die of exhaustion in this way every year. Those who reach the ocean must manoeuvre skilfully to escape predators until they are large enough to defend themselves. Consequently, only one in 1,000 will reach adulthood; a wonderful illustration of nature's ingenuity and fragility.

Bocas del Toro

side of the island, outside the park limits, is a little Guaymíe village named **Salt Creek**. It is hard to get to, however, so those who wish to visit such a community should instead to Isla Cristóbal (see above), which is more accessible. Also outside the park, this time to the west, is the little fishing village of Bastimentos. It has nothing of particular note to attract visitors. The only reason to go there is for the beautiful, wild **Wizard's Beach**, 1 km along a path from the village. Here, the size of the waves makes swimming unsafe, and one is limited to romantic strolls along the shore.

An integral part of Parque Marino de Bastimentos, the **Islas Zapatillas** are entirely surrounded by coral reefs and are reputed for the beauty of their white, sandy beaches. The two islands are lapped by shallow, crystal-clear waters, which are ideal for snorkeling (see p265). An ANAM (INRENARE) research centre on the larger island is used during part of the year for the study of sea turtles.

Parque Internacional La Amistad

Although it is located almost entirely in the province of Bocas del Toro, the most convenient entrance to Parque International La Amistad is in the neighbouring province, Chiriquí. Guided tours of the region also start from there. For this reason, you will find the detailed description of this attraction in the chapter "Province of Chiriquí" (see p221, 240)

Outdoor Activities

Hiking

From Chiriquí to Chiriquí Grande

Finca La Suiza
7am to 9pm
45 km from the Interamericana, entrance on the right-hand side of the road going towards Chiriquí Grande, 3.4 km from Los Planes, Apdo 1152 David
☎ *615-3774*
⇰ *774-4030*
afinis@chiriqui.com

Herbert Brullmann and Monika Kolher will gladly welcome you to the heart of the large **Finca la Suiza**, nestled in the heart of the mountains. They will take you on an approximately six-hour excursion *(B/. 6 per person)* which will allow you to see birds, butterflies and other insects and

waterfalls, all surrounded by exuberant vegetation. The trip is not exactly restful, but you will see magnificent scenery including the Barú Volcano and, on a clear day, the Pacific Ocean. Good walking shoes and a lightweight raincoat are essential on this ecotourism adventure.

Surfing

Playa Bluff

This long beach with brownish sand is famous for large waves that are ideal for surf boarding. However, given the force of the breakers, only true experts can safely ride the waves here. Beginners should exercise utmost caution.

Cycling

Bocas del Toro

Hotel Laguna and the **La Ballena** restaurant rent bicycles by the hour or day. Expect to pay B/. 3 for the first two hours and B/. 1.50 for additional hours.

From Bocas del Toro to Playa Bluff

Except for the streets in the town of Bocas del Toro (barely 20 in number), there are only two roads on the island. The first, a dirt road, goes completely across the island to Boca del Drago, 14 km away. The other, partially paved, follows the coast to Playa Bluff. Barely 8 km long, this second road offers lovely scenic views and allows visitors to see the flora and many of the native birds. With patience and luck, you might catch a glimpse of the amusing white-faced capuchin monkeys that live in the area.

Unfortunately, mid-way along the road, there is an unsghtly dump. Here too, an effort by

the local authorities to improve the environment would be appreciated.
Nevertheless, the rest of the road is enjoyable. With just a few minor hills to climb and some small streams to be forded, you will soon arrive at beautiful Playa Bluff, where signs announce the presence of a restaurant, Finca Verde. The food is very basic and choice is limited so a picnic lunch is in order. One last warning, sun screen and insect repel-

lent are necessities here; but we also advise you not to wear your "Sunday best" clothing and shoes: mud stains from Bocas seem to be indelible!

Scuba Diving and Snorkelling

Bocas del Toro

Bocas Water Sports
Calle 3, next door to the Tourist Bureau
☎ 757-9541

Turtle Divers
Calle 3, near Parque Bolívar
☎ 757-9594

Transparente Tour Boats
Calle 3, at Le Pirate restaurant
☎ 757-9600
☎ 757-9172

All have a good selection of diving equipment for rent; everything from fins, to compressed air tanks and diving masks. Prices vary according to the equipment rented and the time of year.

Cruises

Bocas Water Sports
Calle 3, next door to the Tourist Bureau
☎ 757-9541

Turtle Divers
Calle 3, near Parque Bolívar
☎ 757-9594

Transparente Tour Boats
Calle 3, at Le Pirate restaurant
☎ 757-9600
☎ 757-9172

All three companies offer various excursions leaving from **Bocas del Toro**. The day trip to the **Cayos Zapatillas** which stops on **Cayo Crawl** is one of the most interesting. It provides a complete overview of the flora and fauna of the archipelago.

Those who suffer from seasickness should opt for a visit to **Carenero Island**, to **Solarte** or the little village of **Bastimentos**: the boat rides are shorter and the waters calmer. Unfortunately for those travelling alone, the cost of these excursions is much higher for small groups. For example, an outing to the **Islas Zapatillas**, including a meal, is B/. 15 for those in a group of six or more, but can rise to B/. 75 if the group is not large enough. However, competition is increasing all the time. Do not hesitate to bargain. The crossings are of significant length and the seas are not always calm; so only choose outfits with boats of a decent size, and make sure to wear a lifejacket.

Boca del Drago

While the beach at **Boca del Drago** is somewhat out of the way, it does offer beginner snorkellers the opportunity to observe rich marine life, provided a few safety rules are observed. The only disappointing aspect is that, apart from a few cabanas turned into hotels, and an unidentified little restaurant, there are no services here.

Cayo Crawl

This little island is one of the best places to snorkel. More sheltered than the Islas Zapatillas, the calm, shallow water is perfect for beginners and scuba divers will appreciate the proximity of **Bahia de Almirante**, known for its clear water and absence of waves. Although there is a modest restaurant on Cayo Crawl, we suggest bringing your own provisions along.

Islas Zapatillas

An integral part of the **Parque Maarino de Bastimentos**, the **Islas Zapatillas** are famous for crystal-clear water, ideal for snorkeling. This is a great spot for observing marine life because the islands are on a particularly rich coral plateau. A coral reef only 3 to 5 m deep rings the islands and it is easy to observe red mullet, scalare

(angel fish), grouper, scarus (parrot fish), butterfly fish, crabs and many other species. Outside the reef, strong currents make scuba diving problematic and too dangerous for beginners.

Accommodations

From Chiriquí to Chiriquí Grande

Finca La Suiza
$$
pb, hw
45 km from the Interamericana, entrance on the right hand side of the road going towards Chiriquí Grande, 3.4 km from Los Planes, Apdo 1152 David
☎ *615-3774*
✉ *774-4030*
afinis@chiriqui.com

Herbert and Monica will welcome you to the Finca La Suiza, nestled in the heights and surrounded by luxuriant vegetation. The rooms, located in a newly constructed building, are comfortable and clean and each one has a

terrace with a beautiful view of the mountains. If you like peace and quiet and are interested in birds, butterflies and even insects, don't miss the chance to spend some time here. Unfortunately, the Finca La Suiza is not open all year round, but only between December 1 and May 15, or July 1 and August 30. The owners, who are avid walkers, offer guests the use of several hiking paths on the property (see p264).

Chiriquí Grande

The Hotel Emperador
$
overlooking the pier in Chiriquí Grande, to the left of the main street
☎ **757-9656**
The Emperador is comfortable and has a large balcony with a view of boats coming and going. It is fairly ordinary, but clean, and the staff is friendly.

Isla Colón

Bocas del Toro

Las Brisas
$
⊗, *pb*, ≡, *hw*
Avenide H and Calle 3, east of Ancón Expeditions
☎ **757-9248**
✉ **757-9247**

As the number of hotels in Bocas del Toro is fairly limited, you may have difficulty finding rooms in the area. If so, a solution would be the hotel Las Brisas, where you will find about 30 rooms with basic comforts. Spread out along a lengthy hallway, most of the rooms are sombre, poorly insulated and decorated rather gloomily. Ask for quarters near the dock, as these are the more attractive rooms.

Hotel La Veranda
$
⊗, *sb*
corner Avenida H and Calle 7
☎ *757-9211*
Those on a limited budget who do not mind communal-style lodgings will be treated well by the Canadian hosts at the La Veranda. On the second floor of a large wooden house, there are several rooms ranging from small ones with two beds to more spacious family-style rooms with several beds. Mosquito netting is available for B/. 2 per night. As with most of the houses in Bocas, the rooms open onto a large gallery, in this case equipped with a stove and all the equipment necessary for those who wish to prepare their own breakfast or fix themselves a snack in the afternoon. A friendly "hippy" atmosphere prevails.

The Scarlet
$
pb, bw, ≡, tv
Calle 4 and Avenida C
☎ *757-9290*
The Morales family welcomes guests to their 12-room hotel in

their villa located on a corner of the main street in Bocas. Once again, the rooms extend along a lengthy corridor. Most rooms are bright, with tile floors and a modern, if conventional, décor. This establishment offers the best value in its category.

The Bahia
$
≡, ⊗, *bw, tv*
Calle 3 or Calle Rev Ephraim Alphone
☎ *757-9626*
⊨ *757-9692*
If you arrive by ferry, The Bahia hotel is probably the first building typical of Bocas that you will see. It has a long history, since it was the administrative seat of the famous United Fruit Company when this little village was booming. Now converted to a hotel, the building, made entirely of wood, could stand some serious sprucing up. Thirty rooms, the majority of which have only one fan, open off a long, gloomy corridor. The premises are clean but the rooms are poorly insulated and the décor is dreary. Despite these drawbacks, this inexpensive hotel is a good bet for visitors on a limited budget.

Cocomo on the Sea
$$$
bkfst incl.; ⊗, *sb, bw*
Avenida Norte
☎/⊨ *757-9259*
After unsuccessfully scouring Costa Rica in

search of a peaceful haven, Claus and Dorothy Claassen, from Alberta, Canada, opted for Bocas del Toro, where they opened a small hotel. Built on stilts on the beach, this immaculate, white, wooden building, has only four rooms, two of which face the ocean. Those seeking a restful atmosphere will be delighted by the small terrace overlooking the sea, where they can stretch out in a hammock with a book in between adventures! This charming establishment is attractive and clean beyond reproach. Ample and nourishing breakfasts are served in the owners' house next door in an equally pleasant atmosphere.

Hotel Laguna
$$
pb, ≡, bw, tv, ℝ
corner Calle 3 Av. D
☎ *757-9091*
⊨ *757-9092*
Located on the main street in Bocas, the Laguna has a dozen rooms in a Swiss-style chalet. While the rooms are dark and rather depressing, the ones upstairs display more charm and some even have a pleasant view. The hosts suggest various activities for guests (see p264). Although sanitary facilities are adequate and the premises are immaculate, this hotel is expensive for what it offers.

Bocas del Toro

Ancón Expeditions

$$$

bkfst incl.; pb, hw, ⊗

☎ 757-9226

⌨ 264-5990

A dozen or so clean rooms in an old wooden house built on stilts. The rooms, leading off here and there from a central hallway, are bright and simply decorated. With the exception of two rooms facing the sea, none offers an interesting view. However, there is an ocean view from the spacious open-air room on the main floor (where meals are served). Despite a certain shabbiness, the residence is charming and comfortable. Many rooms were being renovated during our visit.

Swan's Cay

$$$-$$$$

bkfst incl.; pb, hw, ≡, tv, ℝ

corner Calle 3 and Avenide F

☎ 757-9090

☎ 757-9316

⌨ 757-9027

Strolling down the main "artery" in Bocas, visitors will be surprised at the appearance of the brand-new (and imposing) Swan's Cay hotel. The Treccani family's establishment testifies to the beauty inherent to Italian culture. In the main building, there are 20-odd apartments on two floors, opening onto a vast interior hall that is air conditioned and beautifully decorated. In the centre of this hall an elegant staircase leads to a spacious

gallery in warm tones of wood and the respective quarters of the guests. Those who prefer the view of the garden may go to the back of the building, where 15 or so rooms on two floors surround a flowered patio. As for the decoration of the rooms, Señora Treccani has demonstrated excellent taste in a beautiful selection of fabrics for the bedding, while lovely inlaid furniture embellishes the premises. Finally, for those who dream of spending a night in the atmosphere of the roaring twenties, the penthouse suite in the main building is the answer. This hotel offers excellent quality for the price.

Punta Mangrove

Mangrove Inn Eco Resort

$$$$

1/2b, pb, ⊗

Punta Mangrove, 5 min. by boat from Bocas del Toro

☎/⌨ 757-9594

www.bocas.com/mangrove. htm,

www.manninginn@ usa.net

For those who enjoy scuba diving and don't mind isolation, this resort has a series of rustic cabins built on stilts at the edge of the mangroves.

Packages here (*allow B/. 60 to B/. 95/pers*) include lodging, meals, equipment rental and excursions in the archipelago. The only drawback, since the hotel is accessible only by boat, is that visitors are entirely dependent on the establishment for transportation...unless they bring their own boat!

Boca del Drago

Cabañas Estefaña

$$

pb, K, ⊗

on the Boca del Drago beach, south towards Lime Point

☎ 774-3117

Practically built on the beach, these cabañas will suit tourists who travel family-style and for whom comfort is not an absolute priority. In this idyllic but isolated diving setting, meals (based most likely on fish) are prepared in the kitchen corner of the

wooden cottages. For the unskilled fisher, the thoughtful proprietor will furnish the basics. A good insect repellent should be included in the tourist's kit.

Restaurants

Chiriquí Grande

Dally
$
to the right of the pier
The friendly owner of this restaurant prepares, at your request, freshly caught fish after 2pm; a variety of other family-style dishes are also served. This is a charming restaurant and a good place to meet local inhabitants.

Isla Colón

Bocas del Toro

Lakois Place
$
Avenide Norte, between Calle 6 and 7
A small open-air terrace, a few modest tables and chairs scattered here and there and a small bar imaginatively painted – this is the décor of Lakois Place! Although very simple, this locale is a favourite of many Bocatoreños and fine fish and seafood dishes are prepared according to local tradition.

Good quality for the price!

Baia Paradiso
$
Calle 3, across from the Parque Central
As you will have guessed from its sign, the pizzeria-reposteria offers a choice of pizza (unfortunately limited and somewhat lacking in taste) as well as modest family-style dishes. While this is not the place for haute cuisine, it does offer a pleasant terrace facing the park where one can have a light snack. We might add that customers here would appreciate a welcoming smile!

Buena Vista
$$
Calle 1 and facing Calle 2
This small restaurant, managed by an American couple, has an attractive wooden terrace with a view of the ocean. A good vegetarian chilli is available as well as a choice of sandwiches, and of course the traditional hamburger. Portions are generous and English is spoken.

La Ballena
$$
Avenide F
Just beside the elegant Swan's Cay hotel, the La Ballena restaurant serves the catch of the day (unfortunately too often pargo!) accompanied by a good sauce, thanks to the Italian origins of the owner.

Despite a relatively attractive décor and a warm welcome, it is disappointing to note that the personnel does not seem particularly interested in providing good service! Also, the absence of espresso and of tiramisu (so vaunted by the proprietor) was quite a let down.

Le Pirate
$$$
Calle 1, near the corner of Calle 3
This modest restaurant welcomes its customers to the attractive terrace on stilts facing the bay, or to a booth beside the bar. The meals served here, mostly fish and seafood, are simple and presented without frills.

Swan's Cay
$$$
corner Calle 3 and Avanida F
Like the hotel where it is located, the restaurant takes us into another world, that of tables dressed in fine fabrics and set in the purest European tradition, in an elegant décor worthy of the best restaurants in major cities. Even though during our visit the menu was still in the planning stages (for instance, the choice of Italian dishes was relatively limited), the meals served deserved special mention for their flavour and presentation, something rare in Bocas. A somewhat limited choice of fine wines is available.

Isla Carenero

The Ocean Queen
$$
5 min by boat from
Bocas, Isla Carenero,
facing the village of
Bocas, is considered by
the Bocatoreños to
have the best location
in the area. Upon ar-
rival we were surprised
by the large terrace on
stilts. Our curiosity was
piqued! However, the
only valid reason for
coming here is the
beautiful view of Bocas
from the terrace. The
meals, although good
and amply portioned,
are limited to seafood
and the catch of the
day, as well as a few
other family-style
dishes.

Also on stilts, right next
door, the **Pargo Rogo ($)**
serves much the same
fare and has the same
natural "decor".

Entertainment

Isla Colón

Bocas del Toro

El Encanto
Calle 3, beside Bocas Water
Sports
Near the landing dock,
the bar welcomes ama-
teurs of billiards in a
small room facing the
street. Just beside it, a
long hallway leads to a
large, open-air dance
floor where exotic mu-
sic reigns. For those
who simply wish to
relax and sip a glass of
ron con jugo de naranja
(*B/. 0.85*) to the strains
of Panamanian music,
there is also a small
terrace beyond the
dance floor that opens
out onto the bay. The
establishment is some-
what dark and gloomy,
but otherwise typical of
the region.

Buena Vista
Calle 1 facing Calle2
Before calling it a
night, sports-lovers will
want to stop by this
restaurant-bar, where
they can watch the
latest football game. In
fact, the American
owner has equipped
the bar with a large
television screen where
one can catch the latest
sports news direct from
the States. And for
those who like to day-
dream, glass in hand,
there are several tables
on a pleasant terrace
and American music in
the background.

**Bar Restaurant Las
Palmitas**
Avenida Sur, 100 meters from
the dock
For travellers seeking a
change of pace from
the bustle of Calle 3,
this bar offers a modest
terrace on stilts where
one can sip a small *ron*
or a cold Panamanian
beer while enjoying the
soft sea breeze. Sea-
food and fish are on
the menu.

Comarca de San Blas

Located along the northeastern coast of Panamá, in the Caribbean Sea, the Comarca de San Blas is unique in that it is the only province in the country populated exclusively by Amerindians, Kunas to be more specific.

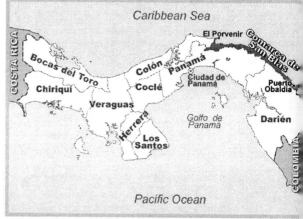

Except for defense, it is also the only province governed exclusively by Amerindians. It is thus classified as a *comarca*, which means region or territory, rather than a province. Besides a long strip of land, barely 10 km wide, extending along the coast to the Colombian border, the Comarca de San Blas consists of an archipelago called the Archipiélago de Las Mulatas. It is made up of some 350 islands and islets, 60 of which are inhabited. Due essentially to a lack of historical documents, little is known about the origins of the Kunas. Certain historians, however, believe they were originally from Colombia and

emigrated to Darién, near the Atlantic coast. In any case, journals left by Spanish explorers reveal that by the 19th century the Kunas had split into two groups: one group lived inland, the other on the islands. This geographic division may have resulted from the different approaches taken by the *caciques* (chiefs) in response to the colonizers, but nothing is certain. Nevertheless, those Kunas wishing to avoid all contact with the intrusive missionar-

ies fled deeper into the heart of the jungle. The difficult living conditions and hostile environment, however, forced the majority of the population to settle on the coast. According to the last census taken by Panamanian authorities, there are 50,000 Kunas living on the islands and only 2,000 spread throughout Darién. About 6,000 Kunas are currently living in the capital.

Before enjoying their autonomy, the Kunas endured a long

series of humiliations. After colonization, they lived under the authority of the new Republic of Panamá when a governor for the territory was nominated in 1915. Severe restrictions on fishing and farming the land proved completely inappropriate for the Kunas, and quickly became a recurring subject of discontent. Also, in their efforts to assimilate the various minorities, the Panamanian authorities wanted to abolish their traditional clothing, the *mola* (see p278), and force parents to send their children to Spanish-language school.

However, it was their attempt to control the territory by deploying police and civil servants to the islands in 1923 that really angered the Kunas. After suffering brutality and the ultimate affront, namely the rape of Kuna women, *cacique* Simrol Colman, on Ailigandí island at the time, declared war. During the month of February 1925, the Tule Republic (in the Kuna language *Tule* refers to Kuna men in general, but also means son of God) was proclaimed, and several police officers were killed, along with their children born of mixed marriages. Several other islands followed Ailigandí's lead, which led to widespread revolt. Panamanian officials reacted by sending in the army, but the troops were intercepted by the Americans, whose warship **Cleveland** had been dispatched to the islands. The United States forced the two sides to negotiate and resolve the conflict. Under an accord reached the same year, the Kunas withdrew their declaration of independence, and the Republic of Panamá agreed to recognize the autonomy of the Amerindians. It was not until 1930 that the accord was ratified in the Panamanian parliament, and 1933 that the Comarca was created.

Fishing, gathering coconuts and making *molas* (see p278) are still the principal activities of the Kuna. For their own alimentary needs they regularly head to the mainland to farm small plots of land across from their islands. Tourism to the islands is constantly increasing and the sale of *molas* to tourists has become a major source of income for the Kuna. Unlike other cases, where tourism has had a negative impact on indigenous communities, the "tourist windfall" here has actually helped preserve the Kuna culture and identity. The Kuna *caciques'* opposition to the establishment of large hotel chains on their islands has undoubtedly been a wise approach.

Finding Your Way Around

Warning: Do not forget that there is a very limited choice of accommodations throughout the region, and that there is no potable water or electricity on the islands. Furthermore, staying on an island, even an uninhabited one, without the permission of a *cacique* is prohibited. A last-minute adventure to these islands could thus be potentially dangerous and above all shows a lack of respect for the indigenous authorities. Before

Comarca de San Blas

heading here, therefore, make sure your accommodations are arranged.

By Plane

The best way to reach the **San Blas Islands** is by plane. There are regular flights to the landing strip on the coast at the edge of the jungle, and from there, small boats take visitors to the various islands. Take note that because of weather conditions, all flights are scheduled early in the morning, starting at 6am. Unless you charter a flight, it is therefore impossible to return on the same day. Weekend flights are particularly busy, so much so that if you plan on travelling at this time you should get to the airport by 4am! Once there, you will need patience and some perseverance to actually get your ticket.

One of the best ways to avoid this headache is to organize your trip through a travel agent.

In general, this will allow you to arrive at the airport later (around 5am), and a Kuna agent will quickly get you your ticket. Various travel agents in the capital can provide you with more details (see p 64).

Note: the following schedules and rates are provided for reference only and are subject to change.

Only one company provides regular service to the islands:

Aero Taxi
Monday to Saturday at 6am
☎ *315-0275*
flies to 15 islands all the way to Puerto Obaldía, near the Colombian border.

Cudidad de Panamá to Puerto Obaldía (direct)
Departure: Mon, Wed and Fri 6am

You can also obtain information from **Aeroperlas**, which purchased the company (see p48).

Albrook Airport to El Porvenir (capital of the Comarca)
Travel Time: 25 min
Cost: (return) approx. B/. 56

Albrook Airport to Puerto Obaldía
Travel Time: 75 min.
Cost: (return) approx. B/. 88

Some of the destinations served:
El Porvenir, Cartí, Río Sidra, Narganá, Río Tigre, Playón Chico, Tupile, Ailigandí, Achutupo, Mamitupo, Ustupo, Mulatupo, Tubuala and Puerto Obaldía.

By Car

There is a coastal road that leads to the Comarca (via El Llano) but this a long journey. Furthermore, the road is unpaved, and passes

no services. Lastly, do not forget that you need permission to enter the Comarca.

Practical Information

Among the numerous travel agencies established in the capital, some offer particularly interesting packages. Here are a few examples:

Eco-Tours
7 Calle 50 Este/Ricardo Arias, near Vía España
☎ *263-3077*
☎ *263-3076*
⇒ *263-3089*
ecotours@pty.com
www.avatar.pty.com/ecotour s/frabome.htm
From the end of December to the end of March, the Eco-Tours Agency organizes a day-trip to the island of Wichubuala every Sunday for B/. 109, including transportation from the airport to and from the island, a guide (English-speaking upon request), breakfast and a night in a hotel in Ciudad de Panamá. This package is particularly well-suited to those with little time. Another interesting option is a tour of Achutupo island with lodging on the marvellous neighbouring island of Uaguitupo.

This costs B/. 165, including transportation, a night at the Dolphin Lodge (*B/. 80 for an extra night, including meals*), four home-made meals, a Kuna guide and visits to various sites (Achutupo, a jungle tour, a Kuna cemetery, etc.). There is no electricity on the island, so you'll be living on Kuna time from sunup to sundown. An unforgettable experience.

Starlite Travel
Av. Roosevelt and Height Avenue, Edificio L-639, Balboa, across from the Canal administration building and beside the McDonald's; Apdo 6-6200, El Dorado
☎ *232-6401*
☎ *272-2474*
₪ *232-6448*
starlite@panama.c-com.net
Among the agencies with competitive prices, Starlite Travel offers various packages including transportation, lodging, meals and excursions in the Comarca. Prices vary from B/. 100 to B/. 178 per person for a night at the San Blas Hotel, the Ani Hotel, the Dolphin Lodge or the Kwadule Hotel (see p281). An agency representative will accompany you to the airport in Ciudad de Panamá (Albrook Airport) and a Kuna guide will welcome you when you reach your destination in San Blas. Friendly service and competent staff.

Jungle Adventures
38 Calle 50 Este/Ricardo Arias
☎ *269-6017*
₪ *263-8261*
iskardup@sinfo.net
www.iskardup.com
If you are looking for adventure, but like your creature comforts, contact Jungle Adventures. For B/. 180 you can spend the night on Iskardup island (*B/. 280 for two nights*) in a comfortable cabin equipped with a shower and electricity produced by solar panels. The tour includes transportation, a guide, a tour of Ukupseni island, a visit to a Kuna cemetery, breakfast, a buffet lunch and a "gourmet" supper.

Exploring

★★★

Kuna Yula (Land of the Kunas)

Imagine more than 300 coral islands sprinkled on a turquoise-blue sea. Loll about on a dreamy beach of fine golden sand on an island all to yourself in the middle of nowhere. Rock yourself to sleep in a hammock slung between two palm trees, to the sound of the palms rustling in the breeze. Dive into crystal-clear waters and discover a world of a million and one vivid colours. Behold the impenetrable jungle that lines the coast, forming a stunning ribbon of emerald off in the distance. In short, this region will delight dreamers in search of a lost paradise. Kuna Yala has much to offer travellers looking for a change of scenery, for it is above all the land of the Kunas, a proud and friendly people.

The main attraction of the Comarca de San Blas is the extraordinary presence of the Kunas, who have preserved their unique culture over hundreds of years. Those interested in indigenous cultures can experience the Kuna way of life without too much difficulty.

The Kunas have fought long and hard to preserve their culture, and are very proud of it, so it is important to follow a few general rules so as not to offend the local population in any way. Since the coming and going of foreigners is controlled by the *cacique*, each visitor is automatically assigned a guide. He or she facilitates your contact with the population and serves as an interpreter since very few Kunas speak Spanish. Plan any visits or excursions off the island with your guide. Possible activities include exploring the village and the beautiful islets with their white-sand beaches, scuba diving,

Welcome to Kuna Yala

After flying over the dense Darién jungle, the tiny eight-seater starts its descent in search of a landing strip hidden somewhere along the narrow ribbon of coastline. To an uninitiated traveller such as myself, the tops of the gigantic tropical trees look as if they are within arm's reach, as if the wheels of the plane are brushing against them! But where is the landing strip? For a moment I imagine it has been swallowed up by the forest, but then suddenly in the distance a narrow clearing appears – is it even paved? The question has barely formed itself in my mind when the plane swoops down to the ground, leaving the jungle behind. As I get off the Islander I am greeted by the smiling face of our Kuna guide, small in stature like all Kunas. I cannot help but stare; even though the scenery that surrounds us is extraordinary, I am transfixed by her garb. Her head is covered with a bright red and yellow scarf, and she is wearing one of the stunning molas I have heard so much about. Her forearms and calves are adorned with tiny strands of colourful beads, a sure sign of coquetry, and a thin black line runs down the bridge of her nose. Barefoot, she leads us to a rickety boat, while the smiling Kuna men bring the bags. The little motorboat shoves out to sea, where only the tops of the palm trees visible on the horizon remind us of dry land. As we approach the islands, we see clusters of bamboo huts with palm roofs on some of them. Clinging to every last square inch of land, they stand harmoniously side by side. As we head toward our destination, we pass several Kuna women paddling canoes between the islands. Always a smile and a friendly wave. Their colourful clothing stands out against the turquoise blue waters, a beautiful sight in itself. All too quickly, we arrive at our island, where we are welcomed by the mother, sisters and brothers of our guide. A macaw perched on a palm tree branch watches in bewilderment. Our hut awaits... welcome to Uaguitipo!

visiting a Kuna cemetery or taking part in an excursion into the jungle. Avoid the rainy months of June, July and August, when the sky is almost continuously overcast.

Kuna Society Today

Contrary to mainland Kunas, who live in families, and islolate themselves from one another, the Kunas of the San Blas islands live in small villages of bamboo huts built on the bare earth and topped by palm roofs. Although concrete frames and houses have been built in recent years, they are still rare (schools, hotels, clinics, etc.). In general, the inhabited islands are over-populated, and it is not unheard-of to find islands with so many huts that virtually all traces of the coastline seem to have vanished.

The traditional single-family dwelling is simply one large room with no partitions or windows. While some Kunas sleep in beds, most sleep in hammocks. Cooking is done in the hut on an open fire. The only agricultural activity is the harvesting of coconuts which are sold to Colombian merchants who visit the islands.

The fruits used in Kuna cuisine come from the mainland. In the early morning, the Kuna men head inland to the various plantations established by each family (in the broad sense of the word). In the afternoon, the men spend their time fishing. Fish and seafood, including the delicious conchas, accompanied by coconut, fried plantains and rice, make up the bulk of Kuna cuisine. While some islands have electricity and running water thanks to a pump, most islands do not have these services. Fresh water thus comes from rivers on the mainland, where it is collected in large barrels by the men and brought to the islands by boat. In some hotels, potable water is flown in straight from the capital.

The administrative capital of the Comarca is El Porvenir. The San Blas islands are divided into groups, each with its own administrative centre. Ailigandí, for example, is the administrative centre for Achutupo, Uaguitipo and many other islands. Like the capital, the centres offer various administrative services, such as a police station, a school, a clinic, etc. Among the important centres, the island of Ailigandí is famous in Kuna history for having been the place where the 1925 revolution began. Several plaques commemorating the Kunas' fight for independence can be found at the police station. You will also see the swastika, the national symbol chosen for the flag of the short-lived Tule Republic. To reach Ailigandí you must have your passport and in some cases pay an admission fee of B/. 1.

Celebrations take place on the 19th, 20th and 21st of February to commemorate the Kuna revolution, and they are particularly lively in Ailigandí. As the Kunas are very proud of their fight to defend their culture, some of them will probably ask you if there are indigenous peoples in your country, and if you answer positively, they will want to know what their rights are! Still on Ailigandí, you can visit the **Instituto Nacional Cultura Ogar Yakun Nega**, an art school where the technique for making the *mola* is taught.

Customs

Supreme power resides with three chiefs elected to represent all Kunas and the interests of the Comarca. These three individuals are chosen by the village chiefs, called *Sáhila*, themselves elected and assisted by "sub-chiefs". The latter have authority over their territory and take care of various matters, like the division of land, family disputes, marriages, etc. Kuna society is essentially matriarchal, and the grandmother, or Mu, is the center of the family. Marriages are not documented and require just a simple ceremony.

Up until the 1950s, marriages were unions of convenience arranged by parents when the children were quite young. Also, it was the female's family who did the choosing. Today the choice is freer, though it must still be approved by the parents, and the husband still has to live with the wife's family. A Kuna man can change islands if he likes, but to marry a woman from there, he must have the permission of the island's chief. Inter-racial marriages are very rare amongst the Kunas and are effectively prohibited. In fact, if a Kuna marries an outsider, the couple must leave the

Comarca. In the history of the isthmus, a number of unfortunate events have underlined this exclusivity; according to some, this rule is necessary to protect the Kuna culture. Between 1625 and 1725, French Huguenots settled in the region and had children with Amerindian women. These mixed-blood children, along with their parents, were all massacred during the Amerindian rebellion against the Spanish in 1726. Another sad example came in 1925, when Panamanian police officers and their children, born of Kuna women, were also killed. The only example of a happy union today is that of American Marvel Iglesias and Lonnie Iglesias, a respected Kuna man, known for having raised the funds necessary for the construction of the hospital in Ailigandí. The couple received permission to settle in Ailigandí in 1933.

As far as religion is concerned, the Kunas believe in a God, creator of the universe, as well as in the powers of the *neles*, healers of sorts who are inspired by superior forces. Their vision of the world is that two parallel universes exist: an invisible one harbouring spirits and the physical life as we know it. Thus, for the Kunas, every being possesses a double personality, one visible and one hidden. The same applies to animals, plants and objects, which have two different names, one for the day and the other for the night. Only a few objects are used during religious ceremonies, including *nuchus* (wooden figures with therapeutic powers that represent particular characters), dyes, leaves and branches, and no major temples or buildings have been consecrated. Each plant, animal, object and even every part of the body has its own aura, which can be beneficial or not.

Young artists can gain inspiration by chanting while burning a piece of a *mola* that belonged to a highly creative person. Stealing, lying, murder and adultery are considered the most reprehensible acts. Among the major religious ceremonies, the one marking a girl's coming of age or a person's death are the most important. However, no stranger is allowed to witness these. Several other religions have influenced the Kunas. For example, although the Kunas do not have any religious holidays, Christmas is celebrated on some islands, and various Christian practices have been adopted here and there.

The oral tradition, village assemblies and the stories and sayings of the chiefs are an important part of everyday life. All sorts of fascinating dances are also part of the local customs. Some of these are performed at tourists' requests. This is most common on the islands of Ailigandí and Playón Chico. On Ailigandí, for example, you may have the chance to take part in an intriguing dance called the *Nogagope*. A dozen people are carried away by lively music played on a bamboo flute and maracas in double time.

Kuna Women

Women are very powerful in Kuna society. The woman is the one who chooses her future husband, and it is with her family that he must live. The birth of a girl is cause for great celebration since it is she who will continue the family.

Separation is accepted, and a woman simply has to put her husband's things outside the hut to let him know that she wants him to leave. The woman is then free to remarry, while the man must obtain the approval of his ex-wife or wait for her to remarry before he can take another wife. Finally it is the wives who take care of expenses. Kuna women generally wear a long skirt with a piece of fabric rolled

Kuna Glossary

tule	man, can also be collective; is also used to designate the Kunas
ai	friend (male)
aimala	friends (male)
dia	friend (female)
diamala	friends (female)
núedi	good day or nice, good
na	hello
deguimalo	goodbye
panemalo	see you tomorrow
an	I
nuga	name
merkey	good stranger
waga	other strangers
eye	yes
suli	no
takey	come here
mútiki	night
nega	house
kas	hammock
tupu	island
ti	water
achu	dog
úa	fish
kanil núchukua	chicken
ogop	coconut
ossi	pineapple
mas chunnat	banana
mesmalat	family
machi	son or daughter
nana	mother
paba	father
tutu	flower
sapi	tree
sapigana	trees
tommo make	to swim
múa make	to float
soul kukualet	plane
uágul	boat
mullu suli	big
pipigua	small

Kuna Glossary

pannabagua	far
ittigi	close
tule poniguale	sick
ukku	hungry
ti koppie	thirsty
kabe	sleep
ti uiet	rain
tada	sun
kuen	one
bo	two
padgua	three
mani	money

breach in tradition, for some village chiefs have permitted residents to wear western clothes. Traditional dress has already disappeared from the islands of Narganá and Corazón de Jesús. Today, the islands found to the west of the Comarca (Atchutupu, Mulatupu, and Ustupu) are considered the most traditional and the *mola* is required dress for the women. The Kuna are a modest and timid people, and do not tolerate nudism. Women are also advised to wear a one-piece bathing suit rather than a bikini, which is considered provocative.

If you want to photograph a Kuna woman, it is **imperative** that you ask her permission first (your guide will help you). You should give her a small compensation of B/. 1 for the "royalties". For a group photo, ask your guide how much you should give. When you purchase something (*mola*, necklace, sculpture, etc.), however, you do not have to pay anything to take a picture of the vendor. Nevertheless, always ask your guide before taking any pictures. Travellers with a video camera are **obliged** to obtain the permission of the chief before filming anything. You will probably be asked for a donation if your request is approved.

around their hips and a short-sleeved blouse with a *mola* sewn on it. They also wear strands of tiny, colourful beads, called *canilleras* or *wini*, on their forearms and calves. Some women wear a gold ring in their nose and have a thin black line drawn down their nose. Ethnologists say that this line is the last vestige of the painting with which they once covered the entire body. Today, it serves a purely cosmetic purpose. During certain festivities, wide necklaces and gold earrings are worn. A married woman must keep her hair short, and she covers it with a bright red scarf with yellow designs.

The majority of Kuna woman bear between 8

and 12 children. While the men spend the morning farming and the afternoon fishing, the women can spend hours sewing the superb *molas*, either for themselves or to sell. It can take several weeks of steady work to make a *mola*. The *canilleras* or *wini* only last a few months and making a new one can take up to five full days of work.

The woman's traditional dress is considered the most prestigious expression of the Kuna culture and is thus jealously safeguarded. Unfortunately, since the middle of the 20th century, there has been a

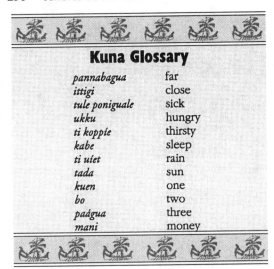

Accommodations

As the cost of accommodations can double or triple depending on the season, availability or any other unpredictable eventuality, we can only provide a general price range. It costs between B/. 100 and B/. 200 per person per day, including transportation, lodging and meals. Also, remember that most hotels have neither electricity nor running water.

Kwadule Eco-Lodge
B/. 180 per person per day, including meals; trips and transportation from Ciudad de Panamá; B/. 90 per person for each successive night
Contact Green World, Apdo 6-1668, El Dorado
☎ *269-6313*
☎ *269-6304*
☎ *269-4198*
≈ *269-6309*
On a small island with a white-sand beach, Kwadule Eco-Lodge is made up of 6 rustic cabins on stilts. Each cabin faces the ocean.

Touring the entire island takes only 5 min on foot.

Hotel San Blas
B/. 115 per person for the 1st night, including meals; trips and transportation from Cudiad de Panamá; B/. 140 for each successive night
Nalunega
☎ *262-5410*
www.copalisbeach.com/critterorp/nalunegaisland.html
This hotel can accommodate up to 40 people, and boasts a beautiful beach where fishing trips and scuba diving are organized. Very basic.

Hotel Anai
B/. 125 per person for the 1st night, including meals; trips and transportation from Ciudad de Panamá; B/. 165 for each successive night
Wichub Wala
☎ *239-3025*
☎ *299-9011*
Ask to speak to Sr. Alberto Gonzalez
www.copalisbeach.com/critterorp/botelanai.html
This hotel has 14 cabañas, as well as a pool and a small restaurant.

Cabañas Kuahidup
B/. 145 per person for the 1st night, including meals; trips and transportation from Ciudad de Panamá; B/. 170 for each successive night
Río Sidra
☎ *227-0872*
Small, rudimentary cabins located on an island of white sand and crystal-clear waters.

Hotel Iskardup
B/. 180 per person for the 1st night, including meals; trips and transportation from Ciudad de Panamá; B/. 180 for each successive night
Iskardup
Only through Jungle Adventure
(see p275)
This hotel has 14 comfortable, bamboo cabañas with a shower and a private bathroom, and electricity provided by solar panels. A buffet-lunch (meat and seafood) and a "gourmet" meal are served on the premises. A wonderful blend of adventure and comfort!

Hotel Dolphin Lodge
B/. 165 per person per day, including meals; trips and transportation from Ciudad de Panamá for the first night; B/. 80 per person for each successive night
Uaguitupo
☎ *220-8898*
On this small island right beside Achutupo, there are six cabañas, only three of which have cement floors and private showers. Each cabin has several large beds, a table and chairs

Comarca de San Blas

and a hammock suspended at the entrance. The shared washrooms with showers and a small washbasin are located in a separate building. You can thus brush your teeth while contemplating the turquoise sea behind you. There is no electricity, but at nightfall an oil lamp is brought to you. Meals are served at a large table on a bamboo terrace with a palm roof. The 270° view of the sea is like something out of Robinson Crusoe.

Shopping

The *mola* is of course the thing to buy on the islands. While exploring a village you will probably see several Kuna women (sometimes even the whole family) waiting in front of their hut, *molas* in hand, in the hopes that you will buy one on your way by.

Do not, under any circumstances, be embarrassed to buy; the Kunas will not be insulted. Everyone is all smiles, often to conceal their shyness.

If you plan to buy a *mola* on your trip to Panamá, buy it here instead of in the capital, since the money goes right to the artist, and you will be contributing to the preservation of this unique art form. Expect to pay between B/. 15 and B/. 40 for a well-made *mola*, and between B/. 20 and B/. 60 for a blouse complete with both panels. You can also buy small *molas* for a few balboas each, and as of recently, much less elaborate, "imitation *molas*" for B/. 5. A selection of gold jewellery (10 carats), like bracelets and earrings, is also available. A simple chain costs about B/. 30.

Mola

The Mola

This word once simply meant clothing in the general sense; today it applies essentially to a part of a Kuna woman's traditional dress, specifically the square piece of fabric sewn on to the blouse. The *mola* is made up of many pieces of fabric of various colours. These pieces are cut out and sewn together using the method known as appliqué, in other words placed on top of one another to create a alternating colour motif. The *mola* is made up of two panels (one worn on the front, the other on the back) with similar motifs but with alternating colours. This use of colours demonstrates the duality of the world vision characterizing Kuna society (see p ?). Certain ethnologists claim that this activity can be traced back to the paintings with which the Kunas used to decorate their bodies. Why this practice was transferred to cloth remains a mystery, though some believe it can be explained by the arrival of the missionaries, who forced the Kunas to wear clothes. The Kuna elders have their own explanation for the origin of the *mola* fabric (see pÊx). Very long ago, an old Kuna woman succeeded in visiting the *Kalu Tiupis*, a secret place reserved exclusively for women. The *kalus* are sacred locations dedicated to different deities and hidden in the centre of one of the invisible layers (eight in all) of the earth, where all the spirits gather. After visiting the Kalu Tiupis where the *mola* was created, the old Kuna woman learned the technique for making the *mola*. When she returned, she was able to teach her knowledge to the village women, knowledge that is still passed on from mother to daughter. Very little is known about the *mola*, and because of the fragility of the fabric, there are few old examples to study. The oldest *mola* is on display at the Museum of Natural History in Washington and dates from 1902. We do know, however, that older motifs were basically geometric and consisted of only a few colours, mainly red, yellow and black. Today, the colours vary as much as the subjects, and usually represent characters, animals or plants. The *mola* is an impressive and creative piece of work, and is the pride of Kuna women.

Across Darién on Foot
(An account of Joëlle Jenny's trip through Darién in 1991)

How long has it been since I left the river? Three hours? Four, maybe? No point in looking at my travel clock, since it stopped working yesterday because of the humidity. I begin to worry: I passed that ridge of mountains a long time ago, and I should have reached the second river a little while after. But how can I be sure? Twice now I have confused the trail – scarcely marked – with tracks made by columns of ants. The first time, I had to go in circles for 10 minutes before getting back to the real trail. The vegetation is so thick I can hardly see the sun. I feel tiny: lost in an ocean of green.

The day is coming to an end. The long thorns covering most of the trunks scratch me whenever I carelessly lean on something. And still there is no *río*. Even walking slowly I should have reached it

long ago. To continue this way would be madness. Better to retrace my steps and go back to the river I left this morning, before I run out of water: in sticky air like this, the body can become dehydrated very quickly.

Now it's night: black as ink. I hook up my hammock between two trees. My pocket flashlight has not survived the humidity any better than the clock did and in any event, I prefer not to take the risk of being spotted. Weeks can go by with no one coming this way, but still it's better to be careful. Despite fatigue, I have trouble getting to sleep. In the pitch darkness of this moonless night, I live only by my senses, fascinated by the noises around me: yelps, shrieks, the shaking of leaves. Monkeys? Pumas? Better not to think about it...
With the dawn, I start

off again, drained by several days of walking. Finally, at the base of a rock, a small trickle of water. What relief! Now I can wash and replenish my supplies! The cares of the night fade quickly: an animal runs by, a bird sings, a plant with blue berries stands out in this emerald universe. Everywhere there is a celebration of life. And early in the afternoon, my last fears take flight as I finally come upon the río I had left the day before. I roll in the water, drunk with the joy of being where I am. No more need to worry: I had been told that if I had any problems, all I needed to do was to follow the river, and after a day or two's walking I would find a native village. Then all I will have to do is find a boat...

Time to cook a little rice, then set off again.

Province of Darién

A dense tropical jungle covers the greater part of Darién, the most isolated and least developed province in Panamá.

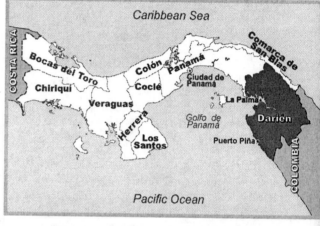

Although the Panamanian and Colombian governments have agreed to establish a ground link between the two countries by extending the Interamericana across Darién, the project has been suspended by the Panamanian government since 1995. In 1984 a route stretched from Yaviza passing 24 km from Parque National Darien. The two governments are apparently having second thoughts about the undertaking, which has been condemned by numerous environmental groups and opposed by several eminent personalities. It is becoming clearer and clearer that the new highway would have a negative impact on the biosphere, and would eventually lead to the destruction of one of humanity's greatest riches. In recognition of the area's inestimable value, UNESCO placed the Parque Nacional Darién on the prestigious list of World Heritage Sites in 1981. Faced with nature's warning signs (the thinning ozone layer, vanished species, depleted soil), human beings are apparently becoming aware that it is necessary to protect the environment for their own good, as well as that of future generations. Somewhat ironically, the famous Interamericana, meant to symbolise friendship between two nations, might not make it farther than Yaviza. Perhaps if it does not, Panamanian and Colombian officials will realize that their countries can also be united by a common goal -- the preservation of some of the most beautiful plant and animal life in the Americas.

Finding Your Way Around

Warning: Although more and more people have been travelling across Darién to Colombia, it is important to note that Panamanian and Colombian officials **strongly advise** visitors not to do so. Not only is the trip physically demanding, but some regions still are not policed and are known to be frequented by drug traffickers. Furthermore, unless you have been given special authorization, crossing the border by this route is considered illegal by both countries, since there is no border station. We recommend enlisting the services of a trained guide for all outings in the park. Their knowledge of the terrain and the local flora and fauna will guarantee you a safe and pleasant trip (see p288).

By Plane

Note: the following schedules and rates are provided for reference only and are subject to change.

Aeroperlas provides regular service in this area, with flights to **Bahía Piña**, **Sambu**, **Yaviza**, **El Real**, **Garachiné**, **Jaqué** and the capital of the province, **La Palma**.

La Palma

Ciudad de Panamá to La Palma
Departure: Mon to Sat 7:50am
Travel Time: 45 min
Cost: B/. 38 one way

La Palma to Ciudad de Panamá
Departure: Mon to Sat 8:45am.

Bahía Piña

Ciudad de Panamá to Bahía Piña
Departure: Tue and Sat 9:30am
Travel Time: approx. 1 hour
Cost: B/. 45 one way

Bahía Piña to Ciudad de Panamá (stop-over in Jacqué)
Departure: Tue, Thu and Sat 10:35am

El Real

Ciudad de Panamá to El Real
Depature: Mon, Wed, Fri 8:45am;
Sat 7:50am (stop-over in La Palma)
Travel Time: approx. 1 hour 20 min
Cost: B/. 40 one way

El Real to Ciudad de Panamá
Departure: Mon, Wed and Fri 9:45am;
Sat 9:20am

Aeroperlas
Ciudad de Panamá
(see p48)

By Car

Keep in mind that there is no road to Colombia that is suitable for motor vehicles, and that it is impossible to drive all the way across Darién. If, however, you would like to explore part of the province of Darién by car, take the Interamericana from Ciudad de Panamá toward Tocumen Airport, and keep heading straight until you reach the village of Chepo, up to which point the road is paved. From Chepo to the village of Metetí, and a short distance beyond, parts of the road are paved and other parts are covered with gravel. You can then take a dirt road to the village of Yaviza, which is as far as you can go by car. The section of road between Chepo and Yaviza is only passable during the dry season, with a 4WD vehicle.

Exploring

Darién's appeal lies mainly in its wealth of plant and animal life. Keep in mind, though, that this region is not an exotic garden where you can safely stroll around observing all sorts of birds and other animals, but rather an actual jungle, where the damp heat and

Province of Darién

Chepo, Ciudad de Panamá

Ipetí
Tortí
Cañazas

Province of Panamá

Comarca de San Blas

Caribbean Sea

N

Carreto
Anachucuna
Puerto Obaldía
La Miel
Aguacate
Rufino
Pinorroa
Acandi

Los Monos
Santa Fé
Río Chucumaque
Boca de Lara
Arretí
Metetí

Bahía de Panamá

González Vásquez
La Palma

Playetta

Canglón

Golfo de San Miguel

Seteganti
Punta Patiño
Chepigana
Río Tuira
Yaviza
El Real

Parque Nacional del Darién

Taimatí

Garachiné
Calorio
Puerto Indio

▲ *Cerro Pírre 1200 m*

Pipirre

Playa de Muerto

Boca de Pavarando
Mamatí

Río Tuira

Caracoles

Parque Nacional del Darién
Río Viejo

Parque Nacional Los Katios

Punta Piña
Bahía Piña
Jaqué
Lucas
Yaramendo

COLOMBIA

Golfo de Panamá

El Guayabo

Cocalito

0   25   50km

© ULYSSES

teeming vegetation make it difficult to get about. Furthermore, it would be a mistake to think that the forest reveals its riches that easily (see J. Jenny's account) (see p 289). In fact, observing exotic birds and other animals requires a thor-

ough knowledge of their behaviour and habitat. To make the most of your visit to the jungle, therefore, it is important to enlist the services of a competent guide and to arrange your accommodations ahead of time. Once you have taken

these precautions, you can fully enjoy this magnificent environment.

During your stay in Darién, you might be lucky enough to come across the indigenous peoples of this province. These include a small community of Kunas, who live mainly on the Atlantic coast (see p275), and the Chocoe, linguistically divided into two groups, the Emberá and the Wounaan. Like the Kunas, the Chocoe now have their own *comarcas* or autonomous regions. There are two of them, located on the outskirts of Parque Nacional del Darién. Comarca Emberá district *Cemaco* lies to the north and Comarca Emberá district *Sambú* to the south.

Unfortunately, very little is known about Chocoe customs, which are still being researched by ethnologists. Chocoe men sometimes stain their entire body (except the top of the face) with a dark-coloured juice, and during certain festivities adorn themselves with animal teeth, feathers and shells. They also wear unusually wide silver bracelets, and earrings in the shape of halfmoons, from which hang a series of other objects of various shapes. These earrings are held in place by two little sticks, which pierce the earlobes and are tied together with a string at the nape of the neck.

Curiously enough, the number of albinos born to Chocoe women appears to be relatively high. These children are believed to have

been conceived supernaturally; born of the moon (according to Chocoe symbolism, the sun represents man and the moon woman), they are most highly venerated when they are female. Like the Kunas, the Chocoes do not mix with other groups (Kunas, Panamanians, etc.), and only unions within the tribe are accepted. They remain among the most isolated and "primitive" indigenous peoples on the planet.

In the capital, La Palma, and in sizeable villages like El Real or Yaviza, the population consists mainly of descendants of *cimarrones* (see p 24), black slaves who escaped during the Spanish colonization. Most took refuge in these areas, which were hard to reach in those years, and established themselves as farmers.

Unfortunately, as a result of continual soil impoverishment on the Azuero peninsula, many farmers have settled in this province, mostly around the huge gulf of San Miguel. Using the same cultivation methods (intensive deforestation and slash and burn), they are currently recreating the same conditions that forced them to move in the first place. This danger is exacerbated by the fact that large forestry multinationals, always on the lookout for high-quality wood,

are pressuring the government, promising jobs and significant financial gains. If the Panamanian government is not careful, a part of Darién risks suffering the same fate as the peninsula. Aside from the Amerindian villages, the Ancón-run stations of Cana and Punta Patiño, and the province's capital (La Palma), which boasts lovely surroundings, most communities in this region have no attractions as such and are of little interest to visitors.

Parks

Parque Nacional Darién

Parque Nacional del Darién is the largest protected park in Panamá, with a surface area of 579,000 ha. Created in 1980, it was a natural addition to Parque Nacional Los Katíos (70,000 ha) on the Colombian side of the border, which was established in 1973. With its coastal swamps, mountains and dense tropical forest, it is considered by experts to cover the most diverse territory of any national park in tropical America. With 2,440 plant and animal species thus far inventoried (and the research continues!), this is one of the richest parks in all of Central America. There are as many as ten different types of vegetation and no less than 23 endemic animal species, including five kinds of felines (including pumas and jaguars). Among the 400 bird species, there is the famous harpy eagle, one of the most powerful raptors on earth. Tapirs and peccaries can also be seen.

The park is home to more than 60% of the mammals found on the entire isthmus. As a result, it was declared a UNESCO Biosphere Reserve in 1983 and classified as a World Heritage Site in 1981. Mining operations have been banned in the park since the introduction of a Panamanian law in 1996. The park is also the source of the gigantic Tuira River, fed by the Río Chucumaque, on whose banks live many Amerindian communities.

Since 1993, Ancón has established two large research centres in the province, one at Punta Piño bordering the gulf of San Miguel, and the other inside Parque Nacional del Darién itself, at Santa Cruz de Cana. Although it primarily hosts scientists, the organization is now open to tourists, to whom it offers educational visits (see

p291). Due to its great diversity of birds, the Cana location is said to be one of the best spots in all of Central America for birdwatching.
Using the services of local guides, amateur ornithologists will have no problem spotting many exotic birds, and even, with a bit of luck, the powerful harpy eagle, symbol of Panamá.

Because of its isolation and inherent dangers (poisonous snakes, disease-carrying mosquitoes), inexperienced visitors are **strongly advised** not to venture into the park alone. The drug traffickers who frequent this region can also pose a serious threat to travellers.

The disappearance of a Canadian tourist several years ago, as well as recent missionary kidnappings in the region illustrate the risks faced by those who wish to get there on their own. For this reason, we have limited our discussion to supervised accommodations that present minimal risks to travellers. Finally, keep in mind that an ANAM permit (see p72) is required to visit the park.

Accommodations

Santa Cruz de Cana

Ancón Expeditions
Calle Elvira Méndez, in front of the Bolsa, Edificio El Dorado
☎ *269-9414*
☎ *269-9415*
≈ *264-3713*
www.ecopanama.com,
travel@ecopanama.com
Through its subsidiary, Ancón, Ancón Expeditions has recently started hosting tourists at its research centre in Santa Cruz de Cana, at the foot of Mount Pirre, within Parque Nacional del Darién itself. In addition to being located in the heart of one of the largest bird reserves in Central America, the centre is close to a former 19th century gold mine. Originally worked by an Englishman, the

mine rapidly fell into disuse once the stores of precious metal were exhausted.

Today, tourists can admire the small locomotive and ovens once used to extract the gold, which are displayed on a grassy plot. Package tours last four days (*B/. 1327 per person*) and include all transportation fees, meals, forest guided hikes and a tour of the mine. There is also the option of an overnight camping trip, sleeping in tents at the summit of Cerro Pirre (1,200m). The rooms at the Ancón station are very modest (no hot water, common washrooms) but renovations are in the works to make them more comfortable. This package will be most appealing to people willing to sacrifice some personal comfort in order to have a unique experience in the wild.

La Palma

Eco-tours
7 Calle 50 Este or Ricardo Arias, near the Vía España
☎ 263-3077
☎ 263-3076
≈ 263-3089
ecotours@pty.com,
www.avatar.pty.com/ecotour
s/fra-bome.btm
The Eco-tours agency organizes excursions into the jungle from La Palma. During the trip, an experienced guide will provide you with all sorts of interesting information on the

tropical forest and the animals living there. You will also visit an Amerindian village (inhabited by Embarás). Accommodation is provided in La Palma, in the comfortable Macaw Lodge. The cost is B/. 335 for one person or B/. 225 per person double occupancy, including return transportation, outings, food and overnight lodging. Visitors short on time can opt for a day-trip by minibus from the capital to the Río Pequení (in Parque Nacional Chagres, in the province of Panamá), site of another Chocoe community. The cost for this outing is B/. 170, including return transportation, a boat trip to the Chocoe village and the services of an experienced guide.

Punta Patiño

Ancón Expeditions
Calle Elvira Méndez, in front of the Bolsa, Edificio El Dorado
☎ 269-9414
☎ 269-9415
≈ 264-3713
www.ecopanama.com,
travel@ecopanama.com
Ancón Expeditions welcomes tourists to the Ancón Research Centre (see p 72) in the Punta Patiño natural reserve on the gulf of San Miguel. The three-day package (*B/. 585 per person*) includes a round-trip plane ticket from the capital to La Palma, the boat trip to the research centre,

meals and several guided hikes.

Several boat excursions are also organized, including one on the Mogué River to visit an Emberá village (see p35). The rooms are located in ten modest *cabañas*. Again, this trip will appeal primarily to those for whom the comforts of home are not a priority.

Piñas Bay

Tropic Star Lodge
pb, ≡, ≈, bw
B/. 2,525 per week per person, including meals, transportation from the capital, and various fishing excursions
635 N. Río Grande Dr., Orlando, FL 32804, U.S.A.
☎ 407-843-0125
☎ 800-682-3424
info@tropicstar.com
If you have a passion for fishing and complete isolation, the Tropic Star Lodge is the place for you. This luxurious fishing club also offers deep-sea fishing packages. A number of world records have been broken here. The place is absolutely beautiful and offers all the comforts of a grand hotel (swimming pool, air conditioning, etc.). Although it is quite expensive, you could be rewarded with the sighting of a celebrity like Julio Iglesias or Anthony Quinn, who are both regular guests here.

Glossary

Consonants

b Is pronounced **b** or sometimes a soft **v**, depending on the region or the person: *bizcocho* (biz-koh-choh or viz-koh-choh).

c As in English, *c* is pronounced as **s** before *i* and *e*: *cerro* (seh-rroh). When it is placed in front of other vowels, it is hard and pronounced as **k**: *carro* (kah-rroh). The *c* is also hard when it comes before a consonant, except before an *h* (see further below).

d Is pronounced like a soft **d**: *dar* (dahr). *D* is usually not pronounced when at the end of a word.

g As with the *c*, *g* is soft before an *i* or an *e*, and is pronounced like a soft **h**: *gente* (hente). In front of other vowels and consonants, the *g* is hard: *golf* (pronounced the same way as in English).

ch Pronounced **ch**, as in English: *leche* (le-che). Like the *ll*, this combination is considered a single letter in the Spanish alphabet, listed separately in dictionaries and telephone directories.

h Is not pronounced: *hora* (oh-ra).

j Is pronounced like a guttural **h**, as in "him".

ll Is pronounced like a hard **y**, as in "yes": *llamar* (yah-mar). In some regions, such as central Colombia, *ll* is pronounced as a soft **g**, as in "mirage" (*Medellín* is pronounced Medegin). Like the *ch*, this combination is considered a single letter in the Spanish alphabet, and is listed separately in dictionaries and telephone directories.

ñ Is pronounced like the **ni** in "onion", or the **ny** in "canyon": *señora* (seh-nyo-rah).

qu Is pronounced **k**: *aquí* (ah-kee).

r Is rolled, as the Irish or Italian pronunciation of **r**.

s Is always pronounced **s** like "sign": *casa* (cah-ssah).

v Is pronounced like a **b**: *vino* (bee-noh).

z Is pronounced like **s**: *paz* (pahss).

Vowels

a Is always pronounced **ah** as in "part", and never **ay** as in "day": *faro* (fah-roh).

e Is pronounced **eh** as in "elf," and never **ey** as in "grey or "ee" as in "key": *helado* (eh-lah-doh].

i Is always pronounced **ee**: *cine* (see-neh).

o Is always pronounced **oh** as in "cone": *copa* (koh-pah).

u   Is always pronounced oo: *universidad* (oo-nee-ver-see-dah).

All other letters are pronounced the same as in English.

Stressing Syllables

In Spanish, syllables are differently stressed. This stress is very important, and emphasizing the right syllable might even be necessary to make yourself understood. If a vowel has an accent, this syllable is the one that should be stressed. If there is no accent, follow this rule:

Stress the second-last syllable of any word that ends with a vowel: *amigo.*

Stress the last syllable of any word that ends in a consonant, except for **s** (plural of nouns and adjectives) or **n** (plural of nouns): *usted* (but *amigos, hablan*).

GREETINGS

Goodbye	*adiós, hasta luego*
Good afternoon and good evening	*buenas tardes*
Hi (casual)	*hola*
Good morning	*buenos días*
Good night	*buenas noches*
Thank-you	*gracias*
Please	*por favor*
You are welcome	*de nada*
Excuse me	*perdone/a*
My name is...	*mi nombre es...*
What is your name?	*¿cómo se llama usted?*
no/yes	*no/sí*
Do you speak English?	*¿habla usted inglés?*
Slower, please	*más despacio, por favor*
I am sorry, I don't speak Spanish	*Lo siento, no hablo español*
How are you?	*¿qué tal?*
I am fine	*estoy bien*
I am American (male/female)	*Soy estadounidense*
I am Australian	*Soy autraliano/a*
I am Belgian	*Soy belga*
I am British (male/female)	*Soy británico/a*
I am Canadian	*Soy canadiense*
I am German (male/female)	*Soy alemán/a*
I am Italian (male/female)	*Soy italiano/a*
I am Swiss	*Soy suizo*
I am a tourist	*Soy turista*
single (m/f)	*soltero/a*
divorced (m/f)	*divorciado/a*
married (m/f)	*casado/a*
friend (m/f)	*amigo/a*
child (m/f)	*niño/a*
husband, wife	*esposo/a*
mother, father	*madre, padre*
brother, sister	*hermano/a*
widower widow	*viudo/a*
I am hungry	*tengo hambre*
I am ill	*estoy enfermo/a*
I am thirsty	*tengo sed*

DIRECTIONS

beside	*al lado de*
to the right	*a la derecha*
to the left	*a la izquierda*
here, there	*aquí, allí*
into, inside	*dentro*
outside	*fuera*
behind	*detrás*
in front of	*delante*
between	*entre*
far from	*lejos de*
Where is ... ?	*¿dónde está ... ?*
To get to ...?	*¿para ir a...?*
near	*cerca de*
straight ahead	*todo recto*

MONEY

money	*dinero / plata*
credit card	*tarjeta de crédito*
exchange	*cambio*
traveller's cheque	*cheque de viaje*
I don't have any money	*no tengo dinero*
The bill, please	*la cuenta, por favor*
receipt	*recibo*

SHOPPING

store	*tienda*
market	*mercado*
open, closed	*abierto/a, cerrado/a*
How much is this?	*¿cuánto es?*
to buy, to sell	*comprar, vender*
the customer	*el / la cliente*
salesman	*vendedor*
saleswoman	*vendedora*
I need...	*necesito...*
I would like...	*yo quisiera...*
batteries	*pilas*
blouse	*blusa*
cameras	*cámaras*
cosmetics and perfumes	*cosméticos y perfumes*
cotton	*algodón*
dress jacket	*saco*
eyeglasses	*lentes, gafas*
fabric	*tela*
film	*película*
gifts	*regalos*
gold	*oro*
handbag	*bolsa*
hat	*sombrero*
jewellery	*joyería*
leather	*cuero, piel*
local crafts	*artesanía*
magazines	*revistas*
newpapers	*periódicos*
pants	*pantalones*
records, cassettes	*discos, casetas*
sandals	*sandalias*

English-Spanish Glossary

shirt	*camisa*
shoes	*zapatos*
silver	*plata*
skirt	*falda*
sun screen products	*productos solares*
T-shirt	*camiseta*
watch	*reloj*
wool	*lana*

MISCELLANEOUS

a little	*poco*
a lot	*mucho*
good (m/f)	*bueno/a*
bad (m/f)	*malo/a*
beautiful (m/f)	*hermoso/a*
pretty (m/f)	*bonito/a*
ugly	*feo*
big	*grande*
tall (m/f)	*alto/a*
small (m/f)	*pequeño/a*
short (length) (m/f)	*corto/a*
short (person) (m/f)	*bajo/a*
cold (m/f)	*frío/a*
hot	*caliente*
dark (m/f)	*oscuro/a*
light (colour)	*claro*
do not touch	*no tocar*
expensive (m/f)	*caro/a*
cheap (m/f)	*barato/a*
fat (m/f)	*gordo/a*
slim, skinny (m/f)	*delgado/a*
heavy (m/f)	*pesado/a*
light (weight) (m/f)	*ligero/a*
less	*menos*
more	*más*
narrow (m/f)	*estrecho/a*
wide (m/f)	*ancho/a*
new (m/f)	*nuevo/a*
old (m/f)	*viejo/a*
nothing	*nada*
something (m/f)	*algo/a*
quickly	*rápidamente*
slowly (m/f)	*despacio/a*
What is this?	*¿qué es esto?*
when?	*¿cuando?*
where?	*¿dónde?*

TIME

in the afternoon, early evening	*por la tarde*
at night	*por la noche*
in the daytime	*por el día*
in the morning	*por la mañana*
minute	*minuto*
month	*mes*
ever	*jamás*
never	*nunca*
now	*ahora*

today	hoy
yesterday	ayer
tomorrow	mañana
What time is it?	¿qué hora es?
hour	hora
week	semana
year	año
Sunday	domingo
Monday	lunes
Tuesday	martes
Wednesday	miércoles
Thursday	jueves
Friday	viernes
Saturday	sábado
January	enero
February	febrero
March	marzo
April	abril
May	mayo
June	junio
July	julio
August	agosto
September	septiembre
October	octubre
November	noviembre
December	diciembre

WEATHER

It is cold	hace frío
It is warm	hace calor
It is very hot	hace mucho calor
sun	sol
It is sunny	hace sol
It is cloudy	está nublado
rain	lluvia
It is raining	está lloviendo
wind	viento
It is windy	hay viento
snow	nieve
damp	húmedo
dry	seco
storm	tormenta
hurricane	huracán

COMMUNICATION

air mail	correos aéreo
collect call	llamada por cobrar
dial the number	marcar el número
area code, country code	código
envelope	sobre
long distance	larga distancia
post office	correo
rate	tarifa
stamps	estampillas
telegram	telegrama
telephone book	un guia telefónica
wait for the tone	esperar la señal

ACTIVITIES

beach	playa
museum or gallery	museo
scuba diving	buceo
to swim	bañarse
to walk around	pasear
hiking	caminata
trail	pista, sendero
cycling	ciclismo
fishing	pesca

TRANSPORTATION

arrival, departure	llegada, salida
on time	a tiempo
cancelled (m/f)	anulado/a
one way ticket	ida
return	regreso
round trip	ida y vuelta
schedule	horario
baggage	equipajes
north, south	norte, sur
east, west	este, oeste
avenue	avenida
street	calle
highway	carretera
expressway	autopista
airplane	avión
airport	aeropuerto
bicycle	bicicleta
boat	barco
bus	bus
bus stop	parada
bus terminal	terminal
train	tren
train crossing	crucero ferrocarril
station	estación
neighbourhood	barrio
collective taxi	colectivo
corner	esquina
express	rápido
safe	seguro/a
be careful	cuidado
car	coche, carro
To rent a car	alquilar un auto
gas	gasolina
gas station	gasolinera
no parking	no estacionar
no passing	no adelantar
parking	parqueo
pedestrian	peaton
road closed, no through traffic	no hay paso
slow down	reduzca velocidad
speed limit	velocidad permitida
stop	alto
stop! (an order)	pare
traffic light	semáforo

ACCOMMODATION

cabin, bungalow	*cabaña*
accommodation	*alojamiento*
double, for two people	*doble*
single, for one person	*sencillo*
high season	*temporada alta*
low season	*temporada baja*
bed	*cama*
floor (first, second...)	*piso*
main floor	*planta baja*
manager	*gerente, jefe*
double bed	*cama matrimonial*
cot	*camita*
bathroom	*baños*
with private bathroom	*con baño privado*
hot water	*agua caliente*
breakfast	*desayuno*
elevator	*ascensor*
air conditioning	*aire acondicionado*
fan	*ventilador, abanico*
pool	*piscina, alberca*
room	*habitación*

NUMBERS

1	*uno*	30	*treinta*
2	*dos*	31	*treinta y uno*
3	*tres*	32	*treinta y dos*
4	*cuatro*	40	*cuarenta*
5	*cinco*	50	*cincuenta*
6	*seis*	60	*sesenta*
7	*siete*	70	*setenta*
8	*ocho*	80	*ochenta*
9	*nueve*	90	*noventa*
10	*diez*	100	*cien*
11	*once*	101	*ciento uno*
12	*doce*	102	*ciento dos*
13	*trece*	200	*doscientos*
14	*catorce*	300	*trescientos*
15	*quince*	400	*quatrocientoa*
16	*dieciséis*	500	*quinientos*
17	*diecisiete*	600	*seiscientos*
18	*dieciocho*	700	*sietecientos*
19	*diecinueve*	800	*ochocientos*
20	*veinte*	900	*novecientos*
21	*veintiuno*	1,000	*mil*
22	*veintidós*	1,100	*mil cien*
23	*veintitrés*	1,200	*mil doscientos*
24	*veinticuatro*	2000	*dos mil*
25	*veinticinco*	3000	*tres mil*
26	*veintiséis*	10,000	*diez mil*
27	*veintisiete*	100,000	*cien mil*
28	*veintiocho*	1,000,000	*un millón*
29	*veintinueve*		

Index

Index

Index